THE EDWARDIANS
AND THEIR HOUSES

THE EDWARDIANS
AND THEIR HOUSES

The New Life of Old England

Timothy Brittain-Catlin

Lund Humphries

First published in 2020 by Lund Humphries, reprinted in 2021

Lund Humphries
Office 3, Book House
261A City Road
London EC1V 1JX
UK

www.lundhumphries.com

All the new photography for this book, unless stated otherwise, is by Robin
Forster and was carried out specially for this book between January and June
2019. © Robin Forster.

http://RobinForster.co.uk/

The author, publisher and photographer would like to express our sincere
thanks to the residents who permitted us to visit their houses for that
purpose and made this book possible.

Copy edited by ABIGAIL GRATER
Designed by ADRIAN HUNT
Set in WINDSOR and KEPLER
Printed in SLOVENIA

The new photography commissioned for this book from Robin Forster was
generously supported by the John S. Cohen Foundation; Marc Fitch Fund;
a Publications Grant from the Paul Mellon Centre for Studies in British Art;
and Sophie Service in celebration of Alastair Service.

Front cover: A detail of King's Close in Biddenham, by M.H. Baillie Scott, *c.* 1909.
Back cover: A detail of Rhinefield House near Brockenhurst by
Romaine-Walker & Tanner, 1888–90.
Frontispiece: A detail of Perrycroft, Colwall, by C.F.A. Voysey, 1893–4.

The production of this book has been made possible by grants from the
Design History Society; the Scouloudi Foundation in association with the
Institute of Historical Research; the Society of Architectural Historians of
Great Britain; and the Vera Brittain Literary Estate.

The University of Kent generously supported both the new photography and
the book production.

for Patrick O'Keeffe

Rickie at once had a rush of sympathy. He, too, looked with reverence at the morsel of Jacobean brickwork, ruddy and beautiful amidst the machine-squared stones of the modern apse. The two men, who had so little in common, were thrilled with patriotism. They rejoiced that their country was great, noble, and old.

'Thank God I'm English,' said Rickie suddenly.

E.M. Forster, *The Longest Journey* (1907)

CONTENTS

———

INTRODUCTION

—

Edwardian domestic architecture was so rich in ideas and so accomplished in execution that interest has not waned since Alastair Service wrote his two books about it over forty years ago. In *Edwardian Architecture and its Origins*, of 1975, he presented a selection of articles, mainly reproduced from the *Architectural Review*, supplemented with perceptive commentary and additional chapters, such as his own on Charles Harrison Townsend. With *Edwardian Architecture* two years later he contributed what has remained the textbook overview of the period. The timing was faultless: we then saw Edwardiana everywhere, from the republication of my grandmother Vera Brittain's *Testament of Youth* in 1978, and the television series that followed it, to the film of Isabel Colegate's *The Shooting Party* in 1985, both of them wartime dramas that were tributes to the 'lost' England of the period immediately beforehand.

In a presumably not unrelated development, English postmodernism in architecture and in cultural criticism got under way too. In 1981 the Hayward Gallery presented an exhibition of the work of Edwin Lutyens, designed by Piers Gough, a leading postmodernist architect. Embarrassment at the indulgence and pretty eclecticism of the period started to wane, and since then many brilliant writers have between them created a substantial mass of monographs, exhibition catalogues, specialist articles and much else. Following Mark Girouard's *Sweetness and Light* (1977), some historians – especially Peter Davey, Clive Aslet and Gavin Stamp, although there were many others – produced memorable books with fabulous, lush photography. Davey's *Arts and Crafts Architecture* (1980, revised 1997) is especially valuable as a sympathetic study of a group of architects as a whole from the viewpoint of a writer who was simultaneously an architect, an architectural historian, a critic and an editor, informed in many cases by conversations with those who knew the protagonists at first hand.

The imagery within these books is important: these Edwardian revivalists were out to beat the modernists at their own game of 'the better picture', with the archives of the magazine *Country Life* providing photographs unparalleled in range and quality when it came to the houses of the period. But in spite of much interesting and rewarding scholarship, there are still significant gaps in our understanding of Edwardian architecture, and our treatment of it looks inadequate when compared to the fresh ways in which historians of the First World War itself have responded to the era in recent years. It is not difficult to make a list of some of the areas that are missing. We have not heard much about what the clients who commissioned houses in that period thought they were doing: why they wanted houses of a certain type, and what they intended to demonstrate through them. We have heard next to nothing about how Edwardian housebuilders related to the history of England in their own buildings, even though contemporary writing made a great deal more than one might expect of the integration of old and new fabric. We have heard little beyond details about how progress in scientific and medical discoveries influenced the designs of homes, even though we know that it affected pretty much everything else. And perhaps most strikingly, we have not yet really taken into account the vast and original range of housebuilding of the years that led up to the War: the seaside villas; the servantless weekend cottages; the rooms for games and sports; the dormy houses for golfers. Behind this question of range there lies too the bigger question of how the Edwardians saw themselves as occupiers of their land and how builders related to the idea of land tenure and ownership itself.

This last point links directly to a further aspect of Edwardian architecture that has not yet received its due: the fact that so many of its most active perpetrators were Liberal Party politicians, those in power or closely related to them, during the period that led up to the War. These people, from the prime minister downwards, built a staggering number of interesting and attractive buildings of all kinds. That degree of investment of both time and money, not to mention thought, is in itself a remarkable characteristic of the period. We are already aware of the significance of the great Victorian churchbuilding and restoration programme of the mid-19th century; we have not yet gone through a similar process to the housebuilding that followed. In a small late-Victorian chapel we might identify a trace of a magnificent structure like William Butterfield's All Saints' church, Margaret Street

(1849–59), or even of a vast cathedral like J.L. Pearson's at Truro (1880–1910); if we can discover the signs of the great mansions in a seaside villa, it will give us another way of grasping the significance of the period as a whole. And just as Victorian churchbuilding was closely related to the politics of the churches – with the Ecclesiologists emerging triumphant – was it also the case that housebuilding related to lay politics? The Liberals of that period had much to say about English history, town and country, land and ownership; surely this emerged in the buildings that represented their various practical endeavours and their daily lives?

Sweetness and Light

Mark Girouard's *Sweetness and Light* signalled a new attitude to the architecture of the decade and half before the War and in particular to the 'Queen Anne' movement of the end of the previous century that influenced it so greatly. As one would expect from its author, then as now perhaps the most influential of all writers on English domestic architecture and the life in it, it also introduced a common-sense view of social history into an area which must have looked to many like a branch of antiquarian nostalgia. At first reading, the most memorable people in the book are those who held what were at the time extreme political and social views: radicals, pacifists, socialists. But looking closely one realises that more mainstream forces were playing the dominant role: the Liberals, a national party. In fact, one of the first figures introduced into the book is a fictional Whig peer Lord Martindale, from Charlotte M. Yonge's 1854 novel *Heartsease*, who rebuilds his Queen Anne mansion – it must surely be that, as it has an 'old red pediment with the white facings' – after its brief and unhappy replacement with a neo-classical mansion.[1]

That provides a major but inexplicitly stated theme of Girouard's book. For Liberals are building everywhere, and indeed as with all social history of architecture, it here is the agency of building – that is, the use of building projects to execute further and wider ambitions – that is the key. For unlike the socialists, the pacifists and the radicals, the Liberals were a party of power, in government for approximately half the period between 1880 and 1914. It was William Forster, the Liberal MP for Bradford, who introduced the 1870 Education Act in W.E. Gladstone's cabinet; and it was William Cowper-Temple, likely to have been the illegitimate son of Lord Palmerston and adopted by him, and a client of William Eden Nesfield, who gave the board schools that followed their

1. (p.8) A detail of George Devey's additions to Hammerfield, Penshurst, Kent, for the inventor James Nasmyth, 1857–9. What made Devey so distinct was that unlike picturesque architects of the previous generation, his houses were designed and constructed using authentic historical vernacular building details.

2. The roots of Edwardian architecture lie in projects by Liberal architects working in the mid- to late 19th century. 29 Exhibition Road in South Kensington, London, was designed in the late 1870s by J.J. Stevenson, one of the most fluent and stylish architects of his day.

character by promoting the amendment named after him which insisted that they should exclude the teaching of the religious denominations.[2] The proliferation of these buildings, and their domination of the urban landscape, still in some places today, in areas of London, turns 'Queen Anne' into something more than an aesthetes' style. Both Forster and Cowper-Temple moved in social circles that were much more radical than they were themselves; similarly, John Passmore Edwards, the proprietor of the pro-'Queen Anne' *Building News*

and briefly Liberal MP for Salisbury in 1880–82, was perhaps more of an idiosyncratic radical at heart.[3]

Some of the leading characters in Girouard's book have explicit Liberal Party links: James Cochran Stevenson, the brother of the architect John James Stevenson, was Liberal MP for Morpeth in 1868–75 as well as an active, building, local politician. He was a member of the Tyne Improvement Commission for more than half a century after 1850 and its chairman for 20 years; at one point the Stevensons' chemical works worked in partnership with Charles Tennant's St Rollox works, providing a link with yet more well-established, well-heeled Liberal builders.[4] John and James's sisters Flora and Louisa were social reformers, active in education, women's suffrage and nursing. J.J Stevenson designed early board schools in London in addition to his influential houses (fig.2). Joshua Nicholson, a significant patron of 'Queen Anne'-style building in Staffordshire, the silk manufacturer who built W.L. Sugden's Leek Institute in 1881–4, was according to his biographer a prominent Liberal and an admirer of Richard Cobden,

3. T.G. Jackson's Lime Tree Walk in Sevenoaks, Kent, of 1878–82, was a harbinger of later Liberal efforts to distribute land fairly to working people, and to provide them with idealised '17th-century' homes. The drawing is by T. Raffles Davison.

the radical and influential Victorian Liberal free-trader, pacifist and land reformer.[5] Thomas Baring, the first Earl of Northbrook, a Liberal and a viceroy of India, commissioned Ernest Newton in 1879 to build a 'Queen Anne' pub and houses 'in abundance' on his estate at Grove Park to the south-east of London; there were several other Liberal MPs who did something similar, as we shall see.[6] And furthermore, some other key developers and architects in Girouard's book have a Liberal tinge to them even if they were not explicitly that: the scheme at Lime Tree Walk in Sevenoaks, Kent, by T.G. Jackson, for example, aimed to provide housing at a fair rental for local workers and was designed in 1878 during a period of debate on land reform (fig.3).[7] Girouard does not mention it, but Jackson at this stage was a Liberal too, and the project grew out of his political beliefs.[8] And although he touched briefly on seaside architecture, and looked at Westgate-on-Sea in Thanet, developed by the builder W. Corbett & Co. with the architect C.N. Beazley from the end of the 1870s, Girouard said little about the overall impact of seaside holiday villa architecture,

but this was the beginning of another story which also eventually came to characterise Edwardian England.[9]

Girouard also looked at the relationship between children's writing and book illustration, in particular, at (in his words) the 'little aesthetic bombs' dropped by Walter Crane, Kate Greenaway and Randolph Caldecott, and the rural idyll they drew which was itself a hybrid of Queen Anne – in the sense of the real period of Queen Anne, who reigned from 1702 to 1714 – and the Regency period approximately a century later (fig.4).[10] The architectural styles of the two were quite different, even if both were 'neo-classical': baroque houses have solid walls, typically red brick, with relatively small windows punched through them; cornices both inside and out are heavy, swagged, somewhat sensuous in feel. The regency ones that we, or perhaps set designers and illustrators, like to remember could by contrast be grey brick or plastered with, at best, light, almost filigree elevations, glazed bow windows, verandahs with cast iron screens, and sometimes gothick touches such as battlements or a cusp or two. Draw all these together and you have the romantic fantasy that is now termed the 'Quality Street' style, apparently first called that by Nicholas Taylor in 1971.[11] The soft pinks and greens of Greenaway's and Caldecott's drawings seem to dominate Girouard's book, even if in fact nearly all the illustrations were printed in black and white. The clever way in which writers for both adults and children referred to houses in their work suggests that something further was going on that needs to be investigated.

I have chosen Liberal Party politicians as a uniting theme because Liberals broadly, however split they were over Irish Home Rule, free trade or empire policy, were all at least to some extent committed to a progressive view on the major defining political debate of the era: land reform. Although the government faced a Liberal Unionist opposition on matters such as the Housing, Town Planning, &c. Act of 1909, the distinction is not a significant or consistent one in regard to the development of houses; clashes between the two tended to be about the details of compensation processes. Liberals of all kinds wanted to reduce the exclusive control of vast estates by private landowners and for a number of reasons: to reduce rural poverty; to provide rural labourers with a secure investment in the area in which they lived; to reduce the likelihood of a further depression; to provide civic rather than religious or aristocratic leadership across the counties; and in towns, to reduce land speculation, and the overcrowding and squalor that followed where private landowners controlled inner-city estates with little incentive to improve their property. The Conservative approach was, generally, to take defensive action by pre-empting more radical reform and to counteract Liberal centrist tendencies.[12] The 1875 Artizans and Labourers Dwellings Improvement Act was a High Tory measure which set out to penalise negligent landowners by allowing compulsory purchase of their land, and it was another Conservative government, under Lord Salisbury, that introduced the 1890 Housing of the Working Classes Act which actively enabled public authorities to build model dwellings on such sites. To the dismay of Conservatives, their local government reforms in the late 1880s resulted in a powerful London County Council in the hands of the Progressive Party; this was in effect a municipal wing of the Liberal Party, controlled by politicians with national status, which by 1900 was already building highly regarded model

4. *Ride a Cock-Horse to Banbury Cross*: one of Randolph Caldecott's 'little aesthetic bombs' from 1895. His houses freely mixed Tudor, 17th-century and Regency styles, a harbinger of the Edwardian style.

5. A view of houses by R. Norman Shaw (and one by E.W. Godwin, to the left) on an advertising poster for Bedford Park, 1877, drawn by the architect Maurice B. Adams.

estates on the sites of slums. There was thus by then a sense among Liberals that the domination of private landowners could change, and that isolated projects such as the private or idealistically communal garden suburbs could suggest, even if little more, the direction of future reform. The 1909 Act, which envisaged town plans and garden suburbs as an instrument of local government, was enabling legislation rather than the introduction of any revolutionary development.

In the meantime, there was also a voracious appetite for the idea of the cosy old English cottage, even a real one rather than a new villa made to resemble one, which filtered down from elevated, cultured people such as the Prime Minister's wife to the many popular publications full of photographs and plans of houses that were well within reach for large sections of the population. In his recent book on the London garden suburb Bedford Park (fig.5), Andrew Saint writes:

> In a proud and independent country with a strong
> sense of its own history, a natural point of reference
> for reformers endeavouring to address such cultural
> or urban issues as the housing problem – as acute in
> the 1870s and '80s as it is today – was to look back
> and see how things were done in order to work out
> how to do things better again. We have become so
> unaccustomed to this historical frame of thinking,
> which Conservatives and Radicals shared, that we are

inclined to view the adoption of a history-based style of architecture as artificial. To many people it seemed at the time perfectly cogent and natural.[13]

The structure of this book

An argument can be made that distinctly Liberal architecture was broadly the architecture of land reform: an image of a widely spread people living contentedly on land they felt they belonged to, picking at symbols such as half-timber and gables that seemed to have come up out of the land rather than being imposed upon it in the way that Palladian houses had been. At the same time many shared an expression of an attitude to buildings that was distinct from that of their parents. We think of the leading Victorians as a scientific generation, with an analytical attitude to work, machinery, ideas, politics, history and even religion. It took a while for this mindset to filter through to the commissioning of expensive, exemplary new buildings, but when it happened there was no mistaking its influence; in fact, several of the major buildings in the book owe their existence to dry forms of cleaning materials, Robert Hudson's dry soap and Charles Tennant's dry bleach, both technical breakthroughs which reduced the costs of labour, time and space. This book starts with the study of one large project, not well known, that was built for a figure who precisely exemplifies this type of late Victorian: an active Liberal, albeit a Liberal Unionist at this stage; a man with a record of pragmatic legislation from the backbenches; extremely rich, hospitable and generous; a busy social personage with a very wide circle of political and scientific acquaintances across the world; and perhaps above all a man with a ceaselessly curious logical, analytical mind, ever interested in what 'England' meant in terms of geology, archaeology, settlement; flora and fauna; public education and pleasure. Lord Avebury's new castle at Kingsgate, on its striking promontory in the far east of Kent, sets the scene for what follows.

Chapter Two looks at houses associated with senior Liberal Party and government members and identifies in them the elements that make them particular to the period. This is intended to indicate the extent to which Liberal politicians themselves were so much at the forefront of progressive building. Chapter Three looks at the enormously rich world of Edwardian publications on house design, which provides a way of seeing how the nature of the profession and its relationship with the public was distinct from that of Victorian England; it looks closely at H. Avray Tipping and Lawrence Weaver to see how exactly their own interests and preferences, and perhaps their precise writing style, played such an influential role. And finally, Chapter Four echoes Girouard's 'little aesthetic bombs' by exploring how various evocations of childhood and magic are more closely related to the real and rational aspects of Edwardian architecture than has hitherto been assumed.

Some explanation is needed as to why this book spends less time on the architects most closely associated with the Edwardian period: Edwin Lutyens, for example. Not everything that Lutyens designed was a resounding success, but many of his buildings are strikingly beautiful – exquisite, even – and people seem to fall in love with them. Yet they tend to reflect Edwardian preoccupations rather than create them. The exception to this pattern is the role that Lutyens played, with Weaver and Edward Hudson, in the professional literature at the time, and I go into this in Chapter Three. There is also the fact that not only has Lutyens already been much written about, the whole way in which he was bound up in the tight social and political circles of the time has been described so well more than twenty years ago by Jane Brown in her *Lutyens and the Edwardians* that there is no chance that I could do it any better, or would want to. Anyone who has become starry-eyed about Lutyens should read her devastating description of how he treated the Hemingways at Ilkley.[14] It will be seen that

Lutyens's buildings are extraordinarily good examples of the innovations that others, perhaps less gratifying as designers, had pioneered. It may well be that this was the reason why Nikolaus Pevsner, engaged in devising the foundation myths of modernism, notoriously did not include Lutyens in his surveys, something for which conservative historians seem never to have forgiven him.

There are many, many attractive, picturesque, photogenic, well-made houses designed in or soon after the Edwardian period. Aslet's *The Last Country Houses* of 1982 remains one of the most memorable and haunting depictions of them, and they can be seen too in countless excellent articles in (mainly) *Country Life* by Stamp, Jeremy Musson, Michael Hall, John Goodall, John Martin Robinson and Mary Miers, which cannot be bettered. This book is trying to do something else. An almost unknown architect like the Mr Lees who converted Lord Carrington's farmyard and potting shed into a sophisticated residence at the start of Chapter Two, will be relatively more important to my version of the story: Augustus Pitt Rivers, a hero of Chapter One, an arch-positivist and a pioneer of modern archaeology, would appreciate why. For the same reason, I have not retold here the stories of the planning and building of Letchworth and the Hampstead Garden Suburb, or indeed the familiar origins of the garden city or suburb movement in general. When the perceptive Tipping wrote that 'Letchworth is a little disappointing . . . there is a lot of very poor building at this first Garden City', he was no doubt speaking for many.[15] I have therefore preferred to concentrate instead on one particular estate, Gidea Park, that seems to me to have something else and just as valuable to add to the history of Edwardian garden suburb developments.

The colour photography taken specially for this book is intended to provide the suggested canon of the most significant new houses in the period leading up to the outbreak of the First World War, wherever it has been possible to access the sites. The emphasis therefore has been on showing as much as possible of the important aspects of these buildings in particular, and complementing them with a stream of original images that were published during the period itself.

Liberals and land

———

The relationships between Liberal Party history, doctrines and legislation and their overall consequence on building and land, from the writings of the rationalising, utilitarian late Georgian philosopher Jeremy Bentham to David Lloyd

George's failed attempts in the wake of the 1909–10 'People's Budget' to subsidise agricultural labourers' wages and municipal rates from a tax on land, have been described in detail in Avner Offer's *Property and Politics 1870–1914* of 1981. At least three of the themes of this book are relevant to the current study. When Offer's book opens, still in Bentham's lifetime, tenure – that is, any form of interest in the ownership of land – is managed beyond any other kind of marketplace; its transactions and rules are the result of historically accumulated and closed privileges and customs, administered by specialist lawyers in specialised courts. Over the course of the century, Liberals and radicals tried to create a 'free trade in land', using a national registry, so that anyone could buy and sell it. In this they were only partially successful, not least because the legal profession succeeded in maintaining its monopoly on transactions. Secondly, Liberals wanted to draw taxation, especially for municipal purposes, from the value of land rather than from tenants or other occupiers of buildings in the freehold ownership of others. This featured increasingly in the rhetoric of Edwardian Liberals – in fact Henry Campbell-Bannerman's first speech as prime minister, addressing a crowd of 9,000 at the Albert Hall in late December 1905, declared that his government wished 'to make the land less a pleasure ground for the rich (loud cheers) and more of a treasure house for the nation (Renewed cheers)'.[16] This was an often repeated theme in the speeches of Lloyd George whose terrifying reputation among Conservatives was to a large extent due to it, especially in the period of the 1909–10 budget debates. And finally, Offer drew attention to what he called the 'transcendental' relationship of Liberals with the land, by which he meant the sense of the sublime occasioned by visits to the countryside; some Liberals, such as Charles Philips Trevelyan and the bird-watching, forest-dwelling Edward Grey, were especially moved by them. Going into and rediscovering rural joys may have seemed like a conquest of Conservative lands and land values akin to roaming rights to some in modern times. Using the terminology of sociologists Offer described these feelings as Liberal 'residues', from which changing policies – 'deviations' – can emerge in varying forms at different times.[17]

The Campbell-Bannerman and H.H. Asquith cabinets from 1905 to 1916 included a variety of personalities, and there is no direct relationship between all Liberals and any particular set of attitudes to land. The idea of central government grants to municipal authorities, eventually adopted by Lloyd George, has its origins in Benjamin Disraeli's attempts, from 1849 onwards, to buy off farmers disadvantaged by the abolition of the corn laws, and what

Offer called his *étatisme*, the building up of an imperial state. A cross-party acceptance of the idea of taxing land separately from buildings, the breaking of a long-held English Conservative taboo, came about through the minority report to the Royal Commission on Local Taxation of 1901, presented by Lord Balfour of Burleigh, Lord Salisbury's high-Tory Secretary of State for Scotland. John Lubbock, from 1900 Lord Avebury, who opens the first chapter of this book, was a Gladstonian Liberal and free trader, who parted from his leader at some personal cost over Home Rule and became a Liberal Unionist; he was elected in 1889 as a Progressive member of the first London County Council, and became its chairman on Lord Rosebery's retirement in 1890. He was then elected by other council members to be one of their aldermen. Yet he vigorously opposed the growth of municipal power, believing it would hand too much tenure in land over to inefficient corporations, and Offer described him as the 'Leader of London Conservatism'. His real radicalism, as we shall see, was from this point onwards transferred to his patronage of architecture. From 1905 he tried to become

6.   (opposite) Henry Campbell-Bannerman, the Liberal leader of the opposition, photographed by George Charles Beresford in 1902.

7.   Herbert Henry Asquith, chancellor of the exchequer and the up-and-coming man on his way to the premiership. Photographed in 1907 by Reginald Haines.

involved, as a private individual and shareholder, in the creation of the area around Smith Square in Westminster, the great set piece of Edwardian Liberal urban planning.

So some prominent Liberals held versions of Conservative viewpoints, while some were distinguished only by political tradition from the socialists; in that respect the Liberals at their high water mark of 1906–10 were very similar to their successors, the Liberal Democrats, precisely a century later (figs 6 and 7). At the same time, it is hard to pin down any possible connection between Liberals and any kind of distinct architectural style, although there is evidence that some of the leading ones, intellectually, shared contemporary architects' love of Tudor and Elizabethan buildings: Charles Masterman, for example, thought that the 16th century produced 'the noblest of English country houses'.[18] This choice had an implicit anti-establishment connotation to it, as arts-and-crafts designers would have been aware. Nearly all descriptions of the designers and architects who followed in the footsteps of William Morris have stressed the fact that they were looking for motifs from vernacular architecture,

especially from buildings that they believed to have been the result of artisan tradition rather than the impositions of an architect; indeed, this is what designers and writers were saying at the time, for example in *Country Life*. As Hermann Muthesius put it in his famous and influential *Das englische Haus* of 1904–5, the 'escape' from the bad architecture of the early 19th century 'consisted in the architects recovering the traditions of the old master-mason, abandoning any suggestion of fine architecture and beginning to build simply and rationally like the old guild-masons'.[19] Yet this familiar narrative does not explain the distinctive forms of Edwardian domestic architecture, in particular the careful mixing of different 17th-century styles within the same building and the intense anti-chronology of their design, the attempt to make buildings look as if they had grown over the years when in fact they had been built as a piece. Offer's concept of Liberal transcendentalism might prove closer to the point.

In a recent text on the Edwardian land question, Paul Readman addresses the prevailing view among historians that 'land, landscape and the rural' have been understood as the core to English national identity, and provides examples of how Conservatives and Liberals alike were concerned with it, for reasons of public health as much as for tenure. But what is yet to be seen is whether this translates into a specific architectural approach and style beyond the work of arts-and-crafts architects who were, with one or two exceptions, only ever at the fringe of mass housebuilding.[20] It seems improbable that there will be any definitive explanation that ties all this together as a distinctly 'Liberal' theory, even if Liberals played the major role in it, but it is gratifying, in view of the argument that I am going to make, that Masterman lived in one of Percy Morley Horder's Walton-on-the-Hill 'Tudor farmhouse' golf houses; and that Trevelyan, who emerges towards the end of Offer's book as a kind of ultimate Liberal Party politician both intellectually and emotionally, commissioned and lived in one of Horace Field's finest 'late 17th-century' houses. As will become clear, it is more gratifying still that Edward Hudson, Lutyens's patron who came to play so important a role in the history of Edwardian houses, was trained as a conveyancing clerk before returning to his family printing firm and thus presumably had some rational and informed knowledge of the basic principles of tenure. But there is no easy pattern: Earl Loreburn, Asquith's first Lord Chancellor, a strong and early voice in support of land registration, retired to nothing other than a stuccoed late Georgian villa in Deal, just the type of thing most architects and writers in this book abhorred more than any other kind of dwelling. Furthermore, some of the finest houses of the late

Victorian and Edwardian period – from Philip Webb's Clouds in Wiltshire of 1877–86, to Lutyens's Greywalls in East Lothian of 1901 – were built by the Wyndhams, a Conservative dynasty, and by the Lytteltons, who were in turn Whigs, Conservatives and Tory-supporting Liberal Unionists.

The Edwardians and realism

In my past writing I have developed Chris Brooks's concept of 'realism' or 'reality' into a theory about why the buildings of the gothic revival look the way they do. Augustus Welby Northmore Pugin had written – it is one of his best-known sayings, presented on page one of his primary theoretical text – that '*there should be no features about a building which are not necessary for convenience, construction, or propriety . . .* the smallest detail should *have a meaning or serve a purpose*'.[21] To this Brooks commented that 'Pugin's response parallels those of Carlyle and Dickens, Ruskin and the Pre-Raphaelites both quantitatively, insisting upon the sheer amount of individual detail, and qualitatively, insisting upon the separable identity of each detail. Every element of the Pugin building is true, true to structure, to function, to material, to a religious meaning; above all, true to itself, its own isolable reality' (fig. 8).[22] 'In spite of the gothic detailing,' wrote Service in his 1975 book, 'there was an underlying rationalism in some of Pugin's secular buildings' – an observation missed by most of Pugin's admirers when scholarship on the subject eventually developed.[23]

My argument has been that this realism was the result of the change in the ways in which architects operated rather than because of any romantic inclinations about gothic castles and cathedrals.[24] These were certainly in the background: even Pugin himself went on copying features from inaccurate illustrations of buildings in books he had seen as a child.[25] But they are never enough for modern architectural practice. To win a public contract from the 1830s onwards, architects or builders were required for the first time to submit itemised specifications which could be priced accurately in advance; this was connected not only with the need to maintain a budget but also the consequence of a series of building failures due to inadequate detailing. The architectural profession responded with a far greater interest

8.   A.W.N. Pugin's rectory, now Pugin Hall, at Rampisham in Dorset, 1847, photographed by Graham Booth in August 2012. The finest of his houses, it provides an emphatic demonstration of his realism, from the smallest detail to its overall form.

in *what* precisely they were designing, and *how* the parts fitted together: this ranged from Pugin's precise explanatory drawings to Alfred Bartholomew's *Specifications for Practical Architecture*, of 1840, which spelled out word for word what an architect needed to specify from the top to the bottom of everyday structures. Gothic architecture demonstrated to the observer what precisely the roles of its elements were: a steep roof and deep eaves explained their purpose in a way that the old brick parapet did not. In time this new accuracy, which was reinforced by, for example, application forms for mortgages, spread out to encompass working drawings and other professional practices. The growing knowledge of building craft methods accumulated by members of the Society for the Protection of Ancient Buildings (SPAB) from the late 1870s was itself an extension of this scientific process: the application of precise knowledge about history, materials and details to the repair and extension of old buildings. During the Edwardian period architects developed a keen interest in the exact prescriptions (and proscriptions) of the building bye-laws, joining campaigns for their reform, and designed new houses accordingly. It is not fanciful to see a parallel between this and the way in which their professional forebears had responded to the raised levels of expectation of their performance and technical knowledge that had brought about the gothic revival two generations beforehand.

None of those gothic-revival architects seems to have described what they were doing as this process continued: they acted professionally and, presumably, increasingly instinctively and they could not have had the perspective of time which would have allowed this kind of self-aware analysis anyway. But we can assume that processes like this are always at work in some form or another. An overall gloss of Offer's conclusions would show that the primary instinct of Liberals in the second half of the 19th century was towards finding a rational concept of land and buildings. The whole Benthamite argument for land registration was precisely that; for reasons that Bentham would have appreciated, the magazine *Country Life* ran its early campaigns for improved cottage dwellings along rational, economic lines which emphasised the rights and duties of landowners. Another area that marks out this wave of realism as being distinct from Pugin's is the informed interest in health: the professional press carried considerable information about this, and elsewhere I have suggested that the uncharacteristic plan and type of Lutyens's Great Maytham of 1909 may have been due to the fact that its clients, who both had a professional interest in laws relating to health at work, would have been very likely to have seen one of the many publications of H. Percy Adams's King Edward

VII Sanatorium at Midhurst in West Sussex.[26] In spite of the memorable title of Roderick Gradidge's *Dream Houses* (1980), one of the best-known books to date on Edwardian domestic architecture, it is yet to be proved that Edwardian patrons were spending so much money on houses primarily to dream either in them or about them.

I have been struck by the role played by scientists and scientific types in the development of what became the most characteristic Edwardian domestic architecture. Webb, who retired from London on 4 January 1901, in the month of Queen Victoria's death, did some of his best work for the industrialist Isaac Lowthian Bell and his family. Andrew Ballantyne and Andrew Law have observed that a house called Hammerfield, near Penshurst in Kent, of 1857–9, which had already been designed 'to look as if it had grown accretively over the years', attracted a scientist buyer, James Nasmyth, the inventor of the steam hammer, who then commissioned George Devey to make it look even more so (see fig.1).[27] These scientific types are not only looking at materials and strata of building, finding in them a representation of the basic rules and types that had been observed in natural phenomena. They are also taking an analytical mirror to English history, extracting lessons from it and restating them eventually in a characteristically Edwardian way.

There are some clear patterns in this attitude. The first one is that Edwardian critics and architects disliked most English 18th-century architecture at least as much as, or more than, they disliked the High Victorian gothic revival. The late Georgian period was associated with the enclosures, and with the pauperisation of the countryside: resentment at these two alone motivated many Liberal land reformers; furthermore, it had been 'an age of negligence' (in Peter Virgin's phrase) in the parishes of the Church of England as the Church itself departed from any sense of providing the heart of a community.[28] The writers of *Country Life* took a clear SPAB view – that is, they thought that old fabric should be respected in rebuilding or remodelling. Yet when an architect they approved of demolished 18th-century or early 19th-century classical work in order to build a new wing, they were happy to see it happen. So much did they dislike the Georgian styles that these astute critics even expressed a fondness for the version of Elizabethan designed by Anthony Salvin, the kind that generally occupies a very insignificant place in architectural history (fig.9). Of the many publications discussed in Chapter Three below, only the *Architectural Review* seems to have had any respect for 18th-century architecture of the plain, Palladian, post-Queen Anne, type. Margot Asquith, who commissioned the restoration of an early 17th-century riverside barn, grew up in a 'Scottish baronial' David Bryce house of 1854–5 called The Glen, in the Borders, and adored it all her life; she recorded in her autobiography that she thought that Robert Smirke's austere neo-classical Whittingehame House (*c*.1817) in East Lothian, where her closest friends the Balfours lived, had the look of a municipal institution about it.[29]

For all her idiosyncrasies and wilfulness, Asquith was in that respect characteristic of her generation of builders. Edwardian domestic architecture is overwhelmingly 17th- or 16th-century in inspiration, to the extent that the *Architectural Review*'s interest in, say, the details of Robert Adam's houses or the 'polite vernacular' doorframes of the houses of Bath should be seen as an act of defiance by artist-architects against the majority view. The very best neo-classical houses of Edwardian England, large and small, such as those by Field,

are late Stuart, not 'Georgian' or 18th-century, in style; and up to the First World War Field's smallest and cheapest houses were designed in his own version of Jacobean vernacular.

Awareness

As with the gothic revivalists, the architects in this book cannot be expected to have been preternaturally aware of the themes of the period and their own contribution to it that have emerged a century later. But it is striking how little they addressed, in their speeches to the Royal Institute of British Architects (RIBA) or the Architectural Association, the principal aspects of house design as it was then executed and seen by anyone who read the trade papers, let alone *Country Life*. They almost never spoke about the most significant of those themes that I identify in this book: there was for example very little reference by these people to the economics of housebuilding, even though this arose again and again in detail in other contemporary discussions during the period. Many of the best-known architects of the time – and they

9. Anthony Salvin de-Georgianised the front elevation of the master's lodge at Trinity College, Cambridge, in 1842–3, providing a new but authentically mediaeval-looking front rather than a historical re-creation.

include Professor Pite, Professor Prior, Professor Ricardo and Professor Lethaby – had little useful to say. They wrote and spoke incessantly about the qualities of modern houses, and their lectures on the subject were reprinted over many pages of the professional and trade press. These were generally vague, speculative, and overly literary, philosophical and artistic, not to mention repetitive; there was much reference to the Morrisian ideals of the cottage lifestyle, of humility and modesty, of common sense, of pottery and pewterware, of largely arcane symbolism, of comparisons that can be made between dress and buildings, and so on: a typical lecture by E.S. Prior will have all of these.[30] Yet these fringe aspects of design that they mentioned explicitly touched the great mass of Edwardian housebuilding only as might a transient fashion.

They took no interest in the allegories between architecture and archaeology; nor did they see any connections between the way in which architecture was discussed by the best contemporary critics and the scientists who restored old buildings, from the zoologist George Herbert Fowler of University College London, who remodelled a cottage in Aspley Guise in Bedfordshire from 1906 with the architect W.H. Cowlishaw for his retirement, to George Darwin, the Cambridge professor of astronomy and experimental philosophy who from 1885 had Stevenson convert the Old Granary there as his home (fig.10). They said nothing about the growing uses of photography for the architect pioneered (in private, admittedly) by Devey. In fact they said almost nothing about altering old houses, which M.H. Baillie Scott did several times very successfully for himself, 'successfully' here meaning well enough for many other architects to imitate. They likewise never addressed in print the almost endlessly repeated phenomenon of houses that mixed the styles of the 17th century, sometimes within a single room, let alone a house, except to attack it, even when they had done it themselves, for example Prior during the period of his many designs inspired by the work of R. Norman Shaw of the 1880s. And they certainly never referred to a new house being designed to look as if it had been remodelled by vernacular builders over centuries. Yet these were everywhere too. To return in detail to many of these famous architects whose work and writings have been exhaustively examined by some of our greatest architectural historians would be, I feel, to go round endlessly in circles.

Indeed, unlike the best journalists they had remarkably little of practical use to say even about the very small houses, sometimes excellent ones, that they designed themselves. Baillie Scott's *Houses and Gardens* of 1904 started with a claim that his ideas were applicable to the cottage as well as to a large house, yet his chapter on children's rooms suggested providing four rooms for them: a day nursery, a schoolroom and a playroom as well as the 'sleeping apartments'; he did not discuss the smallest cottages that were intriguing the professional press until he reached Chapter 36.[31] He wrote that 'the modern Jacobean room . . . must necessarily be a failure' and that 'we have no workman now who would be able to re-create the spirit of the Jacobean age', comments which were demonstrably untrue: his own houses were by then entirely Jacobean in style, as were so many others, as every reader of *Country Life* and the *Architectural Review* was well aware.[32] It is striking too how derisive these architects were of the people who lived in modern houses. In the same book – which is full of beautiful, original, subtle plans and countless ideas – Baillie Scott characterised contemporary villa residences as 'St Mildred's' and 'The Pines', and thought that they should be called 'The Crime' instead; he said that they chose their furniture in order for it to 'pose and smirk'.[33] He also thought that these awful suburban people had their homes designed mainly to impress their own servants, specifically – as he bizarrely put it, moving into E.M. Forster territory – the 'gorgeous male domestic'.[34] That rang a bell. When writing *Bleak Houses* in 2012 I was struck by how much better the novelist Alan Hollinghurst is at describing the ordinary domestic architecture of the period than modernist historians are; he is evidently better too than the actual protagonists were.[35] The architects themselves were, I suppose, more interested in their own development than in other people's houses.

Legacy

Two difficulties have accompanied the writing of this book. The first is that Alastair Service and Osbert Lancaster in their different ways captured the houses of the period so well that I have had to keep reminding myself why it has been necessary to look at them again at all. Furthermore, many of the well-known architects of the period have for some time now been the subject of first-rate studies: Alan Crawford on C.R. Ashbee; Wendy Hitchmough on C.F.A. Voysey; Diane Haigh on Baillie Scott; Trevor Garnham on W.R. Lethaby; James Macaulay on Charles Rennie Mackintosh; David Valinsky on Prior; Sheila Kirk on Webb; and Stamp, Brown and Jane Ridley on Lutyens, now joined by a perceptive and useful book by David Cole. It is now some twenty years since Dean Hawkes produced a critical edition of Barry Parker's *Modern Country Homes in England* and provided a long introductory chapter to it. Some minor figures

10. The Old Granary, Cambridge, photographed by the author in February 2018. Stevenson converted this building as a house for Professor George Darwin in 1885 and made later additions. It is the archetype of the many Edwardian vernacular restorations and remodellings that followed.

are well accounted for too, from Jill Lever on A.T. Bolton in 1984 to Elizabeth McKellar on C.H.B. Quennell in 2007, both in substantial scholarly articles for *Architectural History*.[36]

In contrast to many of these writers, I am making a conscious effort to overcome both the teleology of an approach which emphasises the watershed of the First World War, and one of the so-far unavoidable tenets of modernism, especially one of several which were a rehash of gothic-revival dogma: that architectural styles 'develop'. The typically Edwardian houses in this book neither developed in style, nor were they replaced or superseded by neo-classical, neo-Georgian or proto-modernist ones: they just got better (or worse) at times, depending on the money, talent and interest spent on them. The other styles went on simultaneously or immediately afterwards; as fashion changed they attracted varying degrees of interest, but they did not replace them.

The trajectory of Edwardian building continued well beyond the War in defiance of the modernist theory of architectural history which stands in opposition to common sense, and of everyday observation to anyone who lives in a town. Davey, in his *Arts and Crafts Architecture*, wrote as if it were only the builders' speculative villas and suburban semi-detached that carried on where Baillie Scott and others had left off, but this is not the case: high-class architecture remained Jacobean for a long period after the First World War.[37] Bron-y-dē, the house that Philip Tilden designed for Lloyd George near Churt in Surrey at the beginning of 1922, precisely illustrates the 'archaeological' Jacobean house type that developed during the Edwardian period; so in different ways do the many idiosyncratic interwar Tudor houses designed by architects like Blunden Shadbolt or Ernest Trobridge, both of whom received their professional training around the end of the century. The upmarket 'Stockbrokers' Tudor' architect Edgar Ranger, born in 1888 and working in Broadstairs in Thanet from the mid-1920s up to the mid-1930s, established the high standard of design in the town that others imitated and copied; he also built a flower shop with a crumbling brick and stone motif that

11. A flower shop in Broadstairs by Edgar Ranger, 1925, photographed by the author in April 2013. Many 'Tudor' architects continued to develop Devey's ideas and Edwardian themes well into – and beyond – the interwar period.

12. (opposite) A corner of the courtyard at Brinsop Court, Herefordshire, remodelled and extended by H. Avray Tipping from 1911. The half-timber wing on the left was added by him; its outer walls were faced in stone (see p.141).

was surely taken from Devey's St Alban's Court in Nonington not far away (fig.11; see also fig.49). His small houses have a roughness to them that must be indebted to F.W. Troup's Peasant Art movement studios in Haslemere.[38]

The idea of a style of architecture that was 'lost' as a result of the First World War has no evidence to support it. Traces of Edwardian ideas cropped up in the grander interwar houses constructed from bits and pieces, or ones which reincorporated them, like Amyas Phillips's Bailiffscourt at Climping in West Sussex of 1931–3, not to mention the entire village of Portmeirion in north Wales by Clough Williams-Ellis, an architect who emerged early in the new century and who repeatedly appeared in the professional press in this period and continued to do so until the end of his long life in 1978. Ranger was still designing in freestyle Tudor in the early 1960s. Houses of this kind, large or small, seem to have a perpetual appeal that trumps every attempt at writing them

out of mainstream architectural history.[39] There is therefore no teleology and no 'development' in this book. A further example of how modernist history writing distorted the late Victorian and Edwardian scene is the way in which its critics looked at the fashion amongst arts-and-crafts designers for simplicity and saw it as a harbinger of Gropius's or Le Corbusier's Ripolin-white rooms.[40] But at the time they were no such thing: they demonstrated if anything a hankering after the genteel but modest mid-17th-century protestant interior, as plenty of evidence below will show. There has been much fine scholarship in recent years, for example by Paul Oliver, Mark Swenarton, and from a different perspective by Ballantyne and Law, about the later life of the Edwardian Jacobean style; my contribution is intended specifically to look at what generated it in the first place, and to try to kindle a feeling of what it might have been like to be there at the time, a sense of busyness and action.

1

KINGSGATE:
THE EDWARDIAN LIBERAL
AND HIS CASTLE

———

How doth the Banking Busy Bee
Improve his shining Hours
By studying on Bank Holidays
Strange Insects and Wild flowers!

Punch, 'Fancy Portraits no.96', 1882

I F YOU TAKE A WALK BETWEEN Joss Bay and Kingsgate Bay on the Isle of Thanet at the easternmost tip of Kent, up along the top of the chalk cliffs or even from the sandy beaches below, you can see a building – a castle – that will tell you almost everything that is special about Edwardian domestic architecture. Science; politics; archaeology; style; history; castle; fantasy; magic; golf; a contented people in the land of England: it is all there (fig.13).

Kingsgate Castle was built over the surviving walls of a Georgian folly in 1901–12 by John Lubbock, first Baron Avebury, the possessor of one of the most active and varied scientific minds of the 19th century (see fig.29). He was born in 1834, when William IV was on the throne. When Lubbock was

eight years old, his father told him that a wonderful surprise would be waiting for him that summer in Downe, the west Kent village near Farnborough where the family had their country home. Young Lubbock, excited, thought at first that it must be a pony; but in fact it turned out to be none other than Charles Darwin, already an eminent scientist.[1] This was an encounter that determined the direction of Lubbock's life; in time he became, perhaps, the ultimate Edwardian Liberal: scientific, optimistic, and astonishingly industrious. In addition to introducing Bank Holidays and his work on early closing, he vigorously promoted the first legislation to protect historic buildings. Overall, he pushed through 30 acts of parliament, at least nine of which were considered substantial

13. (p.26) The courtyard at Kingsgate Castle, remodelled in phases for Lord Avebury by W.H. Romaine-Walker in 1901–12. Patches of surviving flint masonry from the Georgian folly are readily identifiable.

14. The Lubbock family outside High Elms, their principal residence, in one of the earliest informal outdoor family daguerreotypes in existence, from 1842. John Lubbock, the future Lord Avebury, is the boy with the cricket bat towards the left-hand end of the house.

by his political supporters in his lifetime.[2] He did these from outside government because he had no time, or perhaps ambition, to take a ministerial role. He became a Liberal Unionist, opposed to Irish Home Rule for intellectual reasons, even at the cost of offending his friend W.E. Gladstone, and sat on the opposition benches after the Liberals won the general election in January 1906. Although he was taken out of Harrow School at the age of 14 to join his father's banking business, he was already as a child methodical and rational; inquisitive and technically ambitious; his greatest political regret must surely have been his failure to introduce a logical, fair system of proportional representation to British parliamentary elections.[3] The boy very soon made a lifelong friend of Darwin, accompanying him on walks around the village; he became especially fond of the Darwin circle, which included the biologist T.H. Huxley, and extended to Huxley's daughter and son-in-law, the prolific if unadventurous gothic-revival architect Frederick Waller who was based in Gloucester. His closest friends tended to come from backgrounds similar to his own, regardless of age – late in life he was badly affected by the death of Sir John Evans, a distinguished archaeologist with an industrialist background, who was more than ten years his senior. Unpretentious in manner, he travelled on the London Underground to accompany his son to the latter's first

day at work, even though he was a well-off and by then widely recognised grandee.[4]

There are two aspects of Lubbock's career that stand out: an absolute conviction of the importance of scientific evidence to decision making of any kind; and the connection between that evidence and the unfolding history of England and its people. His father, Sir John William Lubbock, third baronet, a banker, was elected to the Royal Society in 1829 – at the age of 26 – and throughout his life contributed papers on mathematics and astronomy to learned journals. This elder John Lubbock, says a biographer in a particularly neat phrase, was 'consistently drawn to topics which allowed him to relate mathematical theories with observations that had been collected by practical men with little formal scientific training' – a harbinger of the career of his son.[5] As an undergraduate he had been a friend of the young geologist William Whewell at Trinity College, Cambridge, and this, and other connections with Whewell's fellow scholars, provided the starting point for his various scientific endeavours and debates; in addition, his role as a partner in his own father's London bank, Sir John William Lubbock, Forster & Co., had enabled him to move easily in elevated social circles, culminating in the role of treasurer to the Great Exhibition of 1851. Perhaps for that reason he made the otherwise surprising decision to bring his son swiftly into business circles rather than pursue an academic career.

John William was an enthusiast for technological novelty; an early daguerreotype, of 1842, perhaps the first ever informal outdoor portrait photograph, shows the family outside High Elms, their newly extended country house (fig.14) – a scene in which the figure of his young son John can be seen wielding the cricket bat he had just been given as a birthday present in the April of that year, in that same summer when the Darwins moved to Downe House just the other side of the village. Only the plain Italianate look of the new extension, designed by Philip Hardwick of recent Euston Station fame, a lump of a building that pays only some regard to the style books of the 1830s – Charles Parker's popular *Villa Rustica* of 1832, for example – recalls the Georgian era that had ended five years beforehand. It is the completely inseparable relationship between all the fields of endeavour at which the Lubbocks excelled, whether social, political, historical or scientific, that seems to exemplify the hidden hand of the transformational Victorian elite. Even after the Lubbocks had sold the house – indeed, even after its destruction by fire in 1967 – the site speaks volumes about their achievement, for the estate became a public country park, intended for the enjoyment and subliminal education of a workforce freed, by John Lubbock junior, from the necessity to work every single day of the year that was not a religious holiday.

When some twenty years later this younger Lubbock first stood for parliament, he made some notes of his political ambitions:

1. To promote the study of Science, both in Secondary and Primary Schools;
2. To quicken the payment of the National Debt [he was a banker, after all]; and
3. To secure some additional holidays, and to shorten the hours of labour in shops.[6]

In a note added later he wrote that there had been only one scientist in the House of Commons at the time – the geologist George Poulett Scrope, then towards the end of his political career – but also that he was 'very anxious to carry a measure to prevent the then rapid destruction of ancient monuments' as much as to secure the public holidays. The latter, he wrote, 'met with practically no opposition'.[7] Only a year after his eventual election to parliament, for Maidstone as a Liberal in 1870, did he succeed in promoting the Bank Holidays Act, a name which intentionally carried no nationalistic or religious connotation but simply the fact – the *fact* – that banking transactions otherwise due on the day could be delayed for 24 hours. The Ancient Monuments Protection Act was however a different matter; Lubbock pursued it in vain for the entire period – nine years – in which he was member of parliament for the constituency.

This early episode in the development of what has turned out to be one of the primary characteristics of British culture – that is, the establishment of extremely high standards of building conservation and the endless, often very profitable, promotion of heritage as a national asset – has been described recently by Simon Thurley.[8] Lubbock had been motivated by a threat from housebuilding developers to the site of Avebury, a series of neolithic stone circles west of Marlborough in Wiltshire, some 20 miles (30 kilometres) north of Stonehenge. He bought the land and saved the stones. His interest was, generally, in the most ancient of remains, Romano-British at the latest, rather than in the badly mutilated and perpetually threatened mediaeval monuments that had so intrigued and moved the romantic antiquaries of an earlier generation: in 1865 he had published a book, subsequently much reprinted in different versions, called *Pre-historic Times: As Illustrated by Ancient Remains, and the Manners and Customs of Modern Savages*, as ever combining his research with ethnological observations. As with much else in British politics, the contemporary problem was to do with landownership rather than anything else. Attempts to interfere with the traditional rights of landowners had always been seen as subversive, and Thurley points out that antiquaries – even John Britton whose monumental and (in Britton's words) 'scientific and systematic' efforts at recording and preservation in the 1820s and 1830s – were considered marginal and eccentric because they threatened them.[9] Disraeli's Conservative government of 1874–80 was not going to interfere with land rights and Gladstone's Liberal one that followed was not going to sanction the expense of compulsory purchase, inspection and preservation work. Some independent trusts were already buying up and looking after historic sites: Thurley gives the example of Shakespeare's birthplace in Stratford-upon-Avon, in private hands since 1847 and attracting visitors in numbers large enough to pay for its upkeep. This provided a rival model. It took the appointment of G.J. Shaw-Lefevre as First Commissioner of Works in 1880 for anything to happen, and even then the Ancient Monuments Protection Act of 1882 only allowed the State to receive, rather than compulsorily purchase, such monuments from a published list of 68 or others 'of a like character'.[10] But it was Lubbock's work that had eventually borne fruit.

15. One of countless 18th-century views of Holland House surrounded by the follies, with the Castle above the cliffs to the left, the ruined convent of St Mildred's on the horizon to the right, and the Captain Digby pub, looking like a chapel, just below it to the left.

Mimic desolation

In the meantime, Lubbock had continued his prodigious output of surveys of British phenomena, topographical, botanic, geological and much else, and of the links between them, such as his *On Certain Relations Between Plants and Insects: A Lecture*, of 1873, as well as on proportional representation. It is striking, then, that his principal venture into modern architecture was an attempt to address the irrationality of the early antiquaries, and their riotous predecessors the Hellfire Club, in the early 18th century.

In July 1901, a few months into the reign of King Edward VII, Lord Avebury – as Lubbock had become at the beginning of the previous year – went on holiday to Margate with his wife Alice and son Eric because he had been advised that the boy was in need of 'the tonic air'.[11] They rented a portion of Holland House, then owned by the artist Luke Fildes, a strange and degraded Palladian mansion a few steps from the cliff's edge on Kingsgate Bay, the centrepiece of an intriguing set of mid-18th-century follies, structures that even in their present altered form continue to attract fascination.[12] The house, originally called King's Gate House, had been built in 1762 by Henry Fox, first Baron Holland, the Whig politician and father of Charles James Fox, who had himself decided to settle there for the benefit of his health. It was much illustrated in its original form, mostly inaccurately, even before day trippers from Margate and Ramsgate went off in search of it from the 1820s; its sea front was composed of a tall hexastyle pediment flanked by five-bay, two-storey wings, and there was a grand saloon on the landward side. The walls were built of coursed ashlar flint, which 'being well polish'd & nicely join'd, has the appearance of Black marble', and a copper roof.[13] There is no definitive history of its design, but Hugh Honour wrote about it in *Country Life* in 1953: he attributed it on the basis of an account from 1813 to an amateur architect and politician called Thomas Wynn, with professional assistance from John Vardy, who had designed a great deal around Westminster in the 1750s and may well have known Holland from there.[14] Already by 1825 it was noted that 'the mimic ruins which surrounded it are become real ones'.[15] Honour pointed out that there is a design by Robert Adam for a decorative 'Cieling for Lady Hollands Bed Chamber at Kingsgate, 1767', at Sir John Soane's Museum, and he attributed the design of the follies to Wynn and J.L. Nicholl. There are some traces today of ornamental work on the first floor of Holland House, and of its pair of ornamental pavilion bays; the rest however had been plastered, mutilated and subdivided by the time that Avebury arrived on the scene, and the portico with its columns were long gone. According to his son, it was a surprise to his own family when Fildes took it up as a seaside residence, and apparently a coincidence that the family's London home, the house by Norman Shaw in Melbury Road, bordered on the grounds of Holland House, the first Lord Holland's Jacobean residence.[16]

Just about every account of Kingsgate includes the famous poem by Thomas Gray, which gives some suggestion of what Holland was trying to convey when he chose what was still, when Fildes moved there in 1896, a 'pretty bleak' location, and why he had built the gothic follies, which according to William Gilpin were 'depraved', that were visible in every direction from its windows (fig.15):[17]

Old, and abandoned by each venal friend,
  Here Holland formed the pious resolution
To smuggle a few years, and strive to mend
  A broken character and constitution.

On this congenial spot he fixed his choice;
  Earl Goodwin trembled for his neighbouring sand;
Here sea-gulls scream, and cormorants rejoice,
  And mariners, though shipwrecked, dread to land.

Here reign the blustering North and blighting East,
  No tree is heard to whisper, bird to sing;
Yet Nature could not furnish out the feast,
  Art he invokes new horrors still to bring.

Here mouldering fanes and battlements arise,
  Turrets and arches nodding to their fall,
Unpeopled monast'ries delude our eyes,
  And mimic desolation covers all.

'Ah!' said the sighing peer, 'had Bute been true,
  Nor Mungo's, Rigby's, Bradshaw's friendship vain,
Far better scenes than these had blest our view,
  And realized the beauties which we feign:

'Purged by the sword, and purified by fire,
  Then had we seen proud London's hated walls;
Owls would have hooted in St. Peter's choir,
  And foxes stunk and littered in St. Paul's.'[18]

Holland felt by that time that his career had been ruined by the treachery of his political friends, and his mimic desolation consisted of: a ruined convent, actually the servants' accommodation; a ruined chapel with stables, built as and the surviving part still today a public house called the Captain Digby (or, poetically, 'Oh! The Noble Captain Digby Oh!');[19] a ruined castle, for Lord Holland's stables; the Arx Ruochim (Ruoihm was thought to be the British name for Thanet), a miniature Henrician fortress with a plaque claiming it was built in the fifth century; the King's Gate

16. James Basire portrayed the Kingsgate follies in their original appearance through a series of engravings around 1769. The Castle at this time provided stables for Lord Holland's horses.

itself, a grand gateway across the way down to the bay to commemorate the arrival of King Charles II and the Duke of York in 1683 (at which point the name had been changed from St Bartholomew's Gate); and various towers, forts and monuments, decorative or 'ruined', some of which have fallen into the sea or been felled by storms but nevertheless mostly survive today in some form. James Basire drew and engraved a series of illustrations depicting them around 1769 (fig.16).[20]

Whatever Lord Holland's intentions had been, the Kingsgate follies must have looked to Avebury as to everyone else like an astonishing and confused way of representing history. For much of the 19th century only a very small number of people had any idea of how to interpret or explain genuinely ancient structures. Historic buildings had first been represented accurately in engravings in the pioneering publications of Britton and his illustrator, A.W.N. Pugin's father Auguste Pugin, in the Regency and George IV periods, less than a century previously; what elements of building construction actually did, or why an architect might emphasise or exaggerate them in order to create a coherent architectural style, was an only slightly newer interest, derived from A.W.N. Pugin's realism from the 1840s. In spite of the penetration of the scholarly gothic revival into every corner of England – and Pugin's church of St Augustine, Ramsgate, one of its finest buildings, was only a short trip away from Kingsgate – there was very little sense about how old anything was. The Margate shell grotto, in the nearby town to the north-west, had been 'discovered' (if that is what it was) in the 1830s, but no one had any idea of its age, or of how, if it was an ornamental regency fantasy like so many others, it could have been built without anyone noticing: even today nobody knows what its

17. Holidaymakers from London visit the Kingsgate follies, from Paul Pry's *A Trip to Margate* (*c.*1830).

origins are. So any observer could draw from these curious structures whatever they wanted to. A humorous picture book called *A Trip to Margate by Paul Pry Esq.*, published soon after 1827 – Paul Pry was a generic name for comic writers – includes a vignette of a group of fashionably dressed tourists being introduced by a guide to a ruined gothic tower, with refreshment rooms in the background (fig.17):

> 'Pray can you tell us how old this Ruin is?'
> 'Lord bless you Marm. its all a sham – I dare say it aren't near so old as your Ladyship.'

The refreshment rooms might have been the Captain Digby, the folly-chapel-stable-pub.

There can be little doubt that by the end of the century, Lord Avebury of all people would recognise a Georgian folly when he saw one. But what attracted him to Kingsgate? Perhaps a country seat to suit his title? Even on that first visit to Holland House he 'thought of buying the Castle', and that October he returned to look at it again.[21] At 67 he was ten years older than Lord Holland had been when he had plunged himself into the building of the house and its follies, but it may well be that he was encouraged by news of others who had already made the same step. The London solicitor William Capel Slaughter, founder of Slaughter & May, had moved into a large, plain Italianate (if anything) house called White Ness close by before 1900 to which he eventually made grand improvements, including a colonnaded verandah and ornamental plaster ceiling; he owned the land between his residence and the village of Reading Street.[22] And Clifford Brookes JP, like Slaughter a golf enthusiast, lived at the Convent just to the east of White Ness, originally Lord Holland's 'Convent of St Mildred', which if Basire's illustration is to be believed once incorporated a large ruined gothic window standing on its own at the north-western end of its cloister.

There was another golf player nearby: the journalist and editor Alfred Harmsworth, the founder of the popular *Comic Cuts* magazine. In the late summer of 1890, the 25-year-old Harmsworth, already on the verge of becoming the proprietor of the largest magazine company in the world, had been holidaying in Broadstairs when his horse stopped by a tall garden wall outside the picturesque village of Reading Street, allowing its rider to see into 'as beautiful a garden as Thanet could show'. Entranced, he bought the house as soon as he could, for £4,000 from the profits of his magazine *Answers to Correspondents*, and spent a further £1,600 fitting it up.[23] This was Elmwood, a cement-fronted mid-Victorian villa with older origins. The Harmsworths moved in on 15 April 1891, and Harmsworth himself preferred it to anywhere else he ever lived.[24] As well as playing golf, he spent his time there 'working, fishing, cycling, watching cricket, playing tennis, receiving visits from members of his editorial staffs, relishing the satisfaction of owning a kennel of pedigree Irish terriers, and being able to stroll through his own peach and orchid houses, and having recourse to what an enthusiastic neighbour described as "the finest billiard room in Thanet'", which he had built at the back of the house together with other half-timbered extensions and improvements, as well as a little garden pavilion to work in.[25] In 1898, two years after launching the *Daily Mail,* he bought Joss Farm on the other side of the road down to Joss Bay and the Castle, changed its name to Elmwood Farm, and founded there a popular annual summer camp for poor boys from the London borough of Southwark, which he funded liberally.[26] There were other lively people about with overlapping interests. Harry Hananel Marks, a journalist and former Conservative MP, lived just beyond Harmsworth in a spectacularly ornate half-timbered Victorian mansion of somewhat German appearance, and Fildes himself seems to have run a congenial household, judging by his son's biography.[27] A fine group of Edwardian grandees were thus clustering around the site, aided by convenient trains from Victoria to Broadstairs station.

Avebury attended a soirée at the Castle on the evening of 3 September 1901. Then in early October he went on an elevating tour to North Berwick in East Lothian, where he admired the dramatic ruins of Tantallon Castle on the cliffs above the sea and the 'fine coast' around St Abb's Head. Immediately on returning home three days later he made his decision: 'We have bought Kingsgate Castle for £8250'.[28] That was on 19 October 1901. On the 24th he took the train to Margate, and the following day 'Walker met us at Kingsgate & we discussed plans'.[29]

The Edwardian Kingsgate Castle

⸺

'Walker' was W.H. Romaine-Walker, a London architect at the time in partnership with Francis Besant, and his career too provides an exemplar of the Edwardian professional trajectory. The castle that he and Avebury inspected had been patched up to create a residence, a ramshackle conversion of Lord Holland's picturesque stables. By the mid-19th century irregular rooms and corridors had been added behind its most imposing facades – as had also happened at the Convent – and its courtyard had been partially filled with service buildings (fig.18).

A detailed plan survives showing its arrangement.[30] A wall had been built dividing the complex into two equal-sized parts, each with a courtyard: the north-western one comprised the house, and the south-eastern the stable yard. The house was entered from the north-west, the elevation facing Kingsgate Bay and the Captain Digby illustrated in Basire's print. A central front door where Holland's arch had been led to an entrance hall, with a pair of dining rooms either side towards the corner towers; the southern of these was probably in fact a drawing room, and the northern one was adjacent to the kitchen. Behind them, and facing onto the courtyard, were small bedrooms. There was a library at the northern corner of the range with a closet, presumably an earth closet, adjacent to it. The base of the tall round tower on the seaward side, the centrepiece of Holland's original folly, had been converted into a dressing room. A small staircase led to an upper storey, and photographs of the house show that there were rooms in the first floor of each of the two square towers: their windows had been made since Basire had illustrated it. The other half of the Castle was given over to a stable block at the sea end, and coachhouses and box rooms along the south-eastern front of the yard. There was storage for harnesses and a further room for hay in the southern tower. This was a generous arrangement and it is possible that they had been built like this for Lord Holland himself. Behind the two round towers on the south-western front there was an enclosed kitchen yard with a laundry building and further closets. An oddity of this plan is that although apparently accurate, to the extent of providing room dimensions and some details, it shows these towers as being unaligned: the Ordnance Survey map of 1874 indicates by contrast that they were a symmetrical pair either side of an entrance gate on the landward side.

18. The Castle, as a somewhat ramshackle residence before the Edwardian restoration, seen from the Captain Digby pub on the other side of the bay. A view from 1869.

All this was picturesque and generous in space but impractical for a modern house; although the three principal rooms were in a logical place, there was no reason to suppose that the recent structures and their roofs would have met modern expectations. There were few bedrooms, and some of them were very small; furthermore, the courtyard was divided up into compartments and service rooms. The first decision must have been to agree that this courtyard would be entered from between the round towers on the south-western side and would be restored as the centre of the new residence; the primary accommodation would occupy the same flank of the courtyard as the Victorian house (fig.19). Indeed, Romaine-Walker's new suite of ground-floor rooms followed a similar layout. With the court cleared of the service buildings, a grand new porch would lead from it into a lobby and thence into a hall at the centre of the north-west front (fig.20). Either side of this there was to be a small open anteroom under each of Holland's square towers, and beyond that a dining room on the landward side and a drawing room, again linked to a library, towards the sea. These rooms seem to have been of about the same relatively narrow width as their predecessors, but they opened up from one another to provide a grand

19.   (opposite) The restored entrance towers on the south-western side of the Castle. The new drive led directly to this gate rather than meandering over to the north-west front, as had been the case with the Victorian house.

20.   The courtyard elevation of the residential wing of the Castle, with Avebury's arms over the porch.

sweep across the whole of the front (fig.21). This wing was then doubled in height, and a stair hall beside the main entrance led up to the bedrooms.

The coachhouses were rebuilt as garages on the same location, which led by a door directly into the court opposite the new grand entrance, for Avebury had his eye on purchasing a 'motor' (fig.22). This service area also led into the household office wing, to the right of the pair of entrance towers from the outside, but the kitchen itself must have always been located in the windowless basement below the dining room: a photograph from the Avebury period shows a parapet wall in the courtyard close to the surviving stairs down to what later became a hotel kitchen. Underground kitchens were not unheard of in Edwardian country houses: Ernest George designed one for his last big house, the 'late Elizabethan' Eynsham Hall, Oxfordshire, in 1904.[31] But how

did staff and goods at Kingsgate cross from the service wing into the kitchen without passing intrusively across the formal entrance into the courtyard? There is a second basement below the service wing of the courtyard, and there must have been a tunnel. Tunnelling is easy in areas of soft chalk and Thanet is riddled with them. Avebury installed another one that led down from his entrance hall through the cliff to the bay. At Rhinefield in Hampshire Romaine-Walker had designed a trench between the main house and the service wing along which servants could walk without being seen.[32]

Archaeology

Avebury has been described as one of the 'greatest archaeologists of his generation' in addition to his many other talents.[33] By his second wife Alice he was also the son-in-law of General Augustus Henry Pitt Rivers, described by his biographer Mark Bowden as 'the father of scientific archaeology', a man venerated by Avebury above all others but Darwin.[34] Pitt Rivers's reputation was based on decades of systematic excavation from the late 1860s onwards, especially of prehistoric and Romano-British settlements in Dorset, Wiltshire and the Thames valley, and this close connection throws light on Avebury's choice of architect. For up to 1901, Avebury had shown no particular interest in architecture of any kind, in spite of the fact that his friend Huxley's daughter Jessica was married to Waller, whose Gloucester practice was flourishing.[35] He had stayed with the Wallers when he opened a public library in Gloucester in May 1900; Waller's father had founded a family practice which was already well known for its restoration of old, especially gothic, churches and other buildings. But he did not choose Waller for his own house.

Horace Hutchinson, his biographer, wrote tellingly that for Avebury, 'All the beauties of Nature and of Scenery were objects of love and interest, but he was little attracted, as I think, by the beauties of art', and his interest in the latter was entirely altruistic, that is, what might be called 'handsome is as handsome does'.[36] His friend Fildes had employed Norman

Shaw in London, and it was Shaw who had converted his neighbour Brookes's remodelled Convent behind Fildes's Holland House into a grand retirement home for the London shipowner and art patron Frederick Richards Leyland and his mistress Annie Ellen Wooster in 1891–2; someone – it is not known who – designed a fine terrace of cottages in 17th-century Flemish style, with coursed ashlar knapped flints and red-brick dressings, dated 1901, on Convent land.[37] Avebury probably already knew Ightham Court in west Kent, with Shaw's happy interventions from the 1870s, and where more alterations had taken place in the 1890s.[38] But by 1900 Shaw had almost entirely retired from practice.

Pitt Rivers had spent his final years tending to Rushmore, his house at his estate at Tollard Royal in Wiltshire. He had earlier employed Philip Webb to extend the house, but Webb's proposed new gatehouse proved too expensive for him; instead, Romaine-Walker and his then partner Augustus William Tanner had designed in 1886–7 a pair of half-timbered lodges, one of which had a bay window with battlements, and the other, called the Jubilee Room, functioned as a chapel and was possibly the location of Pitt Rivers's funeral in May 1900 which Avebury attended.[39] Avebury may also have admired the rather different 'Temple of Vesta', a Roman rotunda in the garden, designed by Romaine-Walker and Tanner in 1890, and Pitt Rivers's last domestic building project.[40] These were only small bits and pieces, architecturally, hardly a useful precedent. But, importantly, Romaine-Walker had won the General's confidence. No doubt the fact that Pitt Rivers had once employed Waller and then fallen out with him over payment played a role in this.[41]

Bowden made several points about Pitt Rivers which hint at his importance to architectural history. First of these was his precision and demanding standards: 'the level of supervision of Pitt Rivers' excavations was extremely high by nineteenth-century standards', he has written, as was the detail of his reports.[42] Secondly, one of his many legacies was the use of experimental interpretative and analytical techniques, because understanding the role of findings in a historical narrative was as important as digging them up.[43] M.W. Thompson, another biographer, has written that Pitt Rivers's approach 'clearly altered the whole nature of excavation':

The objectives were quite different: it was not just a tedious removal of soil in order to remove the urn or Roman tessellated pavement but an end in itself. You set out not with the express purpose of making finds of great value, but with the intention of dating the earthwork from small, valueless finds in it, or of

21.   The Castle soon after restoration, viewed from the west. The principal rooms were arranged *en filade* along the flank to the left, with lobbies at the centre and a drawing room (left) and dining room (right) extending as far as the towers.

22.   The service wing of the courtyard. In 1903 the door at the centre led directly to Avebury's 'motor room'; in 1912 Romaine-Walker replaced this with a staff accommodation and garage wing.

studying the life of the people in a settlement from the discarded bones of their domestic animals. Probably indeed you were not quite sure what information would be brought to light by the excavation but – and this is the important point – you were quite confident that significant additions to knowledge could be made in this way.[44]

Interestingly, Pitt Rivers 'did not associate with historians but rather with fellow archaeologists, sociologists, anatomists and anthropologists'.[45] He had probably met Avebury at meetings of the Ethnological Society which Pitt Rivers had joined in 1861.[46]

One way of looking at Kingsgate Castle, then, might be to see it as a kind of archaeological site. The striking thing about it is that from the outside it appears as bleak as the surrounding landscape had ever been (fig.23). The remodelled Castle sat squarely without any compromise with the scrubby, grassy land around it, and certainly no ornamental Victorian garden: Pugin, at his Grange a little way along the coast at Ramsgate, had pioneered this approach more than half a century earlier, but most Victorian architects had been seduced by plants and trees. By moving the front entrance to between the twin towers on the landward side, Avebury could dispense with the curving drive that previously led to the centre of the accommodation wing. At High Elms he had an ornamental Italian garden, but perhaps he did not feel any attraction to it. When he later visited William Waldorf Astor's Hever Castle in west Kent, restored in 1903–7 and enlarged with servants' quarters in the style of a sprawling mediaeval village by Frank Loughborough Pearson, Avebury thought its Italian garden 'rather out of place'; although Hever was 'well done', he seems to have taken more interest in Deal Castle, which was a Henrician rose-plan fort on the county's eastern coast that had been converted into a residence over a period of time and without any Victorian architect's grand plan.[47]

And then there is the flint. Flint was not a 'polite' building material in 1900. Avebury will have known the Roman remains of Rutupiae, Richborough Castle, nearby, not least because the route to Sandwich passed not far from it, and the railway to Deal and Dover almost scrapes its walls. This is what his own Kingsgate Castle most resembles, especially in the early photographs before the creeper took hold along its walls. That is: large chunks of thick flint masonry emerging from the grass. Avebury's Diary notes in several entries his interest in geological strata, and he was struck by a large ammonite in the cliff in Joss Bay just to the south of the Castle.[48] There is an element of these, too. The orthogonal severity of the castle-like windows that Romaine-Walker installed along the principal

front do nothing to ameliorate it, even though towards the courtyard and around the back and sides, and even more so in his other large new buildings, he went in for picturesque compositions. At Kingsgate Avebury might have felt that he was looking at an object, a series of rational building materials, rather than at the facade of a house.

The principal front at Kingsgate dominates the view from across the Bay – not just from the windows of Holland House but from the popular Captain Digby public house that directly faces it – just as an ancient castle might have done, but perhaps with an educational aspect to it, because the day trippers refreshing themselves opposite could surely learn from this view what building was. The castle complements the austerity of the cliffs rather than competing with them. Avebury had very effectively transferred the dignified, somewhat geological imagery of Tantallon Castle that had so impressed him onto his own new residence without compromising its comfort and modern elegance.[49] He paved the terrace towards the sea on the north-eastern side and put up merely a simple iron railing to prevent members of his household from falling off the cliff; the plain semi-circular terrace on the north-west drawing- and dining-room side appeared only towards the end of his life.

The overall idea of the old house was thus retained around what was an almost completely new building. Romaine-Walker and Avebury kept traces of the old walls, especially of the towers, in the new fronts, but they are readily distinguishable from them because Holland had built them with small unknapped flints, and the new work was in knapped flint of a superior quality. The house thus retained its archaeological character, and evident traces of its past, which must have been as desirable to Avebury as it would have been to those who were inclined to a liberal interpretation of William Morris's 1877 manifesto of the Society for the Protection of Ancient Buildings, which called for architects 'to treat our ancient buildings as monuments of a bygone art, created by bygone manners, that modern art cannot meddle with without destroying'.[50] In 1904, when the first stage of the house was complete, Avebury was elected president of the Society of Antiquaries of London.

Avebury must have been excited by progress at the Castle because he came down to see it under construction a number of times, and photographed it in October 1902, the

day after he noted in his diary that the roof was on.[51] These photographs have survived and it is unclear from them what roof that would be, because at this stage the masonry on the house side of the courtyard had been reduced to a stable single-storey height with the exception of the two square towers.[52] He was concerned about the stability of the chalk cliff alongside the Castle and that summer when work was already underway had sought advice from Arthur Rowe, a fellow of the Geological Society of London who had been born in Margate and who had made an early study of the landscape there.[53] Rowe referred him to Mr Latham, the borough engineer, and following a long consultation with him – 'I fear it will be an expensive business' – Avebury approved his plan to build up a tall protective structure of piers and arches the full height and width of the cliff below the building.[54]

Avebury was sufficiently proud of his work at the Castle to record its purchase and rebuilding at the head of the list of the year's achievements that he inscribed into his Diary every December. He seems also to have been anxious to try it out before it was finished. In March 1903 he and Alice were 'much pleased' with it. The following day he joined a committee – of which he was elected president, and Capel Slaughter, Marks, Brookes and Harmsworth as vice-presidents – of a new golf club based around the Harley Tower, one of Holland's follies that lay on Capel Slaughter's land.[55] He paid three more day-long visits to Kingsgate before recording in July, with emphasis, that he 'Slept at Kingsgate for the first time. Irene down with us. There is still a great deal to do.'[56] He returned to London to meet Émile Loubet, the president of the French Republic, then in the middle of his term in office, and the day after that, Loubet, the King and the Duke of York. So it was certainly looking as if his new residence would match the status of himself. In his impatience he arrived back in Kingsgate a week before taking possession, on 13 July 1903, and even then there was a 'great confusion: neither drawing room, dining room, nor Library ready'. Two days later however he dined for the first time in the dining room, and on the 17th 'Sowed the grass in the Courtyard', perhaps himself. He 'Got into the Drawing room' on the 19th, and his eldest son Johnny came down for the weekend. He 'Got into the anteroom' – that is, the central room in the ground-floor suite – on the 29th, and following a day trip to London, 'Got into the Library' on 4 August. The excitement radiates from the page: for all his many family houses, Avebury had never built one himself before. In between these annexations of domestic territory he found time for two visits to the links at Sandwich.

Avebury commissioned professional architectural photography of his new home and from that it is possible

23.   (opposite) The entrance elevation of the Castle soon after Avebury's death and before the hotel extensions. It is striking how much the scene resembled an archaeological site, not only because of the ivy-clad flint walls but also because of the distinct lack of any kind of domestic garden.

24. (opposite, above) The ante-room at the centre of the south-west front, furnished by Lady Avebury. There is a remarkable contrast between the finely detailed Adam interior and the tough castellated exterior of the house.

25. (opposite, below) The drawing room. The rooms were relatively small for a large mansion in which plenty of entertaining took place.

26. The dining room. This was located at the southern corner of the Castle from which it could overlook the drive as well as the sea. By contrast with the ante-room, this was an essay in French baroque. Note the door from an earlier and much older Lubbock house.

to see what the interior looked like (figs 24–26). There was nothing castle-like about it apart from the windows: the style was mostly mid-Georgian, all painted white, with simple mouldings in the panelling which may have been beading applied to the walls; there were ornamental doorcases topped by a domesticated Doric entablature with a triglyph pattern alternating with rosettes, and a delicate narrow cornice ran around the rooms. The ceilings were decorated with simple geometrical plaster garlands, the kind of interpretation of Robert Adam that was readily available at the time from West End decorators. However there were baroque 'late Stuart' flourishes in the plasterwork, and an old door, with

what looked like some Jacobean linenfold panelling in it, was moved from another Avebury residence to provide an entrance into the dining room.[57] In these rooms the Aveburys placed simple 18th-century furniture and a few ornaments, as well as some comfortable chairs and sofas; there were thick curtains – they were needed! – in a Chinese bird and branch pattern. Interestingly, there was no sign in these living rooms of large formal portraits: instead they hung engravings with wide mounts and narrow frames, as in an aesthetic interior. Hutchinson thought that here Alice had 'found opportunity for the exercise of her talent in making "the house beautiful"'.[58] The other type of room they recall might be those of Avebury's many friends at Cambridge where mediaeval buildings – the best-known of which had been restored externally to look more mediaeval than ever before – still retained their 18th-century plaster decoration and joinery. The library, which faced the sea through a new bay window, was panelled like the study of a don.

The other parts of the building did have a prettier air externally. The courtyard, entirely Romaine-Walker's creation, was faced all round with irregular mullioned windows of different types. The arched porch to the lobby that led from it was decorated with a prominent Avebury coat of arms, and to the right there was a huge window that lit the staircase. After grassing the courtyard Avebury paved it, and put a large ornamental flower tub in the centre, and the effect was very attractive (fig.27). The family went there for Christmas in 1906 and on Boxing Day Avebury recorded a characteristically jolly event in his diary: 'Snow. Halloran says the heaviest he has ever known here. We had a little dance for the servants. It was nearly full moon & a beautiful night. The Courtyard with the snow, & the Castle lit up looked lovely.'[59] Although the Aveburys visited the Castle only about four times a year, they generally spent long periods there in the summer and sometimes over Christmas. The Castle's visitors' book is filled with the names of relations and family connections: Lubbocks, Pitt Riverses, Fox-Pitts and Grant Duffs: evidently it was popular for seaside holidays. Sir Edward Poynter, the artist, came in June 1906 and Earl Curzon, former Viceroy of India, in September 1911. Avebury's golfing friends came too: Bernard Darwin, who wrote on golf for *Country Life*, visited in late August 1904. By contrast, Romaine-Walker's name appears in the book only in 1914, after Avebury's death, when he arrived for a visit with the 27-year-old Harry Stuart Goodhart-Rendel.[60]

In 1907 Avebury named rooms in his Castle after his 'scientific friends': Darwin, Joseph Hooker, Huxley, John Tyndall, George Busk, Evans, John Ruskin, his daughter Ursula's father-in-law Sir Mountstuart Grant Duff and Henry

Two Avebury family members or guests stand at the open archway to the terrace that looks out over the English Channel. The archaeological character is maintained by the jagged tower to the right, but Avebury and Romaine-Walker later converted this into further accommodation.

Pelham, a sort of index to Victorian knowledge in itself.[61] The couple's many children often brought friends and in-laws, and the family entertained constantly; the tennis court on the lawn outside the Castle must have been an attraction. Towards the end of a long visit in August 1912, to recuperate from severe illness, Avebury recalled that the Castle had been full almost the whole time, but even that had not prevented him from correcting the proofs of his *Origin of Civilisation* and of a paper called 'Notes on Pollen' for the Journal of the Royal Microscopical Society.[62] All this activity required new building work. In June 1909 Romaine-Walker visited, and with Avebury decided on the immediate building of what at first was called 'the Verandah' but later, and in family albums, the 'cloister': this was an arcade of three gothic arches facing the sea alongside a small irregular round tower, which had been left in its 'ruined' form as a remnant of Holland's stable.[63] Romaine-Walker no doubt encouraged this, because both cloisters and triple arcades had been motifs of his (fig.28; see also fig.31). Here it gave Avebury a quiet place to sit and look out to sea away from the courtyard where, judging by family photographs, the young people liked to spend much of their time; at the same time the tower, which had been left in its 'ruined' form, was built up to provide more rooms above.

In 1910 Avebury bought the triangle of land he called Brookes Corner (it had been part of Clifford Brookes's Convent estate) beyond the end of his entrance drive, so that he could extend it visually and avoid a diversion when motoring to the golf course or the Convent.[64] How much golf he played himself

there is not clear since he did not record all his local games.[65] And then in early 1912, perhaps when it had become clear to him that he would be spending more time there, he decided to replace the old narrow garage wing along the south-east side with a two-storey flat-roofed building that projected towards the service court. This had more spacious garages and what looks like (because of its tall ceiling and large window) a servants' hall on the ground floor, with servants' accommodation above.[66] Avebury and his family enjoyed motor cars and in the family album there is a photograph of one outside the old garage doors.[67] The final addition to the castle in Avebury's day was the clock presented to him on his 79th birthday, which was placed in the gablet above the central courtyard door to the new wing.

Enter the Edwardian architect

Who designed all this? Very little is known about William Henry Romaine-Walker personally beyond what appeared in his obituary notice in the *Builder* in May 1940, and a note published the following month from a former employee, F.R. Jelley (fig.30).[68] These give the impression of a grand old man: he had been one of the oldest Associates of the Royal Institute of British Architects. Jelley recalled that the atmosphere in his office at 6 Old Bond Street in London in 1909 was Dickensian – he said that there 'was an old-world courtesy about the

28. (top) The north-east front of the Castle soon after completion of the 1909 cloister and 1912 staff and garage extensions.

29. Avebury in the drawing room of his Castle in 1909.

place, as though the spirit of the Brothers Cheeryble hovered around those ancient rooms'; that his former employer had always written with a goose quill; and that the office had not been 'contaminated' by either a typewriter or what he called, in inverted commas, 'business English'.[69] Although there was a telephone, the number was omitted from directories so as not to give the impression of an advertisement. Thus Romaine-Walker seemed at the time to have brought a Victorian spirit into the 20th century. But in fact his career was eminently Edwardian, for he had started as a goth, had gone through an arts-and-crafts and almost bohemian stage around the turn of the century, and ended as a classicist: among his practice's final projects were the neo-classical extensions to the Tate Gallery before and after the First World War, and the role of what would now be called executive architect for Edwin Lutyens's 67–68 Pall Mall of 1930–31, the one with the vanishing pilasters that faces St James's Palace. When Avebury found him he was married to Giulietta, née Arditti, but London-born, and living at 3C Hyde Park Mansions near Edgware Road Underground station with their baby daughter Winifride, a nurse, a cook and a chambermaid.[70] The one style he never entered was the 'modern': Jelley recalled that he had once said that 'When I enter a building designed in the so-called modern manner, I always take off my hat. Not out of respect for the building, but out of respect for my hat!'

This story began in the vicarage of St Saviour's church in Pimlico, London. His father John Walker, born in 1823 in Manchester, became the church's first vicar in 1864, and

30. The Edwardian architect: Romaine-Walker in a studio portrait
by Lascelle of Baker Street, from a history of Holy Trinity,
Hastings, of 1934.

lived in the vicarage at 57 St George's Square with his wife
Caroline.[71] William Henry had been born in 1854 in Bury, when
his father was perpetual curate of St Paul's church there.[72] St
Saviour's was 'High' church, designed for the Grosvenor Estate
from 1863 by Thomas Cundy II, ragstone, gothic of course,
'quite large and prosperous', says the *Buildings of England*,
loftier and tighter than typical work of the decade.[73] Young
William was sent to Lancing College, the most imposing of
the middle- and upper-middle-class schools founded by the
Puseyite pamphleteer Nathaniel Woodard near Shoreham
in West Sussex, with buildings by the Tractarians' favourite
architect R.C. Carpenter. This grand gothic complex of
courtyards and gatehouses, still unfinished but already the
scholastic idyll that Pugin had dreamed of, was in use by 1857
and therefore still fairly new when Romaine-Walker (it is not
clear when he adopted the double barrel) was sent there.

From here he joined the office of George Edmund
Street as an articled clerk where according to one account he

worked on drawings for the Law Courts in London, and after
five years opened an office with Street's manager Tanner, ten
years his senior, 'a picturesque personality, quick to anger and
equally quick to forgive' and 'a really good fellow', according
to his obituarist.[74] Street himself, along with Arthur William
Blomfield and John Oldrid Scott, three of the most respected
gothic church architects in the country, signed his nomination
papers to become an Associate of the RIBA on 16 May 1881.[75]
Then the new practice, working from 19 Buckingham Gate,
Adelphi, started from 1882 to attract some attention.[76] His
father, after nearly twenty years in the post, commissioned
him that year to carry out some work to bring St Saviour's up
to the standards expected of a Tractarian place of worship.
That meant improving the chancel with new glass; adding a
blind arcade around its walls with pointed trefoil arches to
provide sedilia-like seating to the north and south, with a
pretty quatrefoil frieze along the top, and a tabernacle-like
reredos; and removing the galleries, always the bugbear of the
revivalists.[77] The result was very gothic in a Puginian way and
the church's appearance greatly lifted.

There followed a few years of small-scale church
improvements. At the large and isolated 13th- and 14th-
century church of St Helen, Cliffe, on the Kentish side of the
Thames Estuary where it starts to widen considerably, they
added in 1884 a richly traceried east window which contrasts
with somewhat stiff earlier restoration work by George
Austin and J.P. St Aubyn, and raised the roofs.[78] The following
year they restored All Saints', Spelsbury, in Oxfordshire,
presumably adding the arcading and ornamental timber roof
in the chancel of what, on the outside, was a plain and blocky
building.[79] In 1887 they designed a new steeple for the church
of St James, Hampton Hill in Middlesex, with ashlar stripes
of pale stone breaking up its rocky mass, and an ornamental
bell storey along the lines of the St Saviour's reredos.[80] In 1889
a commission for a new church turned up – for a permanent
structure to replace an iron church called St Saviour's in
Parkstone, Newtown, near Poole in Dorset.[81] The result, St
Clement's, was a picture-book Pugin model village church,
with 60-degree gables, aisleless with a prominent chancel
and a picturesque bellcote.[82] The probable explanation for
the wide geographical range of locations was that Romaine-
Walker's family, or possibly connections from the Street
office, had provided a number of High Churchmen looking for
improvements and extensions. This is what usually happened.

The first of Romaine-Walker's appearances in the *Builder*
occurred in 1883 with an executed design for a structure of
unusual and somewhat coarse appearance that suggests
that the young goths were ready to experiment. This was for

an extension to an exhibition building on the Trevor Estate between Belgravia and Knightsbridge in London, facing the Hyde Park Barracks, called Humphreys' Hall, a flourishing venue for colourful and exotic shows such as the Food Exhibition as well as the location for a welcome banquet given for the Horse Guards on their return from the Egyptian campaign in 1882.[83] On the main road side the partners designed a row of mansion blocks topped with artists' studios. The style of the building was not gothic at all: maybe an artistic instinct was trying to burst out of it. It had four storeys of red brick, with windows topped with pediments of various unlikely shapes: the first-floor ones either side of the grand entrance arch were made up from a pair of convex curves or adjacent semicircles. The general effect was what James Stevens Curl defines as Flemish mannerist.[84] Other details looked more Dutch, or what was called 'Queen Anne'. At the top of the composition the artists' studios had large north-facing windows, and the centrepiece was a grand Flemish gable with an improbable Venetian window below an ornate pediment, and writhing ogival sides. After this extension the halls continued to prosper, in spite of a serious fire in 1885, presenting the long-running and popular Japanese Native Village exhibition in 1885–7.[85] The same year the partnership designed a new front for a varnish factory at 7 Caledonian Road, near King's Cross station, which has survived.[86] This is Dutch or Flemish too, with brick lower storeys, a picturesque shop front, a row of brick pilasters on the first floor, and tile-hanging in a colour that matches the brickwork below.

Buildings like these are seen as being tail-end Victorian, but they are equally the first stages of Edwardian architecture. At a straightforward level, they are attempts at the Sweetness and Light style the architects would have seen from the hands of the very best architects. Norman Shaw's 68 and 72 Cadogan Square, London, of 1877–9, had the same ornate shaped gables, and in the case of 68 the same flat brick pilasters and fancy window pediments, as the two Romaine-Walker and Tanner commercial buildings, but Shaw had somehow managed to balance the decoration and the flat surfaces of wall to produce a balanced and artistic elevation rather than a jumble. They are likely also to have seen the many illustrations in the professional press of Ernest George's palatial new Buchan Hill, near Crawley in West Sussex, begun in 1882, which also has odd pediments.[87] So it looks as if they were trying too hard to translate their successful and pretty decorative church style with which they had made such a promising start into the new 'Queen Anne'.

They were each, essentially, a different type of person from Shaw: Romaine-Walker, a child of the high noon of the gothic revival, was more than twenty years younger than Shaw, who had been born during the reign of William IV. It looks in retrospect as if they were at that time more attracted to surface and what could be done with it. Thus they could design floriated, 'Decorated' church ornament and Flemish house or shop fronts without the highly prized coherence of form that unites Shaw's buildings of different styles and periods. It is not necessarily true that this was only because they were less talented than he was, which they surely were. It is also that later on in the century, surfaces had lost the connection with natural materials that the revivalists had so prized. The modern debate had started with John Ruskin's *The Seven Lamps of Architecture* and *The Stones of Venice* in 1849–53; Gottfried Semper's *On the Origin of Polychromy in Architecture*, which is about surface and texture, was published in English in 1854, and Owen Jones's *The Grammar of Ornament* in 1856. Prominent public buildings appeared in late century which were covered in 'surface', as it were, for example the Brompton Oratory in Knightsbridge, London, completed by Herbert Gribble in 1884, or William Richmond's mural mosaics with their ungothic shadows and perspectives in St Paul's cathedral, which although of the 1890s, have their origins in a lecture of 1882.[88] Following this argument, Romaine-Walker and Tanner are post-Pugin and post-Shaw.

But they are post- all these for another reason: their patronage. The little village church of St Clement was close to land owned by the Welsh industrialist and politician Ivor Guest, first Baron Wimborne since 1880, a Conservative politician who eventually became a Liberal, married to a daughter of the Conservative seventh Duke of Marlborough. It was Wimborne who had paid nearly all the cost of replacing the old iron church at Parkstone. By 1889, when work began on the church, Romaine-Walker and Tanner had already completed what appears to be their first substantial building after the Humphreys' Hall project: a wing at Wimborne's house, Canford Manor at Canford Magna north of Poole. The house had been begun by Edward Blore in 1825–6, but vastly aggrandised by Charles Barry for Wimborne's father Sir John Guest after 1849: Blore's building became the service quarters and a great hall, a monumental staircase and huge tower – sometimes compared to the Victoria Tower at Westminster – was added.[89] Although low and plain from the outside – minimally Tudor, with a little half-timbering on the gable – Romaine-Walker's new apartments were grand within, with splendid Jacobean smoking and billiard rooms. The smoking room was illustrated in the *Builder* that year, with a full-page plate and short description.[90]

Big houses

How Wimborne found his architects is not clear, but the Royal Academy exhibited in 1886 a drawing by Romaine-Walker entitled 'Mansion at Fetcham', and perhaps Wimborne had seen it.[91] At any rate, from this point onwards the architects' careers took off: they were asked to design a large house to replace the small Rhinefield Lodge, west of Brockenhurst in the New Forest. The client here was Edward Lionel Walker-Munro, née Munro, or perhaps his wife Mabel, née Walker, who paid for it. Mabel was from the family that owned Eastwood Colliery in Nottinghamshire and there does not appear to be any connection with the architect; maybe they had seen Canford Manor, less than 20 miles (30 kilometres) away to the west. Certainly the new Rhinefield, the house that Romaine-Walker and Tanner built for them in 1888–90, could outdo Canford in terms of sheer bravura, and much of Romaine-Walker's later work owed a lot to it stylistically (figs 31–33).

It was a very big house in a more-or-less Jacobean style, set in ornate gardens. At the centre of the garden front there was a large two-storey mullioned window, with an ornamental gable above that looks as if a reredos had been carved into it. To the left, the house becomes romantic Tudor, again two storeys high, with three little octagons (in plan) of different heights projecting from it: the largest one in the centre has that triple gothic arcade in it that was to reappear at Kingsgate. The right-hand part looks more mediaeval, but the whole composition is kept together with a single ridgeline, above which sprout brick Tudor chimneys. There is a long service wing set back to the right on this side. The entrance front resembles an Elizabethan E-plan house with many more angled projections and small upper-storey oriel windows, but the rear of the service wing on the same side has a spectacular tower that easily rivals Canford Manor's. The whole thing looks rather as if Romaine-Walker had taken his clients over to visit Lord Wimborne's house, and they had told him that they wanted one like that, only much bigger. The house was illustrated in the press, with a long description, and views that included its tall mediaeval-type great hall, with a hammerbeam roof, again like Canford's but bigger and better, and with an absolutely vast fireplace (fig.34).[92] There was however one area where the Wimbornes need not have felt outdone: Rhinefield had an electric organ in its minstrels' gallery, 'a device snobs considered frightfully vulgar' according to Jill Franklin. She also points out that there is a little upstairs boudoir where chaperones could keep an eye on proceedings downstairs through a casement window.[93]

The oddity at Rhinefield is a little smoking room in the Moorish style, like the Arab Room that William Burges had designed in about 1880 for the Marquess of Bute at Cardiff Castle: perhaps the Walker-Munros had seen that too. Theirs was not as ornate, but it too was bigger (fig.35). A further project for the Walker-Munros was an extremely grand

31. (previous pages) The garden front of Rhinefield House, near Brockenhurst, Hampshire, by Romaine-Walker & Tanner, 1888–90. This was the first of Romaine-Walker's new large houses, and it displays both the legacy of his apprenticeship under G.E. Street and his theatrical panache.

32. (above) The staircase at Rhinefield. This was one of the architect's most successful creations and, in common with some of his other ideas, prefigured the work of Edwin Lutyens and contemporaries.

33. (opposite) The gatehouse tower at Rhinefield, with traces of Romaine-Walker's early career as a gothic-revival church architect very much in evidence.

34. (above) Rhinefield's Great Hall, as seen in the drawing that Romaine-Walker exhibited at the Royal Academy in 1891 and published that July in the *Builder*.

35. A detail of the Smoking Room at Rhinefield.

gothic church called St Saviour's, in abbey style, faced in Rhinefield stone, in Wilverley Road, Brockenhurst, a building so ambitious that it was not completed until 1961, more than twenty years after Romaine-Walker's death.[94]

It might have been Rhinefield's wonderful picturesque assembly of archaeological elements, exhibited in Romaine-Walker's own drawings at the Royal Academy in 1889 and 1891, that resulted in his taking over from the ailing architect C.J. Phipps for the completion of Her Majesty's Theatre in the Haymarket in London.[95] But he had other links with the London artistic scene. He had a family connection to Augustus Joel Walker, the founder of Walker's Gallery at 118 New Bond Street, and he pursued a parallel career in the 1890s and 1900s as an illustrator of children's books.[96] His subjects do not appear at first sight to have been particularly architectural: they are full of long dresses and winding plants,

and have been compared to the work of contemporary artists such as Arthur Rackham.

At any rate, Rhinefield was soon followed by three projects in quick succession for a wealthy Midlander called Robert Hudson who had inherited a fortune from his father, also Robert, the inventor of 'dry soap', that is, soap powder: a large gothic house set back from Park Lane, the restoration of Medmenham Abbey on the Thames in Buckinghamshire, and a vast residence nearby, even bigger than Rhinefield, all built and completed in 1898–1901.[97] Hudson had earlier commissioned a large half-timbered residence in Birkenhead

36. (opposite, above) Medmenham Abbey, 1898, Romaine-Walker's first substantial work for Robert Hudson, seen from a popular spot for rowing on the Thames west of Marlow in Buckinghamshire. He remodelled the house, including the earlier 'cloister' attached to Sir Francis Dashwood's folly tower, and extended it westwards to include the central white bay. *Country Life* thought that the architect had carried out his work 'with perfect taste and skill'.

37. (opposite, below) The courtyard of Medmenham Abbey. The composition of tower, porch and courtyard, as at Rhinefield, again provided Romaine-Walker with ideal experience for his later work at Kingsgate.

designed by the Liverpool architects Grayson & Ould, but having in the meantime come into his inheritance on the death of his father, and moved south, he was evidently looking for something more impressive.[98] The Elizabethan style of his first new house gives a picture of the type of atmosphere that he was after; he now moved forward a period, to stone-built Jacobean. From the *Builder* it is possible to see that Jacobean-style houses were not common at this period: the best-known ones were either significantly earlier or later; Norman Shaw's Adcote, in Shropshire, was about twenty years old when Hudson employed Romaine-Walker.

The first of these projects, Medmenham Abbey, was apparently no more than a temporary residence until the much bigger house nearby was completed. Hudson had turned first to Philip Webb; but as it turned out, Romaine-Walker was the ideal choice, and furthermore the project was to present him with suitable experience for Kingsgate (figs 36 and 37).[99] A 16th-century chalk-block and flint house, it had been extended by the hell-raising Sir Francis Dashwood, who

38. (opposite, above) Romaine-Walker designed 28 cottages in a picturesque Tudor style for Hudson around Medmenham. *Country Life* praised their generous internal spaces and efficient planning, seeing in them a rational solution to the problems of cottage planning and modernisation that faced its landed readers. This is the garden side of the Bockmer farm cottages to the north of the estate.

39. (opposite, below) The laundry at Medmenham, which was built alongside Hudson's new school and mistresses' houses. 'No trouble or expense has been spared in appointing and fitting the laundry with every modern contrivance', wrote *Country Life*. The easy legibility of the 'Tudor' construction complemented, rather than contrasted with, the rational, functional nature of the activities within.

40. (above) Danesfield House, near Marlow, Buckinghamshire, Romaine-Walker for Hudson, 1899–1901: the entrance courtyard on the north side of the house.

added, according to the *Buildings of England*, a temple with an entrance in the form of a vagina, but, more permanently, a gothic folly, a ruined church tower attached to the front of the house.[100] Romaine-Walker smartened this up and rebuilt the northern part with a smart half-timbered upper

storey with herringbone brick nogging; he also remodelled Dashwood's gothic cloister, as it was called, along the river front.[101] While this was going up, he was already planning Hudson's enormous Danesfield downstream elsewhere on the Medmenham estate, on the site of an early Victorian house that had an Edward Pugin chapel, and designed a number of picturesque cottages in different arts-and-crafts or pre-gothic-revival vernacular styles, some with pretty fireplaces that still have their Conrad Dressler tiles, which the *Buildings of England* authors call 'the most extensive collection of estate buildings in the county' – that is, even outdoing the work of George Devey for the Rothschilds around Cliveden and Mentmore (figs 38 and 39).[102]

Danesfield is vast; it is more disciplined than Medmenham Abbey, with an arcaded symmetrical front that overlooked a formal garden but a grand Tudor entrance under another version of Barry's Canford Manor tower (figs 40 and 41). It is large and white, built of a hard chalk. Its interior has been remodelled more than once, but the original panache

undoubtedly survives.[103] Hudson's taste seems to have been fairly eclectic – perhaps he was influenced by the fact that the London department stores offered furnished showrooms in different styles, all adjacent to one another – which in turn would mean that architectural historians, ever on the lookout for coherence, would turn their noses up at his various creations, however large and splendid they were.[104] Thus Stanhope House off London's Park Lane, the third of his large houses, has always seemed like an oddity to most architectural historians. It looks like a box covered in the thin, blind gothic tracery that historically is associated with the mediaeval Abbot's Lodging at Muchelney in Somerset, an archaeological mixture from the 12th, 15th and early 16th centuries.[105] This heterogeneity continued inside in the case of Hudson's house, as the rooms were in different styles including, improbably, Adam-classical (fig.42).[106]

The connection with Avebury certainly heralded a further boost to Romaine-Walker's practice, which through the first decade of the 20th century was mostly taken up with country-house work. Tanner, who had been since 1883 district surveyor for Hatcham in the London district of Deptford, took on a full-time position in 1896 as district surveyor for an area which now included Rotherhithe and St George's-in-the-East, and he was replaced by Francis Besant. As Romaine-Walker & Besant they continued to design work for churches, some paid for in part by the Wimbornes. Thus in 1902–3 they built St John the Baptist, Heatherlands, Parkstone, which has a plain red-brick exterior but a stunning Roman interior, with carved wreaths in the spandrels of its arcade and a basilica ceiling in two curved sections. At the same time Romaine-Walker was working on the ornate, much-ogied, carved and moulded aisle and sanctuary fittings at J.J. Scoles's church of the Immaculate Conception, in Farm Street, Mayfair, and carried out decorative work at G.F. Bodley and William Burges's

church of St Michael and All Angels in Hove, East Sussex.[107] He also designed the interior of the chapel at Beaumont College, a Jesuit school in Windsor, in a Pompeiian style, and built a plain Italianate house for a Catholic order called the Sisters of the Holy Rood in Camden, London.

Edwardianising

Over this period Romaine-Walker made substantial alterations to large houses, mostly 18th century, turning them into Edwardian country houses often with the addition of ballrooms, gun rooms, and lifts. Making large residences much larger still for these purposes by wrapping them in

41.   The garden front of Danesfield, facing the River Thames. The gaunt white stone has a primitive air to it, so different from the elevations of most contemporary Victorian houses, and would probably have appealed to Avebury if he saw it.

42.   Stanhope House, Hudson's mansion on Park Lane in Mayfair, London, by Romaine-Walker & Besant, 1899–1901. The apparently ahistorical elevations with their shallow traceried panels owe some debt to the surviving fragments of the abbot's lodging at Muchelney in Somerset, a building that early gothic revivalists such as Romaine-Walker's pupil master Street were well aware of.

or enclosing them between extensions was an Edwardian characteristic (fig.43): sometimes the results were positively gargantuan, as for example at Hursley House in Hampshire, by Alexander Marshall Mackenzie, later the architect of the exuberant, baroque Australia House in the Strand, London.[108]

Of Romaine-Walker's own contribution to the genre, much the most original and distinctive was his treatment of Buckland House in Berkshire. This had been a simple Palladian box, designed in about 1757 by John Wood the Younger. In 1910, Romaine-Walker and Besant added wings either side of the same height and in the same style – a very difficult thing to do successfully, and an idea they had experimented with before in 1908–9 for the Earl of Derby's house in Stratford Place off Oxford Street. These wings seem hardly visible from the front, but at the back they project to create a U-shaped facade, providing the residents with a 'state bedroom' on one side, and a billiard and gun room on the other, and lifts in both.[109] He also made tactful alterations to

Wood's long, low wings, and to the porch. He had previously designed a new house, more resembling the 17th-century Wilton House, called Moreton Hall, Warwickshire, in 1905–8; and for that client's brother-in-law Robert Emmett he designed a house nearby that looked like Holland House in London called Moreton Paddox.[110]

The two other projects as grand in style as Buckland were smaller. He designed Sunderland House in Conduit Street in London of which the exterior survives, a large freestanding aristocratic classical town house of the kind that is unusual in England. This was started in 1899, just before Besant joined him, but possibly Besant had a significant hand in its execution as it does not much resemble anything else by

43. Jardine Hall in Dumfriesshire was greatly extended by E.J. May in the mid-1890s in a way that soon became typical for Edwardian houses: note the new billiard and smoking rooms at the dining room end, and the greatly expanded drawing room suite at the other.

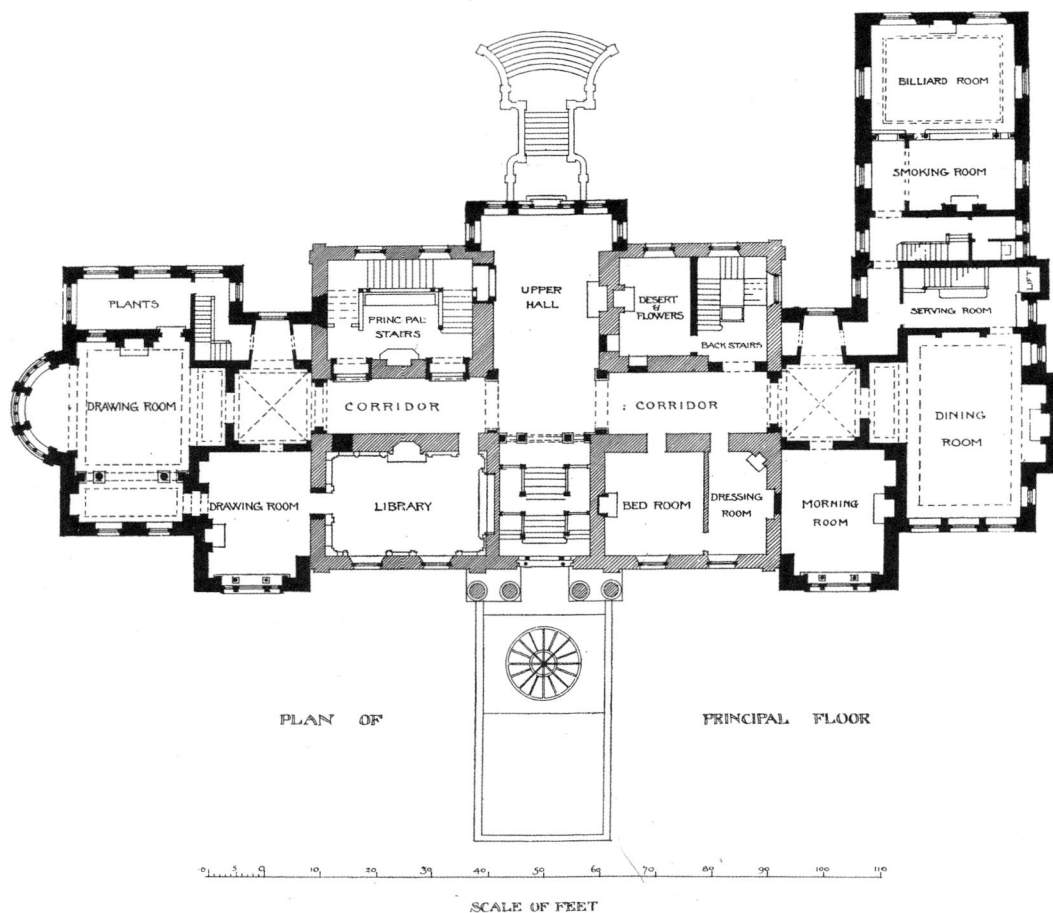

PLAN   OF   PRINCIPAL   FLOOR

SCALE OF FEET

Romaine-Walker except perhaps in its eccentric detailing. The house was a gift from William K. Vanderbilt to his daughter Consuelo on her marriage to the Duke of Marlborough – that is, the nephew of Lady Wimborne.[111] The other designer who played a role there was the French landscape architect Achille Duchêne, but what that could have been in this garden-less project remains unclear. The second was the fitting out of the painted hall at Chatsworth in Derbyshire with a fine new staircase and balustrade in 1911–12. This may possibly have been through an Avebury connection, because the politician usually known as the Marquess of Hartington, father of Chatsworth's owner the Duke of Devonshire, had been one of Avebury's closest friends and was to be an ally in the free trade and tariff reform debates that had ended the era of Conservative government in 1905.[112] There is a decorative game larder with an octagonal plan at Chatsworth which is attributed to Romaine-Walker, perfectly reasonably.[113]

Romaine-Walker had thus entered the list of architects who knew how to service the aristocracy. At Blenheim Palace in Oxfordshire he designed the organ case that sits on the end wall in the Long Library.[114] At Knowsley Hall on the outskirts of Liverpool, the house of the Earls of Derby, in 1908–12 the partners tidied up an undistinguished, long straggling and mostly 18th-century house, creating, as Lord Derby himself tellingly put it, 'more of a restoration to what never existed . . . than an old house', but with a splendid new staircase, and after that he remodelled the stairs and foyer of John Wood the Elder and James Wyatt's Town Hall in Liverpool, perhaps at the Earl's instigation since he had been mayor of the city in 1911.[115] All the while the practice worked on minor alterations and remodelling projects for the nobility or newly rich across Mayfair. He remodelled the interior of 66 Grosvenor Street, reusing old work, for Emmett, his Warwickshire client, in 1900 and he added a 'showy porch' to 19 Upper Brook Street as part of a job for the merchant Arthur W. Davis.[116] Avebury himself moved his London residence to 52 Grosvenor Street in September 1908, but there is no record of any alterations made there.[117] Most of the 'show' was kept for the insides of these houses, and in fact when Romaine-Walker designed a completely new one, in 1912–14 for James de Rothschild at 34 Park Street, he provided a plain, but elegant, 18th-century bow front which looks 20th-century only because it is in the standard red brick of the Grosvenor Estate, rather than the London stock the form is generally associated with. That year he also redesigned the interior of the theatre in the Haymarket. Prospering from all this, he built himself a surprisingly plain Tudor house in Mayfield, East Sussex, in 1902–3, that employed some of the motifs from the

Medmenham cottages: a rendered upper storey over an ashlar base, curvy bargeboards, and an elaborate interior.[118]

By 1910, Romaine-Walker was in a new partnership, this time with Gilbert Jenkins, who had joined his office as an assistant in 1902 when he would have been about 27, and according to his obituary seems to have been responsible for Romaine-Walker's interest in gardens, expressed in those Rackhamesque drawings.[119] They worked together on these not only for the newly aggrandised houses such as Buckland, and a red-brick, Jacobean house called Great Fosters near Egham in Surrey which they smartened up, but also for Mewès & Davis's Luton Hoo near Luton, and a large early 19th-century Hungarian castle that had been built in a conscious attempt at an English gothic-revival style, called at the time Oroszvar but now, in Slovakia, called Rusovce Mansion.[120] Jenkins's obituary refers to a house then called Grianaig, Killay, which appears to be the one now named Glen Hir in the outskirts of Swansea and which has a slightly French neo-classical appearance.[121] But more significantly, they began to take on institutional work of a different kind altogether. In 1906 the art dealer Henry Joseph Duveen evidently asked Romaine-Walker to remodel his house at 128 Park Lane, the third reconstruction in three years, maybe having seen Hudson's Stanhope House emerge from scaffolding further down the street.[122] This did not come off, but in 1909 Duveen's nephew Joseph funded, with his father's bequest, an austere neo-classical extension over a rusticated base alongside the southern side of the Tate Gallery, and this was designed by Romaine-Walker and Jenkins. They continued the range northwards in 1925–7, and in 1935–7 the practice acted as executive architect for the American architect J. Russell Pope's sculpture galleries that run through the centre of the building, as they had done for Lutyens in Pall Mall. Romaine-Walker was now in his 80s and possibly not that active in the practice; his working life spanned from thirty years before the reign of King Edward VII, to thirty years after it.

Romaine-Walker's work was not overlooked at the time and it has been recorded since, sometimes in complimentary terms. Yet the picture of it has never been added up, because architectural history does not tend to dwell on designers who moved broadly from one stream to another without being exemplary in any of the different fields unless, like Oliver Hill, they did it almost from week to week. The kind of people who have been interested in Avebury have not been interested in buildings; the same has been true of the Wimbornes and of Pitt Rivers. Yet Romaine-Walker's houses and churches provide a helpful guide to the architecture of the Edwardian period, and he is as exemplary of it as Avebury is of the

Edwardian client. Kingsgate Castle is in some respects typical, and in others unusual and revealing. Restored castles, for example, were becoming a phenomenon of the period. Amicia de Moubray's *Twentieth Century Castles in Britain* provides a rich and illustrated list of some of the most important: Bamburgh and Lindisfarne in Northumberland, and Hever, Lympne and Allington in Kent, are all buildings of Avebury's period. But of these, only Lord Armstrong's Bamburgh had been started when Avebury bought Kingsgate in 1902, by an antiquarian architect named Charles Ferguson rather than by Norman Shaw of Armstrong's Cragside, and it was not well received.[123] There were many more fine restorations about to materialise across the country, on different scales: Layer Marney, the vast Tudor mansion in Essex, was to be restored, by Chancellor & Son, in 1904–12, and everywhere in the late Victorian and Edwardian period small historic buildings were being adapted and even moved. But Kingsgate is a different type of castle anyway to those which attracted Edwardian money: it was constructed around an 18th-century folly of the kind that high-art architects turned their noses up at. It cannot be ruled out that it was precisely this that attracted not only Avebury but Romaine-Walker, to it; do not forget that Romaine-Walker came to Avebury fresh from Dashwood's Medmenham Abbey.

Another point is that Romaine-Walker's very large castellated Jacobean buildings were not typical stylistically of their period. New castles and Jacobean mansions were not going up much in 1903. R.A. Briggs, who was exceptionally eclectic in his choice of picturesque styles, designed a castellated house at Leamington Spa in Warwickshire that was published in both the *Builder* and the *Architectural Review* in mid-1900 and early 1901 respectively, but it stands out because it was unusual.[124] Four years younger than Romaine-Walker, he designed a vast house at the time that Kingsgate Castle was being transformed – the rebuilding and remodelling of Cowley Manor, between Cheltenham and Gloucester, completed in 1902 and illustrated extensively in the *Architect and Contract Reporter*.[125] This is a version of Cliveden House in Buckinghamshire, not much smaller than the original. Generally, Briggs's medium-sized houses aim for a gentle look. His Cranford House near Leamington Spa is pink brick, Jacobean, castellated, and part half-timbered, complete by 1905, and a good example. He made his name as the designer of the cosy and pretty bungalows on which he published illustrated books; the interiors of these are not always predicable, as his early Pleasaunce Cottage in Dormans Park near East Grinstead, of the late 1880s, shows: its hall is a kind of revealed balloon frame, a soaring double-height

space lined with exposed timber posts and lintels.[126] Briggs's houses sometimes seem to have been designed to capture a feeling, rather than a style, and he illustrated and published them through comfortable vignettes. Interestingly, a Hubert Besant recorded in A. Stuart Gray's *Biographical Dictionary* of Edwardian architects, who worked for Romaine-Walker & Besant, and was presumably a family connection of the latter, did his articles at Briggs's office before joining the partnership as an assistant in 1908.[127] So possibly ideas flowed directly in this way, as they so often do.

In retrospect it seems that this new life of Tudor architecture blurs into something that stretches through from Shaw, via Lutyens, to the all-over-England popular Tudor of the 1920s. In fact it did not happen like that: Shaw's Adcote went up in the 1870s and Dawpool in the 1880s, and by the 1890s he was building splendid classical or neo-Georgian houses. In any case, Romaine-Walker's houses are different in appearance from these earlier well-known examples of the style: they are spikier and more archaeological, with the details and the surfaces flaunted, in an artistic, romantic way that evidently appealed even to the rational Avebury.

George Devey

And here was another link from the pre-Shaw period. Romaine-Walker's enjoyment in the expression of the elements of the old fabric of buildings, at Medmenham Abbey or at Kingsgate for example, not to mention the various internal interventions in the Mayfair houses, owed a great deal to George Devey's extraordinary cottage remodelling at Leicester Square and the new farm buildings at South Park, both in Penshurst in west Kent, back in the late 1840s when Pugin was still alive – a pivotal moment in the history of so many things and especially of archaeological architectural conservation (figs 44–7). The significance of these buildings is that it is not possible to tell in them what is old and what is new; the gothic revivalists never worked like this, not even at their most picturesque. Avebury, later on, was 'delighted' with Penshurst Place, where Devey had also made alterations and interventions to the mostly 14th-century manor house and garden: he wrote this after the first phase of Kingsgate had been completed, and it indicates a consistency in his taste.[128] Possibly he had also seen Devey's cottage work carried out for the Rothschild family in the Vale of Aylesbury at the other end of Buckinghamshire, or any of the series of houses for Liberal MPs: Jill Allibone's monograph concludes that 'there seems

44. Leicester Square, Penshurst, Kent, designed and built around the entry to the churchyard from 1849 for Lord de L'Isle and Dudley. George Devey remodelled and added to an old group of cottages so that it was very hard to distinguish between old and new.

45. The north side of Leicester Square, Penshurst, from the churchyard.

little doubt that Devey was himself a Liberal, and possibly one with radical views'.[129]

Avebury certainly knew Devey's restoration of Walmer Castle, a short distance from Kingsgate, as he occasionally visited the place. The work there was done in 1871–5 for Granville Gower, second Earl Granville, then the Lord Warden of the Cinque Ports, who had been Lord John Russell's foreign secretary in the 1850s and had returned to the same post under Gladstone in 1870. Devey converted the castle into a comfortable, picturesque residence, reusing stone from the remains of Sandown Castle nearby.[130] This last apparently annoyed archaeologists, but in a sense Devey, like Pitt Rivers, understood something that they did not: that archaeology is a continuing scientific narrative, not just a collection of artefacts.[131] There is much in Devey's work that invites more study, including his pioneering use of photography, and his enquiring and rational approach to history; in a way, he seems to have something of Avebury about him. Mark Girouard has described the Penshurst cottages as 'rural archaeology',

46. A corner of Leicester Square, Penshurst. Many architects had remodelled old cottages over the centuries, but the way in which Devey convincingly re-entered the local vernacular, with (mostly) historically correct detailing, was an innovation.

47. In 1850 Devey remodelled South Park, an estate farmyard a mile south of Penshurst, for Sir Henry Hardinge. His work included a new barn, sheds and sties.

intending to convey that they were scientific and revelatory about the nature of the original architecture; in the light of what happened later to Kingsgate Castle, this seems a particularly perceptive observation (fig.48).[132]

Devey's Kentish masterpiece St Alban's Court is in east Kent, near the village of Nonington, and dates to 1875–9. Here he designed for the banker William Hammond a large new house built of red brick over an irregular plinth of stone (fig.49). All around the outside of the main block of the house, this stone seems to crumble into a froth of ashlar block and brick as it rises, interspersed along the two main fronts with coarse buttresses (fig.50). At first this might look random, but with Devey nothing was random: according to Walter Godfrey, who wrote a belated tribute to him in the *Architectural Review*, this design was the result of 'many a long day plotting and planning, altering and revising' with his client.[133] It seems likely therefore that the location of each of the 'floating' bricks and stones was planned, or at any rate the way in which it was to be carried out would have been carefully devised. In doing this, Devey was drawing attention to the individual

48. Devey's drawing for the south garden front of Hammerfield, Penshurst, not exactly as built (compare with fig.1). He drew his work to express its 'archaeological' character, as if he were unpicking and revealing contrasting elements of buildings.

materials, and also, in disrupting their traditional pattern, to the ways in which they had been traditionally used, rather as an archaeologist might find an ancient fragment, of say a lamp or pot or coin, and hold it up on its own for exhibition. Devey had presumably seen – he himself said nothing – that it no longer mattered what was old and what was new. What mattered was what it was made of; what its logic was; how every element related to the one adjacent to it. In this way he could abstract historical elements, such as the idea of the stone, and isolate them so as to emphasise the timelessness of a building; clearly this is the opposite of the claim sometimes made that that St Alban's Court is 'fake-old'. Shaw himself was familiar with Devey's work at Penshurst, at least, and Andrew Saint has noticed that he occasionally imitated Devey's

49. Devey's masterpiece: the south front of St Alban's Court, Nonington, in east Kent, built for William Hammond in 1875–9. This was the most mature and sophisticated example of the architect's characteristic manner of emphasising the physical nature of individual building components, to make one think about them, their history, and their role in a structure.

50. A detail of the west front of St Alban's Court, with (from left to right) the windows lighting Hammond's 'Own Room', the library and the drawing room. A few irregular flared headers appear as the stone crumbles into the brickwork above.

'mannered' method of working his way through materials as he reached from the ground up to the top of the chimneys.[134]

It suits the mid-Victorian mentality very well to see all this in terms of a scientific experiment that abstracts a sense of age and turns it into an objective building block, a demonstration of useful facts, and one that can be done on any scale. One is looking at the construction and one is aware of a sense of history, and yet one is also aware that this is all new and logical. Allibone writes that 'Devey's study of small domestic buildings as an architectural source in the late 1840s seems unparalleled', and he maintained a large collection of architectural photography, both of old buildings and of his own as they were going up, or recently completed.[135] He knew what he was doing.

Many of Devey's ideas seem to have vanished from the way in which architectural history is written; perhaps he has been too complex a character for non-architects to understand what it was all about. Consciously or not, Romaine-Walker was one of the Edwardian figures who kept Devey's architectural ideas alive. In 1904 an architect called Mawson who attended a talk on garden architecture by Mervyn Macartney said that 'he had noticed that whenever the works of George Devey were brought to notice, his name was left out'.[136] The impression is that architects were aware of him, even if few others were.

The pleasures of life

It is striking that all three of Romaine-Walker's major new houses – Kingsgate Castle, Rhinesfield and Danesfield – have been or are today high-class hotels. They are emphatically comfortable and attractive, unusual places. Of the major conversions and reworkings, Holme Lacy in Herefordshire, where he added a ballroom and one of his grand staircases in 1910–11, is now also a smart hotel, and so is Great Fosters.[137] Although the latter two trade on their older historical connections, the imagery and the atmosphere of all these places are Edwardian, and that must be how they appear and are marketed to their guests, for Romaine-Walker can certainly have been said to have captured what was to become a marketable Edwardian image. It is possible to see in his three great works references from the 1830s and 1840s, the period in which architects in their own pattern books and architectural writers in the learned journals placed a great deal of emphasis on comfort, on romance, on historical motifs.[138] John Claudius Loudon wrote of his comprehensive

Encyclopaedia of Cottage, Farm, and Villa Architecture and Furniture of 1833 that 'The great object of this work is, to show how the dwelling of the whole mass of society may be equalized in point of all essential comforts, conveniences and beauties'.[139] The gothic revivalists were not (publically at any rate) interested in any of these as primary motivations for buildings, except for 'convenience' and even then with a somewhat different meaning. Some of this late Georgian pleasure was now evidently on the way back, combined with what had undoubtedly been the gothic revivalists' great achievement, the interest in constructional quality.

It is difficult to look back on Edwardian architecture without seeing it through the prism of its later life as much as of its predecessors. Most of the external walls, and the staircase, of Avebury's Kingsgate Castle remain, but the rest has been very much altered. His widow sold it in 1922, although not to Harmsworth, by now Lord Northcliffe, who had possibly been lusting after it: Avebury had recorded that Garter King of Arms wrote to him in December 1905 to say that he had rejected the then Sir Alfred's application to call himself Lord Kingsgate, which implies that the College of Arms had already heard from both of them on the subject.[140] Northcliffe seems to have had ideas of turning the area into a popular resort, for it was he who converted the private members' golf club into a 'holiday club', that is, a place that tourists could use on a daily, pay-by-visit basis; he also established the Northcliffe Golfing Society – of journalists – which played at North Foreland and brought it to national attention since their games were promoted in their newspapers. In fact the Castle's buyer was North Foreland Hotels Limited, which during its ownership turned it gradually into a resort-de-luxe.

Extensions followed throughout the interwar years.[141] First, the narrow ground-floor principal rooms of the Avebury house were extended by 1924 by doubling them in width towards Kingsgate Bay to become a lounge and hotel dining room; then a semi-circular glass-topped ballroom was added in the middle, directly onto what had been the anteroom. The whole elevation was then extended along the entrance drive with the four-bay, two-storey Coronation Wing. All were faced in flint to match the Avebury building, as was a small single-storey projection at the front to the left of the main gate, perhaps the hotel reception entrance, but cheaper extensions were put up round the back. The Tudor Wing of 1928 projected from the eastern corner of the courtyard, parallel with Avebury's garage and servants' accommodation. This was built of red brick with a half-timbered effect, of a somewhat lower standard of design and construction on the service court

side; then a mostly underground garage for 22 cars appeared beyond the tennis courts. As the Coronation Wing was going up, the hotel built a large set of squash courts in what was described as a Moorish style – it had a bizarre ground-floor arcade of tall narrow gothic arches with a flat reticulated lattice above them.[142] The unworldly Hollywood feel of this evidently attracted the intended clientele. A board signed by hotel guests between 1934 and 1951 includes the names of Laurence Olivier, Constance Cummings, Peggy Ashcroft, Gracie Fields, Merle Oberon and many other celebrities, including the comedy double act Elsie and Doris Waters, who lived locally, as did their brother Jack Warner, later 'Dixon of Dock Green'.[143] Avebury's library survived and was illustrated in the hotel's brochure (although without his name attached to it).

After the Second World War the hotel was converted into flats: the rooms were subdivided, and thus the surviving remnants of the Avebury era were further compromised. The cloisters were enclosed and subdivided into a kitchen and a narrow 'morning room', the latter perhaps because the estate agents could not think what else to do with it; the grand staircase alone has survived in what looks like its original condition.[144] Astonishingly, some fancy plasterwork and Hollywood-gothic sconces, a fireplace and even a chandelier have survived from the hotel period, in the remains of what was once Avebury's drawing room.[145] The carpenter from the nearby village of St Peter's who worked on the conversion was said, locally, to have been the father of the then Conservative chief whip and future prime minister Edward Heath. Even in its post-war condition the building continues to make a profound impression on anyone who sees it, just as it had done when Avebury first saw it and seems immediately to have wanted to buy it.

Some of the thoughts that Avebury expressed when he opened the public library in Gloucester in May 1900 give a picture of his world vision in which imagination and science go hand in hand:

> The greatest discovery of the XIX century is the importance of education . . . There are still some who object to public libraries on account of the expense. But I think they make a mistake even from their own point of view . . . Victor Hugo even said 'He who opens a school closes a prison'. . . . Novels are very interesting, very refreshing & many of them very instructive.[146]

In other words, the creation of narratives was important, just as it had been for his father-in-law, old Pitt Rivers, with his idea that archaeology was not just the study of artefacts but the weaving of a story that bound them together. In his speech Avebury noted that the first six books taken out of the new public library in Birmingham were three novels, a work by Tyndall, another by Huxley, and a technical manual. He went on to point out that 'working men' such as James Watt, Henry Cort, Benjamin Huntsman, Josiah Wedgwood, Richard Bradley, Thomas Telford, David Mushet and James Beaumont Neilson, George Stephenson ('a cowboy & could not read until he was 18'), John Dalton, Michael Faraday, Thomas Newcomen, Richard Arkwright, Humphry Davy and Matthew Boulton ('the father of Birmingham') had all used libraries. With this list of names he painted a picture of the fathers of the 19th century, the new library opening their wisdom for the education of the next generation. His own castle is in that sense a book, from the library of Edwardian houses.

51. The great tower at the entrance to Romaine-Walker's Danesfield.

2

THE LIBERALS AS BUILDERS

—

Will anyone, a hundred years hence, consent to
live in the houses the Victorians built?

H.G. Wells, 1910

CHARLES ROBERT WYNN-CARRINGTON (fig.53),
first and last Earl of Carrington from 1895 and
later Marquess of Lincolnshire, was a different
kind of Liberal from Lord Avebury, but the
house he remodelled from an old farmhouse courtyard is
just as remarkable and expressive of Edwardian domestic
architecture as Kingsgate Castle.

Carrington shared Avebury's devotion to Gladstone
but unlike Avebury, he remained in the party for the whole
of his life, not only working for land reform by reforming
his own estates, but in time through national legislation
that he himself introduced as a member of government.[1]
In 1890 he returned from a period of office as governor of
New South Wales and threw himself into party politics;

then, two years later, he was elected for West St Pancras as
a Progressive member of the London County Council (LCC).
The Progressives, aligned with the radical wing of the Liberal
Party, included Labour leaders and social democrats. His
wife's diary records that he wanted to help Alfred Wallace's
Land Nationalisation Company to buy land to lease on at
reasonable rents.[2] Yet as a close friend of the Prince of Wales,
after whom he named his eldest son, he also moved in court
circles, spending long periods in attendance at Balmoral.

Carrington's primary concern throughout the decades
following the death of his father had been to clear the
mortgages he had inherited and to put his family estate in
order. The Great Depression in English agriculture had lasted
for about twenty years from the mid-1870s. The value of rural

52. (p.66) A detail of the western courtyard garden at Vann, near Hambledon, Surrey. This house, designed by W.D. Caröe for his family in 1907, is one of the finest examples of the Edwardian old-and-new house where it is impossible to distinguish between the eras of building.

53. Charles Robert Wynn-Carrington, Earl of Carrington from 1895 and later Marquess of Lincolnshire, in a late Victorian portrait.

tenancies sank as labourers moved into towns. The result was that landowners lost prestige as well as income, further marked by a series of changes in legislation: the introduction of the secret ballot in 1872; the establishment of the new county councils in 1888; the transfer of some game rights to farmers from proprietors. Affected landowners responded in different ways: some stood for election in the new public authorities; others improved the quality of the housing they offered to tenants, or began to invest in the parish church or school as a way of establishing their status, especially if they felt challenged by the nouveaux riches who had begun to invest in large new houses. Many, even the grandest, had to sell land, sometimes even their core holdings, in order to keep afloat.[3] Carrington's diary noted in December 1896 that 'De L'Isle and Dudley' – that is, Philip Sidney of Penshurst, the second baron – 'is broke . . . a real national misfortune'.[4] Sidney died in Berne in Switzerland two years later. But Carrington himself soldiered on through wise estate planning

which also enabled him to put into practice his deeply held belief that a Liberal government should secure land tenure for those who lived by and on it, and therefore avoid civil discontent and socialist land expropriation.

Like Avebury, Carrington commented on his building campaign in his diaries. Avebury's recorded, mostly, his social and family engagements; but Carrington's were quite different. He repeated jokes, pasted in caricatures of politicians that amused him, added colour to public scandals (including one in which he was implicated himself, after being accused in court by a madwoman of having an affair with her), and uninhibitedly retold political gossip and indiscreet stories. On the death of the Duchess of Teck, her son-in-law the Duke of York, the future King George V, told Carrington that 'It is very hard on me; as it knocks all my shooting on the head'.[5] But on the subject of his land and building endeavours he was precise, to the extent of returning to earlier entries to comment on them.

Once back in England Carrington had started to sell off marginal land from his estates in Wales and Bedfordshire. At the same time, he maintained his largest holdings in south-east Lincolnshire: his mother, the daughter of Lord Willoughby de Eresby, had grown up in Grimsthorpe Castle, between Stamford and Grantham, the splendid baroque north front of which had been designed by John Vanbrugh in the early 1720s.[6] These Lincolnshire holdings produced an income of about £10,000 per annum, and over time they provided the canvas for his establishment of experimental smallholdings.[7] He also had a house in London, at 53 Prince's Gate in South Kensington, and a small castle in north Wales called Gwydir, which he had bought from a cousin on his mother's side as a long-term investment for his son, Albert Edward. He owned land in the Buckinghamshire town of High Wycombe, including much of the undeveloped geographical centre and his own house on the edge of a substantial park to the south. This had been bought by the first Lord Carrington at the end of the 18th century and expensively rebuilt soon afterwards by James Wyatt in a rambling, somewhat mechanical gothick style, with a new name to suit: Wycombe Abbey.[8] The large house with its countless rooms and many expensive roofs, and the staff to maintain all these, posed a threat to Carrington's family fortune, especially if he himself was to be instrumental in improving the rights of tenants at the cost of those of the traditional landowners. Indeed, his diary shows that his plans for Wycombe Abbey were devised with his heir's financial security in mind. The idea was to sell the house – to a newly established girls' school – and to move into a house in the park. In a note subsequently added to the first page of his diary for 1897 Carrington wrote that 'the Wycombe property now free from the incubus of the big house, ought to be a gold mine to the boy'.[9]

In preparation for this, Carrington, his wife Cecilia, five daughters and two-year-old son left the Abbey in July 1896 and moved into a modest farmhouse to the south of it called Daws Hill, itself attached to a late Georgian folly, a fragment of a castellated fort, perhaps by Wyatt (fig.54).[10] His idea at this point was to live there while a relatively small new house went up nearby, on a plateau at the edge of the ridge overlooking the park just beyond a small area of woodland.[11] He found an architect, a Mr Lees, probably William Hewson Lees of Mecklenburgh Square in London, who was a district surveyor in the capital, at one point for parts of St Pancras that Carrington represented on the LCC.[12] But Lees's first plans, presented in August 1897, were too ambitious – Carrington recorded with amazement that his architect had assumed that '"we cannot do with less that 22 bedrooms" !!!!!'.[13] Lady Carrington had found the old farmhouse 'cosy and delightful', so her husband's next idea was to expand it, to 'build a sort of shooting lodge which will take us all in', reusing the agricultural buildings on the site.[14]

Carrington later recorded what happened in a note he added subsequently to his original entry when he had first chosen the site:

> some additions were made to the old farm house. The farm buildings were turned into rooms. – The Cow house becoming a corridor: the cowman's cottage a sitting room: The cart house stable was turned into the oak room, and the big barn into the white drawing room. The 'calving down box' became an 'overflow' kitchen – and the slaughter house a secretarys room – One farm yard was turned into a kitchen court, & the other was terraced, laid down with grass & flowers & shrubs planted.[15]

In December that year, Lady Carrington approved the plans; and the project started in the spring.[16] Some works were carried out to improve access, including new gates to the west on Marlow Road, where two new large boarding houses designed by W.D. Caröe for the already thriving girls' school were threatening to spoil the view. Like many another client, indeed like Avebury, he eventually became impatient with progress on his future 'delightful home', remarking twice that construction was going 'very slowly' after a year on site.[17] The family moved in 'with three servants' on 29 July 1899, and on the 30th Carrington wrote his first diary entry – a story about Disraeli which reflected badly on early Victorian Tories – from his new home.[18]

54. Daws Hill, High Wycombe, Buckinghamshire, from the north-west. As at Medmenham Abbey and Kingsgate Castle, the new work – commissioned by Carrington in the late 1890s – incorporated a Georgian folly, in this case possibly designed by James Wyatt who had created Wycombe Abbey to the north from an older house.

Carrington's description gives little sense of the unusual nature of his house. The farmhouse itself was a compact, deep, two-storey, rendered house with a pretty bow window at the front facing south. To the west of this, and running back northwards down the hill, was the long narrow red-brick range that had housed the barn, the cart-house stable and the other large farmyard spaces (fig.55). Lees's extensions joined the two together with a long single-storey entry hall

55. Daws Hill: the new west front of the former farm buildings, previously (from right to left) the barn, calving-down box and slaughter house.

56. Daws Hill: the new entrance wing occupying the site of the cow house and cowman's cottage. Part of the old farmhouse is visible to the right.

which fronted a garden courtyard to the north (fig.56). The old farmhouse house grew eastwards and westwards, to provide more bedrooms and reception rooms, and the farm buildings were substantially rebuilt in a somewhat heavy Tudor style, with large stone-mullioned bay windows under rendered gables.

Inside, a grand white drawing room now occupied the former barn. In spite of its Tudor windows and the tall Jacobean cupola over it, it was classical in style, with a deep cornice, Corinthian columns and pilasters, decorations by William Chambers of 1760 taken from Carrington House in Whitehall, 12 late 18th-century panels by Angelica Kauffman, and an ornamental white marble fireplace with caryatids (fig.57).[19] It sat in the middle of a sequence of rooms that were linked at their short ends with doors and staircases *en filade* as the floor levels descended down the hill: the sitting room reached from the hall-corridor at the southern end was followed by the large oak room, lined in patched-up Jacobean artisan-mannerist panelling from Gayhurst in the north-east of the county, another Carrington house; this connected to the drawing room, and beyond that there was a further large supper or morning room to the north (fig.58).[20] Apart from the folly walls the complex as a whole looked as if it had been built at different periods of the 16th and 17th centuries, and the interior changed in character from room to room, from 16th to 17th to 18th to 19th, mixing old and new work, up to the fresh and bright end-of-century feeling of the new entrance hall. From the outside it is possible to glimpse the older and coarser brickwork sandwiched between the layers of sharper, newer work (fig.59). Lees's new dining room, attached to the old farmhouse on the other side of the courtyard, was Tudor, with oak beams across the ceiling. There was no stylish overall composition, as there were in so many artistic cottages of the decade.

Carrington's diary over the period of the construction of Daws Hill refers to it on occasion as his shooting box. He travelled a great deal across the country and had no doubt seen the recent shooting boxes of the gentry. He recorded nothing in his diary about how or why he chose his architect: perhaps he had simply met him on LCC business. In a sense his lack of interest in style, which later betrayed itself also in the dull nature of the public buildings he erected or subsidised

57. The interior of the former barn at Daws Hill during the Carrington family residency. Nothing on the inside testified to the history of the room, but this was nevertheless a significant reuse of a former agricultural building.

58. Daws Hill: the former cart-house stable after conversion to the Oak Room. Carrington lined the room with Jacobean panelling from elsewhere, filling in gaps between it with new work. The floral plasterwork seen here is characteristic of the period.

59. The tallest gable of Daws Hill, below the clock tower, was almost all that survived the remodelling to testify to the former barn on the site. Old bricks appear to have been reused and mixed with new ones elsewhere, giving the house an agreeably mottled and irregular appearance.

in the town of High Wycombe, is helpful in that it draws attention to the process that his home had undergone: a more stylish or artistic architect would have made an effort to incorporate the old work more smoothly into the overall scheme. His diary for the period says almost nothing about the architecture of big new houses: he evidently thought that Alfred Rothschild's Halton, a grand French chateau in the Chiltern Hills, was vulgar, and the peculiar underground rooms and corridors at the Duke of Portland's Welbeck Abbey in Nottinghamshire 'horrible' and 'the creation of a mad-man' (which they were).[21] Norman Shaw's Cragside near Rothbury, built in stages over 20 years from the mid-1860s for Lord Armstrong, had also begun as a shooting box; its gradual conversion into a grand house almost completely obscured its modest origins, which lived on mostly in the form of an untidier plan than Shaw would normally have contemplated. But Armstrong was nouveau riche. To convert a farmhouse into the country residence of a person with the political and court status such as that of Carrington was an extraordinary thing to do.

It was however consistent with his career as a land reformer. Andrew Adonis's study of his estate management records that by 1890 he had already granted over 1,400 urban allotments within High Wycombe, and over the ten years that followed a change in the law in 1892 had let some 650 acres (260 hectares) in his Lincolnshire estates in the form of smallholdings, a system of land tenure that he believed would strengthen the security of agricultural tenants to the land and their connection to it.[22] It was also, Carrington maintained, good business. It is thus possible to see Daws Hill as a rational response to the recurring English dream, the 'four acres and a cow', the systematic return of the worker to the land in the form of well-laid-out cottages and gardens, remaking the elements of past buildings with their personal and historical connections into a new, financially and practically rational composition.[23] The mixed style and the unexpected conjunctions of old and new, of 'polite' work with the vernacular, could be seen as an attempt to remake the history of the old house in a new and rational way. In this respect, Carrington was as much a scientist as Avebury. If Kingsgate Castle had been designed by an artistic, gothic-revival-trained architect as a demonstration of building archaeology, Daws Hill was about farming tradition and connection to a landscape; both were about reentering the past and remaking it.

After the sweeping Liberal win in the general election of 1906, when Avebury was sitting on the opposition back benches in the Lords with the Unionists, Carrington faced him as President of the Board of Agriculture and Fisheries, a position similar to the one held by his paternal grandfather under William Pitt. From here he further strengthened the rights of allotment holders, tenants and agricultural labourers: low land values constituted a threat to the tenant, in that the landlord, especially in the Home Counties, could more easily find a city professional in search of a country house to sell his land to, with the result that prices rose above what locals could afford.[24] He became Lord Privy Seal in 1911, and retired from politics with the marquessate of Lincolnshire the following year. In the latter part of his life, bereft of his only 'boy' who had been killed in the Great War and with no further use for a 'gold mine', he parted further from his estate.

As Adonis points out, Carrington was in many respects simply a typical progressive Liberal, albeit a consistent and an unusually generous one, but the house he bequeathed at Daws Hill opened a new chapter: Liberal architecture was as much about the old as it was about the new; as much about the land as about the building on it. Lady Carrington recorded in her diary that King Edward and Queen Alexandra came to see the house in January 1903, planted a pair of cedar trees, and 'took the keenest interest' in their home, as well they might, for Daws Hill was to be an archetype for the Edwardian house.[25]

Old-and-new

The outstanding example of an old-and-new house is Vann, originally Lower Vann Farm, near Hambledon in Surrey (figs 60–64; see also fig.52). The architect for its extensive remodelling, begun in 1907, was Caröe – the same person who Carrington thought was spoiling the view at Daws Hill. Best known for his work in church and cathedral restoration, he was by now practising from his own house and office that were incorporated into his newly completed and monumental Ecclesiastical Commissioners building on the corner of Great College Street and Millbank in Westminster. In the course of his church work he recorded his attitude to restoration: protect all old fittings and good-quality work; replace unsound construction. That sounded like the dogma of the Society for the Protection of Ancient Buildings. But what he actually did at Vann was much more interesting, and annoyed SPAB a great deal.[26]

The house that Caröe bought was a small mediaeval construction that had originally been a single double-height space but which had had a chimney and an upper floor added at a later date. Then, at around the beginning of the 18th century, a small brick wing with tall casements had been added to the southern end. At an angle to it to the north and north-west was a series of agricultural outbuildings, including a barn which was recorded by the assistant Caröe sent to survey it as a plain rectangle. Caröe designed a long wing running east–west at the northern end of the old house, to form a T, providing a new kitchen, scullery and housekeepers' room, an entrance hall from the barn side of the building and a living-room-like 'hall place' – a term much liked by other

60. The eastern garden front at Vann. The mediaeval core lies behind the half-timbered front, and part of the early 18th-century wing can be seen at the extreme left. All the rest is Caröe's work.

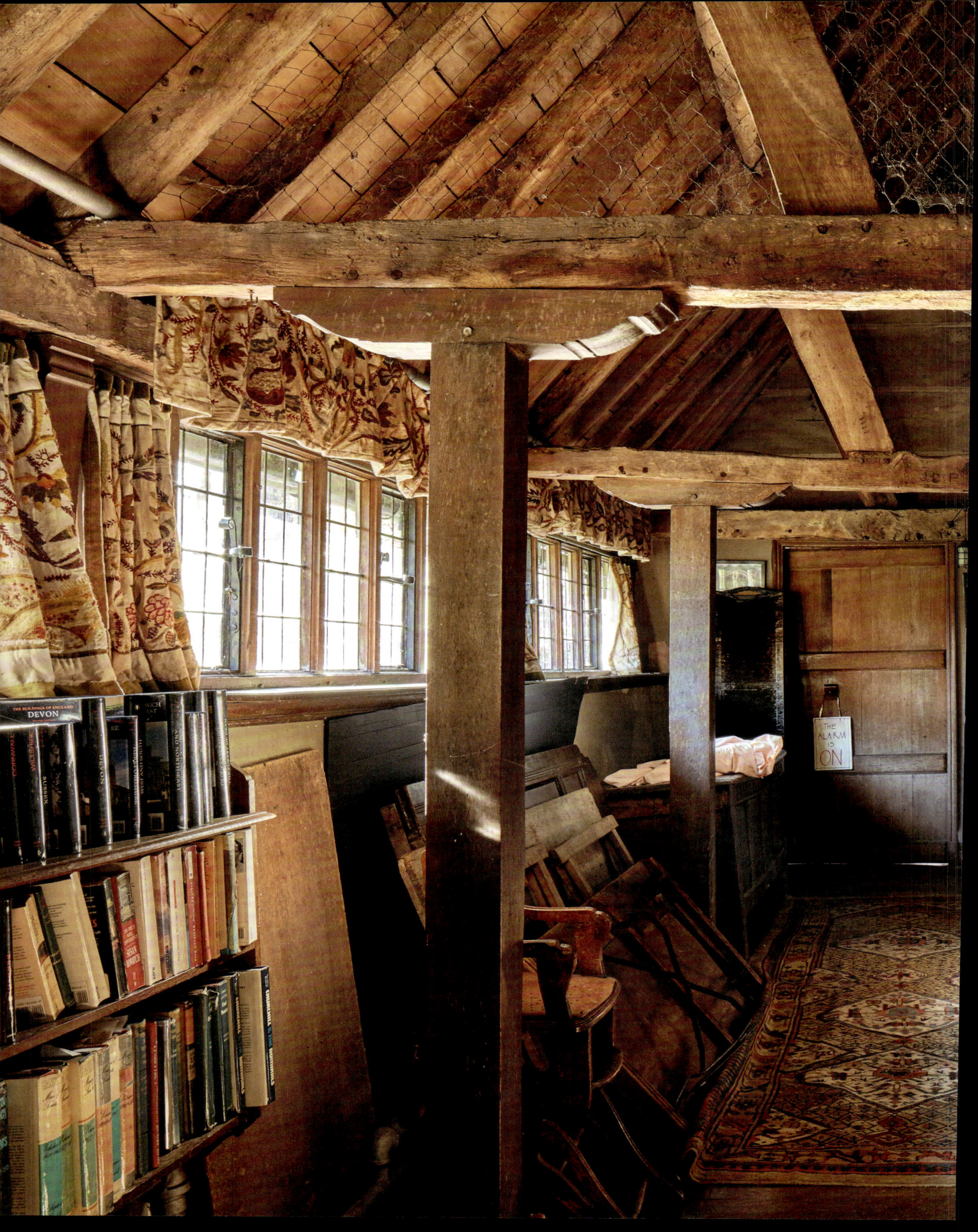
THE BUILDINGS OF ENGLAND
DEVON
THE ALARM IS ON

61. (previous pages) The way through from the hall place to the converted barn at Vann. Caröe himself directed craftsmen on site, at the same time running a busy practice in London.

62. The hall place at Vann. Caröe introduced elements of craft design of the highest quality into his house, some old, and some new. The ornamental ironwork on the door seen here had been moved from a house in Chelsea.

63. A lead water cistern dated 1733 on the garden front at Vann, situated in front of Caröe's new work.

Art Workers' Guild architects, especially M.H. Baillie Scott. Then the northern, entrance, courtyard side was completed with kitchen office buildings and stores. The hall place extended west down along a restored corridor to the barn, which was thus incorporated into the house as a large room for entertaining; Caröe provided it with a big new inglenook and gallery, and a billiard table area occupying about half of the room. He closed off the entrance hall from the rest with a beautiful glazed timber door, and later on other devices were introduced to prevent draughts, but the layout of the hall place and its extensions north and south was essentially a form of open plan that gave the sense, as one moves through it, of spaces – 'places' – that open off from one another, connecting the old with the new (fig.64).

There is one particularly telling detail that Caröe spent some time on which indicates how he was interested in escaping from a SPAB-approved historic restoration. In order to make the plan work in the remodelled upper storey of the mediaeval house, he needed to introduce a corridor that would reach the 18th-century south pavilion. But to do so meant having to cut through one of the old tie beams, blackened by smoke from the period before the fireplace had been introduced. That would have been heresy for an arts-and-crafts restorer. A number of sketches that Caröe himself made show how the tie would be maintained by introducing a hidden iron one at a higher level, with an elegantly curved oak lintel just above head height. In other words, it would be new, of very high technical quality, and designed to look like part of the old structure, but it would not actually be the piece that carried out the constructional role. This is a different approach from applying elements that look like old ones on top of the construction – what the gothic revivalists would have called a 'sham' – because the new timber element referenced both the history of the house and the real tie hidden above it. And down at the barn end, Caröe did rather more than restore it, as it appears and as it is often described; he had to take down one end in order to get the massive billiard table base inside, and he reused the demolished wall plate as a purlin on the rebuilt roof above it. He also turned the internal posts around so that the side that had been abraded by animals over centuries was now facing outwards and less visible. Caröe's interest in the timber detailing expresses itself all over the place; many of the new components were not only industrialised iron ones but also very recent innovations: a proprietary system for partition

walls for example, and vulcanite sheets, masked with timber mouldings that Caröe himself, busy as he was, drew at full size.[27]

Caröe had been a mathematician before serving his articles with the Liverpool architect Edmund Kirby. At Vann one can see the logical, scientific mind at work; he engaged with the problem of rebuilding the house in an unsentimental way, making new details in the spirit of the old ones, and leaving all over it traces of remodelled or cleaned-up features. He had done this with great delicacy when building a new Tudor archbishop's palace in Canterbury in 1897–1901, incorporating and revealing small fragments of buildings that had survived from the mediaeval palace.[28] At Vann, these sometimes sat directly on each other: Caröe remade a

64.   Caröe's ground-floor plan for Vann, May 1907. Pre-existing walls, to the south (right-hand side on the drawing), are marked in grey, and proposed work is in black, but this only hints at the extent of the careful mixing of old and new that Caröe eventually achieved across the house.

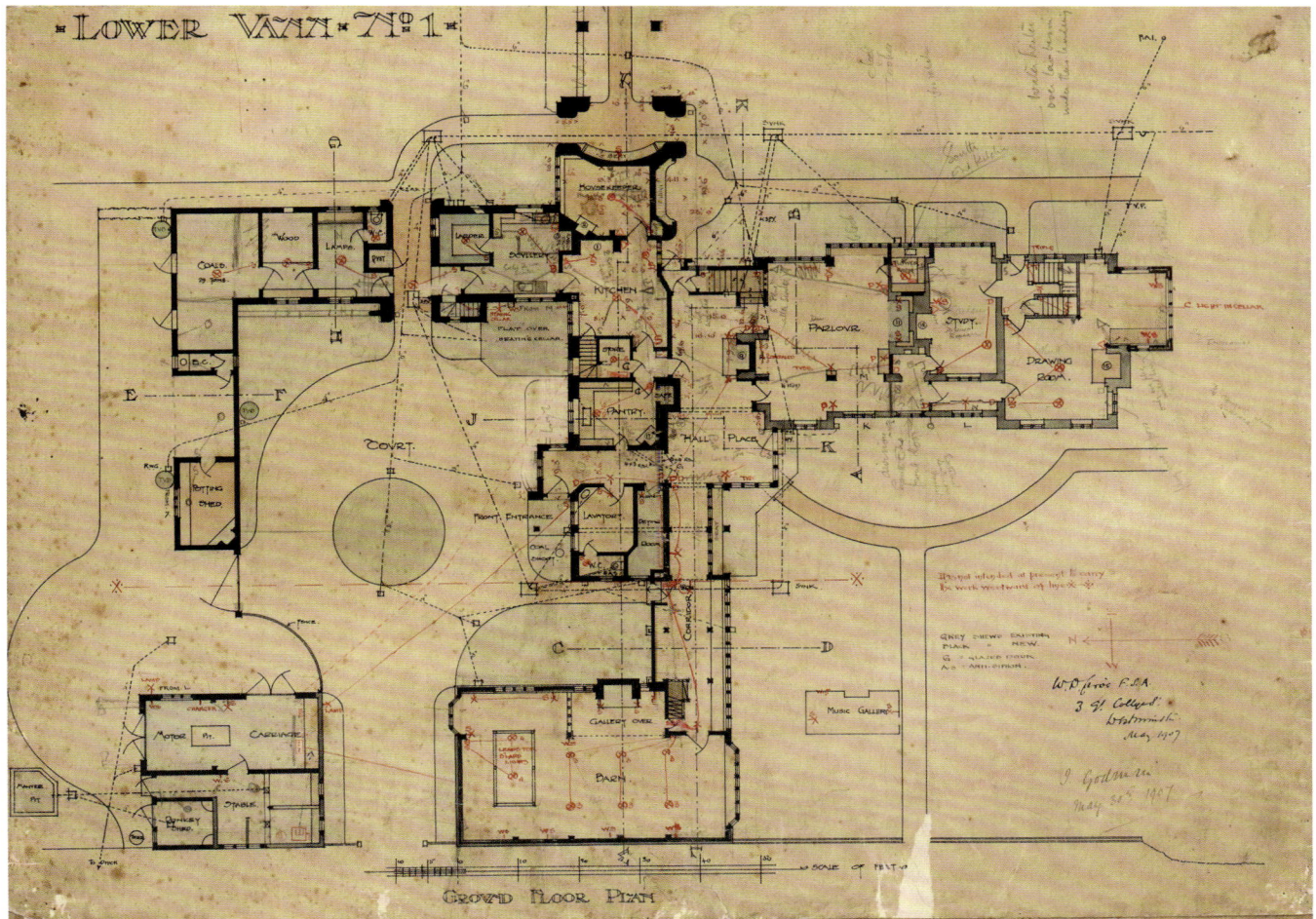

Victorian bay window on the west front by inserting into it new casements with leaded lights held in place by slender oak beads. There is evidence that the artistic elements of the house – the barn room for parties and musical entertainments, the extensions towards the garden with their verandah and pergola stretching out into the garden, the oriental furnishings from the Tibet exhibition at Earl's Court of 1910 – were introduced by Caröe's wife Grace, a friend of the horticulturalist and garden designer Gertrude Jekyll; but everything that can be seen of the house itself, however old its core, is Edwardian, not late Victorian 'arts-and-crafts'.[29] Rosie Ibbotson has identified in the projecting corner bays on the west front of Vann a reflection of the butterfly plan of E.S. Prior's The Barn, Exmouth, of 1896, itself coming on the tail of Norman Shaw's remodelling of Chesters in Northumberland (note that this *was* a remodelling), a plan much admired by the younger generation; but if so, it is so carefully integrated into the body of the house, in a way that mirrors the small-scale integration of old and new details, that it is scarcely more than an intriguing and knowing trace. There is evidence in the construction drawings that Caröe took care to avoid any aggrandising effect: a prominent old arched sliding sash window on a gable wall was for example replaced by a more modest square-headed one. Over a period of time he introduced into his house both new joinery of extremely high quality but also old timber panelling and an ornamental 17th-century plaster ceiling which went into the southern wing. In fact it seems that his greatest interest was in working with the areas where old and new were mixed – the more mixed the better – and he himself moved old features to new locations and added to them. It is very hard to tell from the outside how much of the resulting house is Caröe and how much was there before; it is about the materials as objects, not the chronology or the 'style'. Yet of course the result is all Caröe.

Oliver Caröe says of what is still the family house that his great-grandfather 'calmed the aesthetic' of the antiquarian or archaeological nature of the restored building, modelling its look and feel into what is now the recognisable Surrey style; but he did this through a continuous series of rational design decisions. This process took the house out of the realm of historical reconstruction where each part is judged on its authenticity, SPAB-style, and into a new territory where the whole building became a homogenous fusing of old and new, of the rational with the historical. The somewhat clumsy layering of Daws Hill, which conceivably Caröe had seen when working on the adjacent sites, was here developed into a smooth and consistent way of building. A visitor must know the history and method of the various individual parts but they must also sense the completeness and the general historical analogies, which were mostly 17th century in outline and feel. Thus Vann establishes more clearly than any other house the original nature of Edwardian domestic architecture. It would have been difficult to find a more appropriate house to stand in for E.M. Forster's 'Howards End' in a recent television adaptation: a building that looks as if it were too-good-to-be-true rural English yeoman architecture that is in reality almost exactly the same age as Forster's novel itself.

Vann was included in Lawrence Weaver's *Small Country Houses: Their Repair and Enlargement* of 1914 and with it is another less well-known project that in retrospect appears more significant than it might have done to contemporary readers: The Wharf at Sutton Courtenay, a Berkshire village on the Thames. In 1912 Margot Asquith, the Prime Minister's wife, commissioned a small house from the architect Walter Cave, active in the Art Workers' Guild, for a site in a gap on the village street that backed onto the river.[30] It is not clear how she came to choose him, but she moved in artistic circles which probably overlapped with those of Cave, who had then recently completed a large house in Northamptonshire for the printer and musician Philip Agnew and his family. She might have known about the tactful remodelling carried out by Cave at Bateman's, the writer Rudyard Kipling's house in East Sussex, for a former owner, as it had been published in *Country Life* in 1908.[31] The fact that The Wharf was furnished in the *Country Life* style with sparse, good-quality antique tables and chairs, rugs, and little else, rather suggests that she read it. It is likely that she had at least heard about Daws Hill, since Carrington had been a loyal Liberal on the progressive wing of the party which was brought into government before the party won the 1906 election.

The new house that Cave built for Asquith on the street at Sutton Courtenay was plain and symmetrical, polite village-late-Stuart on the outside (figs 65 and 66). This was not unusual. But turning the riverside barn in its garden into a self-contained cottage, presumably only habitable in the summer, was a revolutionary thing to do: until then, the gentry who wanted to occupy an old building would have had it remodelled – that is, modernised and changed. Asquith called this her 'studio', and it was fitted out with a bedroom above a sitting room (fig.67). There is no indication, in all of her interminably voluble diary or score-settling autobiography, as to why she did it; Weaver implied that this was Cave's idea. His short text, which appeared first as an article in the magazine's supplement and was then converted into a chapter for his book, is uncharacteristically rambling, and appeared to be saying: 'just let old buildings be', although

65. The Wharf, Walter Cave's 'late Stuart' house for Margot Asquith at Sutton Courtenay, then in Berkshire, 1912. The house was the scene of many political and personal events in the period leading up to David Lloyd George's coup against H.H. Asquith which led to him becoming prime minister in 1916.

66. The garden front of The Wharf, facing Margot Asquith's barn and the River Thames.

this was not exactly what had happened in practice.[32] Soon afterwards Asquith bought the 18th-century house next door to her new one on the street front, and Cave joined them together. The sitting room in the new house now directly abutted the unplastered brickwork of the older neighbour, although in fact Cave replaced the original bricks with more authentically Tudor ones; the whole ensemble, with plans and interior views, was eventually published in the *Architectural Review* in May 1924 (figs 68–9).[33] When this extension was complete, Asquith had not only a large living hall in approved arts-and-crafts fashion, but also a roomy bridge parlour where the original kitchen, pantry and scullery had been; she was later frowned on even by her own family for maintaining her lavish bridge parties when the rest of the Liberal leadership had moved into a more austere lifestyle during the War.[34]

67. (opposite) The barn on the riverfront at Sutton Courtenay, restored by Cave in 1912. A case can be made for claiming this as the first 'barn conversion' in the modern sense, a gentrification of an existing structure with minimum intervention for contemporary fashionable living. The sympathetic extension to the right was detailed and completed in 2017 by Nigel and James Roberts following the original design by Elizabeth Collison of Swabey-Collison Architecture.

68. Exposed brickwork and Cave's joinery in the Asquiths' new sitting room in The Wharf where the new house abutted the exterior of an older one. These bricks were, however, inserted by Cave to replace less attractive Georgian ones.

69. The staircase on the street side of The Wharf, designed by Cave. Originally unstained, it was constructed of oak 'just as it came from the joiner's shop', and fixed with timber pegs rather than nails.

70. The Prime Minister's wife *c.*1911, photographed by Baron Adolph de Meyer. In spite of the personal eccentricities of the woman who commissioned it, Margot Asquith's The Wharf provides an archetype for the main themes in Edwardian domestic architecture. She herself gave no clue about what her architectural intentions were.

Like much else that Asquith was associated with, by friends as well as by enemies, the overall house and barn had an unreal quality to them which to her no doubt seemed normal. Herbert Gladstone, Home Secretary from 1905 to 1910, had known her and her youngest sister since their youth; he was hinting at their eccentricity when he recalled them much later as 'great fun, such queer energetic clever characters'.[35] The Asquiths lived in London – at her father Sir Charles Tennant's expense – in a neo-classical splendour at 20 Cavendish Square, in fact preferring to remain there when H.H. Asquith became chancellor in 1905; this was followed by 10 Downing Street in 1908; and only many years later, when she moved to Bedford Square, where she immediately carried out alterations, did she live in the kind of house that most other people she knew were familiar with.[36]

When Tennant died in 1906 he left a substantial fortune to his three sons, two of whom were Liberal Party politicians. The eldest son Edward – MP for Salisbury from 1906 to 1910, married to Pamela Wyndham – inherited The Glen, the baronial mansion built by his father in the Scottish Borders; but the two younger brothers, Harold (known as Jack) and Frank, substantially remodelled old houses in Kent,

71. Lympne Castle from the west, with the mediaeval round tower to the right. The room with the bay window is the new dining room. The left-hand wing was added at a later stage of the remodelling.

72. (opposite) Lympne Castle, Kent, restored and extended by Robert Lorimer for Margot Asquith's brother, Frank Tennant, from 1906. The mediaeval castle is the wing on the right, seen here from the base of the escarpment above Romney Marsh.

conveniently located near golf courses, almost as soon as they came into their inheritance. They both went to top-rank architects, Frank choosing Robert Lorimer to turn the romantic ruins of Lympne Castle on the south-eastern side of Romney Marsh into a comfortable modern residence, and Jack commissioning Edwin Lutyens to rebuild a small and much mutilated early Georgian house of 1721 called Maytham, not far away near Rolvenden, as Great Maytham Hall.

Frank was a sportsman rather than a politician, and evidently more artistically aware than his brothers. He brought Lorimer down from Scotland soon after the latter had carried out work at The Glen after a fire, and altered another Tennant house.[37] From 1906 Lorimer, who at the same time was restoring Rowallan Castle, Ayrshire and building

a new one at Ardkinglas, Argyll, added separate residential and service wings to Lympne so that the old building – a 14th-century hall and tower in an advanced state of decay, perched up on an escarpment with a view to the south across the English Channel – could be repaired and opened up as a kind of museum piece (figs 71 and 72). The residential wing abuts the old castle, but Lorimer arranged the service wing into a picturesque long, low building that formed the edge of a garden courtyard, in a similar style and at the same scale as Romaine-Walker had done at Kingsgate but prettier. Here, though, all the new building was constructed of stone with decorative late gothic tracery in square-headed windows, with red-tiled roofs, reminiscent in colour of Scottish pantiles, and the ornamental plaster and metal work seem Scottish too – in a way, this is an invented 'British' castle that unites English and Scottish history.[38]

Frank's younger brother Jack was MP for Berwickshire from 1894 to 1918, and became parliamentary secretary to the Board of Trade in 1909, the year in which his new house was designed. Great Maytham Hall was rebuilt around the shell of the previous building to form a long, plain symmetrical house in a mid-18th-century style, with a simple plan in which the front door leads straight through the stair hall into the centre of the drawing room and from there to the garden. It has so little of Lutyens's usual spatial complexity or characteristic twisting interior planning that it has disappointed many of his historians. When Weaver wrote about it for Country Life, he focused his text almost entirely on the history of the place rather than the resulting new house. It is possible that he found it dull; but on the other hand he used a telling phrase about Lutyens's work which conveys a great deal about what had happened. Lutyens, he wrote, had 'picked up the thread of early eighteenth century design where Moneypenny [the original builder] had dropped it in 1721'.[39] And indeed what Lutyens had done at a conceptual level (and no doubt had never expressed explicitly) was precisely to reenter the shell of the old Georgian building to expand it, to remake as perfect an imperfect building history that had been interrupted by fire and by unsympathetic alterations. At the same time, it seems possible that the house with its large aligned windows and relatively narrow plan, and its big open spaces between rooms on the upper floor, was designed, under the supervision of Tennant's wife May, a health reformer, in a way that would maximise cross ventilation and help prevent tuberculosis, the disease that had killed many in the family.[40] Thus remade history and scientific progress meld together in a very satisfying way and although the house is plainer than Lympne, it says rather more about its period.

These three building projects, all connected to the Prime Minister's wife and full of original ideas, give some suggestion of the quantity of building generated by prominent members of the Liberal Party and their immediate social circle. There were many more building at a similar rate, and a scale somewhere between Margot's barn and Frank's castle. In the case of the Tennants, it was money from industry rather than anything else that accounted for these houses, indicating how this was funding a level of cultural rebirth. And all three projects were developing the idea that Devey had originally suggested in his work in Penshurst and Nonington: that the aim when building houses was not to emulate old building styles, but to focus on the materials themselves, getting inside their skin so that even large new wings could carry the genes, as it were, of the old house. In fact entirely new houses could be created by emulating this. That is clearly what was happening at Vann; it was the feature of Great Maytham that most interested Weaver and it makes sense at Lympne too. And at Sutton Courtenay Cave had created an intriguing puzzle in which the three separate buildings that form the main elements of the project need to be, but never quite are, fitted together, and so remain in tension with one another.

'Quality Street' comes to life

The architect Edward Warren, then remodelling Lamb House in Rye for the American novelist Henry James, published a letter in the Times newspaper on 25 January 1898 protesting about a private initiative, to which Sir John Lubbock, the future Lord Avebury, was party, to erect large new residences between Millbank and the river, obstructing all views across it from the west, and turning the new section of the embankment into 'a river terrace for the benefit of the highly privileged and presumably high-rented inhabitants of the east front of the new block'. Currently works, wharfs and mills, this area should, he felt, become a park. Warren, who worked from Cowley Street at the heart of the area, went on to draw attention to the 'Hinterland' of the scheme, around St John's church in Smith Square, which its promoters referred to as 'one of the most insanitary districts in London' but which he described as 'some excellent old houses': these were terraces of plain early 18th-century type which at that point were out of fashion.[41] Others objecting to the proposals included the dean and chapter of Westminster Abbey, and C.R. Ashbee, then of the Survey of London committee; these responses were reflected in anguished illustrated articles in the professional

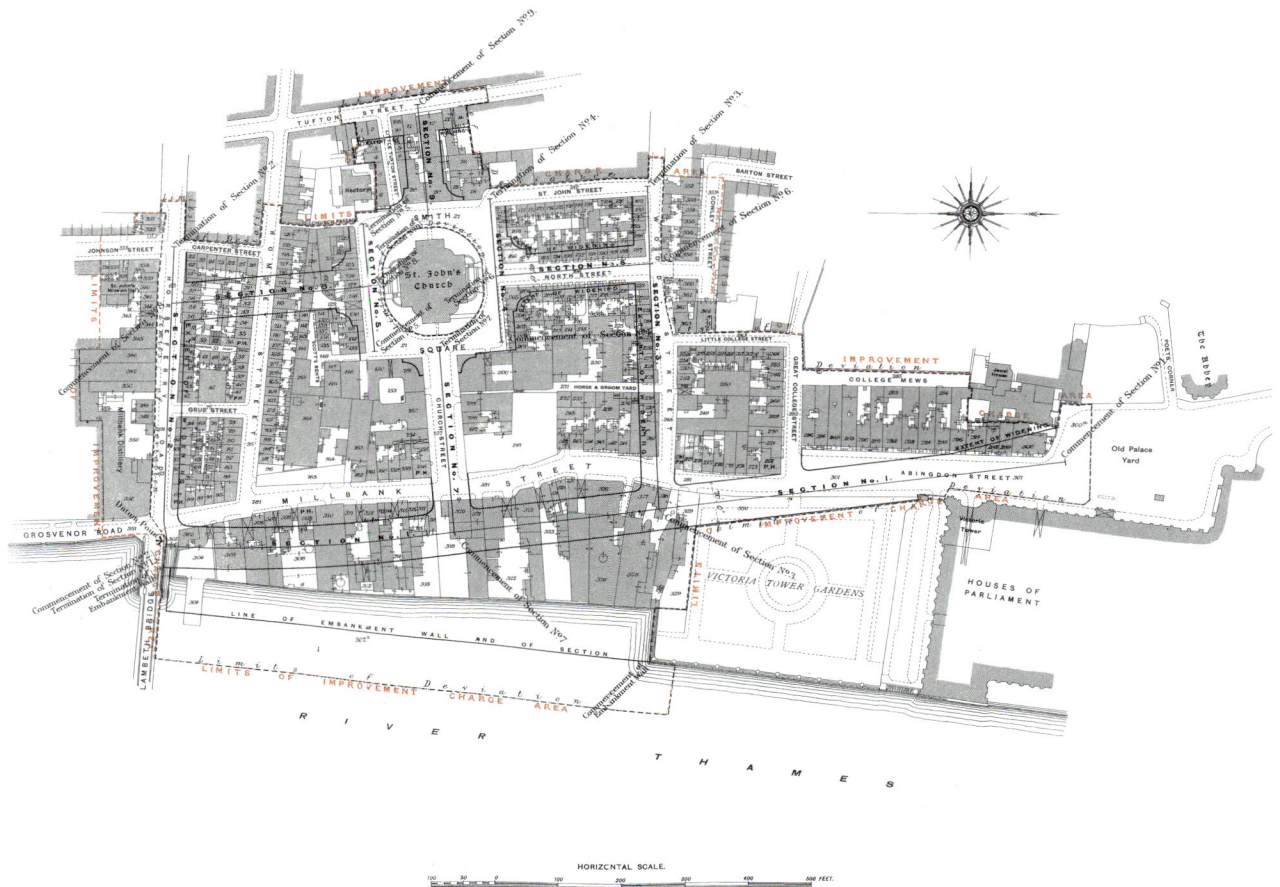

press about the future of pretty streets threatened by road widening and clearances to the south and east of the ancient abbey garden.[42]

In mid-1900 the Conservative and Liberal Unionist coalition responded to this with a public plan which still aimed to demolish the alleged slums but made some concessions to protests; the moving force behind this was G.J. Shaw-Lefevre, once Gladstone's First Commissioner of Works and now a Progressive member of the LCC.[43] The London County Council (Improvements) Act gave the council the right to buy land for street improvements by continuing the embankment south from the Palace of Westminster, clearing the Thames waterfront, and creating large sites for offices without obstructing views of the river. The new act included a plan of November 1899 from the office of the council's chief engineer, Sir Alexander Binnie, to widen and alter the streets inland around Smith Square; and to lease surplus land created through demolition to private developers.[44] The north-east boundary of the development ran along the southern party wall of Warren's own house in Cowley Street. The old houses

73. The proposed street layout around St John's church, Smith Square, from the plan approved with the London County Council (Improvements) Act of 1900. North is to the right. The new Millbank sweeps through the cluster of wharves and works along the river, and four short, broad avenues lead axially towards the church. Note that North Street (now Lord North Street) was to have been rebuilt. Edward Warren, the architect who expressed concern about the development, lived and worked in Cowley Street just outside the plan's boundary, in the house overlaid with the word AREA at top right. Caröe's new Ecclesiastical Commissioners' offices went up on the entire block between Wood Street and Great College Street in 1903–6.

were thus still at risk, and anxiety increased after 1903 as Caröe's Ecclesiastical Commissioners' offices – 'a huge and most aggressive pile', as a writer in the *Architectural Review* described them – began to loom over Millbank on one of the big new office sites.[45] 'The centre of Great College Street . . . is now barbarously threatened,' wrote the *Builders' Journal*, 'two of the houses having been leased to a railway company; and we know what sort of buildings railway companies erect.'[46]

In the end, the large office sites were mostly restricted to the west side of a new riverside avenue facing the greatly lengthened Victoria Tower Gardens; Wood Street was

widened to become the continuation of Great Peter Street; and Smith Square became the focus of a great deal of picturesque activity. In John Rocque's map of 1746, St John's church sat to the western side of an irregular yard, which by the early 20th century had become rectangular in plan, with the church not quite in the centre of it. To its east there were a number of industrial and commercial premises that had spilled across Millbank from the wharves of the river front. The LCC's new plan reorganised the street layout around the square: North Street (now Lord North Street) to the north was to be widened, and matching new short, broad avenues ran west, south and east axially from the church, each terminating at the church end with grand, baroque curved fronts (fig.73).[47] It was not clear from the Act how much of the area was intended to become large offices; the fact that all of the houses in North Street were to be demolished suggests that most of it was. In the end, the North Street houses and the north side of the square itself were saved, perhaps because many of them had been gentrified by politicians; and for the most part up went a better version of what was there before,

74. (opposite) The Trevelyan (left) and Runciman houses, 14–15 Great College Street, designed by Horace Field, at the rear of the Cowley Street site. The Liberal Unionist Alfred Lyttelton lived next door to the right.

75. 4 Cowley Street, Westminster, 1903–4 by Field. These were railway offices, but Field's innovation was to make commercial premises look like the town houses of prosperous Restoration merchants. The opposite side of the street lay within the 1900 redevelopment area.

or what ought to have been, much of it for Liberals, centred on Archer's newly prized masterpiece.[48]

The architects who designed the houses in the new district were some of the finest of the Edwardian era. Horace Field, in partnership with Evelyn Simmons from 1905, played a major role in turning the urban landscape south of the Westminster Abbey precinct up to Smith Square into a stylish, convivial quarter of Queen Anne character. As it happens, Field had been an immediate neighbour of Warren's in the 1890s in Church Row, Hampstead, north of London (George Gilbert Scott Junior lived in the house beyond Field's).[49] The best of the new buildings was actually an office, although

it looked like a house: this was Field's London premises of the North Eastern Railway (NER) at 4 Cowley Street in Westminster, designed in 1903–4, almost as if in defiance of the *Builders' Journal*'s fears for the site. This provided a fitting northern termination to a picturesque, not quite straight axis down North Street towards Smith Square to the south (fig.75).

As part of the same project, Field designed two houses at the rear of the site, on Great College Street, close to Caröe's offices and facing the wall of the abbey gardens (fig.74).[50] Field was commissioned for these by the two leaseholders, Walter Runciman and Charles Philips Trevelyan, both Liberal MPs and NER directors, because the company board was required to vet the designs. Runciman was MP for Dewsbury and the son-in-law of the radical Liberal James Cochran Stevenson; the architect J.J. Stevenson was thus a close connection by marriage. Trevelyan, the son of a Liberal MP himself and 'the scion of a whig family', married one of Isaac Lowthian Bell's 60 grandchildren in 1904, the year in which approval was sought.[51] This came in November 1904, and the whole site

was completed by the end of 1906.[52] Lowthian Bell, resident in Philip Webb's Rounton Grange, was a titanic figure in the north-east of England; he was a director of the NER for 40 years as Liberals including Sir Joseph Pease and Sir Edward Grey acted as chairmen. The NER's vast Christopher Wren-style headquarters in York, by Field and the company architect William Bell, are themselves part of the Liberal history of English architecture.

Many of Field's houses from the period appeared in the professional press, and the elevations, and part of the plan, for the Great College Street pair were published five years later in the *Architects' and Builders' Journal*.[53] They each took the form of a three-and-a-half bay house, the halves being at either end with casement windows half the size of the others. Trevelyan's house, number 14 and the eastern one, had a stone canopy over it, which according to the *Journal* once housed a carving of a horse's head by Eric Aumonier, who worked often for Field. It also had a complicated and theatrical ground-floor arrangement brought about because of the angle of the

76. (opposite) The second Runciman house, 8 Barton Street, facing east along Cowley Street. Field's three developments established the new-old tone for the remodelled Westminster district.

77. A view from the *Architectural Review* in 1903 showing the plain Georgian house that Field replaced. The door at the corner was part of Warren's office at 20 Cowley Street, which sat on an L-shaped site and was divided between Runciman's house and an extended 19 Cowley Street. This, in time, was refaced to look 'early 18th century' (see fig.76).

party wall with the adjoining house. Runciman's had a simpler pediment over the door. The windows were leaded casements in the style of the end of the 17th century and if it were not for the sharpness of the brickwork, the buildings could easily be mistaken for heavily restored houses of that date. Field also exhibited these houses at the Royal Academy summer exhibition in 1906, two years after presenting the Cowley Street railway offices.[54]

In 1907 Runciman was promoted from parliamentary secretary to the Local Government Board to financial secretary to the Treasury; then, when Asquith became prime minister the following year, he was promoted to the cabinet as President of the Board of Education. This seems to have been the springboard for a larger house, which Field then designed

for him on another important urban axis, the end of Barton Street which faced east down Cowley Street towards the railway offices. This house was in the same style as the Great College Street houses and was almost as wide as both of them together; it replaced two flat-fronted buildings, of the plainest and cheapest late 18th-century type (figs 76 and 77).[55]

At the same time the square to the south was fast reverting to the era of Queen Anne as Edwardians were imagining it, even if the baroque convex elevations facing the church never materialised. In 1908–9, Detmar Blow (a former 'unofficial' apprentice of Philip Webb) and Fernand Billerey designed a grand, tall house for Lady Agnew, the subject of one of John Singer Sargent's most famous portraits and the wife of a former Liberal Unionist MP, at number 10 in its north-east corner, as well as a smaller adjoining house to the south for her sister Dorothy Vernon, all occupying the site of a gas meter works.[56] The architects' first design for this was conventionally late 17th-century classical, with a stone front lined with Corinthian pilasters. Perhaps the council vetoed the material, for the executed design was brick-faced and most unusual in terms of composition, almost as if it were a fragment of a building by Vanbrugh. It wrapped itself around the site with a narrow northern bay on the new set-back building line, a 45-degree angled section to take the corner, and two further bays along the eastern side of the square; the centrepiece in the angled part was a deeply recessed tall, narrow archway with a flamboyant ornamental keystone.[57] When the elevations changed, the plan did too, likewise becoming more baroque, with an elliptical entrance hall and a large room for entertaining on each of the two floors above.[58]

Soon afterwards Field designed a pair of grand classical residences for two more Liberal MPs, Russell Rea and his son Walter Rea, adjacent to the Vernon house and incorporating the corner with the new Dean Stanley Street on the eastern side of the square: the style now reflected the church opposite.[59] Russell Rea had already been a valuable client for Field on his home territory in Hampstead: he lived at 22 Lyndhurst Road, one of Field's early tile-hung villas in the style of Norman Shaw, and in 1897 Field had designed a group of three houses next door for him and Russell Scott, perhaps as an investment, in an early 18th-century style with formal fronts and irregular, village-vernacular backs topped by a fin-de-siècle mansard roof.[60] Walter Rea's new house faced the square, and turned the corner towards the river, and Russell Rea's smaller one sat on Dean Stanley Street between that and Westminster House, British American Tobacco's large Millbank premises which were going up at the same time. The houses formed a single substantial block and were

78. The drawing room of Walter Rea's 12 Smith Square, by Field and Evelyn Simmons, from Mervyn Macartney's *Recent Domestic Architecture*, vol.5 (1912). The style was typical of Field, and the early loss of these houses for an extension of a commercial office block was a tragedy for the Edwardian character of the square.

79. (opposite) Looking south towards St John's church, Smith Square, from Field's 4 Cowley Street. The corners with the former Wood Street were remade as part of a straightened, widened Great Peter Street, with the pair designed by Lutyens for Sir Henry Norman and Francis McLaren on the left, joined in 1929–32 by a further group by Oliver Hill, second right. Lord North Street, directly ahead, otherwise survived intact.

ingeniously designed with an open colonnade linking the two residences at street level: to achieve this, Field had to convince the district surveyor to allow him to omit a party wall across the middle of it for 'artistic' reasons.[61] The pretty, panelled, white-painted drawing-room interiors of both houses were widely published (fig.78).[62] Thus in May 1915 there were four senior Liberals living in Field houses in Westminster. But there were several more in new houses designed by other first-rate architects, to a considerable extent copying Field's style, especially the shutters.

On the other side of St John's church, a large house by Lutyens was going up at 36 Smith Square, on another of the corners created by the Act's new street layout. Reginald McKenna, an English MP for a Welsh constituency and a Congregationalist, was married to the niece of Lutyens's collaborator and friend Gertrude Jekyll. He rose rapidly in government as financial secretary to the Treasury in 1905 and then, in the cabinet, briefly as President of the Board of Education before Runciman; with the ascent of Asquith, he became First Lord of the Admiralty and in 1911, Home Secretary. Lutyens designed one of his many buildings that had a plain, severe exterior, more or less based on English late 17th-century sources, but with a circuitous interior sequence around a staircase deep inside the building. Then, from 1913, up went Thorney House on the opposite side of Dean Trench Street, externally similar but plainer and more conventional inside. This was by Ernest Empson for Stanley Christopherson,

the sportsman-stockbroker.[63] For connections of McKenna's through his wife, Lutyens designed the red-brick semi-detached pair on the widened and straightened Great Peter Street; these houses like McKenna's have plain 'late Stuart' fronts and plans dominated by complex stair arrangements. The Corner House, on the Cowley Street side, was designed for Sir Henry Norman, who was Liberal MP for Blackburn, and 8 Little College Street adjoining was for Francis McLaren, Liberal MP for Spalding, both elected in 1910.[64] This ensemble further enhanced the axis between Field's offices on Cowley Street and Smith Square (fig.79). Another remarkable house in the immediate area was 1 Dean Trench Street, on the corner of Tufton Street, designed by H.S. Goodhart-Rendel for Robert Adeane in 1912 in a style that somewhat recalled the work of the German architect Heinrich Tessenow.[65]

At Vann Caröe had created a new Edwardian house by working with and into the fabric of the old farmhouse so that the old and new were not exactly indistinguishable but certainly inseparable. As appreciation for the plain old 18th-century houses grew, the area around Smith Square ended up as a homogenous mixture of the old and the new, both altered because of their effect on each other. This came about, ironically, as a result of a campaign to save this part of the city from encroachment by buildings like the office block designed by Caröe; it was ironic too, that Warren's former plain Georgian offices, part of which sat on the site of Field's Barton Street house, were eventually rebuilt and remodelled

together with numbers 18 and 19 Cowley Street into a new 'Queen Anne' mansion. Warren thus sits at the start and the end of this story, and some of the best new houses in the area deployed features that he had already chosen for himself for his widely published Breach House, his own residence, at Cholsey, above the Thames Valley near Wallingford in Oxfordshire: late 17th-century casement windows with panels below them; shutters; and colonnades.[66] This house became in time a setting for Bloomsbury Group rendezvous through connections of his wife.

Old-new and new-old

Horace Field's work set the tone which still dominates the new Westminster precinct, even after the early demolition of the two Rea houses (and the Agnew ones) in 1928–9 for the landwards extension of Westminster House.[67] He was an 'artistic' architect (to use the term he repeated across his career) from Hampstead and member of the Art Workers' Guild who built a great deal during the Edwardian period; as money ebbed away from expensive domestic architecture during and after the War his output and status diminished.[68] His most lasting influence was the design of branches for Lloyds Bank which then was undergoing a great expansion from its base in the Midlands following a number of amalgamations.[69] He had designed a pretty but not much imitated branch on Rosslyn Hill in Hampstead in an ornamental Franco-Flemish style, and then a short series of small ones that were inspired by, or at any rate reimagined, small urban post-Restoration merchants' houses: those at Wealdstone (in red brick) and Okehampton (in Portland stone) were published and then adapted by other architects for bank branches all over England. It had been Field's idea to make commercial premises look like houses, and the Cowley Street offices were an important archetype.

But Field achieved something else, just as significant: he designed new houses that looked as if they had been altered over centuries, including within. The elements of the style he used could be found in a lavish illustrated book he published in 1905, effectively an encyclopaedia of all of them. This was

·THE·MANOR·HOVSE·POVLTON·IN·THE·COVNTY·OF·GLOVCESTER·

XXVII

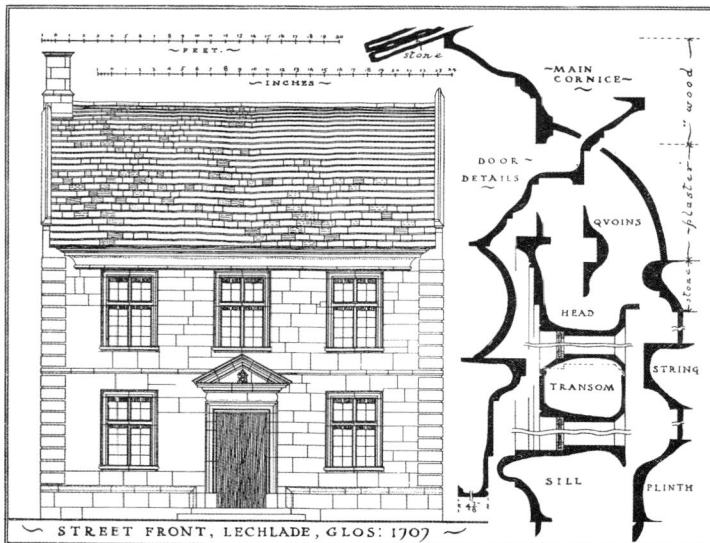

STREET FRONT, LECHLADE, GLOS: 1707

T.R.B. 1904

80. The opening plate of Field and Bunney's *English Domestic Architecture of the XVII and XVIII Centuries* (1905). The book provided architects with countless models for exactly the type of house that they were now asked to design. This drawing of 1904, by Bunney, illustrated the wall-to-window proportions, swept roofs and understated classical detailing that soon became popular.

81. A Queen Anne period street front in Lechlade, drawn by T.R. Bridson for Field and Bunney's book. Some drawings included details and sections.

82. Field, right, in retirement in 1936 with his family at Stuttles, his cottage in Rye. Note the Tuscan mutules on the gazebo.

English Domestic Architecture of the XVII and XVIII Centuries, written with his then assistant Michael Bunney, which included drawings, photographs and details of buildings by the authors and others from the large 18th-century Carshalton House in Surrey to the tiny Tomkins Almshouses in Abingdon in Oxfordshire. *Country Life* gave it a 'cordial welcome', and it provided enthusiasts for 17th- and then, in turn, 18th-century architecture with countless precedents for their own designs, and most likely accounted for the high regard in which Field was held by contributors to the magazines (figs 80 and 81).[70] A copy has been found that carries not only the signature of the Liverpool architect Leonard Barnish, but also the bookplate of one his clients, W.H. Lever, the future Lord Leverhulme.[71] Field's introduction claims that English architecture had a lost 'tradition' in the form of the buildings that emerged through the hands of craftsmen over the course of about a century from the point at which a new wing had been built at Cranborne Manor in Dorset in 1647, his first example of a structure that had merged classicism into English vernacular building. Over the course of this period, the imported academic classical models were developed into practical buildings for the English climate and building materials, with tall roofs, chimney and dormers, and with mullions developing from gothic ancestors to accommodate practical novelties such as double-hung vertical sliding sash windows. In this way he established that authentic

English houses were actually an amalgam of different but sympathetically related styles and adaptations of them. The authors appended nearly 190 illustrations, including drawings by Temple Moore and Adrian Gilbert Scott, showing mostly small buildings in this style from across England. Like many contemporary Art Workers' Guild 'brethren', Field had found a way of remaining faithful to Pugin's insistence on the quality of construction whilst escaping from the gothic revival. He claimed in his book that his attitude was 'conservative', yet in practice he was pioneering the type of reverse archaeology that characterises much Edwardian housebuilding.[72] The revered Webb had worked by defining at the start of every new project its 'Idea', by which he meant, as Sheila Kirk has explained, a choice of an appropriate historic building type as a conceptual model for a new building.[73] In a way, Field was mixing 'Ideas' drawn from the research for his book in the designs for his new buildings and creating his own archaeology that way.

Field was a golfer and designed golf clubhouses and nearby villas for gentlemen who otherwise lived in London; he eventually retired to Rye, where he could play, if he wished, with Reginald Blomfield, A.W. Blomfield's nephew, who lived in a big house that commanded the heights above his small one (fig.82). There is a concentration of Field's golf cottages and villas around Hook Heath, to the west of Woking in Surrey which, with the many others that were built in the

BEDROOM 1 · BEDROOM 1 · BEDROOM 1
BEDROOM 2 · BEDROOM 3 · BEDROOM 2 · BEDROOM 3 · BEDROOM 3 · BEDROOM 2
BEDRM 1 · BEDROOM 3 · BEDROOM 3 · BEDROOM 1 · BEDRM 1
BEDROOM 2 · BEDROOM 2

SCULLERY · SCULLERY · SCULLERY
LIVING ROOM · KITCHEN · KITCHEN · LIVING ROOM · KITCHEN · LIVING ROOM · LAUNDRY
KITCHEN · KITCHEN · SCULLERY
SCULLERY · LARDER
LIVING ROOM · GRASS · GRASS · LIVING ROOM

BED FOR FLOWERS

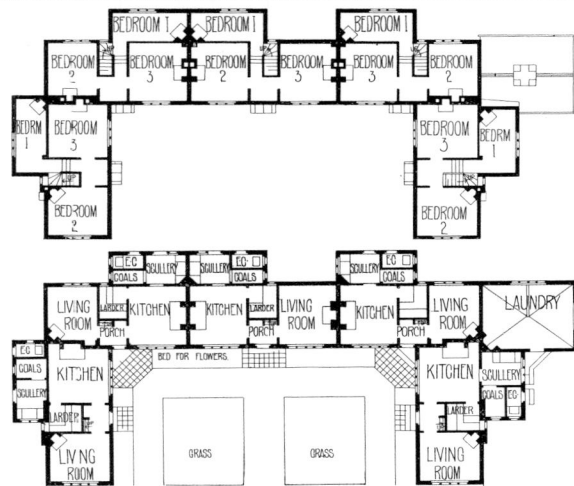

GROUP OF FIVE COTTAGES AT WOKING, SURREY.
HORACE FIELD, Architect.

83.   Field's Milford development in Hook Heath, Surrey, from J.H. Elder-
Duncan's *Country Cottages and Week-End Homes* (1906). Lawrence
Weaver noted that these homes, which had been built for labourers,
were occupied as weekend homes by 'people of educated taste',
including Emery Walker and T.J. Cobden-Sanderson.

area during the period, gives a strong picture of what an
upmarket Edwardian weekend suburb looks like, and how a
style different from the urbane 'Quality Street' of Westminster
was deployed – on the outside, at any rate (fig.83). The largest
house that Field built there was also the first: Hook Hill, for
Henry Fisher Cox, a stockbroker with progressive opinions
and who had earlier been editor of the liberal journal *The
Examiner*.[74] His daughter Katherine 'Ka' Cox, later the lover
of the poet Rupert Brooke and subsequently the daughter-in-
law of a Liberal MP and the mother of Mark Arnold-Forster,
grew up there (figs 84 and 85). Field then designed three other
houses on adjacent land, including South Hill for himself –
a white-rendered, thatched cottage, adorned with a
sentimental inscription which Aumonier carved above
the door (fig.86).[75]

Field's weekend golf cottages at this stage were in a
rural style made up from roughcast gables, tile-hanging and

Tudor mullioned windows, but the interiors were in places
no different from those of his grand London houses. The
exterior of the Hookerel, one of the houses in the group, gives
no indication of the lush 18th-century timber mouldings,
pillars and arches inside, or indeed that the rooms were
once furnished in the finest Edwardian minimal taste, with
widely spaced ceramic plates and vases elegantly spaced out
on shelves and ledges (fig.87). What Field had done here was
precisely to give the impression that he was addressing a past
history: from a stylistic point of view, this was an early 18th-
century interior worked into a Tudor house.

South Hill had a formal entrance hall with a pair of
arches, one of which formed a niche for 'an enchanting little
figure of Narcissus' – Weaver described this arrangement as
having 'gracious severity' – and a sophisticated plan overall.[76]
He seems to have done this wherever he could, even within
a plain small cottage called Kerri, now gone, in Arkley near
Barnet, which had a formal entry hall with what appears
to have been a pair of arches to a vaulted rear passage.[77]
Others were doing this at the same time: Field's almost exact
contemporary E. Guy Dawber did it on a minor scale for
himself at Long Wittenham in Berkshire, with decorative
ceilings in 17th-century style within a 'Tudor' house, and
Lutyens pulled it off magnificently in 1908 in Whalton Manor
in Northumberland when he inserted a series of grand lobbies
and rooms, including an upper hall with an ornamental
plaster ceiling and a circular dining room, into a row of
four 18th-century cottages in a village street. These ornate
cottages demonstrate how little the best Edwardian domestic
architecture had to do with the gothic-revival concept of
'development'. After the War, Field returned to Hook Heath
to extend and rebuild Hook Heath Farm, a house that had
been designed by another architect 20 years previously on
the site of what had once been the only inhabitable building
in the area. In addition to a short new wing he added not
only 'early 19th-century' interiors but a 'late 17th-century'
domed staircase hall within what on the outside now looked,
intentionally, like a clumsy succession of extensions in slightly
different vernacular styles.[78] The interior of Hook Heath Farm
must have come as a surprise to visitors: Field will certainly
have known the baroque staircase hidden within the plain
(and at that point plainer still) exterior of Ashburnham House
in Westminster, and perhaps the idea came from there. The
element of surprise in all these houses that either rework or
appear to rework history must surely have been an important
factor in their design, as was, no doubt, the element of camp
these encounters occasionally evoked. Contrived elements
of both surprise and theatricality in expensive buildings have

84. Brockhurst, the former Hook Hill, an early house by Field designed in 1893 for Henry Fisher Cox. Note the Tuscan colonnade inserted into an otherwise 'Tudor' cottage.

85. A panel at Brockhurst commemorates the craftsmen who designed and built the house.

86. (below) South Hill, Field's own golf cottage on the slopes below Brockhurst, published in the 1911 volume of Mervyn Macartney's *Recent English Domestic Architecture*.

87. (right) Another of Field's high-class 'Queen Anne' interiors, hidden within a plain tile-hung and rendered exterior, 'Jacobean' if anything: Hookerel, one of a cluster of houses near his own golfing weekend cottage on Hook Heath, in W. Shaw Sparrow's *Flats, Urban Houses and Cottage Homes* (1906).

88. (opposite) Field's cottage has been extended and remodelled, partly by the architect himself, and has lost its original thatch, but his studio, left under the hipped roof, has survived.

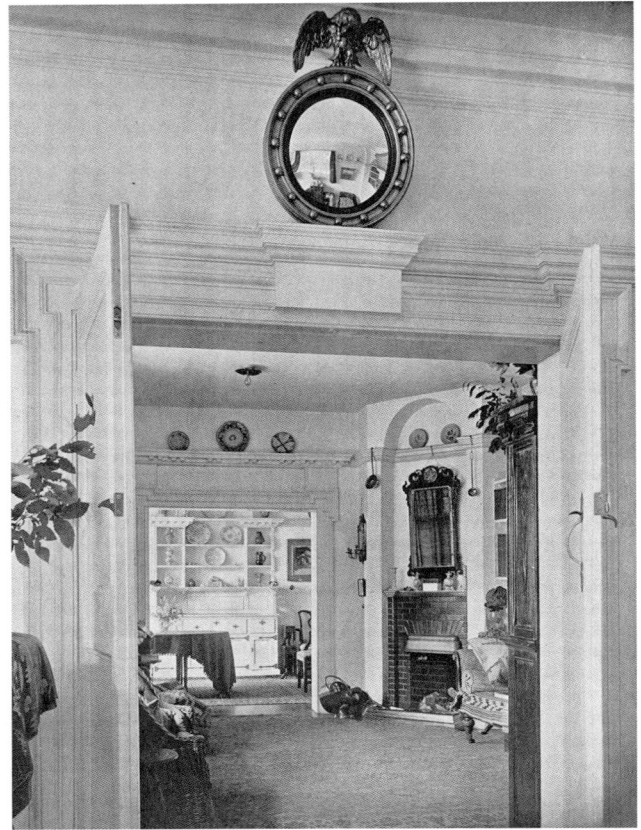

occurred throughout all periods of architecture, and the Edwardian era was no exception.

Thus for those who had no old farmhouse to convert, with no past history to rediscover or to remake, it was possible to build one from scratch. Herbert Gladstone, the Victorian prime minister's youngest child, built himself a home like this in 1899. He too was a golfer, and he chose a site immediately facing the beach at a recent, still under-developed resort called Littlestone-on-Sea along the coast of Romney Marsh between Hythe and Dungeness. This was ideally located between the Littlestone and Greatstone links, and Gladstone, a convivial host and guest, built Sandycroft,

> a comfortable bachelor house, the arrangements of which gave his relatives great interest, and the doors of which opened readily alike to relatives and friends. It was 'the very snuggest house', wrote one guest; 'all too beautiful', wrote another; 'all so dainty, Mother – doesn't it smell good? – so homey', observed a third, who was shortly afterwards catching shrimps upon the shore. Visitors were very frequent, Gladstones, Drews, Lytteltons, Asquiths, Balfours, not the least.[79]

Like Carrington, Gladstone chose an architect of no great distinction: in this case, John Cash, who had started his career in 1874 as an articled clerk to Edward Shewbrooks in Newcastle upon Tyne, worked for the country-house architect Ralph Selden Wornum in London for ten years, and by the time that Gladstone employed him, had completed a plain red-brick public library in Harlesden in Middlesex under his own name, but little else.[80] Yet the house was, when built, a demonstration that the spirit of George Devey was alive, in *fin-de-siècle* form. On the front facing the sea it was two storeys high, in red brick with a contrasting diaper pattern; it had one three-sided bay window, and another that was composed of four vertical sliding sash windows in a continuous row, projecting slightly, late Georgian in style (figs 89 and 90). There was a gablet over the parapet of each of the two unmatching shallow wings, and the front door was in a small extension to the side, under a baroque canopy.[81] The inland side of the house was if anything vernacular Queen Anne, rising to three storeys under irregular gables and a hip. Thus a small house combined elements from at least three centuries, drawing attention to each feature in turn. It could easily have been the result of a series of minor

remodellings of a Tudor farmhouse as it became increasingly gentrified. The Littlestone golf course was however very soon surpassed in prestige by the one at Rye, founded ('with a grand dinner, of which my chief recollection is that at our table we had a magnum of '63 port') by Blomfield, a former Littlestone player.[82] Many middle-class sports developed in the Edwardian period, bringing with them new buildings of various kinds; Blomfield himself was an energetic tennis player without the patience or money for cricket, and unsurprisingly became an enthusiast for the technique called the 'overhead smash'.[83] But it was the golf course that was the key element in the development of Edwardian architecture, bringing, as at Kingsgate, all manner of people together in a way that generated new houses.

Suburban

According to Michael and Eleanor Brock, the civil servant Maurice Hankey and his wife 'arriving at Sutton Courtenay from Walton Heath on a Sunday in November 1916, noticed with amusement the contrast between the suburbanism of the Ll.G. household and the ultra-smart fashionableness of the Asquiths' home'.[84] Ll.G. – the Secretary of State for War David Lloyd George, about to pounce on the premiership – lived in a villa in Wimbledon but when playing golf stayed at a house at Walton-on-the-Hill, the development north of Walton Heath golf course, designed for him in 1912–13 by Percy Morley Horder, as did his cabinet ally Charles Masterman. They had been put there on favourable leases by the newspaper proprietor George Allardice Riddell, co-owner of the course since 1905 and described by the biographer John Grigg as 'Lloyd George's Boswell'.[85]

Walton Heath golf club owns a photograph of the three of them playing golf together, with Lloyd George's son Gwilym. Lloyd George became a member in 1907; the Liberal MP Winston Churchill joined in 1910.[86] By the time of Hankey's visit Masterman was out of parliament, but he had been Lloyd George's adviser and then financial secretary to the Treasury from 1912, a supporter of the chancellor's land taxation campaign on the progressive wing of the party, and a member of the Christian Social Union.[87] His wife Lucy was the niece of Alfred Lyttelton, twice Lutyens's client (at

89. Herbert Gladstone's weekend golf party house at Littlestone-on-Sea of 1899, which survives today although without its chimneys and gablets. John Cash's design was made up from elements derived from George Devey, including the variety of window types and the diaper brickwork, and late Victorian elements such as the 'Queen Anne' front door. The back looked completely different.

90. The interior of the Gladstone house, as illustrated by Cash in his chapter 'The Home and its Decorative Essentials', in W. Shaw Sparrow's *The British Home of To-day* (1904). The convivial atmosphere of Gladstone's house parties evidently belied its austere appearance.

Greywalls in Gullane, East Lothian, by Muirfield golf course, and in 1906 at Wittersham in Kent, near Rye), the widower of Margot Asquith's sister Laura, and, according to Jane Brown, the *fons et origo* of the Edwardian golfing mania.[88] Thus this cluster of mutual interests connected by marriage or by party politics, or both, at this point all located in Walton Heath and the houses at Walton-on-the-Hill, provides an insight into the Edwardian Liberal building world: the small, tight social and professional circles; the prevalence of Liberals of all kinds and the occasional Conservative; the mixture of high-minded progressives with careerists; the newspaper proprietors (whose role included keeping members of rival party factions away from one another, for example McKenna from Lloyd George); the golf club and links; and the concomitant high-

91. Pinfold Manor, formerly Cliftondown, was built in 1913 for Lloyd George by George Allardice Riddell. This was one of Percy Morley Horder's more successful house designs, probably because its overall form was simple and coherent. Lloyd George's ally Charles Masterman lived in another Morley Horder house a short distance to the west.

class suburban development, all under an hour by railway from central London.[89] Northcliffe was a member too.

In fact the large collection of buildings designed for these golfers makes Walton-on-the-Hill a kind of epitome of Edwardian Liberal suburban housebuilding. David Metcalfe's comprehensive study, *The Architectural Development of Walton-on-the-Hill, Surrey, from 1900 to 1930*, identifies 12 projects by Morley Horder and nearly thirty by an architect called L. Stanley Crosbie who worked there between 1906 and 1930. In addition there were houses by E.J. May; Niven & Wigglesworth; and Dawber.[90] Not all the newcomers were Liberals or politicians: Metcalfe's list of residents includes Anthony Hope, the author of the 1894 novel *The Prisoner of Zenda*, who lived there from 1914, but it was the golfers who generated new building types.[91] Riddell commissioned a dormy house – that is, a place for overnight accommodation

– from Lutyens in 1906, which Lutyens set in a pretty flower garden. This circle was thus linked to *Country Life*, for Lutyens had been introduced to Riddell, at this point the managing director of the *News of the World*, by Edward Hudson, the co-proprietor of the magazine, in which Riddell had a controlling interest, some years previously when the latter, originally a solicitor, had advised him on an employment dispute.[92]

Lloyd George's house, Cliftondown, called Pinfold Manor from 1922, was discreetly located off a track on the western side of Duffield's Lane, the route that led south-west from the village of Tadworth towards the golf course (fig.91). Riddell bought and developed the land around what is now called Nursery Road, and his other houses, including Churchfield for Masterman, were built as a group close by, several by Morley Horder, forming a kind of protective cordon around Lloyd George at the centre. The largest house, Chussex to the south-west, was designed by Lutyens for the cricketer W.H. Fowler, who laid out the golf course at Walton Heath, with 17th-century elevations in different styles: William and Mary for the garden front and a vernacular type for the entrance, the reverse of the arrangement used by Field at 19–21 Lyndhurst Road and by Cash at Littlestone.[93] Lutyens may have originally made the sketches from which Morley Horder designed the houses for the two politicians: the most likely course of events was that Riddell started out with Lutyens as architect and then, as his project turned essentially into a multi-unit speculative development, went to a cheaper or less busy designer to realise them, or, as Brown suggests, one with less problematic relatives, for Lutyens's sister-in-law Constance was an active suffragette.[94] Morley Horder had already published photographs of a substantial golf cottage he had designed in Leatherhead, 'practically open to the links', in J.H. Elder-Duncan's widely circulated *Country Cottages and Week-End Homes* in 1906, so he would have been a reasonable choice of architect to approach.[95]

Morley Horder, the son of a Congregationalist minister in Torquay, had started practice in the mid-1890s after serving his articles over a short period with Devey; Jill Allibone has pointed out that he will have owed this opportunity to a family connection, as he was the nephew of Devey's biggest client, the Liberal MP, Congregationalist and Temperance supporter Samuel Morley, of Hall Place.[96] In time Morley Horder became best known as an institutional architect, his friendship with the prospering retail pharmacist (and Liberal) Jesse Boot eventually leading to the design of the grand new campus for the University of Nottingham and, in 1926, for a large plain Georgian apartment block on the south side of London's new Smith Square.[97] Although he was, according to a biographer, a person of exaggerated artistic temperament himself, and a member of the Art Workers' Guild from 1916, his buildings are at their most satisfactory when he strayed the least from attractive and easily identifiable models, for he had none of the original flair of Field, let alone of Lutyens; he did once attempt a Devey-like irregular treatment with irregular stone quoins and random rubble set in brickwork, at Little Court, in Charminster in Dorset, of 1909, which otherwise looked remarkably like Cliftondown; it would have looked better had it been more Devey-like still.[98] In time he caught the eye of Weaver who, with direct access to all the fashionable architects of the period, chose him to remodel his own house at 38 Hamilton Terrace in St John's Wood, London, perhaps for reasons of convenience since Morley Horder lived further down at number 6. The result, written up not by Weaver but by R. Randal Phillips after the War, was imaginative in planning but peculiar in appearance; he brought the main entrance down to basement level and turned the front porch into a study.[99]

Indeed, Morley Horder's career is full of aesthetic misfires. Too often his houses had that stiff look of the villas of the 1880s and early 1890s. Sometimes he simply copied

more than might seem decent; his Hengrove, in Wendover, Buckinghamshire, published in 1911, took its plan with surprisingly little variation from Lutyens's Orchards in Surrey, which had been extensively published in both *Country Life* and the *Architectural Review*.[100] Morley Horder himself and his own work appears so much in, for example, the *Builders' Journal* that the possibility arises that he was simply very good at sending material in.[101] In 1912, when Cliftondown was going up, he designed Cheshunt College in Cambridge, the first of his larger buildings, as a pretty gothic courtyard with an irregular mixture of ashlar stone and red brick around an entrance tower that he had copied from Devey, but small modern houses were harder for him to carry off. He tried, like Devey, and perhaps along lines suggested by Lutyens, to marry brick gables with timber-boarded ones, and narrow vertical sliding sash windows with broad casements of quite different proportions. The results are usually somewhat unresolved. Brown describes Cliftondown as 'a disappointing house which offers just gleams of the real thing', but at least it is true that the house as Morley Horder designed it, but for its stiffness, looks like a farmhouse that has been altered at various times, and that was almost certainly the desired effect.[102] The plan consisted of a simple row of three living rooms facing south, with a hall, passage and modest service rooms behind.[103] The short-lived Lane's End, another of his large houses in Walton-on-the-Hill and located off Chuck's Lane at some distance from the rest of the houses, was extensively published in the *Builders' Journal* in 1910, but by contrast he also designed a pair of small semi-detached cottages, at 31–33 Meadow Walk, an otherwise 'bye-law' street of modest homes to the north-east of the new villas.[104]

Other government ministers were also involved in building or restoring houses, at quite different scales. The austere Grey, foreign secretary for most of the Asquith government, built a tin cottage on the Itchen for himself and his wife to enjoy the simple life, the fishing and the birdsong.[105] By contrast, Earl Kitchener, not really a Liberal but briefly Asquith's Secretary of State for War until his disappearance in 1916, initiated in 1911 a sumptuous comprehensive remodelling by Blow & Billerey of Broome Park south of Canterbury, a large mannerist house of the 1630s with virtuoso ornamental brickwork and a James Wyatt saloon; he installed new interiors on the ground floor, most of which became one enormous gallery in a mixture of ornate early Jacobean styles, and a staircase from a house in Essex (figs 92 and 93).[106] Ivor Guest, the son of Romaine-Walker's client at Canford, and like his father a Unionist who became a Liberal, provided Lutyens with decades of work in Ashby St Ledgers, not only

92. The south front of Broome Park, near Barham, Kent: a remodelling of 1911 by Blow & Billerey of an early 17th-century house. Only the top left and right gables are original: the architects rebuilt all the rest to remove or obscure Georgian alterations that included an 18th-century bow-fronted saloon at the centre.

93. Earl Kitchener's new gallery at Broome Park, with details derived from Elizabethan and Jacobean houses of different dates: the ceiling, with its tiny figures standing above plaster pendants, was modelled after the one in the great parlour of Broughton Castle, Oxfordshire, of 1599.

remodelling and extending a large manor house but also designing estate buildings, including a pretty thatched terrace.

Every minister must have seen small new villas, socially or otherwise. Harry Isaacs, who was implicated with his brother Rufus, Asquith's attorney general, in the Marconi scandal in 1912, moved in its wake first to Brighton and then to Kingsgate, of all places, where a small, sparse, isolated estate of villas was going up just beyond the bay to the north-west of Avebury's castle. It was from this address – Greywood, Marine Drive, on the corner of Fitzroy Avenue, about 160 yards (150 metres) west of Lord Holland's Arx Ruachim, and with a view of nothing except the grubby waters at the mouth of the Thames Estuary – that Rufus, the former ambassador-extraordinary and high commissioner to Washington and future Viceroy of India, who lived in Curzon Street in Mayfair, wrote to congratulate Lloyd George on the award of his Order of Merit in August 1919.[107]

This sequence of buildings by Liberal grandees had a distinguished afterlife. Lloyd George, by then prime minister, commissioned a house from Philip Tilden after the War, in Churt in Surrey, and perhaps happy with his previous experience again lived in a place that resembled an unresolved farmhouse, but this time with grandiose interiors; he ended up shortly before his death at Tŷ Newydd in north-west Wales, in a genuinely old rural building that had been lightly remodelled by Clough Williams-Ellis to resemble, like so many other of that architect's buildings, a vaguely Georgian doll's house. Margot Asquith, who hated Lloyd George with a greater passion than any other, even before the coup in which her husband lost his job, would have been gratified had she lived to see it. McKenna left politics for the Midland Bank once Lloyd George had become prime minister. As Chairman after the War, he was able to commission its Piccadilly branch, two large offices buildings and a City headquarters from Lutyens. One of the office buildings was that in Pall Mall for which Lutyens designed the elevations and W.H. Romaine-Walker's practice the rest. As it turned out, Christopherson, McKenna's former neighbour in Smith Square, became first his deputy and then his successor.[108]

Voysey

It is possible to look at the familiar work of architects who have entered the canon and see traits in them that relate to themes in political Liberalism. It is possible also to see how interest in them seems to surpass changing fashion, or why

they have attracted entirely opposing interpretations. Charles Francis Annesley Voysey, another member of the Art Workers' Guild, is one of these; he was seen in his own day as a kind of artist-architect; then, as a 'pioneer of modern design'; and now he is back to where he was before. He designed several houses for current or future Liberal MPs: 12, 14 and 16 Hans Road, in South Kensington, one as a residence and two as a speculation for Archibald Grove, in 1891; Perrycroft near Malvern in 1893–4 for J.W. Wilson (fig.94); and Lowicks in Surrey (1894), as well as a remodelling of his Chelsea home (1906) and a children's playground in Kensal Green (1913), for E.J. Horniman, the son of the founder of the Horniman Museum (fig.95). He also designed a home for the American-born writer Julian Sturgis; for the publisher Algernon Methuen; and for the up-and-coming sage H.G. Wells. There is no other single architect whose clients included so broad and impressive a collection of Liberal and progressive worthies: 'Everybody's maiden aunt had a little Voysey house somewhere', said Goodhart-Rendel, who did not like him.[109] He also designed a house for a golfer, Sydney Claridge Turner, in Frinton in 1905 which was located only about 200 yards (180 metres) from both the links and the tennis club.[110]

It is possible that all these wanted an eccentric white house as if it were a fashionable piece of art: that would appear to be the impression from most writing on Voysey. But in fact Voysey's white buildings can be understood as something quite different and his own eccentric, counter-intuitive writing on his architecture paradoxically does provide some guide to his intentions. He spoke about his sparkling, alert, white houses – buildings which could not help attract attention when they were on full view and in striking contrast to their neighbours, as his buildings in Turnham Green and Barons Court in west London were – as if they were quiet things, 'laying down to sleep', when to the average eye they clearly were not. In his book *Individuality* he describes them in terms of strings of abstract qualities that at first sight do not appear to explain them: 'reverence, love, justice, mercy, honesty, candour, generosity, humility, order and dignity', and so forth.[111] Architects cannot always identify the qualities in their buildings which are appealing to others, and they also cannot by definition point out where their future influence will lie; all the same, his own descriptions seem unusually improbable. Yet in fact it is quite possible to see Voysey's pert white houses, which in some respects were so revolutionary, as being precisely embodiments of those calm abstract qualities.

Once again the key lies in Devey. Voysey historians, especially modernist ones, have pointed out that the young Voysey worked for the hospital architect Henry Saxon Snell,

and this perhaps is what introduced him not only to the idea of white clean buildings, but possibly also to the methodology of a large practice which helps some young architects start their independent careers on a well-organised footing and enables them to expand their client base and productivity. But Voysey worked for Snell only briefly. He worked much longer for Devey at the start of his career, and went on copying Devey devices afterwards, considerably more successfully and organically than Morley Horder ever managed. As Wendy Hitchmough has described, Devey, a supporter of Voysey's father's Theistic Church, evidently took young Voysey under his wing, toured sites with him, and entrusted him with some small projects from start to finish, the most beneficial start imaginable to a professional career.[112] In his early work, for example his 'Country House with an Octagonal Hall' of 1889, he reproduced one of Devey's characteristic gable patterns; and in both that and a sanatorium design from the earliest years of his independent practice, he decorated his brick walls

with Devey-like diaper patterns – in fact, a Pugin motif which Devey had no doubt knowingly adopted.[113] Devey's assistant James Williams related one of the most telling stories that has come down from the years of Voysey's early training: 'On discovering poor construction work, which was excused on the grounds that it could not be seen, Devey is reported to have blasted a foreman: "What, not seen? I should be ashamed for the birds to see it".[114] Hitchmough notes that the same importance of craftsmanship in every detail became seminal to Voysey's work.[115] It becomes clearer what 'honesty', 'candour' and 'humility', at least, have to do with Voysey's outlook.

These are Puginian concepts in building, but they are also Jacobean, in the way that most people had understood them, at least since Joseph Nash's popular *The Mansions of England in the Olden Time* from the 1830s. Nash's illustrations

HOVSE · AT · SWANAGE · FOR · A · SVIRO · ESQRE

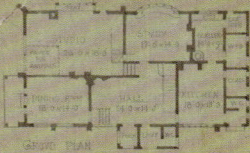

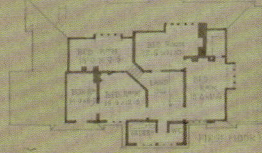

HOVSE · FOR · THE · REVD · C · VOYSEY · BA · PLATTS · LANE
HAMPSTEAD

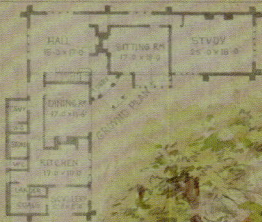

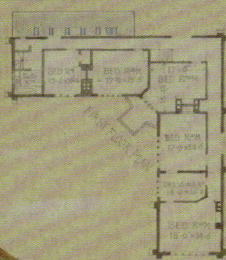

HOVSE · AT · FRENSHAM · SVRREY · FOR · F.J. HORNIMAN · ESQRE

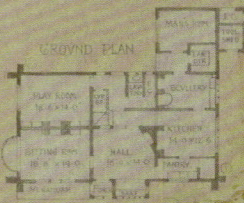

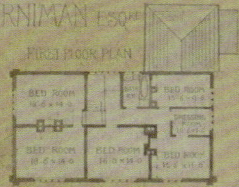

95. (opposite) A drawing by Voysey of three of his houses: Hill Close, Alfred Sutro's house at Studland Bay, near Swanage, Dorset; Annesley Lodge, for his father, in Platt's Lane, Hampstead, both of 1895; and, at the bottom, Lowicks, Frensham, Surrey, of 1894, for the future Progressive London County Council member and Liberal MP E.J. Horniman.

96. Not all Voysey's houses were white, and some referred directly back to Devey's version of Jacobean. This unexecuted design of 1899 for a house in Bracknell Gardens, Hampstead, was one of the few colour plates in Shaw Sparrow's *The British Home of To-day*.

tell a great story about what England is supposed to stand for – hospitality, restfulness, colourfulness and joyfulness. The book was extremely popular and it provided the background for the era's bestsellers, the historical novels of Walter Scott; the magazine *The Studio* republished it in 1906, with an introduction by the architect C. Harrison Townsend who drew on Tudor tower gateways in his own work.[116] Like much else, the early 19th-century Jacobean revival – or more specifically the Tudor gothic revival, which coincided precisely with the reign of King William IV – was knocked down hard by the gothic revivalists who, in common with most high-art critics since, hated it for its slapdash glue-and-lacquer decoration and lack of interest in structural purity. But these buildings were attractive, calm, evocative and romantic. Part of Devey's genius lay in the fact that he resolved these appealing aspects of vernacular Jacobean architecture with a Puginian discipline and coherence. In so doing he created an architecture which went on appealing to different types of people over a very long period of time. And part of Voysey's was that he inherited Devey's own discipline and coherence along with his originality.

Voysey was a Jacobean-revival architect: this is the key to his brilliant career as a designer (figs 96 and 97). Specifically, his achievement was to reconcile his radicalism – his white houses – with a degree of conservatism in the incorporation into them of historical ideas drawn from Jacobean houses. This was to take Field's 'new-old' approach to a conceptual level. Many of his characteristic motifs are Jacobean: the simple stone mullions of so many bay windows;

the enormous chimneys; the ogee roofs, for example of the gatehouse to Merlshanger (later Greyfriars), the Sturgis house on the Hog's Back at Puttenham outside Guildford, or over the projecting drawing- and dining-room inglenook at Norney near Shackleford, both of 1897 in Surrey; even the hall panelling at Norney, which stops a foot (30 centimetres) short of the ceiling and the strange curved pediment over the front door there.[117] The horizontal proportions, which distinguish Jacobean-revival houses from Puginian gothic ones; the curious pairs or rows of brackets carved with grotesque faces, such as those between shallow projecting oriel windows at Perrycroft (see fig.178): these are the late 19th-century versions of the artisan mannerist carvings which parade across the Jacobean hall screen at Hatfield House and elsewhere. Voysey was able to take other profoundly English sources, for example the late 15th-century prior's lodging at Much Wenlock with its vast roof and rows of continuous windows, and incorporate them into his houses. Perhaps he tried to escape his 'trademark' white render: *The Studio* reported that he wanted to build The Pastures, at North Luffenham, from local stone, but his client Miss Conant would not let him.[118] It was often held up as a criticism of much early 20th-century suburban housing that it was a thin copy of Voysey's work, and Voysey himself would no doubt have been horrified by the superficial nature of much of it, but in a sense it was one of the great achievements of Liberal England: that this abstracted representation of the great buildings of the nation's past could be so effortlessly and so cheaply displayed across the smallest of houses.

Houses for the many

Liberals, politicians or otherwise, introduced new types of house beyond models for suburban and seaside villas, golf dormy houses and the like. They also introduced altogether different types of house, or housing, ones which would reach a much larger part of the population than bespoke houses ever could.

The crisis in conditions for rural labourers was paralleled by a similar one in the cities: in addition to the old problem of overcrowding by negligent landowners, there was a severe shortage of housing for the lowly paid, who might sometimes, especially in the case of women, have been from middle-class backgrounds. From the 1880s, philanthropic organisations of both political traditions started to fund hostels for men and women which provided basic sleeping accommodation, sometimes just a cubicle, but at best relatively generous communal areas; the YMCA did this, with Arthur Beresford Pite, an evangelical Christian who was a 'brother' of the Art Workers' Guild, as architect, but so did Lady Brabazon, whose family was High Church and High Tory.[119] Some specialist types of housing also began to emerge. John Lewis, the founder of the Oxford Street department store, elected as a Progressive member of the LCC for West Marylebone in 1901 and 1904, built in 1914 a large block in Bolsover Street to house his shop workers in decent-sized twin bedrooms, with built-in storage, and a dining room, club room and lounge on the lower floors. Lewis was an admirer of the social reformer Edwin Chadwick and named his building the Chadwickham.[120] It was located alongside St Clement's House, a women's hostel of 1911 and one of Lady Brabazon's ventures, creating together a 'Georgian' street elevation 24 bays long. The Edwardian period also saw the construction of large new buildings to provide institutionalised versions of traditional charitable housing; in 1901 Niven & Wigglesworth designed the Passmore Edwards Sailors' Palace on the Commercial Road in Limehouse, in London's docklands, a finely detailed Elizabethan residential hostel for the British and Foreign Sailors' Society, in stripes of red brick and Portland stone, with excellent decorative leadwork and sculpture; the Society had formerly used a small late Georgian building no bigger than a private house

in Newell Street nearby.[121] Clusters of very large institutional buildings had been a feature of mid- to late Victorian suburbs and seaside towns; this type of development was a new version, more urbane and more humane.[122] According to a biographer, Lewis spent some time in prison in 1903 as a result of his battle against the Portland Estate, his freeholder, which he considered to be an unfair landlord.[123]

The difference between these and what can be seen as specifically Liberal Party or Progressive Party projects was that the latter came from the political control of the London County Council which they held from its inauguration in 1889 until the Moderates or Municipal Reform Party – the Conservatives, that is – won the elections of 1907. The Housing of the Working Classes Act of 1890 empowered public authorities not only to purchase slums but also to redevelop them, and without the earlier requirement to rehouse the same number of tenants or indeed the same type of tenant on the site. The council was under the same obligation as any other body to fund its activities on a thrifty basis, and a 'Chadwickhamist' like Lewis would have expected that the cost of accommodation should not deprive residents of a motivation to earn a living. The results, notably the Boundary Street and Millbank estates, have been ably described by Susan Beattie and are well known; it is striking that the Boundary Street estate buildings took the names of Thames villages, consciously rooting new blocks of unfamiliar appearance into the mileposts of the city's river.[124] These buildings were if anything Dutch in style, stripy and with ornamental gables following the fashion of the Queen Anne revival of Norman Shaw, rather than the new vernacular artisan Jacobean of the Liberals. Nevertheless, they should be seen as Liberal Party architecture and townscape when they occupied whole blocks and provided small public gardens. Carrington became chairman of the council's working-class housing committee in 1903, and that year the council completed the construction of Carrington House in Deptford, designed by the council's superintending architect W.E. Riley, with accommodation for 800 and pleasant, airy public rooms. The front of the building married the Georgian style of their inner-London buildings – unavoidable when there were rows of cubicles behind – with a prominent tall gable above continuous vertical bays of shallow, smooth oriel windows, stylistic features drawn from buildings by Art Workers' Guild architects such as Voysey and Leonard Stokes (for whom the LCC architect Charles Canning Winmill had worked).[125]

Even better known than the history of Progressive Party LCC housing is the story of the Edwardian development of Ebenezer Howard's Garden City at Letchworth in

97. (opposite) The entrance court of Perrycroft. When looked at analytically, Voysey's most characteristic elevations are compositions of 'Tudor' elements: strip windows, ornamental towers, prominent porches and large chimneys.

Hertfordshire, and of Henrietta Barnett's Hampstead Garden Suburb, both independent ventures that pioneered solutions to land reform problems. Lloyd George's 'People's Budget' of 1909 proposed land taxes, including one on the capital value of undeveloped land, and one on the unearned increment of land values, which meant that the party was laying the foundations for state control. But in the meantime, these campaigns required powerful private sponsorship, and Howard was supported by Ralph Neville, Liberal MP for Liverpool Exchange from 1887 to 1895. Barnett's project was enabled in the form she envisaged it by the passing of a private member's bill, the Hampstead Garden Suburb Act of 1906, which allowed her to escape the technical restrictions of the building bye-laws, and she had the support of Lyttelton, who was the president of her Garden Suburb Trust. In 1909, in a debate on amendments to his new Housing, Town Planning, &c. Act, John Burns, the president of the Local Government Board, referred to Barnett's experience as an example of how expensive private legislation could be when there was no comprehensive, statutory town planning system.[126]

But there are reasons why these two projects, for all their subsequent significance in terms of post-war land and planning with hindsight towards the 1947 Town and Country Planning Act, are less important to the present study. They do indicate how progressive thinkers in alliance with the Liberal Party in government were becoming more ambitious about turning private assets into public ones, tackling the apparently unsolvable problems of land control and speculation in a country which had been governed into the 1890s by prime ministers from the house of parliament that had been composed of landowners since the Middle Ages. But Letchworth and Hampstead Garden Suburb were primarily organised planning schemes rather than projects for groups of attractive and appealing houses; so controlled and intense were the homogeneity and inorganic nature of their planning layouts that neither was to contribute much to the real development of the characteristically Edwardian suburb across most parts of Britain in layout or in architectural appearance. The subsequent importance of these projects to planning history has also obscured the fact that these two best-known garden developments were mainly seen at the time as the marginal occupation of eccentrics – the place where Osbert Lancaster's New Woman, as she still seemed in 1938, cycled off to 'an interesting meeting of the Fabian Society', firmly in socialist territory at some remove from the mainstream of English Liberalism, let alone the speculative suburban developer.[127] Hampstead Garden Suburb did in fact provide a comfortable home for the New Woman very

different from the urban hostels, with some typological relationship to new women's residential colleges: Waterlow Court, a Tudor courtyard with cosy bed-sitting rooms, a communal hall and cloisters, was designed by Baillie Scott in 1908–9 and became one of his favourite buildings.[128] But this was not a model that would be feasibly imitated.

Landowners with means, and sometimes with philanthropic intentions, had often established attractive private residential estates, usually with leasehold plots, on their land; it is generally the case in property development that better amenities can raise the relative profit that an investor can make. Devey had been commissioned in the late 1870s to design an estate like this near Northampton by the landowner, the Liberal fifth Earl Spencer.[129] This had followed the launch of the best-known example of a garden suburb before the ones established on the communitarian economic and financial lines suggested by Howard: Bedford Park, near Chiswick in West London, in 1875. Jonathan Carr, Bedford Park's founder, was a radical Liberal who had been steeped in land reform all his adult life, since (possibly) having been an assistant to the philosopher John Stuart Mill in his parliamentary election campaign in the Westminster constituency in 1865.[130] Carr commissioned houses from E.W. Godwin and then Norman Shaw; he built community facilities in the form of a co-operative shop, a pub, tennis courts and a club, so that residents would have a feeling of belonging. But he sold the plots leasehold, or simply let the houses, which were in the Queen Anne style, so in spite of the scale and the attractiveness of the venture, this was still a Victorian and not a proto-Edwardian venture (see fig.5).[131]

Housing, Town Planning, &c.

In August 1907 and 1908 the Liberal government passed Carrington's Small Holdings and Allotments Acts which permitted county authorities to buy land for those purposes and compelled landowners to sell in some circumstances; under the second act, a public authority could register as proprietor and act indirectly or directly as landlord, a significant change.[132] Earlier Conservative legislation had failed to take off in practice because Conservative-controlled counties had been reluctant to operate compulsory purchase, and it had been lack of agreement on this question that had traditionally hampered progress of any political intention to support the development of land in the public interest. If political support was to be forthcoming, the government would have to devise legislation that emphasised the advantages to landowners and private developers as much as to public agencies. Until that happened, Liberals could only change the built face of Britain house by house. In the meantime, the Liberal intention was to extend these powers in order to create a standard, national, process by which it would be possible, even if not compulsory, for urban and rural district councils to create controlled suburban environments.

The bill that was eventually enacted, on 3 December 1909, under the awkward title of the Housing, Town Planning, &c. Act, combined housing quality with town planning structures.[133] The first part of the Act set higher standards for new houses, in effect outlawing the use of most basements for residential purposes, and all back-to-back housing; it also made it easier for a local authority to borrow money to buy land for housing and to replace or improve existing buildings. The fact that this was included in legislation primarily aimed at something bigger indicates how Liberals intended to sell their town planning initiatives. One Liberal MP from the 1906 intake, Henry Vivian, a former carpenter and passionate campaigner for co-operative activity, had already initiated what is considered to be the first co-operative garden suburb actually to take shape on the ground at Brentham, north of the west London suburb of Ealing, from 1901. He helped draft the new legislation, which was then introduced to the House of Commons by Burns, Britain's first working-class cabinet member, now occupying the grand new imperial government buildings on the corner of Parliament Street and Parliament Square.[134]

The Liverpool Corporation Act of 1902 had enabled that city to require a 'scheme', to be approved by the Local Government Board, before granting permission for new streets and housing.[135] Part Two of the 1909 Act broadened this to introduce the concept of town planning into British law on a national basis (the Act was applicable, with variations, in Scotland too). The mechanism was that a local authority could on its own, or with a developer or landowner, apply to the Board for authorisation to draw up a plan 'with the general object of securing proper sanitary conditions, amenity and convenience in connexion with the laying out and use of the land and of any neighbouring lands'.[136] This was significant for at least two major reasons, as was pointed out in a lucid commentary in the *Architectural Review* by Thomas Adams, a Liberal who had become the first secretary of the Garden City Association.[137] First, the Board had the means, which the local authorities did not, to provide a degree of 'architectural and expert supervision for these schemes'. That should in time lead to the idea that there was a national interest, and a national competence, in seeing schemes of this kind emerge

– a novelty in Britain. Once the Board had approved a plan, a local authority could borrow money on the same favourable terms used for slum clearance described in the earlier part of the Act.

Second, the Act also enabled authorities to make variations to existing restrictive bye-laws on heights and materials.[138] This could introduce a form of aesthetic control that had up to now been seen in foreign cities or in major civic schemes such as Kingsway in London, but never in suburban housing. As Adams pointed out, the ability to make these variations could bring down the cost of development where denser housing was architecturally desirable, especially if the 'amenity' was enhanced. Where the value of land rose as a result of development, as it usually did, the Act entitled local authorities to take half of the difference.[139] There could now, where local authorities wanted it, be a kind of imposition of Liberal taste. The lack of compulsion meant that most authorities did not adopt plans like this; but on the other hand, this type of planning was at least possible. Where both local politicians and landowners wanted it to happen, it now could, so long as the two sides collaborated. If a council failed to act, the Board could intervene.[140] The Board established a Town Planning Department to provide precisely the type of national 'architectural and expert supervision' that Adams had hoped for – and Adams himself was immediately appointed to it.[141]

Thus the old system requiring an act of parliament for almost every individual planning intervention was finally overthrown, a significant achievement for the Liberals. The parliamentary debates that accompanied the passage of the bill provide a window into the considerations of its proponents and the arguments that they had to face. Burns provided statistics to show that in areas where back-to-back housing prevailed, the average age at death among 'operative labourers and their families' was 19, as against 44 for 'gentlemen and the professional classes'.[142] New plans would have to demonstrate a balance of green and open spaces within them, as Burns found himself countering opposition fears that the Act would enable an authority to build homes for the urban poor 'in the middle of Kensington Gardens'.[143] The Act would furthermore require that houses were maintained in a fit state for human occupation: it would create a 'revolution', he said, in housing.[144] He was supported by the health reformer Sir Walter Foster, Liberal MP for Ilkeston, a former professor of medicine and Gladstone's last parliamentary secretary to the Local Government Board; Foster believed that that the new planning system would only work if the Board was expanded considerably to support it, and if there were sufficient medical officers of health to police housing standards.[145] He thought these could be supported by future taxes from the increase in land values, since raising the rates to do this would be unpopular. Essentially, the new legislation would introduce a system recognisable a hundred years later, something quite different from the various specific enabling acts passed in the previous century.

It is striking that the concept that a public authority should wish to enforce a high level of amenity in housing, based on rational, scientific principles, appears to have been widely accepted across the House: the opposition spokesman was Lyttelton, who not surprisingly, given his role as Barnett's president at Hampstead Garden Suburb, referred to the bill as 'so excellent in its principles and intentions . . . in many respects'.[146] It was the idea of a planning process that he supported. Unionist objections came on grounds of opposition to the role of the Board, rather than the local authority, as the final arbiter of schemes, and to the processes by which a landowner would be compensated for compulsory purchase if his own building plans were subverted by central government.[147] What, Lyttelton asked, if a landowner had made a very fine scheme for 'a cricket ground . . . in a most admirable manner', yet a local authority wished to purchase that same land for housing? The Labour MP Fred Jowett objected to the bill on the basis that it would produce more housing such as that at Letchworth and Hampstead Garden Suburb but not 'affect the general question' of providing more decent houses for working people, in retrospect a justified complaint.[148] The unsuccessful House of Lords amendments that ensued followed similar lines of attack.

In summing up, Masterman, secretary to the Board, said in his characteristically glum manner that 'I believe it will probably be long before we see the lessons we have learned in the garden suburb being universally adopted by the local authorities, or even by private owners in this country'.[149] In his last words, he said: 'We have heard a great deal lately in the last few months of the defence of an Englishman's home; here we are concerned with the preliminary requirement that the Englishman should have a home to defend.'[150] There is something thrilling in imagining Lyttelton and Masterman, whom we know from their individual architectural connections, appearing together in the same theatrical arena of the House of Commons. Given the closeness of the protagonists to the work of Barry Parker and Raymond Unwin, who had laid out Letchworth and Hampstead Garden Suburb, it could be clearly envisaged what the Liberal homescape would look like: rational; educated; healthy; green, and pleasant; English.

Gidea Park

As it happens, the suburb that best expresses Edwardian domestic architecture was a private initiative on conventional lines in terms of ownership but with the participation of several key figures from the garden suburb movement: Gidea Park, in Romford in Essex, the suburb built from 1910 on land purchased originally by the former barrister and political activist Herbert Raphael.[151]

Perhaps this particular combination is what makes the suburb so much more valuable as a model than Letchworth or Hampstead; furthermore, unlike in the controlled developments, there seems to have been no attempt at censoring or regulating the design of the houses: what we see is what a large number of capable Edwardian designers and their builders chose to put up for sale. Raphael had been a Progressive Party member of the LCC until 1892, when he had been replaced by Carrington. He bought Gidea Hall in 1897 and with it 450 acres (180 hectares), of which a large part to the east was leased to the recently founded Romford Golf Links; in 1902 he gave 15 acres (6 hectares) to Romford urban district council to form a small park to the west. This left the central area, beyond the house and park itself, for other purposes. In the landslide of 1906 Raphael was finally elected to parliament, as the member for South Derbyshire; then in 1909, with the new Act in view, he formed the Gidea Hall Development Company with two others, the architect-MP John Tudor Walters, Liberal member for Sheffield Brightside, and Charles McCurdy, a director of the Hampstead Garden Suburb Trust (who became a Liberal MP in 1910) to develop the remaining central part of the site. In July 1910 the suburb was formally announced, and a month later a competition launched to design houses for it.

The idea was to build an exhibition of model houses for sale, 'show houses' in today's parlance, which would mostly cost either £375 or £500 to build including the contractors' profits and architects' fees, making this a more realistic exercise than an earlier one at Letchworth.[152] The plots were sold mostly to architects in partnership with a building contractor, and those wishing to compete for a prize were to submit designs by the end of October 1910; if their plans were approved, the houses were to be built at their own expense. About a hundred and fifty of the designs 'satisfied the standard of taste which had been set up', as Weaver put it.[153] The judges were Dawber, H.V. Lanchester and Mervyn Macartney. The names are significant: Dawber, then vice-president of the Royal Institute of British Architects, was a

98. £500 houses in Reed Pond Walk, Gidea Park, designed by (left to right) Edwin Gunn, Reginald T. Longden, Cecil A. Sharp ('architecturally based upon ideas prevalent during Tudor times') and C.M. Crickmer. The overall effect was – as its planners had evidently intended – of an idealised 'Tudor' village.

99. 54 Parkway, Geoffry Lucas's first-prize-winning £500 house: a bay window has been added, and the house was originally whitewashed. Its style was unusual for Gidea Park, but the neat plan, which Weaver thought was the result of the architect's 'long apprenticeship' in small house design, won over the judges.

practitioner of the style which mixed grand interiors with cottage walls; Lanchester was editor of the *Builder*, and Macartney of the *Architectural Review*, and of its series of special volumes on recent large houses. Then further equally distinguished assessors were brought in to award another five prizes for furnished interiors and other categories: Ernest Gimson, Halsey Ricardo, Charles Spooner, Cave and Weaver.

A street layout was devised. Lutyens may have been consulted, as he had been for an abortive earlier attempt to expand the suburb greatly to the east, but it is not clear who did it in the end; probably Parker & Unwin, whose expertise in this area was unrivalled, or their assistant Charles Wade. Parker & Unwin had recently designed the most recent phase of Brentham and were busy at Letchworth and Hampstead; possibly they wanted to distance themselves from a commercial project. This was in any case a fairly small site, divided into two parts. In the area to the north of Gidea Hall there was room for three short east–west streets running between roads that bounded the new park and the golf course, one of which ran around a large planted reed pond. In the southern section, which lay between the main road and what was originally called Squirrel's Heath and Gidea Park railway station, there were to be three north–south streets with short connections between them, and a shopping centre by the station itself.

The exhibition ran from June to September 1911 and as the official exhibition guide makes clear, there were two main attractions for builders and buyers. First, the site was going to remain largely green, and protected. Second, it would also mark the rebirth of the Tudor glories of old Gidea Hall, which had stood near the site until its replacement by a gaunt, 18th-century neo-classical mansion. In fact from the historical section of the guide – entitled 'Gidea Park of To-Day' – one would think that the old house was still there: it says a great deal about the Tudor past and nothing at all about the Georgian building beyond a tiny view. Elsewhere the guide's author wrote that Raphael's plan

preserves, in every other direction, and in perpetuity, from destruction or disturbance scenes which have been a background for English history for so many centuries. The old order changeth, but nothing may now happen in the landscape of Gidea Park to trouble the shade of its old master, who stood 'contente with contrye qvyet life,' or of his grandson, who wrote that 'a garden is the purest of human pleasures, the greatest refreshment of the spirit without which buildings and palaces are but gross handiworks.'[154]

The old master referred to was, of course, the builder of the Tudor house. The catalogue had thus reversed back into time, before the construction of the 18th-century successor, and remade the subsequent history of the place as if the neo-classical interloper had never existed.

The entire atmosphere of the place, its founders, planners, judges and leading architects, emerged from the busy world of Edwardian romantic idealists and Art Workers' Guild brethren but at the same time owed nothing to the progressive economics of Howardian land reform. It is by the richness of its little houses that it should be judged (fig.98). Surprisingly, the winning £500 cottage, designed by Geoffry Lucas, at 54 Parkway facing Raphael Park, was cottage-Georgian, symmetrical like a doll's house and with a plan that pleased the judges (fig.99). There was a very small number of other 'Georgian' houses, almost none of which were entered for the competition. Overlooking the golf course, there was a group of four Wrenian villas with ornate doorways by Ronald P. Jones (fig.100), and in Squirrels' Heath Avenue, one of the long north–south streets in the southern part, there were six houses, originally intended to be 12, by C.R. Ashbee in association with Gripper & Stevenson (the latter Ernest Gabriel Stevenson, a former student at the Chipping Campden School of Arts and Crafts who had been Ashbee's assistant in 1902–7, remembered for looking after the office cat); these too were doll's-house Georgian, with tall ornamental chimneys, a kind of village-Vanbrugh.[155] The only other 'Georgian' design of distinction, if Georgian is the right description of it, was by Williams-Ellis (fig.101). This was a curious design that might have been more suitable for an ornamental garden pavilion, slightly French but looking as if the architect had studied the illustration in Field and Bunney's book of the Latin School at Aylesbury of 1719.[156] Unable to hold back, the small flat formal front was ornamented, according to Richard Haslam, with details borrowed from Wren's Royal Hospital, Chelsea, and inside there was overstated classical detailing, giving it the unsatisfactory thinly camp air associated with the architect.[157] Williams-Ellis published this house in

100. (opposite, above) Ronald P. Jones, who had written on Harvey Lonsdale Elmes and Decimus Burton for the *Architectural Review*, designed a group of four more-or-less 'Georgian' houses on Heath Drive. He explained in the exhibition catalogue that these were 'an attempt to give practical expression to the theories of the "suburb house" advanced by Professor Reilly'. This would have been seen at the time as an avant-garde design.

101. (opposite, below) Clough Williams-Ellis's house at 23 Reed Pond Walk: this was his first building to achieve wide publicity, and his future trademarks, such as the shallow, slightly 'French', facade are already visible. The house had a flat roof and an octagonal 'dining parlour'.

Weaver's *'Country Life' Book of Cottages* and elsewhere, and it launched his career: Weaver wrote cautiously that the house 'shows thought and a fresh outlook on the problems involved', perhaps puzzled by it.[158]

Nearly all the other houses however were in a vernacular Jacobean style. Even Bunney, in partnership with Clifford Makins whilst still apparently Field's assistant, designed explicitly 'Tudor' houses with half-timbered gables, including several prominent ones at the southern end of Heath Drive. Reginald Longden, an architect to date best known for his Nonconformist chapels, designed several houses at Gidea Park, one of which was featured and praised in Weaver's book and in the first of the two articles he wrote about the exhibition for supplements to *Country Life* in June 1911.[159] This building sat in the estate's prize position at a corner of Reed Pond Walk where it widened for the wild central garden, and won second prize in the £500 category. It was described as 'characteristic of a fine period of English cottage architecture' and this must have endeared it to the landowners and judges (fig.102).[160] The house was built of brick, with ornamental

102. Longden's second-prize-winning house, in red brick, at a key site on Reed Pond Walk. Weaver praised the architect for designing a 17th-century-type cottage without 'haphazard quaintnesses'. Beyond it, to the right, is one of two cottages by Parker & Unwin.

103. (opposite, above) Crickmer's first-prize-winning entry for the cheaper cottage category at Gidea Park, celebrated in *The 'Country Life' Book of Cottages* (1913). Later owners added more windows to its somewhat gaunt street front.

104. (opposite, below) Parker & Unwin's other house, at 41 Heath Drive. This was not a competition entry and Weaver did not appear to notice it, but its plan, which included a small study hall, was one of the most accomplished in the exhibition.

chimneys and a little half-timbering filled with brick nogging. The top award for the cheaper house went to C.M. Crickmer, who had worked for Parker & Unwin in Letchworth and already won prizes in the Urban Cottages Exhibition of 1907 (fig.103). At Gidea Park he designed a white-rendered cottage that featured one of the most popular architectural features of the estate, the tall narrow bay with a stair window on the front elevation; perhaps he won because the design could be built effectively in pairs, and thus even more cheaply, but looked balanced on its own. All the houses in the exhibition were generally either rendered or faced with red-brown brick; very few mixed the two, although Longden did. Most had broad gables: a stylish, continental-looking one by van 't Hoff & Maxwell is almost all gable. Another common feature was the tall brick chimney, sometimes ornamented. Several architects tried to a greater or lesser extent to design open or partly open plans: maybe, in part, because they wanted to attract the judges' attention. A.P. Starkey's house at 20 Meadway originally had no ground-floor windows at all on the street front ('Mahomedan' in inspiration, thought Weaver).[161]

There were some established names: Parker & Unwin built two houses with clever layouts, one on Reed Pond Walk with a front door that gave straight into a living hall and one on Heath Drive (fig.104); and Baillie Scott designed the architectural triumph of the estate, a pair of linked houses with a characteristically ambitious open plan, and ornamental

pargetting representing hops on the exterior (fig.105). The interior was decorated with Baillie Scott's own fabrics made by the Deutsche Werkstätten in Hellerau, Dresden, and the furniture came from Heal's of London, some designed by the architect himself.[162] Baillie Scott had been designing original 'Tudor', sometimes even 'mediaeval' houses with sophisticated open plans for some ten years; although he liked to keep himself apart from fashionable practitioners, he must have been an inspiration for many of the younger architects.

A map of the area indicates that there were building lines along the front, and possibly one at the side, but Gidea Park provides a clear picture of Edwardian architects left to their own devices in every other respect apart from cost. Because most of the architects chose a coherent vernacular style – derived from Essex village houses from the 17th century, by the look of it – the effect is coherent, but as a streetscape it does not provide particularly photogenic views: all the emphasis is on the individual houses themselves, and the communality comes from the pervading greenery, the neat and pretty gardens, the tall chimneys and the combination in many places of timber and brick.

It is worth remembering that these houses are notably well planned inside: not so much in terms of the relationship of the rooms to one another (although that too, in places) but more because of the careful dispositions of doors, windows, storage space for different purposes and staircases. Each one provided in its own way logical, rational solutions to specific problems of modern life in a small home. In fact it is possible to say that what the architects under the direction of Raphael, Tudor Walters and McCurdy had done was to go back into the atmosphere of the lost Tudor mansion house, 'picked up its thread' as Weaver might have said, identified and reinvented its lost atmosphere, and then built this out in the most educated, rational, informed way. More people than ever before now had accurate information regarding the cost of a new house: the ceaseless publication of model cottage types and design competition results over previous years had seen to that. Not only did architects now know how to design practical and comfortable houses in a variety unknown up to then; they also knew, from the many publications of the period, and no doubt in many cases too from weekend bicycling and sketching trips of the sort so many recorded, precisely what the components were for in authentic 16th- and 17th-century vernacular houses.

105.   (opposite) M.H. Baillie-Scott designed a £375 house, right, linked to a £500 one, left. Weaver, an admirer, regretted that the architect had sacrificed reasonable head room on the upper floor to achieve the required artistic elevation, but this pair with its sumptuous interiors from Hellerau and Heal's was the tour-de-force of Gidea Park.

106.   26 Reed Pond Walk, by Thomas Millwood Wilson, later a prolific architect of branches of Lloyds Bank.

'It is almost impossible to over-rate the value of an enterprise like the Romford suburb, which brings together in one place, on a commercial basis and without the deadening hindrance of the ultra-aesthetic person, a collection of houses of a high average of architectural merit', summarised Weaver. 'The people who live in the houses . . . will begin to talk architecture'.[163] The exhibition launched the public reputations of several architects: Tilden, who after the War went on to build for Churchill as well as for Lloyd George, designed a picturesque whitewashed house in Meadway with coarse, rustic, gothic detailing on its front; W. Curtis Green, up to this point an architect for electric tramway companies, on a prime site at the corner of Meadway and Heath Drive; Thomas Millwood Wilson, a former apprentice of J.J. Stevenson and the prolific designer of Lloyds Bank branches in both Fieldian and Tudor styles, on Reed Pond Walk (fig.106); and, a short distance to the north in the narrower part of the street, A. Randall Wells, a Letchworth Cottage Competition prizewinner who had recently been W.R. Lethaby's and then Prior's assistant but had to date built very little under his own name apart from the distinctly Lethabyesque church

107. The interior of 40 Parkway, Gidea Park, a £500 house by Forbes & Tate; the coarse brickwork of some interiors, including this 'Dutch fireplace', evidently disgusted younger neo-Georgians. Note Holbein's portrait of Henry VIII. The contrasting late 17th-century portrait of an infanta over the other fireplace shows how interior decorators, as much as architects, were consciously mixing the early baroque with Tudor and Jacobean motifs.

108. (opposite) Robert Lorimer's new entrance court at Lympne Castle, already merging imperceptibly into the remaining mediaeval fabric of the old building, back left.

at Kempley in Gloucestershire. Jones, the architect of the group of baroque houses, published soon after a book on Nonconformist architecture, and in 1927 designed his finest building, a Wrenian Unitarian chapel in Cambridge.[164]

Not everyone approved of it. Stanley Adshead, professor of Civic Design at the University of Liverpool and one of the voices who shaped what became the prevailing view that highly controlled environments like that of Letchworth were historically more important, wrote scathingly of it in the *Town Planning Review*: already a propagandist for Georgian styles and just starting the design of the 'Regency' Duchy of Cornwall Estate in Kennington, south London, he thought that most of the Gidea Park houses demonstrated 'a fruitless effort . . . to combine modern proportions, modern comforts and old-world effects', and that rooms should be arranged symmetrically, fireplaces should be 'refined', and internally exposed brickwork 'should not be allowed' (fig.107). Possibly he was right in thinking that T.R. Bridson's house in Reed Pond Walk, 'which might suit a prehistoric cave-dweller', had gone too far, since Bridson's is one of the very few houses in the suburb which has been replaced.[165] C.H. Reilly, the head of Adshead's school, asked at a town planning conference in 1910 whether it was 'entirely appropriate' that garden-suburb houses should be 'based on the early mediaeval type of cottage, with high-pitched roof and gables, rather than on

the later Georgian types, with flatter roof and sash windows, which are found so sedately set round many a village green and contribute so largely to its sober restful character?'[166]

But to say that houses should be easy on the eye is a simple argument to make, and not one that does justice to the sophisticated make-up of these houses. Gidea Park was literate, educated and rational. You could also do the same thing at any scale. At an only slightly later LCC estate, at Old Oak in north Hammersmith, west London, where construction prices were necessarily kept low, houses were designed in mixed Georgian and Tudor styles, sometimes one transposed directly over the other.[167] On the other hand, one of Stevenson's last houses, 9 Palace Green in Kensington, of 1903, is a vast mansion but it uses the same devices, a large 'Tudor' mullioned hall window holding together the centre of an otherwise free-style composition. The archaeology of Jacobean England had become the new narrative of the era, and with only a short hiatus of about thirty years in mid-century, new housing estates were built everywhere that followed the architectural style of Gidea Park, not least because one of the estate's protagonists, Tudor Walters, later produced the report that lay behind so much of it.[168] At the launch of Gidea Park, Burns wrote that it was 'a model and an exemplar that in the next fifty years will be greatly followed. This Garden Suburb exalts the British Ideal of the home.'[169] He was right.

3

THE CULTURE OF
EDWARDIAN HOUSE-BUILDING

—

Altogether there was never a more seductive method
of dreaming away the time than in looking at these
photographs, and sometimes the dreams come true.

Bernard Darwin, 1947

PAPER ARCHITECTURE IS NOT real architecture, but the culture of Edwardian housebuilding generated a literary genre which is inseparable from it: just as Lawrence Weaver had predicted, people began to 'talk architecture'. The Gidea Park exhibition of 1911 was commemorated in a detailed and comprehensive catalogue prepared for it 'by the exhibition committee' – the editors' names are unknown, but the large group named in it include Arthur T. Keen, the president of the Architectural Association; Leonard Stokes, then president of the Royal Institute of British Architects; J. St Loe Strachey, the editor of the *Spectator* and a proponent of cheap cottages; and one of the developers, J. Tudor Walters. This exhibition book, 146 pages long with a further 18 pages of advertisements, provides

therefore not only an unrivalled statement of the quality, sensitivity and originality of Edwardian domestic architecture at the peak of its achievement but also a record of how it was described in print. Architects such as C.R. Ashbee and M.H. Baillie Scott who were already well known appeared within the text as equals to others who were in the early stages of their careers or whose achievements had not yet been recognised.

The book's historical chapter has been referred to, but its centrepiece was the catalogue section which provided details on an equal basis for each of the 140 new houses: floor plans; a vignette of the exterior; and a short statement listing its attractions directly to potential purchasers, which in most cases meant its practical domestic conveniences. From these it is possible to see what a relatively small, cheap house now

PARKWAY. Class I. No. 208.
Architect :—GEOFFRY LUCAS, F.R.I.B.A.
Builders :—W. MOSS & SONS.

ACCOMMODATION.—On the Ground Floor is a roomy Entrance Hall, with Store and Hat and Coat Cupboard. The wide and easy-going Staircase, without winders, is screened from view of Front Door, and convenient for service. The

Kitchen is well fitted with Store Cupboard and shelving, and screened from the Entrance Hall. The Scullery is fully fitted with sink, draining board, plate-rack, shelving, copper, and position for gas cooker.

On the First Floor there are a large and light Landing, three Bedrooms, with space for double beds, good-sized Bathroom, with lavatory basin, and large, warmed hanging and linen closet.

On the Second Floor is a large Bedroom, with fireplace, roomy Box Store and Cistern Room.

There is a tiled dado to the Bathroom, red-tiled cills inside windows of Kitchen, Scullery, Bathroom, etc., and red quarry tiled floor in Hall and Scullery, and cement floor in Larder. Glazed tiled hearths to fireplaces.

GENERAL DESIGN.—The general treatment is of symmetrical and simple character. The whole house is contained within four square walls, without outbuildings. Attention has been paid in the design to economical use of space within the walls, general convenience of plan, privacy of Kitchen, Bathroom, etc., simplicity of roofing and exterior design, the whole tending to economy of up-keep and service.

ASPECT.—The house faces south-west, so that all rooms obtain sunshine during a portion of the day.

PARKWAY. Class I. No. 209.
Architect :—S. B. K. CAULFIELD, F.R.I.B.A. (Messrs. SPOONER & CAULFIELD).
Builders :—G. E. HOUGH & Co.

THIS House has a large Drawing Room (21' long, nearly 12' wide), with a window facing south-west, overlooking the Park, and French casements opening into the garden at the back. A fair-sized Dining Room (13' long, 10' 6" wide) also overlooking the Park. The Kitchen has been arranged together with the other offices to facilitate house work as much as possible. There

are four good Bedrooms on the First Floor, a Bathroom, and W.C. The stairs end in a fairly spacious landing. A linen cupboard, with the hot water circulator in it, is placed over the Kitchen. The idea of the design is to secure, as far as may be, the comfortable home-like look of the English eighteenth century houses, with modern conveniences.

PARKWAY. Class I. No. 210.
Architects :—BURGESS & MYERS.
Builders :—W. MOSS & SONS.

BUILT in brickwork, and finished with cement rough-cast, the Roof being covered with red sand-faced tiles, the external woodwork painted cream to match rough-cast.

The Sitting Rooms on Ground Floor open from a roomy Hall. The Drawing Room has a cosy ingle nook, with a fireside seat, and a door opens on to a wide Verandah facing the Garden. The Kitchen premises are well shut off from the rest of the house, while the Kitchen is so placed as to be quite handy for serving. Good Scullery and Larder accommodation is provided.

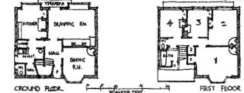

The First Floor comprises four Bedrooms, all of which have fireplaces and large cupboards, while a separate Linen Cupboard is provided on Landing. Maids' hot and cold taps are provided on First Floor.

PARKWAY. Class I. No. 211.
Architects :—BURGESS & MYERS.
Builders :—G. E. HOUGH & Co.

THE external walls are built of brick in double thickness, with a cavity between, and faced with mottled red bricks. The Roof covered with red sand-faced tiles. The elevations are rendered formal by windows being regularly placed.
The Ground Floor is designed to form a roomy Entrance Hall, octagonal in shape, from which the

109. (p.120) The porch at Tuesley Court, now Ladywell Convent, near Godalming, Surrey, by E. Guy Dawber, 1910. Dawber made frequent appearances in the publications of the time, and here the hints of Scottish and French detailing suggest how Tudor architecture might have developed had history followed a different path.

110. A typical spread from the Gidea Park *Book of the Exhibition of Houses and Cottages* (1911). This one includes Lucas's prize-winning house in the £500 category (top left). Note the remarkable degree of detail about the designs in the text even in presenting very small houses.

required to make it sellable. Most entries made reference to the provision of hot water, of storage spaces, and solid-wood casements; coal stores accessible from inside; draining boards and cosy inglenooks (as if this last was a practical installation, as indeed it could be). Many of the smaller homes had living-kitchens, with cooking taking place in an adjacent room which previously would have been the scullery alone – a sign of things to come. The plans and perspectives were drawn in each architect's office and overall it is hard to think of a more comprehensive statement of how sophisticated cottage design had become, and how much the focus of intense and

informed interest: there had probably never been a period when so much effort had been put into refining the quality of the rooms and their precise relationship to one another, their cupboards, ventilation and heating.

No two houses are the same inside; the authors of the exhibition catalogue entries, probably the architects themselves, and no doubt the judges had something different to say about all of them. At 8 Reed Pond Walk, by Mauchlen & Weightman, 'the Bathroom faces east, thus getting the morning sun'; 'A Hot-Air cupboard opens from the Staircase' at 3 Meadway, and 'Maids' hot and cold taps are provided on First Floor' at 58 Parkway, both by Burgess & Myers.[1] Some went further and hinted at what would now be called 'lifestyle': G. Berkeley Wills's house in Balgores Lane, for example, 'has been designed for a middle-class tenant or as a golfer's cottage', and J.D. and H. Mathews' contribution nearby included an integral bicycle store, as did several others.[2] More ambitiously, the description of Percy B. Houfton's cottage in Meadway starts with the announcement that 'The feature of this cottage is "open planning"', although this actually meant cross-lighting and through ventilation.[3] To read the catalogue whilst glancing at the images and announcements in the advertising section, the fireplaces, the pretty gardens, the 'Anaglypta beam and joist decorations', the 'Best Bedrooms', is to re-enter the Edwardian house (fig.110).

But in fact the long catalogue and historical sections are only two of several significant chapters in the exhibition book. There are also details of the exhibition: how it was set up; how to get there; where cream teas will be available; and some amusing cartoons criticising jerry-built old houses ('No one builds such houses now. The LCC is too clever').[4] Illustrations of the interiors of the houses show tasteful, uncluttered, 17th-century-type interiors: brick fireplaces; good furniture; only a few ornaments (see fig.107).[5] John Burns was photographed with construction workers.[6] Near the start came a collection of short articles by a variety of writers and political activists, nearly all active Liberals or radicals, including H.G. Wells and Arnold Bennett, who were also members of the committee, entitled 'What is wrong with your house and how it is to be bettered'. The first of these came from the architect-turned-novelist Thomas Hardy whose contribution, reproduced in his own handwriting, called for servants' apartments 'sufficiently divided by party-walls & sound-proof floors', and 'an independent bath-room to each bedroom'.[7] Bennett criticised 'primitive ventilation': 'England is the country in which rattling windows make night hideous'.[8] He decried the provision of an over-large entry hall which raised 'false hopes as to the scale of the rest of it', but the playwright Arthur Pinero on the other hand preferred a 'spacious and comfortable living-hall' to the 'abomination' of the drawing-room.[9] Millicent Fawcett, having consulted her sister and 'another lady', wanted to see pipes protected against frost damage.[10] Jerome K. Jerome hoped for better wall insulation; A.C. Benson thought that central heating was the chief recent improvement to house design.[11] Several writers, most bluntly a committee member called J.W. Robertson Scott who wrote about country cottages under the pen name 'Home Counties', called for women to plan modern houses, since it was women who were mostly confined to them. What is interesting about all of this is the fact that these writers took so informed an interest in these details or indeed that they even bothered to reply to the editors' requests to send in their musings on such things. Or that the competition organisers thought that having a famous novelist write about central heating was a useful way of promoting an exhibition of houses. Their involvement is a sign that housebuilding and cheap cottages had entered literary culture. And this had happened thanks to one protagonist in particular: *Country Life*.

Country Life

There were many rival and complementary weekly and monthly professional publications that presented architecture in detail during the long Edwardian period, but *Country Life* stands out for a number of reasons. Uniquely, its co-proprietor Edward Hudson and Peter Anderson Graham, its editor from 1900 to 1925, developed and presented a sophisticated and coherent picture of what the modern cottage and in turn the medium or larger house should be like over the whole of the first decade of the century, and beyond. These were remarkable people; Hudson provided a guiding hand, looking 'at every picture' according to his furniture contributor Ralph Edwards, and Graham wrote (in fact, dictated) 'an astonishingly large proportion of the paper' himself, from its agricultural notes to its book reviews.[12] Weaver became the first professional critic of modern architecture of the 20th century. But there were several other factors.

First, the magazine addressed the tone of its articles towards the interests of landowners rather than towards the architects who were doing the designing; that meant that it gave equal weight to all of the various factors behind housebuilding, not least its long-term economics, and the relative financial returns on the building of labourers' cottages. These considerations, usually absent from histories of Edwardian houses, underlay everything. Perhaps Avebury had first heard of W.H. Romaine-Walker through an article on Robert Hudson's estate buildings at Medmenham during Graham's first year as editor; if so, he would no doubt have been as impressed by their rational organisation, investment and planning, and their technical equipment, as by their picturesque Tudor-cottage styles (see figs 38 and 39). This is early 19th-century realism applied to late 19th-century buildings in a different and appealing way. Second, *Country Life* drew material from a large range of sources, rather than simply from images sent to them by the architects themselves: in fact it provided a proper narrative commentary on many aspects of a house and the life in it that the professional press did not. Its two architectural writers – H. Avray Tipping and, from mid-1909, Weaver – wrote with a clarity of purpose and consistency unmatched by the regular contributors to any other paper about houses: what they were for; what they should be like; how they should be built; what their historical role was and remained; what the point of old buildings was.[13]

Even before the appearance of these two central characters, it is striking how intelligent and well informed the regular contributors were. Bernard Darwin, the grandson of the famous naturalist and the nephew of George Darwin, the client for J.J. Stevenson's 1885 Cambridge granary, joined as assistant to the golf editor in 1908 and wrote a perceptive memoir of the magazine for its 50th anniversary nearly 40 years later. In it he describes how his boss, Horace G. Hutchinson, 'wrote the golf; but that was a small part of what he did'; as well as his knowledge of shooting and fishing, Hutchinson not only knew 'the right kind of subjects but also the right kind of people and the right kind of houses', and, as Hudson's 'stout ally', played an invaluable role in establishing the magazine in the first place.[14] Darwin wrote that Hutchinson was also an informed naturalist himself, which possibly accounts as much as his golf for his friendship with Avebury and the otherwise improbable fact that he eventually became Avebury's first biographer. *Country Life* was, according to legend, founded on Walton Heath golf course; this says more about golf courses than it says about *Country Life*.[15]

Although Hudson seems to have kept his political opinions to himself, the two other major figures associated with the magazine were Liberals: George Newnes, and George Allardice Riddell, the developer of Walton Heath. On the magazine's founding in 1897, the debonair Newnes, a haberdasher turned journalist, was perhaps at a loose end, during an interval between sitting as Liberal MP for Newmarket (until 1895) and Swansea (from 1900), although he was by now the owner of the Liberal *Westminster Gazette*.[16] It was the partnership between Newnes's own publishing company, George Newnes Ltd, and Hudson's family printing firm Hudson & Kearns that created *Country Life*. A Liberal of a different type, Riddell was not at first financially associated with the magazine, but he appears to have been in on the project at its inception, and from 1910 took over Newnes's firm.[17] He was something of a rogue and a sharp operator by comparison with his high-minded predecessor there.[18] Thus, in spite of the later image of the magazine as a weekly for the landed classes, enhanced by its aristocratic portraits and coverage of expensive hobbies, it was in reality a Liberal paper, its controlling interests ranging from the high-minded Nonconformist wing to the radical and populist.

It thus supported some aspects of land reform. Margot Asquith, at this point the wife of the Shadow Chancellor of the Exchequer and not an uncontroversial person, appeared on the cover of the magazine in 1904, and her sister-in-law Pamela Tennant, née Wyndham, followed a year later. A leading article welcomed Earl Carrington's appointment as President of the Board of Agriculture following the change of government at the end of 1905, by declaring that he 'possesses ideas that have often been expressed in these pages'; the

magazine supported Carrington's campaign to increase rural smallholdings, and published model schemes.[19] The new Foreign Secretary Edward Grey was 'a private citizen with a singularly attractive personality'.[20] When the magazine reported that H.H. Asquith thought that suffragists should be like lady golfers, in 1906, it was not clear whether it was the writer or Asquith himself who was being sarcastic.[21]

Although never stated as such, this political attitude presumably accounted for the fact that the magazine ran a coherent and increasingly planned campaign to improve rural housing and extend smallholdings, even before the end of the tenure of Hudson's first editor J.E. Vincent (poached by the *Times* in 1900 to cover the forthcoming visit of the Duke of York to Australia).[22] The only other general-readership periodical to do this over the long term was Strachey's *Spectator*, the first large-circulation magazine to launch the subject in the first place, at the end of 1899: the rest of the extensive architectural press never made more than a passing reference to the subject.

Early architectural coverage

Country Life was first published in January 1897 as *Country Life with which is incorporated Racing Illustrated*, and subsequently as *Country Life Illustrated*. Its architectural interests were there from the start. John Leyland, already a prolific author on landscapes and gardens, wrote about the moated mediaeval and Tudor Baddesley Clinton, near Warwick, in the first issue, and his article was immediately followed by the first of Hutchinson's genial yarns, 'After-Dinner Golf'.[23] Then in February photographs accompanying an article on the Fairfield Stud concentrated to a surprising extent on the stable buildings. By the end of the year, readers had seen the work of George Devey: Leyland wrote about two houses where Devey had made significant alterations – Penshurst Place, and Ascott in Wing, Buckinghamshire, a farmhouse converted into a shooting box, although he did not mention the name of the architect. Then in November Lucy Hardy wrote first about cottage gardens, with images of picturesque cottages, and then on deserted houses, with some atmospheric photographs of them.[24] The first of the articles given the series title 'Country Homes' was on Albury Park, to which A.W.N. Pugin had added a service wing as well as remodelling the interior and making other changes and additions between 1843 and 1849 – which also means that Pugin was the first recent architect named by the magazine: a testament to the revival of interest in him

Four Beeches, 3 Denbridge Road, Bickley Park, then in Kent (now London), 1906, by C.H.B. Quennell for himself. Quennell was displaced from his position as *Country Life*'s 'official' architect once Edward Hudson had latched on to better designers, but this house has matured beautifully with age. H. Avray Tipping described it as having 'the welcome air of a country farm' and rightly pointed out that the original black-and-white photography failed to do it justice.

at the time.[25] The first contemporary architect to be reviewed was Pugin's admirer C.F.A. Voysey, in early 1898, in a piece on a substantial house (misleadingly called 'The Cottage') at Dovercourt near Bishop's Itchington in Warwickshire: this might have been expected, because at that period and for some years to come Voysey was the most published and the most imitated designer of those who became the canonical Edwardian architects.[26] But specifically, all this suggests that the magazine's architectural interests were already wider, and its architectural photography more significant, than is sometimes thought before the later stage in which it developed its reputation as the contemporary country-house magazine. There was exceptional photography by C.J. Cornish in articles on foresters' cottages and ancient water-mills in 1898, and his further contributions were important too: 'Village Houses for Holiday Homes' was about restoring timber-framed houses.[27]

Thus the appearance of C.H.B. Quennell in August 1898 as a kind of modern house architect to the magazine, with his 'A Little House with a Big Room' – the first in a short series of

'Houses for People with Hobbies', more or less in Baillie Scott style – would have appeared logical to readers.[28] In his mid-20s at the time, he had escaped his builder father's home in Kennington to become a member of the Junior Art Workers' Guild; he emerges from his son's unforgiving autobiography as an affectedly arty figure, rather as Percy Morley Horder was said to have been.[29] He had worked first for James Brydon and then after a couple of years as an assistant to the free-style architect Henry Wilson, and he had only that year commenced independent practice; he was designing some small houses for speculative builders in Highgate and then on and around Redington Road in Hampstead, of which he later made a high-quality picture book. Unlike the 'Big Room' house, these, and

112. The staircase hall of Four Beeches has likewise hardly changed since Quennell designed it.

113. Decorative panels on the ceiling of the parlour of Four Beeches. This
114. type of plasterwork with floral motifs was typical of good-quality
115. Edwardian domestic architecture, and the rough surface surrounding each one was intentional, although apparently exaggerated by the craftsmen in execution.

116. 1 Denbridge Road, Bickley Park, by Quennell: it is not obvious today that the 'late Stuart' motifs, such as the emphatic brick quoins and deep eaves soffit, were innovative and artistic. Both Quennell and Ernest Newton designed several houses in the immediate area, creating an upmarket Edwardian village.

his own villa 'Four Beeches' in Bickley Park, near Bromley to the south of London, of 1906, were mostly plain brick houses, some with rendered upper storeys and Ipswich windows, related in style to the contemporary houses nearby by Ernest Newton, but presumably cheaper (figs 111–116).[30]

The enduring feeling with Quennell has always been that he failed to live up to the high standards he seemed to suggest, or of those he admired, especially after having being named as an 'excellent designer' of furniture by Hermann Muthesius. He eventually had to leave Four Beeches with its lively and fun top-floor nursery, the subject of another *Country Life* article, for a cheap house of his own design so ugly that he once overheard strangers laughing at it.[31] A recent view is that his experimental modern architecture has been ignored, made tragic by the fact that he was 'a notably hard worker'.[32] Yet much of the importance of *Country Life*'s role in architectural history lies in small houses, and with apparently marginal designers like Quennell who have been subsequently overlooked by historians.

Quennell's occasional contributions to the magazine continued for a few years more, and no doubt he took a lot of trouble over them, but they tend not to stick in the mind. Hudson, according to Darwin, was the one who dealt with 'country houses, architecture, pictures and furniture' and it may be that Quennell's ebbing from publication came about as Hudson asserted himself or as Tipping and Weaver raised architectural standards. Hudson was already the friend

and client of Edwin Lutyens, and the godfather of Lutyens's daughter Barbara, one of the few non-aristocratic children to be portrayed in the magazine (at least three times, in fact).[33] At any rate, the period 1900–01 is the key one. In conventional architectural history terms, it was when Hudson published his first major Lutyens house: Munstead Wood, the Surrey home of Gertrude Jekyll, in February 1900; unconventionally, the editors and contributors now set out the series of ideas that were to carry them through the decade. These came out crisply and regularly in different ways.

In the last fortnight of 1899 the magazine had published two major articles. The first, on 23 December, was a long illustrated article on the village of Penshurst, with Devey's finest cottages and the slightly later forge photographed to their best advantage (fig.117).[34] In January 1900 there was an article on the recent temperance clubhouse at the centre of the village of Penshurst which had been designed by the rector's son, M. Maberly Smith, in a more or less Deveyesque style, with red brickwork rising up through irregular stonework and a contrasting half-timbered wing (fig.118).[35] In June, those who paid attention to the supplement will have seen an illustration of Blythwood, a house in the centre of the Essex village of Stansted Mountfitchet that had been rebuilt by W.D. Caröe as a substantial 'Tudor' mansion for the dairy pioneer James Blyth, an old cottage on the site becoming the new entrance hall; in fact, the beginning of the remodelling campaign at Blythwood predated that at Daws Hill by more

than ten years.[36] Blyth also built a substantial model dairy and yard at the back of his garden.[37] Then in August and September came the pair of long, illustrated articles on the Medmenham estate buildings.[38] An article in February 1901 reviewed a dairy cottage in Anglesey.[39] All of this provides the context for an observation by *Country Life*'s then architectural editor Mark Girouard on his return to Penshurst in 1971: that the very founding of the magazine was 'the natural culmination of the Devey frame of mind'.[40]

Realism, cheap cottages and English history

Country Life's brilliance lay in the way in which it both published charming old buildings of all kinds that had an historical air about them and at the same time pioneered economic, rational building and rational planning, especially for agricultural landowners: in this way it captured the essential balance between the practical and the dreamy that characterises the decade. In the week that followed the article on Deveyfied Penshurst, the magazine launched its parallel and complementary campaign for improved country cottages. The editor or someone in his office had seen a letter to the *Spectator* in November 1899 from a don called Rev. F.W. Bussell from Brasenose College, Oxford, claiming to have built a semi-detached pair of agricultural workers' cottages for £200 and supplying details.[41] The *Spectator* had earlier in the month published a long article on the problems of rural housing following interest in the subject by the *Daily News*, so the subject was in the air.[42] From this point on, however, the general observations described in the original *Spectator* article increasingly took on a more analytical air.

Bussell's letter was reproduced by *Country Life*, together with his house plans, thus initiating first, an energetic correspondence from readers, and secondly, the first of the magazine's attempts to design or promote the improved design of cottages of this kind.[43] In January and February 1900 there were articles on the subject, the latter one calling for readers to send in letters.[44] Evidently they did,

because 'correspondence . . . streamed in from all parts of the country'.[45] The magazine called on both Quennell and Lutyens to design; there was no sign that Lutyens responded, but Quennell's scheme in a Norman Shaw cottage style was published with rent calculations and figures showing that it met the Board of Agriculture's requirements for borrowing: early articles on the subject in the magazine included tables of calculations, in a way not dissimilar to those through which Ebenezer Howard had presented his case for garden cities.[46] Interest in the subject moved on to pointing out exactly how the standard building bye-laws adopted by local authorities made it difficult to remodel old cottages sympathetically: these in effect required all new rural building to look like urban terraces, the traces of which survive all around the country and tend to stick out in old Ordnance Survey maps.[47] In two issues in February 1901 the magazine published related correspondence, including a letter from someone signing themselves 'Disgusted'; it then launched a series called 'The Building Bye-Laws', which on 23 February lamented that they prevented the use of traditional building methods such as cob, wattle-and-daub, soft chalk and mud, as well as timber-frame construction.[48] The letters continued to flow in, many illustrated with plans and suggestions. In fact, from 1901 the Local Government Board occasionally published new model bye-laws for rural areas, perhaps in response to this outbreak of interest in them from landowners, but it was not until further legal changes in 1907–9 that local authorities began to respond to them.[49]

At the same time, *Country Life* carried articles over the course of the first decade of the 20th century which focused on the elements of the design of small buildings, looking carefully and rationally at windows, chimneys and building materials in different combinations, in thematic photographic essays and in articles. This was unique in both the general and the professional press, and it reached an influential readership. From this, the magazine went on to establish what became one of the great national archetypes: the modern 'Tudor' cottage.

What happened over this period was that these two major aspects of building design – the Devey one that emphasised materials and forms over age and consistent historical style, and which applied to houses large and small, and the exacting interest in the details of labourers' cottages – began to merge into a single theme. It is striking that when the magazine discussed Old Place, Lindfield, 'completely remodelled over 20 years by Mr Kempe', the stained-glass designer, it made no attempt to distinguish between new and old work, for the distinction evidently did not matter to its

117.   George Devey's saddler's shop at Penshurst. An unsigned article in *Country Life* in December 1899 thought this building, then almost completely covered in creeper, to be 'very beautiful'.

118.   M. Maberly Smith's temperance clubhouse at Penshurst, 1899, with irregular patterns in stone and brick that echoed Devey's work. The architect's father was rector of the parish.

119. The stairs at Fulbrook, near Godalming in Surrey, designed in 1896–9: one of Edwin Lutyens's earliest houses, photographed here for *Country Life* in 1903. Readers of the magazine, and of the professional press, repeatedly saw this contrast between a 'Tudor' exterior and a lush, glossy white classical interior throughout the Edwardian period.

writer.[50] As coverage of old houses became more ambitious, the magazine showed not merely picturesque houses, as it had always done, but specifically those with juxtapositions of building from historical periods; so December 1901 saw an article on Cranborne Manor in Dorset, with its combination of both early and late 17th-century work, and the following month it featured Spains Hall near Finchingfield in Essex, which has elevations in strongly contrasting styles, and which had also been recently remodelled, a fact which the article did not mention.[51] Presenting houses with these mixed styles was one of the dominant and most consistent characteristics of *Country Life* during the decade. Sometimes these had almost the full set of possibilities from ancient to recent: for example Combe Abbey in Warwickshire, with its large William Eden Nesfield east wing that comprised a remade Norman cloister at its base and a chateau roofline above it.[52]

A picture then began to develop of where this might take the buildings of the future. When Lutyens's Fulbrook, near Godalming in Surrey, appeared in January 1903, featuring on one page a pair of external views of a '16th-century' farmhouse exterior, and on another the hall and stairway of the same house in a glossy white, slightly French, late Stuart neo-classical style, it will have been obvious to readers that this was continuing what had become a conventional way

of making a house rather than, say, an outrageous gesture by a one-off genius – an aspect of the context of Lutyens's work that has been downplayed by later historians of him (fig.119). Indeed, the sequence at Folly Farm, at Sulhamstead in Berkshire, where Lutyens took a 17th-century cottage that had been transformed into a 19th-century house and added styles first from 150 years beforehand (in 1906), and then 150 years before that (in 1912) is, when seen in the context of the old houses favoured by *Country Life*, a relatively simple conceit. His design in an article about the need for a sympathetic replacement for an old bridge over the Thames at Sonning in Berkshire, published in September and October 1902, might be one of his least-known works, but because it incorporated old and new seamlessly together, it might equally be one of his most significant.[53] The choice of subject tells us that Hudson was behind it, as the site was just west of Deanery Garden, the recently completed house designed for him by Lutyens. In fact Hudson managed to sneak his own house repeatedly into the pages of the magazine, for example as the backdrop to a photograph in an article about his garden (where it appeared without being named); in a strange essay on 're-countrified' England by Frederick Greenwood, where it was the only recent house in a series of images of picturesque ones; and over many pages as one of the 'Houses for People with Hobbies'.[54]

120. (above) *Country Life* presented an almost continuous sequence of details of Jacobean joinery, providing architects (including Lutyens) with an inexhaustible supply of ideas. These Jacobean newel posts at Methley Hall, Yorkshire, appeared in May 1907.

121. A newel post at F.W. Troup's Sandhouse, near Witley in Surrey, 1910. This house was fitted with a particularly fine set of timber, iron and lead details drawn from Tudor precedents. See also fig.32.

Lutyens spent so much time with Hudson that it is not really possible to work out who was influencing whom, and in what respect. But the suspension of 'development', the throwing off of that last shibboleth of the gothic revival, which in any case had been alien to Pugin's realism, and the picking of details from historic buildings that worked well, seem to have been common to both of them. In fact recent writers on Lutyens have noticed that he drew extensively from contemporary architects as much as from historic ones: David Cole's photographic survey of the houses of this period identifies features developed from ideas by E.S. Prior, Charles Rennie Mackintosh, and Arthur Mackmurdo, among others; to this can be added that Lutyens's 'Wrennaissance' was itself an accomplished version of what Horace Field had been doing early in his career.[55] The secret of his success seems to have been that he designed their ideas better than they did. At Marshcourt in Hampshire, from 1901, Lutyens designed a wall

base with irregularly placed, disintegrating areas of clunch, flint and red tile in the manner of Devey's St Alban's Court, but more self-consciously artistic (and the white stone and bays echoed Romaine-Walker's recent Danesfield (see fig.41)). In time, *Country Life* – to be exact, the perceptive Tipping – saw that Philip Webb had done this all along. At Great Tangley Manor in Surrey, when making additions in 1893–4 to a half-timbered Elizabethan house for Wickham Flower, a member of the Society for the Protection of Ancient Buildings, Webb inserted a strongly geometrical, bold white fireplace from Vanbrugh into a dark new low-ceilinged, heavily beamed 'Jacobean' library; and he referred to Vanbrugh when extending elsewhere, for example at Exning House in Suffolk in 1894–6.[56] Great Tangley was one of the first large houses to appear in *Country Life*, in July 1898.[57]

Was it that library that Lutyens was referring to when, in a *Country Life* tribute after Webb's death in 1915, he wrote

122. The Ship Room at Lindisfarne Castle, converted by Lutyens for Hudson in 1902–3 and photographed for *Country Life* in 1913. In 1909 the magazine published a photograph of just such a hanging ship, in a church in Fife.

that the freshness and originality of one of Webb's houses led him to think it had been made by a 'young man'?[58] Could it have been his transformative moment? Great Tangley is near Wonersh, deep into Lutyens's Surrey home territory. Lutyens thought that this cathartic event had occurred in 1891, which was a couple of years before the room was designed, but he might have misremembered it, and in any case there were plenty of other recent projects by Webb for him to see. Lutyens repeatedly adapted the unexecuted design by Webb of 1885 for General Pitt Rivers's gatehouse, so much so that Webb's drawing now looks more Lutyens than Webb, and he also occasionally copied elements of the related front elevation of Webb's Smeaton Manor, Yorkshire, of 1876–9.[59] Christopher Hussey told a famous story that Lutyens made fun of his own former employer, Ernest George, by saying that he used to return from holiday with 'overflowing sketchbooks' which he would then raid for picturesque details; yet he differed from this himself only in that (like Pugin before him) he committed the details to memory rather than accumulated sketches.[60] In a chapter on Homewood at Knebworth in Hertfordshire, designed by Lutyens *c.*1901–2, Weaver described the architect's

approach as 'an organic fusion of differing motives' – by 'motives' presumably meaning what would now be spelled as 'motifs'.[61] One historical type that Lutyens repeatedly used, in common with several others, including, eventually, Tipping himself, was the Wealden house, especially the version with a recessed central bay carrying an ornamental half-timbered upper storey: Devey had revived this for the pair of cottages on Rogues Hill outside Penshurst in the 1860s or 1870s (see fig.177), and Lutyens did it time and time again, or referred to it in variations such as the gallery on the north side of Munstead Wood.[62]

These images of Lutyens's houses sat within a continuous stream of closely related architectural ideas. The house that followed the publication of Fulbrook, with its contrasting styles, was the Vyne in Hampshire, which has reception rooms in both Tudor and the mid-17th-century artisan manner, a Corinthian portico by John Webb, and a grand, severe classical staircase from about 1770.[63] The magazine twice published photographs of South Wraxhall Manor in Wiltshire, where there is a neo-classical Tuscan loggia inserted in about 1720 into a late 16th-century wing, which implies that this line of thought had been pursued consciously by the editor, proprietor, writer, or all three.[64] Lutyens quoted this feature on the roadside elevation of his Tigbourne Court near Witley in Surrey, in 1899, which further suggests that the magazine looked for historical examples to provide a context for its modern buildings. Overall, however, the most detailed images in *Country Life* from across the decade were of ornate Jacobean interiors, some very fancy indeed, and it is striking to what extent Lutyens must have based some of his detailing on these.[65] There are many decorative 17th-century newel posts with chequer patterns, fretwork and the like, which Lutyens was still recalling in, for example, his Benson Court at Magdalene College, Cambridge, in the early 1930s (figs 120 and 121).[66] Most remarkably, an image of Kinghorn church in Fife from September 1909 sent in by a reader shows a model of a ship hanging from a vaulted ceiling, just as it does in a famous interior photograph of Lindisfarne Castle, which Lutyens had remodelled in 1902–3 (fig.122).[67] Which came first? Did Hudson choose his photographs to suit his idol, or the other way around?

Conversion and restoration

It was surely through this continuous, consistent presentation of historical and recent work side-by-side over a decade, so merged that distinction between the two was impossible, that architects awoke one by one to the idea of the old-new and the new-old house: no other publication promoted the idea in this way. Furthermore, it was applicable at any scale. As the large Lutyens houses began to roll out across the pages of the magazine, and as in the wake of the new rural standards the interest in bye-law reform abated somewhat, *Country Life* increasingly promoted the idea of buying and restoring old village houses as weekend cottages: the intentions behind this were to revive the fortunes of pretty but poor villages, and to encourage townspeople with taste and money to take an interest in them. This went well with the magazine's campaign for better rural housing in general, and indeed as time went by, some houses were advertised in the magazine or elsewhere as equally suiting both servant-less weekenders and agricultural workers. An article in June 1903 on 'The Week-End Cottage' illustrated only picturesque old ones, but two years later the magazine was publishing 'before and after' examples of houses transformed for these purposes.[68] This was in the air beyond the pages of the magazine: Field designed tile-hung or rendered houses like this for Surrey landowners, for example

around three sides of a courtyard in an area of nurseries south of his own home at Hook Heath near Woking (see fig.83), as well as a relatively expensive pair, at £600, north-east of Ripley, both soon after 1896.[69] It had been this subject that had provided the pretext for that article on Voysey's 'Cottage' at Dovercourt.

It was also this theme that introduced E. Guy Dawber, Field's almost exact contemporary, born just over two weeks later than him, in the summer of 1861. Dawber's public career went on to overshadow Field's, and his vernacular buildings, often in Cotswold Jacobean styles, soon appeared regularly in most architectural magazines, usually in sympathetic perspectives.[70] Dawber's first contribution was for a pair of cottages that 'combine the comfort of the old ones with a convenient and simple plan', essentially one of the magazine's mottos for the rest of the decade.[71] Dawber, who had left the office of Ernest George for Gloucestershire because of eye strain, became a specialist in the vernacular detailing of the area, and produced construction sketches and notes for the Cotswolds edition in a series of books on old cottages published by Batsford, this one in 1905.[72] In mid-decade he designed a whole village for the Earl of Harrowby, also featured in the magazine.[73] According to John Betjeman, Voysey thought that Dawber's work was too 'peasant-like'; certainly it could be quite rough on the outside.[74] Another relative newcomer to appear in the magazine was Detmar Blow, a SPAB adherent, who sent in a letter to show off his restored 'old Sussex cottage' in 1905.[75]

Thus at this point the magazine's flow of large Lutyens houses was punctuated with high-quality cottage work, with names of architects which would crop up long afterwards in cottage books of various kinds: one was W.A. Forsyth, in partnership with the Architectural Association's headmaster H.P.G. Maule, who became a conservation architect of distinction and added a sympathetic residential wing to Daws Hill for Wycombe Abbey School.[76] A correspondent called B.G., noticing this recurrent theme, sent in a plan and photograph of a Kentish oast house that had been converted into a weekend cottage.[77] Perhaps Reginald Blomfield had seen it before designing a similar conversion of a double oast house at Godinton, west of Ashford, in 1907, one of several estates where he was combining professional advice with 'some excellent days' shooting' (fig.123).[78] In that year, during what one of his biographers calls a phase of 'slightly more meticulous approach to historical detail' when in partnership with James Scott, Clough Williams-Ellis converted an unusual oast building, with a pair of towers and an elongated plan at first sight straight out of the late 18th-century symbolic

OLD GROUND PLAN

S. ELEVATION AS ALTERED

OLD 1ST FLOOR PLAN.

10 5 0   10   20   30   40   50   60

TOOL HOUSE   POTTING SHED

GROUND FLOOR PLAN
AS ALTERED

COMMON ROOM   BED RM. 2

PANTRY   BED RM. 3

BED ROOM 1.

BED ROOM 4

FIRST FLOOR PLAN
AS ALTERED

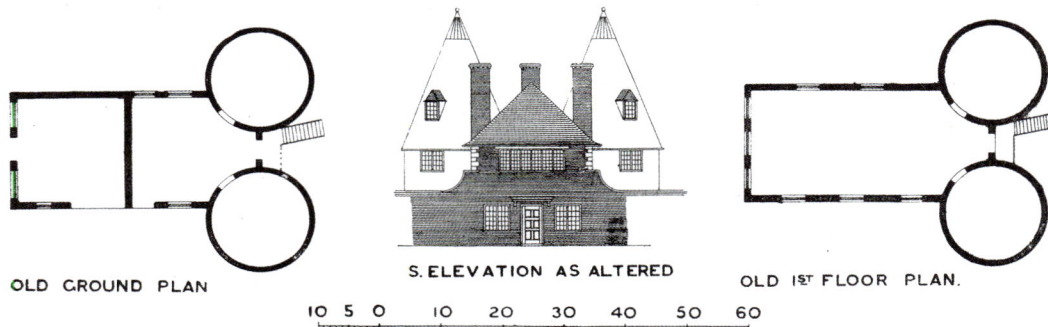

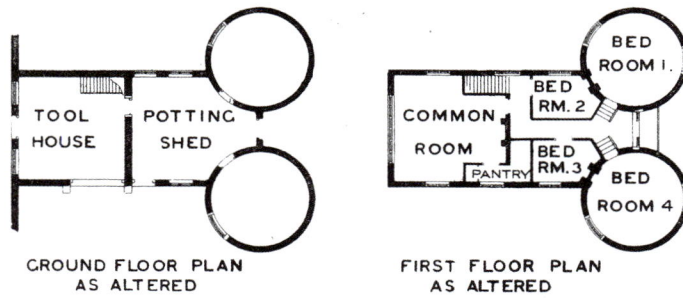

FIG. 254.—PLANS SHOWING
OAST-HOUSE BEFORE AND
AFTER CONVERSION INTO
BOTHIE.

Reginald Blomfield, A.R.A.

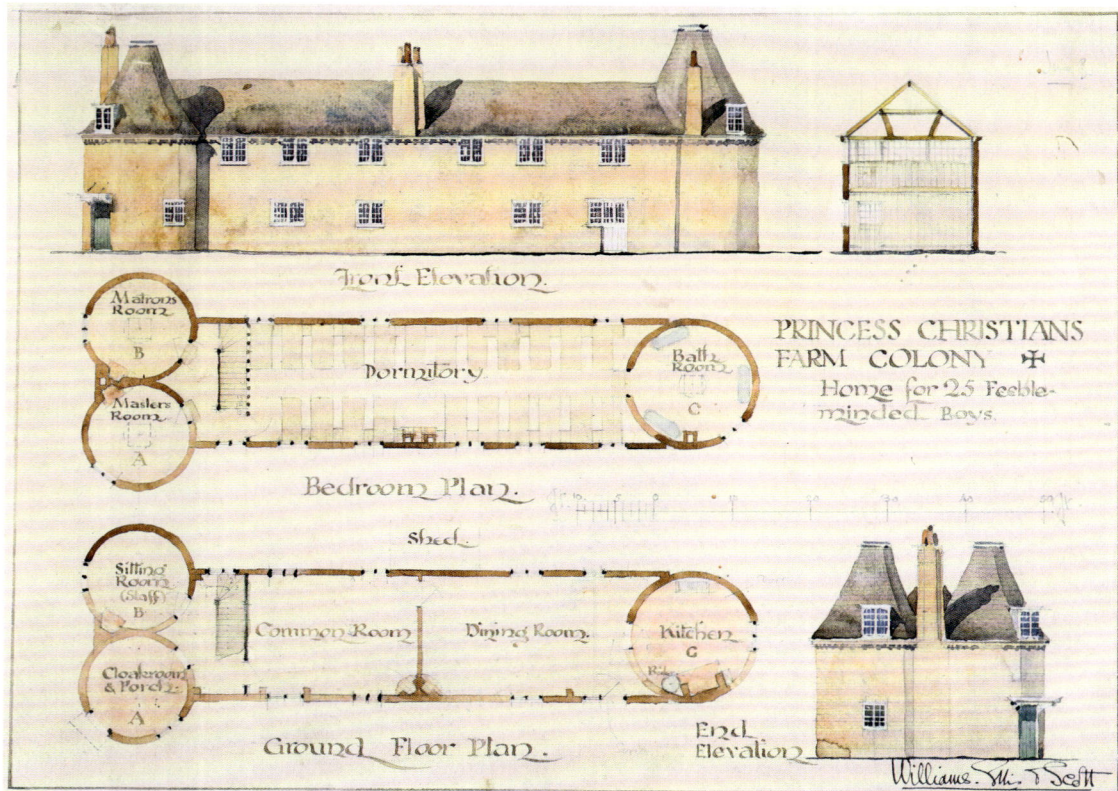

Front Elevation.

Matrons Room
B

Masters Room
A

Dormitory

Bath Room
C

Bedroom Plan.

Shed.

Sitting Room (Staff)
B

Cloakroom & Porch
A

Common Room   Dining Room.

Kitchen
G

Ground Floor Plan.

End Elevation.

PRINCESS CHRISTIANS
FARM COLONY ☩
Home for 25 Feeble-
minded Boys.

Williams. & T. Scott

architecture of Claude-Nicolas Ledoux, for Princess Christian's Farm Colony at Hildenborough (fig.124).[79]

Thus the oast house conversion is another Edwardian building type. Old cottages which might well have once housed animals as well as people had always been patched up, repaired, altered and remodelled, sometimes by well-known or promising architects but usually simply to make them habitable; but Stevenson's granary was the first prominent example of an agricultural building converted for comfortable residential use (see fig.10). Stevenson continued to work on the house until 1894 when he incorporated it into an artistic reworking of a vernacular building on the landward side.[80] The appearance of projects like this in *Country Life* might denote respectability, but there are similar examples elsewhere. At Layer Marney Tower in Essex, Chancellor & Son converted a fine 16th-century stable block into a 'long gallery' for entertainments around 1910, an example which does not appear to have been published at the time.[81] The practice of Niven & Wigglesworth, in partnership with a Blomfield graduate called Harold Falkner of Farnham between about 1896 and 1902, specialised in gentrifying old cottages; they published two in J.H. Elder-Duncan's *Country Cottages and Week-End Homes* of 1906, one of which had previously consisted of three tiny sitting rooms and a large hop kiln and store.[82] The upper part of the kiln was turned into a studio, and the house included a workshop and dark room, so this was clearly an 'artistic' project (fig.125).[83] Mill conversions appear: there was a large one by Forsyth & Maule at Stedham, near Midhurst in Sussex, in the *Architectural Review* for April 1911 (fig.126), but the origins of Unsworth & Triggs's cottage at Petersfield in Hampshire, 'built almost wholly from the very admirable materials . . . which already existed on the site in the form of the wreckage of an older house', were in a mill, too (fig.127).[84] Possibly the windmill conversion is also an Edwardian phenomenon, although these were inhabited by eccentric individuals rather than by the agricultural tenants of large landowners and hence appeared less in the magazines.[85] By 1913, Weaver's *'Country Life' Book of Cottages*, which was mainly taken up with new ones, included a short chapter on repairs, illustrating cottages restored by Williams-Ellis on his Glasfryn estate in Caernarvonshire, and others by C.R. Ashbee at Broad Campden in Gloucestershire, and by Tipping in Monmouthshire. All of these were projects by benevolent landowners for labourers, so their status lay somewhere between the upgraded cottage and the artistic house. In August 1907 the law was changed to ensure that homes converted from structures originally built for agricultural or other purposes would comply with the bye-laws as if they

VIEW FROM THE SIDE.

· OLD · PLAN ·

GROUND FLOOR·PLAN·   ·FIRST FLOR·PLAN·

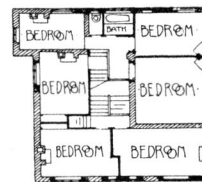

PLANS BEFORE AND AFTER ALTERATION.

THE DIAL HOUSE, SHORTFIELD COMMON, FARNHAM.
NIVEN, WIGGLESWORTH and FALKNER, Architects.

Another example of excellent adaptive work. The blacked-in walls show how little structural partition work has been necessitated. Cost, new, from £850 to £1,500. See p. 81.

123.   (opposite, above) Reginald Blomfield's oast house conversion at Godinton in mid-Kent, of 1907, described as for use as a 'bothie' but more probably for weekend guests who came for golf or shooting.

124.   (opposite, below) Clough Williams-Ellis and James Scott's executed design for Princess Christian's Farm Colony, Hildenborough, Kent, *c.*1910: note the circular bathroom at the right-hand end. There is some evidence that working with the elemental forms of vernacular buildings encouraged Edwardian architects to move away from conventional plans.

125.   Niven & Wigglesworth worked in partnership with a Farnham architect, Harold Falkner, between about 1896 and 1902, and built and remodelled many houses around the town. The Dial House has an unusual plan that emerged from working with existing fabric, shown in black in this plan from J.H. Elder-Duncan's *Country Cottages and Week-End Homes* (1906).

126. A watermill at Stedham, near Midhurst in West Sussex, converted into a home by Forsyth & Maule, and published in the *Architectural Review* in 1911. The same architects later made tactful extensions to Daws Hill after the Carringtons sold it to Wycombe Abbey School.

127. The right-hand wing of this cottage near Petersfield in Hampshire was constructed from the materials of a derelict house and mill by the local practice Unsworth & Triggs some time before 1913. The recent left-hand extension is a worthy addition in the same spirit. Photographed by Hugh Routh.

were new dwellings, indicating that local authorities were thinking about the process.[86] *Country Life* liked Dutch scenes, whether of landscapes, of houses or of people in traditional costume, and an article in March 1906 entitled 'The Land of Homeliness' was illustrated with a fine photograph of two 'Zeeland girls cleaning copper' in an austere room, almost the epitome of pan-north-European domestic protestantism.[87] It can be seen as a hint of what its writers hoped that interiors of these houses might be like.

Country Life made, then, little distinction when describing old and new; that also seems to suit the odd fact that it occasionally failed to mention any architect's name, even when describing a large new addition or, indeed, a big house that the editors approved of, such as G.F. Bodley and Thomas Garner's stupendous Hewell Grange, covered enthusiastically in August 1903.[88] It is worth stating how much this approach lies beyond the version of architectural history that contemporaries were attempting to record at the time. W.R. Lethaby, for example, gave a lecture in 1910 at the Royal Institute of British Architects in which he said that

> we have passed into a scientific age, and the old practical arts, introduced instinctively, belong to an entirely different era . . . the living stem of architecture has always been rooted in the spirit of active

experiment and adventure for the further satisfaction of needs and desires.[89]

And then by way of conclusion: 'We hope to combine the two realities, the reality of natural necessity and common experience with the reality of the philosophers, which is the idea, and to reconcile Science with Art.'[90] In comments made during the discussion that followed the presentation of his paper and were added later to the main body of his text, he further said: 'Now we, the best of us, are trying to build things which shall *look like* farm-houses and look like cottages, and so on.'[91] If this means anything – which it may not – it is saying that the realism of the 19th-century architects whom Lethaby admired was in danger of being substituted for picturesque mimicry. Yet this was demonstrably not the case with the influential high-art architects and their many imitators published by *Country Life* whose work was scientific in the sense of being researched, rational, and often analytical, and not actually concerned with either personality (apart from Lutyens) or imitative style. The magazine maintained a rational economic view of building, building repair and estate management, and village restoration, thus establishing an essential new facet of English positivist architecture: the buildings they liked made financial sense for landowners. Furthermore, the historical accounts given in the magazine, even before Tipping and Weaver, were of the highest quality. It was however the Lethaby version, words and theories rather than actual buildings, and part of the founding myth of modernism, which went on to dominate every mainstream description of the period ever since. As Blomfield later sighed, in the course of his assault on *Modernismus*, 'It is easy to spin words in support of a prevailing fashion.'[92]

Tipping

It is possible that the way in which Hudson conveyed his ideas about new houses in his magazine was through his contributor Tipping, who had taken a first in Modern History at Oxford University and whom Bernard Darwin described as having 'an essentially scholarly quality' (fig.128).[93] Tipping

certainly set a very high standard for historical writing on domestic architecture in the magazine; he was a gardening writer who was a frustrated architect, designing very little on his own beyond one magnificent service wing for a Tudor house in Herefordshire and various small structures for his own estates, helped by a young architect George Kitchin, his closest friend.[94] Kitchin's name appeared in the magazine before Tipping's, as the architect of a remodelled, picturesque old cottage at Compton near Winchester in December 1900: perhaps Tipping wrote it, as at this point he must have been contributing anonymously.

By 1907 articles in the magazine were, mostly, signed, but that does not mean that the authors are identifiable, or even that the editor necessarily knew who they were: Bernard Darwin wrote that Graham was surprised to discover that a contributor called 'Fiona Macleod' was a man.[95] Tipping became architectural editor that year and appeared sometimes as 'T', but increasingly under his full name. His first identified appearance came in April 1907; in the course of an article on Zuylestein, between Utrecht and Arnhem, he observed that:

> Matter-of-fact England, busy with its material needs, has only excelled in art and architecture when kindled and fed by outside influences. When cut off from continental imaginativeness and intellectualism . . . it has tended to revert to the characteristics of its first Teutonic settlers, whom Carlyle somewhat brutally described as 'a gluttonous race of Jutes and Anglo-Saxons lumbering on in pot-bellied indifference'.[96]

Tipping was in the Netherlands, the principal continental source of the kind of historical English architecture that he liked; possibly the reason why he and others disliked plain Palladianism and the like was precisely because they were, in common with the equally disapproved-of gothic revival, too affected, too English, too insular – and almost impossible to adapt inventively.

A month later he combined several of *Country Life*'s preoccupations in a single piece on one of Lutyens's least-known houses, Millmead in Bramley, Surrey, some details of the windows of which had been determined by the building bye-laws: 'Mr Lutyens . . . deserves our grateful thanks for showing us how perfect a thing a little country house on a tiny plot of ground can be made and how a "sordid half acre"

128.   H. Avray Tipping in the garden of Mathern Palace in Monmouthshire, photographed by *Country Life* in 1910.

129. Before and after views of one of Tipping's estate cottages on his Mounton estate near Chepstow, Monmouthshire, drawn by his architect friend George Kitchin, and included as an exemplar in Lawrence Weaver's *'Country Life' Book of Cottages*, 1913.

can be transformed into an earthly paradise.'[97] Millmead is a little house hidden behind a wall as Deanery Garden was, in the style of Tigbourne Court, with a late 17th-century type of house grafted on to a 'Jacobean' one. The wing that ran along the entrance court was in the early style, and the stern entry pavilion straight ahead was 'end of 17th'; the garden front, formal and symmetrical, is French 'beginning of 18th'. Yet Tipping deemed none of this unusual or significant enough to be pointed out explicitly. His own house, Mounton in Herefordshire, designed soon afterwards with a young amanuensis and Dawber graduate called E.C. Francis, was 'Tudor' on the outside but with a 'mid-18th-century' dining room within, some genuinely old elements from Tipping's family home in Brasted incorporated into it.[98]

One of the magazine's most interesting observations appears in an anonymous article in late 1905 about a remote house called The Wyck, near St Ippolyts south of Hitchin in Hertfordshire, which had been almost totally rebuilt by its owner, A.L. Allen. It looked like a picturesque, half-timbered cottage too neat to be old (see figs 168 and 191). The author, probably again Tipping, wrote that it had been 'created out of fragments of the old' and went on to say that the house 'is, indeed, a regeneration and constitution, and certain quaint old cottages have gone to the making of it'.[99] Recycling old houses as part of new ones was not unusual in Edwardian England, but the word 'regeneration' is significant. Pugin had written in 1841 that 'the smaller detached houses which the present state of society has generated, should possess a peculiar character' – in other words, that they should reflect contemporary requirements rather than imitate old ones.[100] And indeed, there is a constant theme in some Edwardian writing, especially Tipping's, of regenerating a house from what remains of its authentic past.

In a way that is unusual for historians and critics, Tipping could combine interpretation and practice, usually through his current amanuensis Kitchin: the article 'Two Renovated Cottages in Monmouthshire' was an account of a project he carried out on his Mathern Palace estate near Chepstow in Monmouthshire (figs 128 and 129).[101] Kitchin at this point, in 1908, was still restoring and remodelling his Compton cottage; Helena Gerrish's outstanding biography of Tipping records that he loved this place, and wrote about it in his *English Gardens*.[102] It was very probably Tipping who presented Kitchin's designs for small homesteads in the magazine a few months later, at a time when Carrington's smallholding campaign was much in the news.[103]

With Tipping's emergence as a named writer came many more long illustrated articles on recent or new cottage-like

homes, to the extent that the magazine now became the only publication which featured them in this way. He also introduced repeated references to SPAB, and made SPAB jokes.[104] He was revealed as a writer on Lutyens, introducing Little Thakeham in West Sussex, of 1902–3, in 1909 (fig.130).[105] It was Tipping who wrote about Ernest Gimson's cottage at Sapperton west of Cirencester in Gloucestershire, 'an *entente cordiale* between the utilitarian and the beautiful'.[106] His article was the first in what became the well-known series 'Lesser Country Houses of To-Day', the subsequent subjects of which were Gimson's other cottage in the village; a vicarage by Maberly Smith, the Deveyesque architect from Penshurst;

and Douglas Murray's Meadow Cottage near Amberley in West Sussex.[107] This last was built on a Jacobean plan and in part from reclaimed building materials in order to retain,

130. *Country Life's* famous view of the hall at Lutyens's Little Thakeham, West Sussex, taken in 1909, six years after the building's completion. The architect's innovation here was not so much the mixture of 17th-century styles but the use of external elements within a drawing room.

131. (opposite) Tipping comprehensively remodelled the mediaeval and Tudor Brinsop Court, Herefordshire, for his friend Hubert Astley from 1911, and designed this service wing along its east side. Its courtyard elevation behind is half-timbered, closely studded (see fig.12).

as the architect put it, 'the simple beauty and dignity of 16th and 17th Century work', and Tipping thought that there had been a 'most happy conjunction of the old and new'; elsewhere Tipping referred to this mixed style as being like 'a Quaker lady's silk dress', that is, well made and in good taste, but simple.[108] This description would suit very well one of Tipping's own later designs, for the elegant, austere stone office wing he added to Brinsop Court in Herefordshire from 1911 (fig.131).[109]

Weaver

It was with the appointment of Weaver rather than with the publication of work by Quennell or Lutyens that the magazine's interest in rational and realist design began to crystallise into a coherent argument, almost a set of instructions, about how to build a house. From September 1909 he had been contributing weekly articles on contemporary architecture to *Country Life*, quite possibly to allow Tipping to free up more time for his restoration work at Mathern Palace, his gardens, his books for the Country Life Library which seem to have generated good royalties, and his other activities.[110] Weaver was perfectly capable of continuing and developing Tipping's own two most influential ideas: that whether something was 'old' or 'new' did not matter, an interesting line to take for a scholar and an historian; and secondly, that a new house could be generated from an old one. Tipping re-emerged from time to time, for example in September 1910 to contribute one of his most revealing observations on this second subject, in relation to Tudor House at Broadway in Worcestershire, which was being remodelled and extended by Charles Mallows.[111] Here, Mallows had found a fragment of an old staircase and regenerated, as it were, a new one out of it, rather as a gardener might take a cutting and nurse it to fruition. Similarly, he praised Edward Warren's rebuilding of Headley Court, Epsom, Surrey, which was raised 'almost on original lines' and incorporated Jacobean panelling and brickwork, and a new wing at Notgrove Manor in Gloucestershire by A.N. Prentice, designed

in a tactful Cotswold style over old foundations and where the junctions between old and new walls were indistinguishable.[112]

The transition from Tipping to Weaver was achieved so smoothly that it is hard to tell the difference between their writing. When a combination of old and new was done too brutally, both writers would protest – as Weaver did, for instance, when reviewing the 1908–10 restoration of the Tudor merchant's house Paycocke's in Coggeshall, Essex (fig.133).[113] But it is striking what little value they attached to Georgian architecture of any kind, especially where its original erection had entailed the loss of something older. It is at first a shock to see Weaver describe the replacement of an Elizabethan wing at Normanby Hall in Lincolnshire with a new building by Robert Smirke as a 'crime'.[114] This was the attitude that led that same year to the article about the history of Gidea Hall which had ignored the classical house as if it had not been there. A review by Blomfield of some articles in 1906 bluntly described Palladio, Inigo Jones and Christopher Wren as 'ancient history': he himself was a Francophile.[115] It was, after all, at precisely this period that the layout of the new streets around Smith Square proposed the demolition of entire terraces of Georgian houses in order to remake the area as an idealised piece of Queen Anne townscape.[116]

So Weaver 'picked up the thread', to repeat again his own revealing description of how Lutyens had rebuilt Jack Tennant's Great Maytham Hall on 18th-century foundations. He generally wrote about the new houses, and many of *Country Life*'s later descriptions, some very long, of Lutyens's houses were by him. He had less interest in gardens – Tipping wrote these. It was apparently Weaver who introduced a series of architectural competitions for houses, so that the results could be analysed in the magazine. Most significantly he wrote books about houses which were at least as much about the text as they were about the pictures, something that departed from the magazine's original aims.

Weaver is a remarkable 20th-century figure: he was technically astute but also aware of the power and purpose of history. It is telling that his knighthood, in 1920, was in recognition of his 'very effective' war work in the supplies

132. Weaver, photographed by Walter Stoneman in 1920. Weaver's rational and perceptive mind made more of an impact on domestic architecture and its interpretation before the First World War than any number of the well-known leaders of the profession.

133. The 1908–10 restoration of Paycocke's, in Coggeshall, Essex, for Noel Buxton, by the Maldon architect P.M. Beaumont and local woodcarver E.W. Beckwith, was considered by *Country Life* to have been overdone, and something of a warning, for it recreated an historical past without developing it.

division of the Ministry of Agriculture.[117] He had developed an interest in historic leadwork when working as a commercial traveller selling builders' ironmongery, and before joining *Country Life* he had written about it in a series of illustrated articles for the *Architectural Review*.[118] He was publishing a great deal for *Country Life* in a consistent and disciplined style very soon after his appointment: between 1910 and 1914 he produced on average more than one article a week.[119] One of the first new houses he wrote about was an extraordinary building called Sandhouse, Witley, in a blunt, rationalised Elizabethan style by F.W. Troup, just over a mile (under 2 kilometres) from Lutyens's Tigbourne Court but very different from it in appearance.[120] Troup had trained with J.J. Stevenson in the late 1880s, and then with Brydon, and he was one of the

few early Art Workers' Guild stalwarts without a connection to Shaw. Sandhouse was built for Joseph King, a Liberal MP since January 1910 and a supporter of the Haslemere Peasant Art movement, and appropriately has a gaunt, slightly atavistic appearance to both of its long elevations: walls of red brick

134. The dining room at Sandhouse, photographed for the *Architectural Review* in 1903. By setting decorative elements against brick or white-painted backgrounds, designers could draw attention to their qualities and enhance their value.

135. Troup's Sandhouse, seen from the garden on the south side of the house. Part of the savage power of this elevation, which once would have appeared very raw, is due to the fact that the windows are not evenly aligned with the brick diaper work – a Devey device.

B25

NETHER SWELL MANOR IN GLOUCESTERSHIRE, THE SEAT OF SIR JOHN MURRAY SCOTT, BART. IT IS BUILT OF LOCAL STONE WITH STONE MULLIONED WINDOWS, THE ROOFING OF STONE SLATES

E. Guy Dawber, Architect

contrast with pale blue diaper work made from flare ends, derived from Pugin's or Devey's version of Elizabethan (fig.135; see also fig.50).[121] Troup designed fine leadwork for the house, one of the trademarks of his early buildings and restoration work, and that is perhaps what had attracted Weaver to it.[122] The interior also had a consciously primitive look to it, originally with a gaudy frieze by Godfrey Blount (fig.134).[123]

A fortnight after covering Lorimer's reconstructed Lympne Castle, Weaver praised Dawber's Nether Swell Manor, in Gloucestershire, of 1903 – probably his best-known house, in part because of the mixture of old and new styles: Cotswold vernacular on the outside but with sophisticated French detailing within (figs 136 and 137).[124] Tipping's protégé was taking clear and explicit steps to establish a canon. The first article attributed to him by name was on the Hampshire

136. E. Guy Dawber's work could be uneven in quality, but Nether Swell, near Stow-on-the-Wold, Gloucestershire, 1903, is a fine house that also looks from the outside as if it could actually be 17th century but for the sharpness of the stone. This drawing was one of his contributions to *The British Home of To-day* (1904).

137. Nether Swell: this detail of the drawing room shows how remarkable the Edwardian contrast of interior and exterior styles could be. The interior designer was Marcel Boulanger, who was working at the same time for the Ritz Hotel in London. A photograph from the *Architectural Review*, January 1906.

138. Percy Morley Horder's work was often representative of what better middle-range architects were doing. At 'Inverleith', 13 Lime Tree Road, Norwich, in 1908–9, designed with A.G. Wyand, he inserted a new '18th-century' interior (incorporating old fittings from the recently demolished Norwich Union headquarters) into a new and notably cheap 'Tudor-vernacular' house.

manor house Avon Tyrrell as rebuilt by Lethaby in 1891, and he consistently praised the architects he called 'the giants', for example covering Webb's New Place and Standen, and Shaw's Dawpool and Chesters, between 1910 and 1912, long after they were built, and in the conspicuous absence of other houses of the late Victorian period, as well as including occasional references to them in articles about other buildings.[125] Everybody liked Webb's Clouds: Wilfrid Scawen Blunt had written about it in a long article for *Country Life* in 1904.[126] And in Weaver's words, Shaw's was a 'long life devoted to the uplifting of domestic architecture from the slough into which it had fallen'.[127] It is worth remembering that some of Shaw's best work had consisted of the remodelling of old houses: Flete in Devon, of 1878–80, as well as Chesters and Cragside. This was a slight but significant modification to Hermann Muthesius's opinion in *Das englische Haus*, published in Berlin in 1904–5, that Nesfield was 'far above the level of his time', and that Shaw was 'the first of the modern architects' full of 'ease and brilliance', which in time became precisely the line of descent that was adopted in outline form by modernist historians.[128] But Weaver could do what Muthesius in Berlin could not: turn this into a practical prescription for modern houses for contemporary British architects, and introduce Devey as a master builder whose work went beyond historical reference and style. At the same time,

however, Weaver laid down some hostages to fortune, making a distinction between Victorian work, which he thought too self-conscious to represent the spirit of its age, and therefore dispensable in restoration, and that of other periods, which did: conservationists have prioritised some eras or types of historical building over others ever since.[129]

The competitions that *Country Life* organised reflect Weaver's energy and activity, and they show a change in emphasis from landlord interests to architectural ones. The first of these was held at the end of 1912, with the results published in December that year and the following June; the judges were Weaver, Lutyens and A.T. Bolton. There was a competition for the design of a house in Sussex, in June 1913, won by W. Curtis Green, and then two for cottages. Then came the much heralded and grandly titled 'Country Life National Competition for Cottage Design', announced the following December. In 1914 there was a 'Golf Architecture Competition', reported in the main part of the magazine rather than in the supplement to which by this time much coverage of small recent buildings – in fact nearly all of Weaver's best-known articles – had been relegated. In addition, Weaver wrote about other competitions, such as the Gidea Park one.

Weaver is usually cited nowadays in relation to his country-house books – *Small Country Houses of To-Day*, of 1911, and his *Houses and Gardens by E.L. Lutyens*, of 1913. The

61.—GROUND AND FIRST FLOOR PLANS.

62.—THE SOUTH SIDE.

139. Walter Godfrey, who had written admiringly on Devey in 1907, turned this cottage at Chailey in East Sussex into a substantial house. Weaver thought that it illustrated two key points: the creation of a new entrance, and the re-use of old materials. The list description of 1952 describes this as a 16th-century building.

former, which was mainly a republication of articles written by himself and Tipping, introduced readers who might not have seen the original to houses by Sidney Barnsley, Walter Cave, E.J. May, Troup and Kitchin, and many more; in several cases, such as Walter Brierley, Bolton, Field, and Quennell, these were homes designed for the architects' own families. Thrown in towards the end was Webb's Red House; Weaver described its architect as 'epoch-making', and the rest of the architecture of the 1850s as 'the lowest depths of aesthetic degradation'.[130] All the houses in the book were in styles familiar to *Country Life* readers: of the 48, none were Georgian. The closest to it were three late Stuart-style houses designed in the second half of the previous decade: Newton's Luckley in Wokingham, Berkshire, which was genteelly vernacular; the grander Old Pound House in Wimbledon, Surrey, by George Hubbard and Albert W. Moore; and Cave's Bengeo House near Hertford. Nearly all had identifiable *Country Life* motifs, large or small: Dawber's Coldicote in Moreton-in-Marsh, Gloucestershire, of 1904–5, had ornamental Jacobean newel heads like

lanterns of the sort readers had repeatedly seen, as did Baillie Scott's Undershaw in Guildford of 1908–9, and Dawber used similar devices many times again. Luckley had interiors that contrasted with the Regency-cottage character of the outside: a Jacobean hall, and a fancy-French white neo-classical drawing room, both with variants of his triple-arch motif above a fireplace. Two of the houses were located by Walton Heath golf course, and Field's own golf-weekend retreat at Hook Hill was included. Morley Horder was represented by four houses, one (in partnership with A.G. Wyand) with a particularly strong contrast between its plain 'Tudor' exterior and his old-new '18th-century' interior (fig.138).[131]

The last six entries in the book were remodellings and extensions, following a section by Weaver called 'On the Repair and Alteration of Old Houses'. This subject soon provided him with enough material for a substantial volume called *Small Country Houses: Their Repair and Enlargement* which came out in 1914, altogether a didactic book which concentrated his observations on the subject. His strongly

CHAPTER XX.—THE COTTAGE, CHARLTON, OXON.

Mr. F. E. Smith's Hunting-box and Its Enlargement by Mr. Alan James—
A New Building Sandwiched Between Two Old Cottages—The Planning of
Alterations Based on Compromises—William Morris on Cotswold Building—
Oxfordshire Building Traditions.

A LITTLE decorative lead panel over the entrance door of The Cottage, Charlton, reveals in symbolic fashion to the passer-by the chief pursuits of Mr. F. E. Smith, K.C., M.P. A lamp and a book hint at his brilliant study and practice of the Law, a prancing horse marks his devotion to hunting, while Mrs. F. E. Smith is represented by a marguerite. When he first took The Cottage as a hunting-box it consisted only of the creeper-clad block to the right of the present entrance (Fig. 171). At first no more was done than to build stables and a coach-house, and to begin the laying out of the garden, which has since developed so prettily under its owners' hands. From then onward additions have been made frequently. First came a verandah and a new bedroom over the dining-room in 1908. A year later an addition was made at the south end to the kitchen offices and nursery. North of the house, and divided from it by a gap of about twenty feet, was an old cottage, which Mr. Smith acquired. The problem then put before Mr. Alan James was to connect the two buildings by a new intermediate

168.—THE ENTRANCE DOOR.

140. Weaver introduces F.E. Smith's hunting box at Charlton in Oxfordshire, complete with giant order and imposing ornamental door surround, as a 'cottage'. The architect was the young Alan James, and the work was carried out in stages from 1908.

worded introduction attacked 'over-restoration' or false restoration of various kinds, using Paycocke's as its prime example, and he repeatedly referred to SPAB in the context of work he approved of. What this suggests is that he, and Tipping, were now looking at houses as if they were churches, faced with the same questions of repair versus restoration or rebuilding. The book included both Vann and the Asquiths' Wharf, and a couple of Tipping's articles: the Old House, Aspley Guise, Bedfordshire, the 16th-century timber cottage restored by W.H. Cowlishaw for G.H. Herbert; and nearby Aspley House, a Queen Anne building where Blomfield had made 'conservative repairs' in the manner now assumed by

many much younger architects (fig.139). In this book one can find many of *Country Life's* enthusiasms: at Stonewall Cottage, near Tunbridge Wells, Morley Horder was about to convert an oast house into a billiard room and playroom; at Little Pednor Farm in Chesham, 'more New than Old', Edwin Forbes had recently inserted a South Wraxhall-like Tuscan loggia into a new wing that otherwise looked Tudor; at Wolverton Court near Stratford-upon-Avon, Williams-Ellis had applied one of his doll's-house fronts, tall, rendered, pilastered with idiosyncratic capitals and a fancy oval dormer, 'that recalls 1700', between a half-timbered wing that looked picturesque-1600 on one side and plain-and-practical-1800

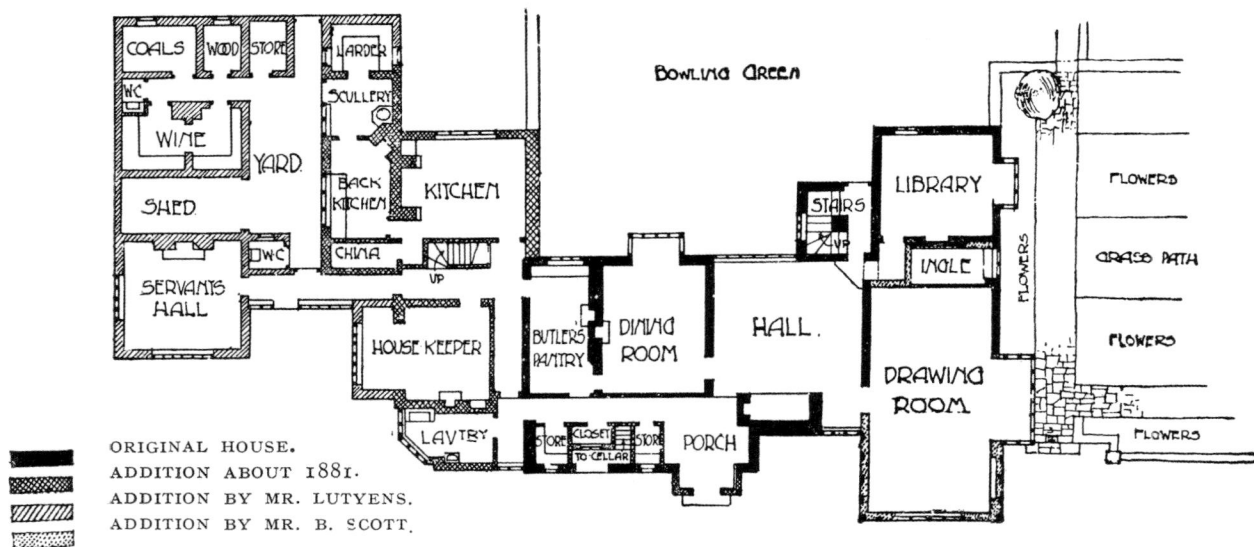

141. The form of the original five-room cottage at the core of Rake Manor, Milford, Surrey, vanished under extensions by Lutyens (in 1897) and M.H. Baillie Scott (in 1910), among others; the latter replaced a substantial chimney breast with his characteristic ingle (on the right), and only the form of the old hall more or less survived.

on the other.[132] A further theme that would now have been familiar was the alteration of a pair of cottages in stages from 1908 by an architect called Alan James on the village street at Charlton in Oxfordshire for another grand personage, in this case the politician and barrister F.E. Smith, who when the book came out was probably best known for having recently defended Dr Crippen's mistress Ethel le Neve at his trial for murder. The two old buildings were linked with a taller and grander block, at the centre of which was a pedimented door surround of collegiate appearance, with some echo to it of the monumental one at Smith's Oxford college Wadham, topped by a cherub in an aedicule; the other alterations mostly consisted of the addition of a large library at the back, and some modernisation of the kitchen offices (fig.140). As with Weaver's lesser country houses book, all the houses were supplied with plans; from this one can see how subtle interventions could be, especially in a large building such as Rake Manor in Milford, Surrey, where both Lutyens and Baillie Scott had had a hand in remodelling it, in 1897 and 1910 respectively (fig.141).

Of Weaver's many other contributions at this period, as author and as editor of the Country Life Library, one further deserves some discussion. The 'Country Life' Book of Cottages of 1913 commences with an introduction blunter, even angrier, than the one that followed in his cottage repair book. The 1909 Housing, Town Planning, &c. Act had actually reduced the number of available cheap cottages for rural labourers, as (he wrote) 1,689 were demolished to build a mere 153 new ones; Carrington's Small Holdings Acts had indeed successfully created many new buildings – 'more than all the other Housing Acts put together', but only for a certain class of person, and not the most in need.[133] The rest of the book follows a distinct trajectory: Weaver begins with further detailed studies of the cheapest cottages, and then makes a study of the work of an architect, A.H. Clough, who specialised in their design, and includes an entire specification from him. He then moves up through price levels, passing on the way the Gidea Park £375 and £600 prizewinners, and Country Life's own 1912 competition for a £600 cottage: the principal winners of this one were if anything 'Regency' or, in the case of a design by Patrick Abercrombie, 'the Regent's Park manner so studiously developed at the Liverpool School of Architecture', reflecting (as Weaver more than hints) the preferences of his two fellow judges, Lutyens and Bolton.[134]

It was Bolton who had written the succession of articles before the War on the big 18th-century neo-classical houses that had been remodelled by Robert Adam – Bowood in Wiltshire, Compton Verney in Warwickshire, and Kenwood in Middlesex – and he was the author of a book that year on Inigo Jones's early 'Jacobean' architecture.[135] As a book reviewer, probably either Tipping or Weaver, had regretfully pointed out in 1911, in relation to H.S. Goodhart-Rendel's

142. Halsey Ricardo's house for Ernest Debenham at 8 Addison Road, Kensington, London, 1905–7. Alastair Service observed that 'The popularity of classical architecture and the quiet neo-Georgian domestic style of Ernest Newton forced even some of the most idealistic Arts and Crafts architects to flirt with things they had rejected.'

Dene Place at West Horsley near Guildford, 'the pendulum is certainly swinging in the direction of Greek refinements associated with the names of Soane and Wilkins, when one sees in a 20th-century house the thin and desiccated detail and slender sash bars associated with the early 19th century'.

Very few cottages of the kind that follow across the rest of the book however were any kind of Georgian until the conclusion, featuring Lutyens and Michael Bunney at Hampstead; there are sections on repair and alteration, and grouping, and a final chapter on village planning. Weaver had identified Reginald T. Longden as an able architect at Gidea Park; the *Book of Cottages* singled out his recent isolated cottage then on Brampton Farm, and now an extraordinary survival on the edge of a roundabout outside Newcastle-under-Lyme, which provides all the exemplary characteristics of the houses he liked: ageless; dateless; Tudor; timber and brick; modelled and expressive of its parts; realist in its details.[136] What one sees repeatedly is that with a more technical mind than Tipping, he repeatedly drew on the realist tradition of expressive and practical craftsmanship in order to promote an architecture which responded very closely to what his readers experienced and needed. Historical eras were recalled through a kind of catalogue of distinct, well-functioning parts. He tended in his writing to move very fast into descriptions of costs; his cottage book insisted that it was a 'record of fact' that would distinguish it from the many picture books on similar subjects now available.[137] The architects promoted by *Country Life* stand a century later with their reputations intact, and some of the more minor ones – Dawber, Quennell, Geoffry Lucas, Curtis Green, Prentice, Cyril Farey (who twice won second prize in the magazine's competitions) – are clearly representative of the better work of their era, and were greatly published elsewhere at the time.

Indeed, when seen together with the other publications of the period, there is very little missing from *Country Life*, in addition to much that could not be gauged elsewhere. It captured the range of stances towards domestic architecture from the sentimental vignette approach to the rational calculations of the landowning cottage-builders. It covered the renewed interest in traditional forms of building – Morley

Horder designed a house in clay lump at Garboldisham in Norfolk, and Williams-Ellis was building up enough experience to publish a post-War book on cob, pisé and stabilised earth.[138] New building types emerged in its pages: seaside cottages; golf club houses; rural farm-building conversions.[139] There was also the phenomenon of well-known or ambitious architects wanting to show that they could solve the problem of the design of the small and cheap house: Weaver's *Book of Cottages* included for example a thatched cottage competing for the £600 cottage competition, by Blow and his partner Fernand Billerey, who had become known in the meantime for their grand, high-society commissions such as Lord Kitchener's 'Dutch' and Dutchified Broome Park in Kent (see fig.92), and his work for Edward Tennant and the Duke of Westminster.[140] Weaver's *The House and its Equipment* of 1912, much of it written by himself and Quennell, provided a guide as useful as any of the technical manuals of the era, and also included a chapter by Tipping on outdoor dining, a sign that living in the garden was no longer the preserve of cranks from Letchworth Garden City.[141] Here there were articles not just by Newton on domestic architecture, Halsey Ricardo on colour, Gertrude Jekyll on gardens and Troup on plasterwork, but also by architect-specialists on refrigeration, lighting systems, air gas and acetylene, dry rot and reinforced concrete. Ricardo's thrillingly colourful Debenham House in Addison Road, Kensington of 1905–7 had by this time been widely published (fig.142).

Hudson, Graham, Tipping and Weaver created and refined their era, and documented it to an exceptional level. The towering historical figure whom Weaver most resembles is the high rationalist John Claudius Loudon: as Weaver wrote in his book on cottage repairs and alterations, 'Building needs, in fact, to be brought back into the normal current of intelligent thought, instead of being relegated to the limbo of technical mysteries' – precisely the kind of observation Loudon might have made himself nearly a century beforehand – and the synthesis of architecture with other forms of aesthetic, literary and technical culture reached a zenith under his authorship.[142] In a memoir published after Weaver's early death in 1930, Williams-Ellis wrote that he questioned '*details* in every department of life, but not the fundamental'.[143] But it was precisely that, the imaginative but utterly rational remaking of the past in practice, that was the key to Edwardian architecture. It seems paradoxical, but it is the case, that the stiffness of late Victorian 'Tudor' blossomed into the romantic lush Edwardian version thanks to an interest in building details, just as it had been an interest in building details that had created Pugin's gothic revival.

The Architectural Review

The only other publication that maintained a coherent editorial position across the Edwardian period was the *Architectural Review*, which was published from the end of 1896 – a month before *Country Life* – although intermittently at first; they shared a further characteristic, which is that the *Review* too featured Webb's work at length in its early numbers.[144] It was a monthly magazine aimed at architects with many fewer pages than *Country Life*, although it did have some similarities: the photography, layout, paper and printing quality were of a high artistic standard from the start. It soon incorporated supplements with reproductions of designs by architects that had been exhibited at the Royal Academy. The magazine was interested in all forms of architecture and not houses alone, but many of its editors were, primarily, house architects, and so domestic architecture featured greatly, with quite small houses occupying whole pages in the way that the major public projects did – Liverpool cathedral, and the LCC's Kingsway and Aldwych project, for example. It also reported on substantial housing developments such as at Letchworth Garden City, and its cheap cottages exhibitions of 1905 and 1907, with long two-part articles, by Mervyn Macartney and H. Kempton Dyson (fig.143).[145] In addition, by mid-decade it

143. Percy Houfton's prize-winning £150 cottage, designed for the 1905 competition devised by J. St Loe Strachey of the *Spectator* to encourage the building of cheap but healthy cottages for agricultural labourers.

had started publishing illustrated books on recent domestic architecture, as well as on the details of historical buildings.

The *Review* was, according to Blomfield, the idea of Mallows who acted as an editorial assistant in its early days.[146] It emerged from a string of unsuccessful initiatives and, after failing itself, was published from April 1901 by Percy Hastings of Technical Journals Ltd, of Fetter Lane in the City of London.[147] The first editor, at least nominally, was Henry Wilson, a close friend of Troup, who lasted until October 1901; he was then replaced by D.S. MacColl. It was edited in practice by an advisory committee dominated by former Norman Shaw employees; Shaw himself sat on it, at least in theory, although he apparently claimed later that he did not know how he had got there. The main perk for the committee members, until it became too expensive, was a series of 'excellent luncheons' at the Savoy Hotel. As financial exigencies set in, the committee was likewise reduced to a much smaller group comprising John Belcher, Macartney, Blomfield and MacColl, of whom Macartney and Blomfield, according to Goodhart-Rendel, 'played first fiddle'.[148] Then in 1905 Hastings replaced MacColl with Macartney without consultation, whereupon Blomfield and Belcher resigned, although Blomfield's reliability in this account is somewhat compromised by the fact that in his memoirs he failed to mention Wilson at all in relation to the magazine.[149] People fell by the wayside somewhat when Blomfield took a dim view of them, and the impression from his *Memoirs* is that Wilson was a bit too off-beat.[150] But he fared better than 'a muscular little red-headed man' who had annoyed Blomfield during the latter's characteristically haphazard architectural education: 'I went for him with a low tackle, after a brief but vigorous struggle got him where I wanted, and spanked him soundly.'[151] 'He was an impatient man', Goodhart-Rendel told Nikolaus Pevsner, 'always ready for a fight, to the very end of his days.'[152]

Judging by the output, for articles were generally signed, the other members who remained active included the Art Workers Ricardo, Gerald Horsley, May, Prior and Newton, and thus Blomfield's original aim of establishing a *Gazette des Beaux-Arts* appeared frustrated, at least for the time being.[153] The first of its houses from the established arts-and-crafts canon was Prior's The Barn, in Exmouth.[154] Alan Powers has noticed that it was a group dominated by these first-generation *Review* people who, as members of the RIBA's first Board of Architectural Education in 1905, 'agreed . . . that architecture should be taught from the principles of materials and construction without reference to existing styles', which indicates an awareness of the mixed historical motifs that most architects were now combining within a single building,

at least as much as any sense that tradition was important to architectural education.[155] The *Review* called A.W. Blomfield's version of classical architecture, with windows like those of the Elizabethan mansion Hardwick Hall in Derbyshire, 'modern'.[156]

One valuable feature of the *Review* was its long, detailed and very often perceptive biographical articles. Paul Waterhouse wrote the first of these, on the life and career of Pugin, in 1897–8, presumably at Wilson's invitation, for Wilson had trained with J.D. Sedding, whose admiration for Pugin was unequalled except by Voysey.[157] There were others on George Gilbert Scott (by Martin Shaw Briggs); George Frederick Bodley (by Warren, who had worked for him); William Butterfield and John Francis Bentley (both by Ricardo); and others: these perhaps balanced for the editors the emerging 18th-century preferences of the magazine as a whole.[158] It was in the *Review* that Walter Godfrey wrote his three-part tribute to Devey, the only detailed description of his life and work in existence until 1991, and even then not quite first hand, as Godfrey was relying on the records and reminiscences of Devey's assistant and successor James Williams.[159]

The new classicists

In January 1900 a writer called George Trobridge who referred during an article on church restoration to 'the pseudo-classical "taste"' of earlier architects was clearly in a minority, because the same issue carried quite a few recent and historical examples of it.[160] The magazine's enthusiasm for classical buildings had been launched in the first volume which had included a set of detailed photographs and drawings of the Georgian Brewers' Hall in the City of London.[161] The *Review* soon maintained a long-term series called 'The Practical Exemplar of Architecture', which provided readers with measured drawings and photographs of details of mainly Georgian buildings; Macartney later put these out as books, and they became, according to Peter Davey, 'one of the most influential forces in the movement towards Classicism'.[162] It also ran a series on the work of Georgian architects including Robert Adam; and Ronald P. Jones, the Wren of Gidea Park, and who had designed a sports pavilion in Oxford in the form of a cottage with an attached Tuscan loggia, wrote on Harvey Lonsdale Elmes and Decimus Burton.[163] Mowbray A. Green wrote about the doorways of Bath, while a two-part series on London street architecture linked Georgian London with the Millbank Estate.[164] It may have been the case that the *Review*'s editors were consciously

AT ANGLEY PARK, CREMBROOK

PART OF THE SMOKING-ROOM

Mervyn Macartney, Architect

countering the continual supply of Tudor examples in the pages of *Country Life*; as Pugin and John Britton had known, as indeed did Field, architects require a steady supply of historical material if they are to launch a revival of any kind. By 1910, the 'Quality Street' houses going up in the environs of Smith Square, and the renewed interest in the old 18th-century terraces in the district – indeed, the eventual survival of a good number of them – were testifying to the effect that the *Review* was having, and to the extent that it reflected changing opinions outside the profession.

It seems likely that Prior, who contributed anonymously to the magazine, played a part in the *Review*'s stylistic manifesto; Davey has pointed out that it promoted his Cambridge Medical Schools in 1904 with its 'overt' classical styling.[165] All this had started some time before Field and Bunney published their *English Domestic Architecture of the XVII and XVIII Centuries* in 1905, and well before the architectural press beyond the *Review* started to show a preponderance of classical buildings. Buildings designed by the active editors, Blomfield's late Stuart predelictions aside, were not generally '18th-century'. Macartney had grown up in

144. Mervyn Macartney's short-lived work at Angley Park, Cranbrook, in west Kent, of about 1904, included this smoking room which combined what Osbert Lancaster later called 'the exasperating gap' where 'Jacobean' panelling stopped short of the top of the wall with classical detailing in timber and a pale 'Queen Anne' ceiling.

Devey's west Kent and began as a 'Tudor' architect (fig.144). His houses were nearly all '17th-century', mostly vernacular variants: an example is Welders House, Chalfont St Peter, in Buckinghamshire, designed in 1898 for his father-in-law C.T. Ritchie, the Conservative former President of the Board of Trade who had reformed local government during Lord Salisbury's ministry. Occasionally he experimented with grand late Stuart, as befitted the Surveyor to the Fabric of St Paul's cathedral, the post he held from 1906. Horsley, best known for St Paul's Girls' School in Hammersmith, London, designed an extension to Balcombe Place in West Sussex in castellated 'Tudor', which like the almost contemporary Kingsgate Castle was an unusual thing to do at the time for a prestigious project.[166]

Ricardo, rambling disappointingly in 1897, wrote that 'We turn to the works of the Elizabethan period with a sigh – with a tenderness, wistful and pathetic, for the chords of the heart

145. Newton's magnificent new wing at Oldcastle, Dallington, in East Sussex. This house opened the fifth volume of Macartney's *Recent English Domestic Architecture* (1912). 'It is no small achievement to have blended in such a perfect harmony so great a variety of materials,' he wrote.

on which they are struck are still in us, though withered with the weight of three hundred years, and they answer now only in the whisper of harmonies from out the world of phantasy'.[167] Yet for several years to come, beyond the world of the editorial board of the *Architectural Review*, it was actually fine new 18th-century-style domestic architecture that was so rare as to be 'out of the world of phantasy', and the *Review*'s editors, if suggesting otherwise, were being disingenuous.

From 1908 Macartney published a selection of the best available photographs of new and remodelled houses, sometimes padded out with his own work and Newton's, and accompanied by a short descriptive text, in a series of volumes called *Recent English Domestic Architecture*. The first of these, alone, included parallel texts in French and German: Ricardo had reviewed Muthesius's *Die englische Baukunst der Gegenwart* in 1901 and no doubt understood the significance of it.[168] These were high-quality picture books with few words, and provide a reasonably comprehensive overview of the houses of the decade, especially the larger ones, as well as more evidence of architects who may only have been

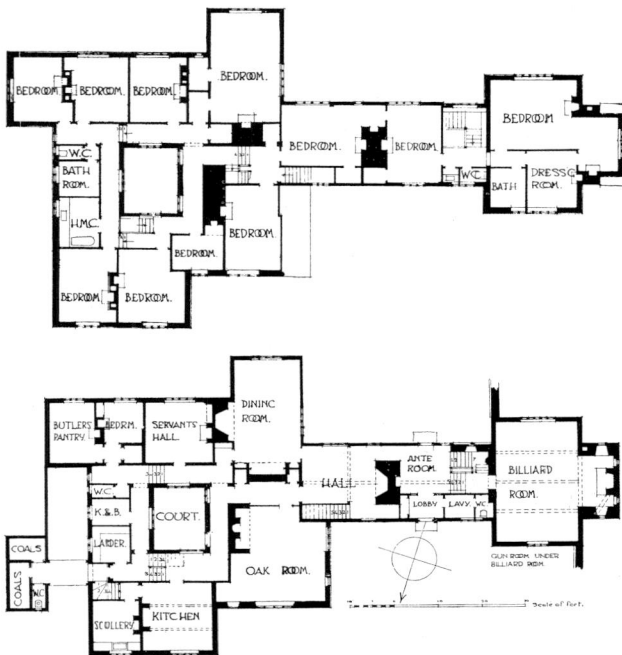

146. Oldcastle: 'Wherever possible,' Macartney continued, 'the old work has been preserved.' The large areas of masonry around the chimney-breasts indicate where this old work survived.

mentioned in passing by *Country Life* but who seem to have been approved by the *Review*: Oswald P. Milne; W.H. Bidlake; Blow & Billerey; H.R. & B.A. Poulter; Warren. The first volume included work by H. Buckland and E. Haywood-Farmer of Birmingham who built at Edgbaston and Bournville, and Thomas Collcutt, well known for his public buildings in London but whose houses had been picked up by Muthesius. Some of these volumes include useful observations, although not always aware ones. The second volume of 1909, for example, remarks at length on the fact that the tax proposals of Lloyd George's 'People's Budget' depressed the stock market and thus the incentive to build new houses; but it also notes that as a consequence, the previous year had been 'a period of marking time', whereas in fact the impact of Hudson and Tipping's views on housebuilding was clearly having an impact in terms of style, and 1908 had been something of an *annus mirabilis* for their 'Tudor' mode of building, just as it was for the Liberal government. Indeed, Macartney went on to point out, even if he did not acknowledge the source of the idea, that 'refinement and artistic perception will find means of individual expression as much in the form and manner of using materials as in the materials themselves', and went on to explain how closely the examples in the volume were related to their localities.[169] Several of *Country*

Life's favoured architects were featured with enough generous photograph coverage of their work to show that they had broader appeal without the patronage of Hudson: Quennell features occasionally, for example, as do Brierley and Morley Horder, and Forsyth & Maule as architects of new farm buildings. The magazine however featured several architects whose work was probably too eccentric for *Country Life*: apart from Ricardo, these included Prior, T.H. Lyon and Pite. It is striking how little interest Edgar Wood's flat-roofed houses – Dalnyreed near Barley in Hertfordshire as well as Upmeads in Stafford, of 1908 – seem to have elicited from the magazine at the time: in fact, Weaver had more to say about Upmeads than did the *Architectural Review*.[170]

From these books, it is both possible to see *Country Life* themes presented without having attention drawn to them. The 1909 volume featured a new farmhouse at Astonbury near Knebworth by Forsyth & Maule that could easily have been early 17th century, with no comment suggesting that this was unusual.[171] Rural houses in the early volumes are almost all vernacular 'Jacobean', some with 'late Tudor' E plans and others irregular with gables, bay windows, jostling chimneys, patches of half-timbering still half-imitating Devey, and variations on Wealden houses; even Blomfield made a very large Devey-like extension to a modest house at Wyphurst, north of Cranleigh in Surrey.[172] So the *Review* was still finding it difficult to find a decent number of houses in the style it was championing. There were however some and, surprisingly, they came from the high-art, high-craft architects: Brierley's Normanby Hall wing of 1904; Newton's short-lived Ardenrun Place near Blindley Heath in Surrey, of 1906–9, which had been photographed for *Country Life* but not used (see fig.160); and Dawber's Conkwell Grange, at Limpley Stoke near Bath, of 1907. By 1912, when Tipping and Weaver's viewpoint was clearly established, Macartney launched his fifth volume with views and plans of Newton's Oldcastle, Dallington, East Sussex, a 1910 remodelling of an old house which although slightly reminiscent of the style of his former pupil master Norman Shaw was not otherwise typical for him (figs 145 and 146).[173] A few pages later came Dawber's Tuesley Court near Godalming, built in the same year, which has a plain brick 'Jacobean' exterior, but a 'late 17th-century parlour', an artisan-mannerist inglenook arch in the billiard room, and arty fireplace surrounds (figs 147 and 148; see also fig.109).[174] Other recent houses in the volume include Percy Scott Worthington's extensive remodelling of Kerfield, near Knutsford in Cheshire, a plain Georgian house, and there are interiors by Frank Chesterton to the late 18th-century Codicote Lodge between Knebworth and Welwyn

147. The garden front of Dawber's Tuesley Court. The style here was more conventionally English than at the front of the house (see fig.109).

148. The drawing room at Tuesley Court. With Dawber, the contrast between the 'Tudor' exterior and the refined neo-classical interiors was often quite extreme. Dawber frequently used ornamental ceiling plasterwork and the type seen here was particularly popular during the decade.

149. The garden front of Upper Warren, a house by Lucas in Royston, Hertfordshire. The main part of the house is unchanged since readers of the *Builders' Journal* saw the architect's drawing of it in June 1902. Lucas lived in Hitchin and built many houses in the area.

150. A detail of the entrance front of Lucas's Yewlands in Hoddesdon, Hertfordshire, 1910: the ornamental leadwork in the windows is part of the original design. Weaver thought that the house 'errs perhaps on the side of restlessness caused by the many materials employed', but the technical quality of Lucas's work here and across his career was highly regarded.

151. (opposite) Mandeville, built in 1908, was designed by Baillie Scott and stands on the site adjacent to Yewlands. Although not one of his well-known houses, it is an exceptional building that combines a Tudor sense of form with cleverly detailed brickwork – that rises in waves over the windows, before resolving itself back to the horizontal below the upper cills – and gutters that carry the Biblical inscription 'Except the Lord build the house, they labour in vain that build it' in Latin.

in Hertfordshire that are if anything in a James Wyatt style, something that would not have been countenanced a few years beforehand.[175]

There are some town houses in Macartney's compilations. The first one included Balfour & Turner's Eaton Terrace in Belgravia, and Blomfield contributed to the fifth volume a baroque entrance hall of a house in Upper Grosvenor Street in London. The appearance of these draws attention to how rare new town houses were in any publication, in spite of the wave of expensive improvements made by leaseholders in Mayfair and Westminster, possibly because the west London estates controlled the appearance of their houses to the extent that only minimal variations were permitted from the Georgian or Queen Anne templates.[176] The Portland Estate in Marylebone, known from 1901 as the Howard de Walden Estate, seems to have allowed more

leeway than others, with decorative house fronts in and around Harley Street, but nothing too Tudor would have been permitted; Webb's 1 Palace Green in Kensington of 1867–8 had to be severely compromised before the Commissioners of Woods and Forests would allow it, as did E.W. Godwin's house for J.M. Whistler in Tite Street in 1877, so this was a restriction that London architects were fully aware of.[177] A very ornate, partly 'Tudor', partly 'late 17th-century' house by F.M. Elgood at 34 Weymouth Street is a rare exception.[178] Another factor would have been that the aristocratic clients of the expensive houses would generally have been reluctant to see their homes appearing in trade papers, especially since the most interesting work is often within, and some architects such as Cave designed rooms for these in a richer style than one might have expected from their exteriors. Arnold Mitchell's drawing for his three houses at 24–28 Basil Street in London made the composition seem a great deal more like that of the suburban houses he was building at the time, but in reality, with the deep red brick replacing the gentle pink of his watercolour, they looked quite different.[179]

The professional periodicals

Had Avebury in 1900 come across a copy of the *RIBA Journal*, the *Builders' Journal*, the *Builder*, the *Building News*, the *British Architect*, the *Architect*, probably even the *Architectural Review*, or any of the others, he would have been none the wiser about what he wanted from his architect. A look into the *Builders' Journal* at the very beginning of that year would have revealed an article illustrated with photographs and drawings of nudes – 'the male form in its perfection is, perhaps, the finest study, the grandest in construction', as the author, the architect A.R. Jemmett put it – immediately following a startling photograph of Jean-Baptiste Carpeaux's sculpture of naked frolics on the face of Paris's Palais Garnier.[180] The extensive architectural press was buzzing, even at a time when housebuilding was depressed. It was likewise unfocused. The difference between these and the two principal magazines above is that they included a much more varied range of material; in any case, neither *Country Life* nor the *Architectural Review* was

particularly concerned with small suburban villas unless they were by the best designers.

As well as construction and contract news, including announcements and competitions, there were also reports on lectures and tours, giving a picture of professional preoccupations at the time; where the *Architectural Review* reported favourably on Muthesius, the *Builders' Journal* looked at the more outré German architecture and asked on its front page whether it had 'gone mad', with its 'unhealthy craving after novelty' in its details.[181] The magazine carried a series entitled 'Men Who Build', one headed by a smouldering photograph of Morley Horder, who appeared again a few years later as 'Architect of the Day' with a further portrait, this time in pencil.[182] There was correspondence on architectural news at the time, with some personal reminiscences of older generations; there was a period, for example, when Stokes (who according to Blomfield had 'a somewhat grim sense of humour' and was 'quite uncomprising in manner') was sending in furious, obsessive letters to the *Builders' Journal*

152. Charles Mallows's Three Gables, Biddenham, near Bedford, designed for his future father-in-law in 1900. Mallows's own skill as a draughtsman in pencil belies the fact that his houses were also conceived to be beautifully coloured in reality, set in beautiful gardens. Mallows later lived here himself.

153. (opposite, above) F.L. Griggs's drawing of Three Gables is one of the most striking images of Edwardian architecture. The house and drawing were widely published.

154. (opposite, below) Mallows's own view of Three Gables, which appeared in the *Studio* in January 1910, is rather different, but in fact captures more accurately the rustic feel of the front of the house.

about the fate of Brydon's original design for the government offices on the north side of Parliament Square, executed to a modified design after his death by Henry Tanner, architect to the Office of Works.[183] Tanner seems to have been a bugbear: Blythe House, his vast Post Office Savings Bank in Hammersmith of 1899–1903, was 'the greatest artistic failure that the Office of Works have created since the completion of

HOUSE AND GARDEN AT BIDDENHAM NEAR BEDFORD, *for* H.J.PEACOCK Esq., C.E.MALLOWS *and* GROCOCK, Archts.

the bankruptcy courts'.[184] A further interesting feature was the occasional reference to houses by British architects working abroad: in 1904 Mitchell published a model of a cottage designed for King Leopold, near Ostend, and W. Campbell Jones a country house near Brussels of distinctly West Kentish appearance.[185]

It is presumably the case that the continuous stream of buildings was for the most part simply made up from those sent in by enterprising architects; nevertheless, some patterns emerge from this. Many of these were what Weaver called the 'blouse and skirt' style: those with a brick ground floor under a gabled upper storey covered in pebbledash or a pale render (not necessarily white, as old photographs suggest) or tiles; these sometimes had applied-half-timber gables and generally heavy details, especially around windows and eaves.[186] This is the style, which Osbert Lancaster later called 'Wimbledon Transitional', that the smarter periodicals managed to keep out of their pages but which dominate the more modest Edwardian suburbs: E.M. Forster's novel *The Longest Journey* of 1907 refers mockingly to the 'villa in Guildford and his mother's half-acre of garden' of a pathetic, sobbing schoolboy – that would have been one of those.[187] In fact from reviewing the magazines as a whole it is possible almost to see these

155. Mallows's *Studio* article was entitled 'Country Cottages and their Gardens', and was illustrated with many of the soft pencil drawings at which he excelled. He himself designed this pair of cottages along a garden wall.

suburbs growing up around many Surrey towns, as well as at Enfield, Stanmore, Pinner, Northwood and Totteridge in Middlesex, at Four Oaks outside Sutton Coldfield, and at many seaside locations elsewhere, from Hunstanton to Torbay.

Another pattern clear from the professional press is the fact that that Voysey dominates their pages in the early years of the century: either his own buildings, in drawings or photographs, or the many imitations of his work. Some of these added elements of their own. The most distinguished of these were the cottage and town planning pioneers Barry Parker and Raymond Unwin, who combined a Voysey appearance with interiors from Baillie Scott: the inglenooks and open plans they designed were entirely logical, given the architectural and urban qualities they promoted, and they were also, according to Diane Haigh, annoying to Baillie Scott himself when he discovered that they were doing it.[188] They even presented houses using Baillie Scott's style of

watercolour, for example of the interior of their Hill Top in Caterham, in Walter Shaw Sparrow's *Flats, Urban Houses and Cottage Homes* of 1906. They repeated this Voysey-without, Baillie-Scott-within formula in the smaller of their two cottages at Gidea Park and in Hampstead Garden Suburb, but also at many places elsewhere and on a larger scale: a house outside Chesterfield, and another at Whirriestone, near Rochdale, of 1907–9, which appeared in Macartney's volumes.[189] They did it too at the substantial Kildare Lodge in Minehead, of 1903, and outside the town a year later they included Voysey features, buttresses and chimneys, in a large new thatched cottage.[190] Macartney's first volume concluded with an unusual essay by Worthington in this style: a recent house called Ashley Green, near the village of Clappersgate near Ambleside in Westmorland, perhaps more Baillie Scott than Voysey.[191] And Voysey was everywhere in the cheap villas. This continued for some time and only began to ebb as the

156. John W. Simpson's 1904 design for a house at 2 Moultrie Road, Rugby seems to have been made up from all of the elements used by Edwardian architects in a single small building, from the Wealden house to the Voysey-inspired eaves and weathercock, with the addition of a Mackintosh-like drawing style (the architect was Scottish-born but brought up in Brighton). The *Dictionary of Scottish Architects* notes that his style was refreshed when he was joined by Maxwell Ayrton the following year. The pair later designed the 1924–5 British Empire Exhibition buildings at Wembley.

classical revival took hold and the copyists aimed for Lutyens instead: the *Builders' Journal* published distinctly Lutyensesque schemes by Deane & Braddell, and by Niven, Wigglesworth & Falkner, over two consecutive weeks in June 1910.[192]

The weekly *Builders' Journal and Architectural Record*, which like the *Architectural Review* was published from 1901 by Technical Journals Ltd, was the most representative of the architectural world around it, for it placed the villa architects' work within a continuous stream of high-art domestic architecture; not just Voysey himself, but Dawber (regularly), Newton, and Macartney's much exposed Frithwood House in Northwood in Middlesex.[193] Sometimes these were works by these architects that did not have the purity admired by Hudson or the *Review*: Dawber's Donnington Hurst, near Newbury, Berkshire, and his Park Down (or Walwood House) near Banstead, Surrey, for the military engineer Francis Acland, with their ornamental external plasterwork, are different kinds of house from the strictly vernacular, good-taste, Nether Swell and Coldicote; and Newton's The Leasowes in Four Oaks, Sutton Coldfield, with its tower, dome, half dome, tile-hanging and half-timbering had none of the 'high level of refinement' praised by Muthesius.[194] The magazine likewise published a house by Prentice which was much coarser and fancier in detail than the ones that were publicised by the high-art magazines.[195] The weekly publication and its supplement of illustrations also had space for architects who were clearly well regarded at the time but little in evidence elsewhere: it published for example C. Harrison Townsend's large, half-timbered and tile-hung

Dickhurst, in the style of Norman Shaw, east of Haslemere in West Sussex, in March 1901, and his Cliff Towers, a fine seaside house near Salcombe in Devon with a round tower along its entrance front, the following month.[196] It also published consistently good work by architects and practices it took an interest in, particularly Penty & Penty of York, and Brewill & Baily of Nottingham. Buckland's work appeared in the *Builders' Journal* before his auspicious entry into Macartney's annual volumes.[197] The magazine also regularly presented Lucas's work, mostly houses in and around Hitchin in Hertfordshire, including a double plate of the house on the Warren in Royston (figs 149 and 150).[198]

The best drawings were however by Mallows, and they featured regularly: what Lucas, Mitchell and Mallows had in common is a romantic and picturesque air that *Country Life* and the *Review* might have thought superficial (figs 152–55). Some of the better Wimbledon Transitional architects – that is, those with a lighter and more artistic touch – such as T. Phillips Figgis and A. Jessop Hardwick, who were to appear in the domestic architecture books of mid- and late decade, appear in the *Builders' Journal* more than in other publications. The *Journal* occasionally offered houses that seem to combine all the characteristics of the period into a single building. A suburban house at 2 Moultrie Road, Rugby, designed in 1904 by John W. Simpson, had many of them: a Tuscan porch, below a 'Wealden' half-timbered bay; Voysey roughcast, Voysey eaves and a Voysey weathercock; 'Tudor' chimneys; slate tiles, stone and render, better in the drawing than in reality (fig.156).[199] This was exhibited at the

Royal Academy summer exhibition in 1904 and the other professional magazines picked it up too.[200]

Given the exposure afforded to some of the best architects, it is likely that the *Builders' Journal* saw itself as closer to the *Review* than to the rest of the trade press; it is telling that in August 1902 it announced forthcoming 'improvements' in its illustrations and appearance, and in 1910 it merged its illustrated supplements into the body of the magazine.[201] The other journals were printed onto coarser paper, and their editorial direction was much less clear, although some had interests and hobby-horses. The weekly *Architect*, properly *The Architect and Contract Reporter*, published lectures and long articles, including on bye-law reform and the Cheap Cottages Exhibition in 1905, and large illustrations, often double spreads. The *British Architect*, also weekly and about 16 pages long, was printed on cheap paper which discoloured, and its full-page illustrations sometimes lost their titles when cropped for binding. It included building contract news and occasionally very brief summaries of papers given at institutions. It featured public projects, especially for the big baroque institutions of mid-decade, the Lambeth Town Hall competition entries and the Methodist Central Hall, which overpowered the domestic architecture submitted or selected. It had been this paper that first published the work of Voysey, in December 1888.[202] The lesser-known architects whom it now featured are interesting in that they provide further evidence for the fact that they were combining the features approved of by the high-art papers in a simple and sometimes crude way: over the decade the paper repeatedly featured an architect called James Ransome who was building eclectic villas like this in Wimbledon and other new suburbs elsewhere; and R. Heywood Haslam copied not only Voysey's architectural style but also his way of drawing and lettering.[203] The editors of the *British Architect* knew where they stood in relation to their upmarket rivals: a review of the architecture gallery at the Royal Academy summer exhibition was moderately sarcastic about the *Architectural Review* architects who appeared in it.[204] Very much unlike the other papers, they regularly included coarsely drawn vignettes of their featured houses by T. Raffles Davison: these were called the 'Rambling Sketches' and were enlivened with pipe smokers and relaxed ladies. They continued (as did the contributions of Ransome) over the whole of the decade. When Davison drew a Lutyens house it did not resemble one at all.[205]

Here and elsewhere in the architectural press there is little message or narrative about domestic architecture. The same is true of the *RIBA Journal*, in spite of its many illustrious lectures and debates, and useful discussions of technical innovations or legislative changes, because it saw itself as a journal of record, not of creating debate. Since the beginning of the 20th century was also the time when many of the gothic generation were dying out, the institute's official publication included long obituaries full of retrospective thoughts. The *Builder* of the period was similar, with long and methodical discussions on every aspect of design, historical, technical and legal; it also carried unpaginated supplements of illustrations but its large brownish 'ink-photo' reproduction was unattractive, and there was little sign of editorial direction regarding the appearance, planning and detailing of new houses. Here and there indications of current interests can be found in its pages: C.E. Bateman gave a long lecture on the small house, with two fine double spreads of plans and elevations. His emphasis was on practical construction, and he confessed to his audience that they might find this 'dry and uninteresting'.[206] This recognition of the practical side of housebuilding 'strikes a true note', sighed Newton, when the lecture was finally over, 'yet the result may be an uninteresting building devoid of any character or quality', thus missing the point.[207] Beresford Pite and Bolton were in the audience. In fact the editors did occasionally include interesting material, such as a design for an early art-nouveau cottage in Bickley by Curtis Green, who had been a draughtsman at the magazine for a period in 1897, and he returned five years later, in partnership with A.C. Dickie, with a pair of houses in Chislehurst, south-east of London, rendered and somewhat confused in composition.[208] A thorough article of 1905 on E. Turner Powell's Great House Court, a large new house in East Grinstead, West Sussex, built in Elizabethan style from old materials, probably marks the arrival of the type of architecture where the actual age of the elements no longer mattered to the readers of the purely trade press; and additions to Piper's Corner, High Wycombe, Buckinghamshire, by L. Rome Guthrie, from the 1909 Royal Academy exhibition, was one where the styles are so mixed – Tuscan, Tudor, in this case possibly Dutch as well – that the building gives the impression of having been altered over a long period of time rather than erected as a piece.[209]

Books and other publications

The remarkable range of publishing on house design and the consistent quality of it were key characteristics of the Edwardian period. Even the monthly *Studio*, founded in 1893, and which was not intended to be an architectural paper,

increasingly carried articles on houses over the decade. It 'went to the arty people' (Goodhart-Rendel again), and published colour plates of high quality for its articles (*Country Life* did so from 1911, and even then, only to illustrate furniture) (fig.157).[210] At this point and for at least the next five years, the style of much that was presented in the magazine was strongly art nouveau, and all its architects were those who saw themselves as artistic. There are watercolours in the Baillie Scott style, by him and by others. Ashbee wrote about his cottage and shop buildings for the Dromenagh Estate at Iver Heath, giving a great deal of attention to the landscape, and illustrated by plans and elevations but also by two perspectives by F.L. Griggs (fig.158).[211] In fact the impression is that its coverage of buildings grew from an interest in gardens, on which Prior wrote a series in 1900, including a view of his Barn in Exmouth.[212] It was in this combination of landscape and cottages with artistic architects that the magazine made its early mark on architectural publishing. Voysey was published here, and a long article on cottages included high-quality architectural photography of buildings by Blow, Spooner, and Dunn & Watson, and the pair by Field at Ripley.[213] It followed this with an article on children's book illustration by John Hassell, including a beautiful colour illustration of red-brick cottages with smoking chimneys at Bank, by the road from Lyndhurst to Bournemouth in the New Forest.[214] By mid-decade, when the fashion for art nouveau

157. One of Arnold Mitchell's picturesque houses, accorded the rare honour of a colour plate in the *Studio* in October 1909. This was designed for a site in Troon, Ayrshire.

158. In October 1905 the *Studio* ran an article by C.R. Ashbee on his designs for the Dromenagh Estate at Iver Heath, Buckinghamshire. Little Coppice, 1903, was built for £875 for Helen Wrightson, who was 'beautiful, intellectual and untidy', according to Ashbee's biographer Alan Crawford. The drawing is by Griggs.

SURREY COTTAGES · NIVEN AND WIGGLESWORTH ·ARCHITECTS

·ARDENRVN PLACE · SVRREY·
· THE ENTRANCE PORCH ·

159. Cottages at Byfleet, Surrey, by Niven & Wigglesworth in a view drawn by Lucas – after Falkner's departure from the partnership – in the regular *Studio* feature 'Some Recent Designs in Domestic Architecture', December 1905. The few cottages that were illustrated here were generally little-known examples of the best type of representative contemporary work. In the case of these ones, 'there was no especial effort made in the direction of cheapness'.

160. Newton's design for Ardenrun Place in Surrey, exhibited at the Royal Academy and subsequently reproduced in the *Studio*. The house was built in 1906–9 and became the residence of the racing driver Woolf Barnato before its destruction by fire in 1933.

had receded, the magazine presented an annual round-up of recent domestic architecture, and this in turn meant that the same familiar houses – by Dawber, Newton, Mitchell, Niven & Wigglesworth, Lucas and Mallows – began to appear here too. The canon of Edwardian architects and of their characteristic stylistic motifs was so clearly established by 1910 that it could be seen easily across all publications (figs 159 and 160).

These included a large number of books devoted to the design of the small house: not usually analytical, but giving a useful picture of how terminology was employed at the time. The *Builders' Journal* admired the illustrations in Maurice B. Adams's *Modern Cottage Architecture* of 1904, but thought that the text was 'uninstructive'; in fact it provides a record of what contemporary practitioners meant by 'the artistic cottage' and the '"week-end" cottage' (still in inverted commas), and what the commonly accepted standards were for bathrooms and kitchens, and it went into a second edition in 1912.[215] 'One is getting a little tired of large publications with

161. Welburn Hall, Kirkbymoorside, Yorkshire, designed by Walter H. Brierley and built in 1890–93 and 1895, incorporating and remodelling the early 17th-century wing (with the polygonal bay).

162. The interior of the small dining room at Welburn Hall, where Brierley seamlessly mixed old and new materials. These two photographs were reproduced in W. Shaw Sparrow's *The British Home of To-day* (1904).

rather indiscriminate pictures of week-end cottages,' wrote the *Review* in 1907, in a notice of a book edited by W. Shaw Sparrow.[216] Shaw Sparrow himself eventually contributed three of them, by the look of it funded at least in part by the advertising supplements from the furnishing shop Waring's that they included. His *The British Home of To-day: A Book of Modern Domestic Architecture & the Applied Arts* of 1904 was a compilation of large recent houses, some reproduced in

attractive watercolours, set within 'Literary Contents' mostly contributed by the architects and designers themselves (figs 161 and 162). Thus Mitchell wrote 'Plans for the Home'; Dawber 'The Home from Outside'; Norman Shaw himself 'The Home and its Dwelling Rooms'; and Macartney 'The Home and its Halls'. The artist Frank Brangwyn, with the architect Harold Cooper, contributed 'The Homes and its Bedrooms', and Herbert Gladstone's architect John Cash – in a rare emergence

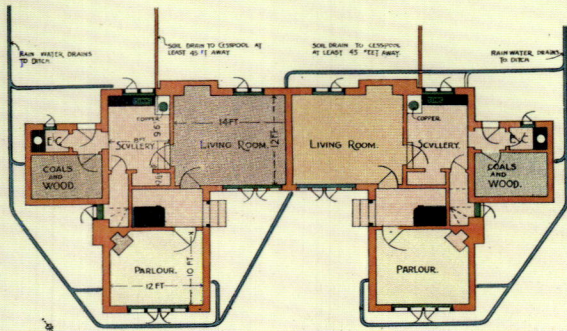

GROUND FLOOR PLANS   FRONT ELEVATION.   SIDE ELEVATION.

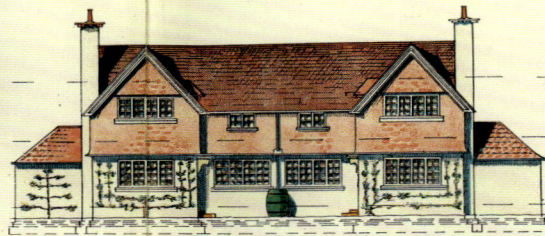

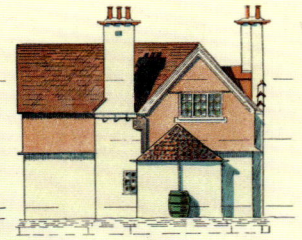

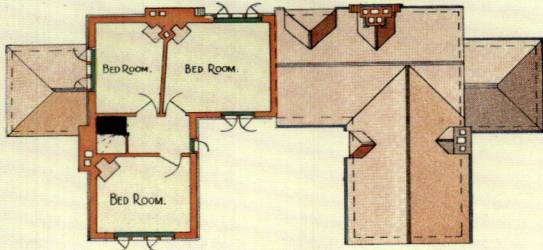

FIRST FLOOR, AND ROOF PLAN.   BACK ELEVATION.   SECTION A·A

SCALE OF   FEET.

PAIR OF COTTAGES AT BRAMLEY, NEAR GUILDFORD, FOR HENRY KEENE, ESQ.   Horace Field, Architect   BUILT AT A COST OF £665 THE PAIR. REPRODUCED FROM THE ORIGINAL DESIGN

from publishing obscurity – 'The Home and its Decorative Essentials', which were to be absolutely minimal. Everything here was in the mainstream of arts-and-crafts writing, with attention to details such as hearth brushes and table ornaments, and some of the houses were more than ten years old.

Shaw Sparrow took reproduction and artistic format seriously, and in 1906 he published a companion volume called *The Modern Home*, in which an appeal was made to 'a very much wider public'. This was firstly because the houses illustrated were generally very much smaller, including for example tiny semi-detached cottages by the architects who were by now familiar, or even famous, from their appearances in the *Review* and *Country Life*, but also because to illustrate them the book included 22 sheets of architectural drawings in 'flat tints', which he called 'a new and original experiment' carried out with the printer Carl Hentschel Ltd, 'the leading and largest firm of photo-engravers in the world', as it titled itself.[217] This gave the outlines of the little houses not only clarity and precision but also something of the character of

children's-book illustrations; in Field's drawing of his Bramley cottages, every branch of the delicate espaliered shrubs along the walls is beautifully delineated, as are his picturesque rainwater butts (fig.163). Bidlake replaced Dawber as the contributor on 'The House from the Outside', and the second billed author was Ricardo on 'The Interior and its Furniture'. Bidlake wrote bluntly that

> We do not want a new style. We are reverent as a people, and we are not only proud of the heritage which our fathers have left us, but we wish to feel that our dwelling houses trace the lineage also from those of old time, and echo by their similar disposition of stone gable or mullioned window some of the romance that attaches to old buildings.

The same sentiment pervades the modern house plan.[218] Following the pattern established by Norman Shaw and admired by Muthesius, this last generally had a large hall on the mediaeval pattern. It is worth recalling that Pugin's

163. (opposite) Cottages at Bramley, Surrey, *c.*1900, by Horace Field, from Shaw Sparrow's *The Modern Home* (1906), the successor volume to *The British Home of Today*, and an example of the printer Carl Hentschel's 'flat prints' on shiny yellow paper.

164. A thatched cottage at Bury, Sussex, by Charles Spooner, whose cottages and vernacular remodellings (unlike his rather stiff villas) were works of great subtlety and originality. Elder-Duncan wrote that 'every endeavour was made to preserve the harmony of the old work'.

revolutionary pinwheel houses of the 1840s, which had so great an effect on house planning across the country, had no such thing.[219] But late Victorian and Edwardian halls often incorporated Pugin-like staircases, or at any rate the base of them, because Pugin's sense of movement across a house was too powerful and useful a motif to abandon, and too much related in modern upper-middle and upper-class living to the etiquette and propriety associated with the different uses of rooms and the relationships between them; and they were also at least to an equal degree exactly what Bidlake said they were: romantic. An architect called A. Winter Rose drew Weaver's attention with the remodelling of Morton House in Hatfield, replacing a Georgian stair corridor with a Pugin-type hall, and this in a late 17th-century house.[220]

Shaw Sparrow's third book – the one that had occasioned some sarcasm, and some unfavourable reference to its images – was his *Flats, Urban Houses and Cottage Homes*. In fact this is a useful publication because of the detailed attention given to flats and town houses which had received little overall critique elsewhere. Some of the larger blocks had ingenious plans, with multi-faceted light wells that maximised daylight to kitchens and service areas. A chapter by Edwin T. Hall, then vice-president of the RIBA, compared their layouts with those in Paris. There were some ornate interiors, and coverage of flats converted from old houses. It was indeed, as the *Review* conceded, 'a book worth getting and keeping, and,

need we say, a notable five-shillingworth'.[221] A comparable publication was J.H. Elder-Duncan's *Country Cottages and Week-End Homes* of 1906. The editor was the secretary to the advisory committee of the *Review*, so it was not hard for him to find, as the title page proclaims, 'numerous illustrations and plans of cottages by well-known architects'. The standard of presentation was however considerably lower than Shaw Sparrow's: there was more emphasis here on the quantity of information. Elder-Duncan grouped his cottages by cost, and not by style or any of the theoretical premises that Lethaby, Pite or Ricardo addressed in the papers that they gave to the professional institutes, and he wrote introductions to each level: the Edwardian client could by this point easily be aware of the prices of buildings for houses of different sizes. For each chapter he introduced examples of recent houses of all kinds, from the *Review*'s favourites to blouses-and-skirts from little-known names, all with plans drawn by their architects rather than standardised, and photographs of interiors and exteriors. There was a reflection of the upmarket interest in using immediately local or traditional building materials: a £550 house in local red brick by Francis Bacon at Burghclere in Hampshire called Little Gravels was thatched in rye straw, with some ingenuity in its detailing: there is much evidence of architects taking an interest in this across the country, perhaps in the light of the changes to the bye-laws (fig.164).[222] Some of the other architects will by now have been familiar to readers of the professional press: here were Quennell and Morley Horder each with six houses, Brewill & Baily and Niven & Wigglesworth each with five (fig.165) and Hardwick with three. There is a sense of well-being throughout all these houses.

These books, like the magazines, largely ignored the subject of the bungalow. On the rare occasions when one was mentioned, it often turns out to be simply a small or low-ceilinged cottage like any other. A bungalow occupies more land and requires relatively more roof than the cheapest two-storey houses that *Country Life* and the others publishers were interested in, and furthermore the word, let alone the type, was possibly considered low class or unprofessional unless referring to a house in India.[223] This possibility is reinforced by a design by William Henry White for a single-storey house in Elder-Duncan's 1907 book for Oetzmann & Co., a cabinetmaker which wanted to move into housebuilding; White's perspective of it was the vignette type, with a lady in a hat under a tree, a sign of aiming for a non-professional audience.

Beyond the magazines

A feature of this period is that architects published fine-quality books illustrated with drawings and photographs of their own houses: Newton and Quennell did this, anticipating the period when architects' monographs became design objects in their own right.[224] Newton's included 62 plates, with many of his houses in south-east London suburbs of Bexley and Chislehurst; Quennell's included his Hampstead houses, and his Bickley ones; the latter, when seen together with Newton's, gave a picture of how the new suburban areas within commuting distance to London were building up. Baillie Scott did rather more: his *Houses and Gardens*, written with his partner A. Edgar Beresford, included a manifesto for open planning and integrated gardens and living rooms. In 1910–12 Parker wrote a series of 29 articles on 'Modern Country Homes in England' for an American magazine called *The Craftsman*, intending to make a book of them.[225]

In addition, this was a period when a very large number of books were published on the qualities of historic building: Field and Bunney's *English Domestic Architecture of the XVII and XVIII Centuries*, the most highly regarded of all, has been mentioned above. When Field had the budget for ornamental classical work, he did it magnificently, and the *Review*'s coverage of Shaw Sparrow's *Flats, Urban Houses and Cottage Homes* welcomed the inclusion of his North Eastern Railway

company offices in Cowley Street, even though it was clearly not a house, because it was a 'refined and scholarly work inside and out, and pleasant on the pages of any book'.[226] A second substantial book was Thomas Garner's monumental and posthumous *Domestic Architecture of England during the Tudor Period*, completed in 1911.[227] The subscribers to this included Baillie Scott, R.A. Briggs, Bunney, Caröe, Cave, Curtis Green, Dawber, Jones, Lorimer, Lucas, Lutyens, Newton, Niven & Wigglesworth, and Shaw, although not Field, Quennell or Voysey. The first plate was of the prior's lodging in Much Wenlock; Layer Marney Tower was also covered thoroughly, although no mention was made of Chancellor's recent restoration and additions which Garner, who died in 1906, might have known about.[228] The book's success resulted in a second edition in 1929. Architects also wrote books about architects: Maxwell Ayrton, who had worked for Lutyens and at this early point in his career was a Lutyensesque architect, published on his former employer, for example; and small-scale spin-offs as well as substantial ones emerged directly from magazine articles, such as Alfred W. Clapham and Godfrey's *Some Famous Buildings and their Story*, from the *Architectural Review*.[229]

Country Life published books on furnishing, antiques, gardening and sport as well as on architecture: a list at the back of Weaver's cottage book had more than forty on these subjects, including five by Jekyll. In 1897 Henry George Batsford joined his late father's small firm and turned it into the country's principal architectural publisher, from textbooks to studies of picturesque old buildings, to modern guides and technical manuals, all illustrated in drawings and photographs. His offices were in High Holborn, appropriately enough since that had been the location of Josiah Taylor's famous bookshop in the early 19th century, the source of many of the villa pattern books at the time.[230] Batsford's biographer has pointed out that he had been taught science by H.G. Wells when at school.[231] Dawber's cottage book of 1905 has been mentioned, and before that he wrote one on Kent and Sussex; possibly he then became too busy to continue, for Curtis Green contributed the text and sketches to a similar volume about Surrey in 1908. These carried photographs by W. Galsworthy Davie, but James Parkinson also illustrated one, on Shropshire, Herefordshire and Cheshire, with a text by E.A. Ould, of Robert Hudson's first architects Grayson & Ould. In addition to these, Batsford published books of different types and sizes on specific aspects of old houses, for example *Old English Doorways*, again with Galsworthy Davie's photographs, in 1903: this must be related to the contemporary interest *Country Life* was showing in building details. It was Batsford

165. The Paddock, Ruskington, Lincolnshire, by Brewill & Baily, and drawn by Lucas. There is nothing in the elevation or plan to suggest it, but this was apparently the remodelling of an existing cottage, and the 'blouse and skirt effect' was due to the need to render the upper parts of old walls to keep the heat in.

who published Newton's and Quennell's books and Garner's Tudor one, as well as *Modern Cottage Architecture*, by Maurice B. Adams, the veteran editor of the *Building News*. The newspapers contributed to this interest in different ways; Northcliffe's *Daily Mail* launched its Ideal Home competition in 1908, and William Wands's winning design, symmetrical, classical and looking like a golf club house, which was built in Abersoch in Caernarvonshire, was published in Macartney's fourth volume.[232]

In addition, countless authors and literary writers published on historical or simply picturesque or romantic architecture. Many local antiquarians and historians wrote about their towns: *The Old Houses of Shrewsbury* of 1911, by H.E Forrest, 'Hon Sec. Caradoc and Severn Valley Field Club, Author of "The Fauna of North Wales"; "Fauna of Shropshire", etc' is typical: it combined historical background and a walking tour with detailed descriptions of buildings, invaluable today for conservationists, and was illustrated by

his daughter with a Miss Moses. Arthur Martin's *The Small House: Its Architecture and Surroundings*, similarly illustrated with photographs by his brother, the Rev. J.S. Martin, was published in 1906, with a new edition three years later; it was aimed at the common-sense, 'average Englishman in search of a house', but for all this lack of pretention it was illustrated by photographs and plans of good-quality medium-sized and small houses, although only one with a credit to the architect, May.[233] The trade press welcomed it for its easy literary style, and the *Manchester Guardian* called it 'an excellent little book, simple, practical and to the point'.[234]

At this end of the market, Batsford manuals were joined by books written by those with experience of the new science of town planning. Unwin was in the forefront of these, and his writing includes a commentary on the 1909 Act, the authoritative contemporary professional view on it ever since; it seems likely, given his background in socialism and Carpenteriana, that like William Morris he had decided that the printed word was as effective a means of reform as artistic endeavour, and this was a very long book.[235] J.S. Nettlefold, the chairman of the Birmingham Corporation Housing Committee, published his *Practical Housing* at the Garden City Press, Letchworth, in 1908, its many illustrations

including plans and sections of streets and comparisons with planning in other parts of the world. P.H. Ditchfield, the rector of Barkham near Wokingham, long-term secretary of the Berkshire Archaeological Society and a contributor to the Victoria County History of Berkshire, wrote sentimental books for Batsford and Methuen with literary and artistic collaborators: *Memorials of Old Kent* (1907); *Memorials of Old London* (1908); *The Charm of the English Village* (1908); *Vanishing England* (1910); *The Manor Houses of England* (1910). In retrospect it seems that there might have been a sense for architects who came across them that the appeal of Tudor architecture was in danger of being seen as a short-cut to nostalgia. In such quantities it might also have been predictable and boring for many, and nudged the *Architectural Review*'s classical campaign a stage further.

Muthesius

Given the century-long influence of his writing on British architecture, it is impossible to conclude without referring to Hermann Muthesius. His direct influence on the

166. Thomas Collcutt's The Croft, Totteridge, now in the London Borough of Barnet, of 1898, identified as a significant recent house by Hermann Muthesius. It was designed to look as if it had been constructed in phases over centuries. Photographed by the author in April 2018.

contemporary architecture of the time must be limited, because his monumental *Das englische Haus* in 1904–5, and his picture book *Landhaus und Garten* of 1907, with its long section on high-quality recent English houses, were published only in German, in Berlin and Munich respectively; so only the connoisseurs, but not the mass of villa builders, will have seen them. What makes Muthesius's writing interesting is that he managed to arrange the various ideas common to Edwardian housebuilding into an organised and mostly chronological commentary, which also provides a comprehensive record of the use of rooms by upper-middle-class clients, and the technical fitting out and standards that they required. And in so doing he had a sharp eye for discerning which houses best demonstrated the most interesting tendencies, even if he did not necessarily say so explicitly.

The line of descent that Muthesius assembled in *Das englische Haus* was very similar to that of Tipping and Weaver's *Country Life*, which it mostly predates in terms of publication. It was from 'the brilliant' Pugin, and then through Webb and Shaw, that British architecture was transformed: no doubt the imperial German embassy in London had subscribed to the magazine.[236] Where he deviates from it is in the importance he gave to Voysey, whom he evidently found to be a genuinely thrilling designer; in fact he launched the British section of his *Landhaus und Garten* with the unusual rear view of Voysey's house on the Hog's Back at Puttenham for Julian Sturgis. The first hundred or so pages of the first volume of his greatest work are about the history of the English house from pre-mediaeval times onwards, and as Muthesius reached the present day, he departed from his chronological account in order to stress the importance of vernacular architecture over the centuries to what he called the 'scientific' approach to house design.[237]

The whole first section on the 'Development of the modern English house', entitled 'The Earlier Architects', is the one that in art historical terms fixed the story of British late 19th-century architecture. This part ends, however, with one of the architects not generally referred to in that canon, and who is best known now for his lush commercial work: Collcutt, the architect of the English Opera House, now the Palace Theatre, in Cambridge Circus in London (1888–91), and of the Savoy Hotel (1886–9 and 1903–04), as well as the Imperial Institute in South Kensington (1887–93), and like Webb and Romaine-Walker a former pupil of George Edmund Street. In that context Muthesius's conclusion of his grand narrative with the inclusion of a pair of his smaller houses seems at first surprising. The very last is a drawing of The Gables, in Fifield in Oxfordshire, of 1893–4, but the final photograph is a revealing one: this was The Croft, Collcutt's own house in Totteridge, north of London, of 1898 (fig.166).[238] The combination of the building materials – a little ornamental plasterwork in a Jacobean artisan mannerist style as well as brick, stone, render and half-timbering – make this look as if it had been built gradually, and not all at once. To the left of the entrance front there is a service stair corridor at an angle linking the former kitchen offices wing to the house that surely had been intended to look as if it had been added later, for the plan within is contrived. Muthesius had, whether by intention or not, displayed one of the most telling attributes of Edwardian housebuilding: that it was possible to go back into the past and to start it running again towards the present day, but this time better.

167.   A door handle and plate from Mallow's Three Gables, Biddenham.

4

THE PEOPLE'S MAGIC

—

'Where are we going?' they asked the Ball, and it
answered with a sparkling green and red smile—
'To the most delightful place in the world.'
'What's it called?' asked Selim.
'It's called Wheredoyouwanttogoto,'
the Ball answered, and on they went.

E. Nesbit, 1901

EDWARDIAN AUTHORS OF ALL KINDS repeatedly touched on the idea of returning to and remaking the past; maybe this was in part due to the spread of a wider concept of the purpose and interpretation of archaeology that Augustus Pitt Rivers had promoted.[1] George Bernard Shaw's play *Pygmalion* was written in 1912 and it followed this pattern in two ways. The first is that it remade the classical story as familiarly set out by the Roman poet Ovid, so that Eliza, Shaw's modern Galatea, fails to marry the man who created her – to Shaw's emancipated way of thinking an improvement on the original. But it is possible to look beyond this and see that he was also writing about the possibility of one human being entering the mind or the soul of someone else, using scientific methods to remake her

as someone different, in this case more fulfilled, than she had originally been. This is a reasonable allegory to what architects were doing at that period to old cottages. In fact, the cottages are much more Eliza than they are Galatea, because they were always real; like Eliza they were scorned until rational, modern, educated people took them out of the gutter.

The best and most aware writers occasionally remade the past like this in ways that seem to capture even more of an architectural story. In *Harding's Luck* of 1909, the children's author E. Nesbit, who had been in love with Shaw, tells the story of Dickie Harding, a lame child from the slums of Deptford, full of initiative and adventure; thanks to a family charm he has inherited from his late father, he moves back and forth between 1906 and 1606, where he becomes Richard

Arden. This type of going backward or forward is a recurrent theme for Nesbit; her characters and narrators wonder how history can be made in this way, and how an entire past, a back story, can be created for those who find themselves suddenly living in a different era – as well they might. In the second part of the book the narrative becomes increasingly fantastical, and merges characters and events with those of her previous novel *The House of Arden*, of 1908. In both stories, a young brother and sister called Edred and Elfrida join Dickie in a search for hidden treasure within the walls of Arden Castle, their ancestral home, in order to bring about its restoration.

From 1893 Nesbit kept a holiday home in Dymchurch in Kent, on the edge of Romney Marsh, and she knew the area well.[2] Arden, with its bailey and ruined chapel, just outside 'a very bright town by the sea', might have been based on Saltwood Castle near Hythe. In Nesbit's novel 'there were red roofs at one side . . . where a house had been built among the ruins', as there was at Saltwood, which before post-war restoration had a patched-up residence of the 1880s occupying part of it.[3] There is a suspicion, however, that her description

168. (p.172) A corner of The Wyck, near St Ippolyts, Hertfordshire, incorporating mediaeval or Tudor, recycled, Victorian and Edwardian, and recent work: it is impossible to distinguish between the different periods.

169. The vivid red roofs of Frank Tennant's Lympne Castle, seen here on the service wing which was visible from the street. E. Nesbit's castle restoration stories were not as fantastical as they might seem today.

had also been inspired by Lympne Castle, for unlike Saltwood Arden was perched on the very edge of the Downs looking towards the sea, and furthermore the Tennants' new house within it had prominent and unusual red roofs (fig.169).[4] Indeed, the fact that Nesbit refers to the children wanting to build 'nice dry warm cosy cottages for the tenants' nearby after they had taken over the castle themselves, a joke made more than once, is a reminder that as an impoverished upper-middle-class Fabian, she did not mind poking fun at the well-connected, self-made Liberal gentry: Thomas Fisher Unwin, who published many of her books, was the son-in-law of Richard Cobden, the Victorian radical.[5] Given the proximity of the dates, it seems likely too that the 'wonderland of Italian scenery' that surrounded the building at the centre of her 'Enchanted Castle', in her book of that name of 1907, was inspired by the Italian garden with marble nymphs nearby that William Waldorf Astor was then creating at the newly re-Tudorised Hever, the one that Lord Avebury had found out of place.[6]

Nesbit, like her hero Charles Dickens, was not particularly consistent with her architectural or topographical descriptions, and at the end of *Harding's Luck* Arden Castle reverts to how she had originally described it in her earlier book: around a courtyard; on the edge of a cliff; by the sea; surrounded by sand and a warren of smugglers' caves. Exactly like Kingsgate, in fact. The nearest town to Arden Castle is called Cliffville, not unlike Cliftonville, just west of Kingsgate Castle; and Nesbit's Dymchurch appeared in her stories as Lymchurch. Nesbit had certainly visited Thanet and she might, like so many other day trippers, have seen Avebury's castle herself.[7] But the point of this is that the magical restoration of castles in her stories was not an act of imagination alone: it was a fact. Hever Castle had been restored by the time of *Harding's Luck*; Sir Martin Conway was just getting going at Allington, also in Kent, not to mention Hudson at Lindisfarne and many other examples elsewhere in England.[8]

All this might testify to Nesbit's affection for the Kent coast and her politically keen awareness of the grandees who were moving into it. But *Harding's Luck* for the most part is about the redeeming qualities of Jacobean life and the urge to escape from the idea of history as being a place in the past alone. The author's disgust for the revolting nature of urban slum life, the 'horrid little houses' from which Dickie first emerges, is balanced throughout the book by the descriptions of the early 17th century to which he occasionally returns – the beautiful house with its long, low stone-mullioned windows; its gardens; its greenery; its elegant river barges festooned with flowers. From this ravishing past, this 'magic world' in which Dickie is no longer lame, he brings forward in time various objects of redemption for Jim Beale, the tramp and beggar who has adopted him.[9] Even when her story is set in the present, Nesbit takes elements from that version of the past with the same aim: the first act in modern London that starts to change their fortunes comes after Beale has thrown his coat over a puddle for a grand lady in imitation of Sir Walter Raleigh, and is rewarded with a generous tip.[10]

It is also from the past that Dickie brings forward a new skill he has learned there as a joiner, and in the present he makes expensive mahogany boxes from discarded sofa legs and can thus embark on his road to fortune. The past is thus not only beautiful but 'real' in the way that its artefacts make possible real change in modern life; by the end of the story, 'Beale was a new man, a man that Dickie had made'.[11] Indeed, an explicit theme repeated at length through all this is that it is not clear which of the Jacobean past and the Edwardian present is the reality, or which Dickie's dream: perhaps both; perhaps neither – a device used by later children's novelists such as Catherine Storr (born in 1913) and Philippa Pearce (in 1920) in order to emphasise the metaphorical nature of their stories. In other words, the passing of time has no significance to the story. It does not matter whether something is old or not; history is not a working out, a developing theme that goes only one way.

Precisely the same can be said about the Edwardians' attitude to their Jacobean houses. The socialist Nesbit and the patrician-radical-Liberal Carrington could no doubt both have agreed that making new houses for the industrious labourer, houses that smelled of hewn timber and fresh mortar as they had done three hundred years previously, was a way of establishing a new English political covenant with the people and the land. Dickie's Jacobean house lay over the site of the modern slums, the 'streaks of dull yellow and filthy brown' where he had grown up: redemption comes to the building and the place as much as to the people in it.[12] The process by which this happens is 'real'; the resulting redemption is 'magic'.

The language of magic and of escape preoccupied all manner of people during this period, and flashes of it appear in interesting places. Peter Quennell said that his architect father hated the 'little grey streets' of his Kennington upbringing, as well as 'Dickens' little grey people' in them; they may have been better than the 'horrid little houses' of Deptford but he could not wait to escape from them (curiously, Nesbit remembered her own childhood house in Lower Kennington Lane 'as an Eden' that had been demolished to build houses like the Quennells').[13] Of his father's developments at Bickley, Peter Quennell wrote in his memoir that he remembered

> picnicking with my nurse in a flowery meadow full
> of buttercups, meadow-sweet and cow-parsley, and,
> as we left, seeing a cart arrive, which rolled heavily
> across the grass and discharged a load of bricks. It
> occurred to me – and the thought was saddening;
> even then I had learned to regret the past – that I
> should never picnic there again. Otherwise I greatly
> enjoyed watching brand-new houses spring up.[14]

This would have been in about 1906, and it is likewise possible to see in it the curious backwards-and-forwards child-like

THE KING HAD TURNED INTO A VILLA RESIDENCE.

170. Claude A. Shepperson's illustration to E. Nesbit's 'The Cockatoucan'. Given the author's penchant for anti-establishment jokes, this could well be a reference to King Edward VII himself.

171. Mr Hipp, Tommy Hipp and Mabel the guinea pig enjoying the seaside. An early children's book illustration by W.H. Romaine-Walker.

emotions of regret and excitement that follow Nesbit's characters, even her many comic ones, throughout her stories, so that they are perpetually conflicted.

Alison Lurie's analysis of Nesbit's use of magic points out that its narrative power derives from being conveyed through real experiences of other places, rather than 'becoming sentimental and escapist'.[15] Indeed, the realistic, unpretentious, unpreachy dialogue of Nesbit's naughty or adventurous children runs parallel to the ways in which architecture was described in the professional press as a real thing, as a series of technical processes married with respect for quality and reality. It is telling that the climax of *The Enchanted Castle* arrives when a statue which has come to life explains to the puzzled children that a magic ring that has caused so much havoc by granting their wishes in a haphazard way needs only to be told *exactly* what the wish is: then it will be granted perfectly satisfactorily.[16] As Avebury had said at that library opening in Gloucester, 'Novels are very

interesting, very refreshing & many of them very instructive'.[17] Nesbit's magical buildings, like Avebury's Kingsgate, are very instructive not only about the real-life castles of her day but also of the motives of those that built them. In one of her comic short stories, a king turns into 'a villa residence, replete with every modern convenience', which could be a delightfully absurd evocation of Edward VII at hard, vulgar Sandringham (fig.170).[18]

Nesbit's stories have illustrations that are sometimes comic and sometimes romantic. The latter are often similar in style to those submitted by architects to the professional press and the Royal Academy exhibitions. Several architects drew romantic perspective views for others; both Charles Mallows and Geoffry Lucas freelanced for the Nottingham practice of Brewill & Baily, for example (see fig.165).[19] Others chose artists who specialised in romantic views: F.L. Griggs, who was perpetually impoverished, evidently found work like this because he crops up several times (see figs 153 and 158).[20] Avebury's architect W.H. Romaine-Walker, whom his friends likened to Dickens's Mr Cheeryble, had a parallel career as a writer and illustrator of fantastical children's books; in an early one of 1893, *Mr Hipp or Three Friends in Search of Pleasure*, the hippopotamus of the title takes Tommy Hipp and a guinea pig called Mabel on a seaside holiday. It is a silly and jolly story, delineated in simple lines and colours (fig.171).

At the turn of the century the London publisher John Lane was specialising, through its Bodley Head imprint, in high-quality editions of children's stories: strange insects and wild, anthropomorphic flowers were everywhere. *Fairies I Have Met* (1910), by Mrs Rodolph Stawell and illustrated by Edmund Dulac, was a typical one. According to an advertisement for it, Dulac's drawings 'possessed the real romantic quality which ordinary mortals leave behind them in the schoolroom'.[21] For the Bodley Head, Romaine-Walker provided the illustrations to Charles Young's *Tales of Jack & Jane* (1906 – 'very artistically drawn and coloured . . . humorous and imaginative') and *Nightcaps for the Babies* (1907), as well as for their 1907 edition of Lewis Carroll's *Alice's Adventures in Wonderland*.[22] Drawings like these add to Romaine-Walker's 'Cheeryble' image that Jelley had recalled and show a playful side to his character (fig.174). The backdrop for the Mad Hatter's tea party is a thatched cottage with hares' ears as chimneys. One undated drawing by Romaine-Walker called *Hauling the Figurehead* shows a boat house that resembles a church (fig.175). This is not as surprising as it might sound, because his *Builder* 1883 debut had been

preceded a few months earlier by the magazine's publication of a set of designs by an architect called Charles H. Cooke for lifeboat stations that do indeed have bellcotes, aisles and in one case even a chancel arch. So as with Nesbit, an apparently fantastical depiction was in fact almost precisely real.

The suburban landscapes designed by Edwardian architects, by the sea or around golf courses, were ways of realising dreams about having fun. Wheredoyouwanttogoto, in Nesbit's story, is the seaside, a perpetual holiday eventually turned into an ugly, dusty street when the children start behaving like squabbling adults. The Edwardian ideal is that the ugly is turned into the beautiful, and stays like that. The fact that Chequers Court in Buckinghamshire is so familiar now as an official residence of the prime minister should not

172. Comic heraldic newel post finials on Robert Lorimer's principal
173. staircase at Lympne Castle. This style of ornamental work is intrinsic to Edwardian house design.

174. Romaine-Walker's later, more theatrical illustrations reflect the passion for fairies and flowers that became very popular with Edwardian families. This one is called *An Exotic Garden*. Courtesy Chris Beetles Gallery, St James's, London, WWW.CHRISBEETLES.COM

175. *Hauling the Figurehead*, by Romaine-Walker. He, in common with other artists, had looked back into his own past for inspiration: the fact that the boat house here looks like a gothic church is less surprising than it might appear because designs of exactly that kind had appeared in the *Builder* shortly before his own debut there, in 1883. Courtesy Chris Beetles Gallery, St James's, London, WWW.CHRISBEETLES.COM

obscure the fact that it was a romantic remaking of 1909–10 by Reginald Blomfield of a Tudor mansion spoiled in the early 19th century, built over the foundations of a mediaeval house, with modern kitchens and with a beautiful garden designed by H. Avray Tipping.[23] Sir Arthur Lee, who gave it to the state, was a Conservative turned Liberal; and the first prime minister to enjoy it, from late 1917, was David Lloyd George. Blomfield designed what he called 'protuberances' onto the new ceilings so that people would think that they were 16th century.[24] It was a comfortable show house for grand parties. Lee stipulated that the house could never be changed. It has thus remained that perpetual, fantastical, Edwardian long weekend.

One of the most famous of all children's stories about remaking people is Frances Hodgson Burnett's *The Secret Garden*, of 1911 (fig.176). In this, a spoilt young orphan is sent to live with her uncle in a big house in a remote part of Yorkshire; she discovers her late aunt's locked and abandoned walled garden and together with her sickly cousin she remakes it: both she, and he, are remade themselves as healthy people in the process. Burnett wrote the story after hearing a false report that the walled garden at Maytham Hall which she had once leased had been destroyed and replaced by a cabbage patch when Lutyens created his big new house for Jack Tennant; the garden and house had been her favourite places and this was her way of recreating them.[25] The lasting appeal of this story is sometimes thought to be due to the way in which it touched on so many Edwardian preoccupations. *Country Life* took however a somewhat sardonic attitude to it on publication: their book reviewer commented that 'If this resolves itself somewhat into a "Christian Science" story, it is doubtless none the worse for that'.[26]

176. 'A boy was sitting under a tree, playing on a rough wooden pipe': Mary first encounters Dickon in one of Charles Robinson's illustrations to Frances Hodgson Burnett's *The Secret Garden* (1911). The story is about redemption through nature, but it is also about remaking people as healthy and fit, just as Shaw's *Pygmalion* (1912) is about remaking Eliza.

It is interesting in that light that the magazine had asked Frederick Greenwood to contribute the article on 're-countrified England' in 1904, the one in which Hudson's Deanery Garden had made one of its surreptitious appearances. Greenwood was the author of *Imagination in Dreams* of 1894, an attempt to make an argument for rationalising the irrational. Greenwood's argument was that dreams, representing pure imagination, were a representation of intuition – in other words, that the dreamers see pictures of things or undergo experiences which relate in some way to their intuition about what they have been through in reality. There is no augury, no divine or other message in them:

dreams are rationalised, but still mainly incomprehensible, reactions to events.[27] Greenwood claimed in his book that these ideas, which he had previously published in the *Contemporary Review* and the *New Review*, had been 'favoured with a good deal of attention'.[28] That would certainly be consistent with the evidence of the architecture of the period. The Tudor and Jacobean houses of Gidea Park, for example, reflect this explicitly, and architects and developers were aware of it at the time: the exhibition catalogue captioned a view of a group of picturesque half-timbered Tudor houses in Heath Drive with the words 'Real oak timber in real cottages' – that is, the houses were dreamy and romantic in their historical references but all the same they were real, they were rational, they were new and they were actually there.[29]

Structured intuition

There is therefore a sense that this rationalised, structured intuition was playing a part in the design of new and remodelled Edwardian houses. The rather stiff new houses that appeared in the *Builder* of 1883 that Romaine-Walker and his young contemporaries will have seen did themselves look like assemblies made from parts of different houses, albeit mostly Elizabethan or Tudor ones: they were the result of architects copying the work of Norman Shaw. But by the end of the century, the masterful way in which George Devey had earlier handled these assemblies had filtered through to a wide audience; the respectful references to his work in the architectural press generally testify to this, as do the ways in which Devey devices crop up in buildings. There are examples too of how what were presented as characteristic local building forms in the evocative Batsford books were adapted and moved as Devey had adapted and moved the Wealden house type (fig.177): Gillian Whitley Roberts has recently shown that William Weller, an Edwardian architect in suburban Wolverhampton, was using in new buildings a type of timber front called 'Salopian', which was supposedly old, but in fact is likely to have dated from imaginative late 19th-century remodellings.[30] The buildings Weller designed in this Devey way were greatly superior in quality to those he produced before or later.

Herbert Gladstone's Deveyesque house at Littlestone-on-Sea, with its pert diaper brickwork and sharply delineated historical detailing from different periods, is a good example precisely because his architect John Cash was not well known; beyond his contribution to Walter Shaw Sparrow's book,

177. 1–3 Rogues Hill, near Penshurst, Kent, designed by George Devey in the 1860s or 1870s for Lord De L'Isle and Dudley. This was Devey's reinvention of the Wealden house type and it was much imitated over subsequent decades.

he does not appear to have put his own thoughts into print. The principal aspect of it that pins it down into the late 1890s is the touch of late 17th-century styling in the bay windows and above the front door. Unlike earlier assembly buildings, all this is dry, clear, slightly austere. Something was attracting architects to this type of juxtaposition of constructional motifs even before *Country Life* noticed it, and Tipping's championing of a distinct set of exemplary projects from a Society for the Protection of Ancient Buildings perspective – Webb at Great Tangley, Shaw at Flete or Chesters, other recent country-house remodellings – had all generated a sense from the recent past of what a house should look like. Popular 18th- and early 19th-century architectural illustrations, from James Basire's engravings of Kingsgate to the work of the influential illustrators of Charles Nodier's great *Voyages pittoresques et romantiques dans l'ancienne France* published over several decades from 1820, had romanticised buildings with picturesque landscapes and figures; A.W.N. Pugin had not been immune to it, but he, Devey and the realists had pulled hard in the opposite direction from the 1840s onwards to convey facts about buildings and their materials, sometimes without much apparent regard for the coherence of their own compositions.

It seems that for most consumers of it, Edwardian domestic architecture succeeded in resolving the conflict between these two poles, the rational and the sentimental,

both equally attractive to the great mass of people who design or build with limited creative imagination of their own. This is where the 'structured intuition' may have been running. The result was more than a decade of houses beautifully poised between the two. W.R. Lethaby, according to J.W. Mackail, lived 'not with his head in the clouds, but with his head in air which had something superterrestial about it; and when he descended to the ordinary levels of earth he was often like someone who had strayed into darkness'; that conveys a sense of someone reconciling two extremes.[31] E.S. Prior's houses, which according to his texts aspired to high-art ambitions, looked as if they were made out of rubble. Edwin Lutyens's long appeal may be due to the fact that such pretty houses were designed by someone who took a fastidious approach to the technical details of construction. The same could be said of the best, most appealing and original church architecture of the period, by Henry Wilson and C. Harrison Townsend: it was simultaneously earthy and ethereal, and that is where their mystic quality comes from. Ideas like these will easily have filtered down the profession: T. Phillips Figgis, an exemplary but little-recognised Edwardian suburban villa architect, had worked with Wilson on the design for the Ladbroke Grove public library in north Kensington, London, in 1891–4.

With this in mind, it is possible to re-evaluate the leading architects of the period in order to see what else, beyond what has already been written about them, may

have contributed to the impact that they had at the time. C.F.A. Voysey is the single architect whose work stands up to any manner of reinterpretation. No other architect was as imitated as Voysey during the Edwardian period, in presentation and even lettering of drawings as much as in style. What made him so appealing? He presented his elevations and perspectives as if they were illustrations for children's stories; yet his architectural method was derived directly from Devey, and indirectly, like Devey's, from Pugin. By placing finely reduced architectural elements against the white backdrop of his rendered walls, he was drawing attention to them as individual objects. Thus at Perrycroft outside Malvern his oriel brackets look as if they have been reduced from the uprights of a Tudor hall screen; against the white background each one is individually read and understood (figs 178 and 179). Greyfriars (formerly Merlshanger), the large Sturgis house on the Hog's Back outside Guildford, is usually illustrated by Voysey's long, low perspective, but the other side of the house was quite

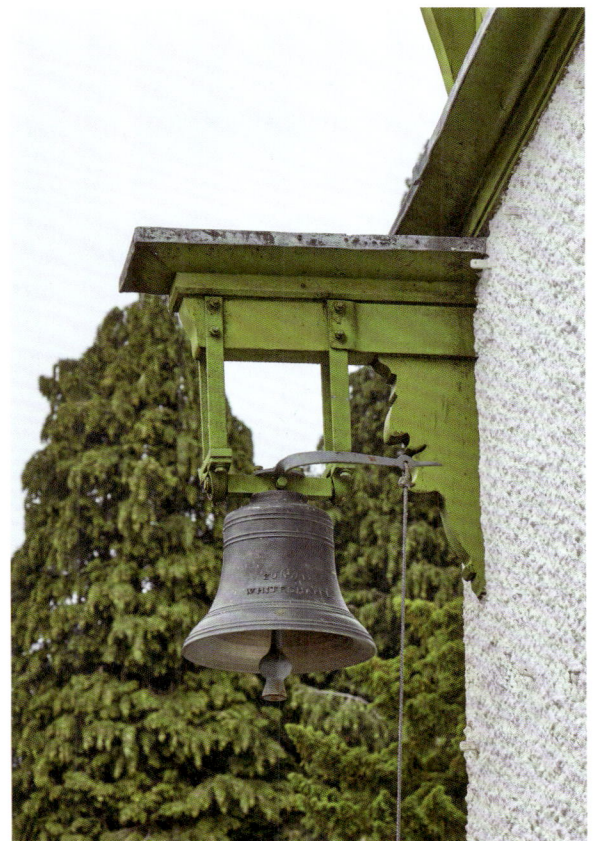

178. Oriel brackets at Perrycroft, near Malvern: by using the white walls as a canvas, C.F.A. Voysey could emphasise both the individual character and the structural role of his grotesque profiles.

179. Another grotesque face at Perrycroft, this time acting as a bracket for the front door bell.

different, an assembly of distinct elements including a square corner tower, like the one of the 1560s at Cotehele in Cornwall: it looks as if Greyfriars particularly interested Muthesius, who chose this unfamiliar view for the start of the British section in *Landhaus und Garten*.[32] Thus Voysey could convey on the outside of a building elements from the inside that are associated with hospitality and warmth, qualities that were important to him, drawing attention to them as objects but also playing out to the public eye some aspect of the historical past. The single Jacobean bow window he inserted into the front of an existing house 73 Fitzjohn's Avenue in Hampstead shows how a brilliant and unexpected device can transform an entire building (fig.180). In the course of remodelling the interior of this plain brick Victorian house, Voysey formed a new hallway that widened from the door like a flask in plan, with a fireplace behind columns in a narrow section to the side, lit by an angled bay that faced the door; he added a long, low bay-window projection to the side of the long drawing room, and the new stone-mullioned bow window lit

the dining room at the front. This bow, and the porch with its angled bay, emerge on the outside as if they were pushing through from within, as if the surface of the brick house has ruptured as some alien forms burst through it, a signal of the riot the architect has caused inside.[33] This approach has much in common with contemporary European art nouveau. Critics who disliked that would refer to Hector Guimard's or Victor

180. 73 Fitzjohn's Avenue, Hampstead, 1901–3. The ground-floor bow window and porch frame are almost all that survive of Voysey's remodelling of this mid-Victorian house following a 1938 makeover, but they still convey magnificently the distinctive characteristics of Edwardian architecture: the careful mixing of different periods of building, and the clever juxtaposition of unfamiliar elements to create something entirely new.

181. (opposite) An apparently unexecuted design by Voysey of 1898 for a house at Limpsfield, Surrey, for C.A. Sewell, illustrated for Shaw Sparrow's *The Modern Home* (1906) in one of the experimental colour plates. The clarity of the reproduction and the architect's characteristic colouring show the way in which he used white walls to emphasise his detailing.

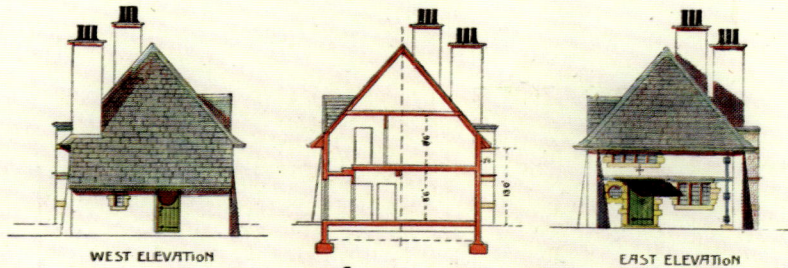

WEST ELEVATION

EAST ELEVATION

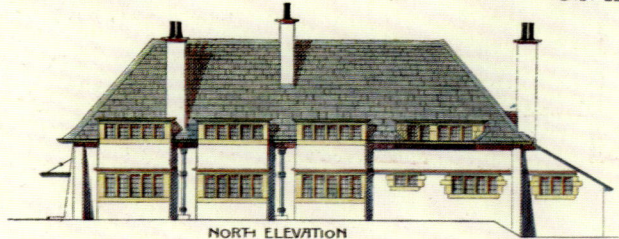

NORTH ELEVATION

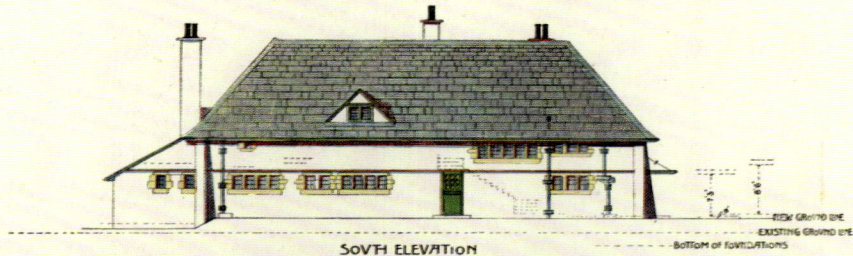

SOVTH ELEVATION

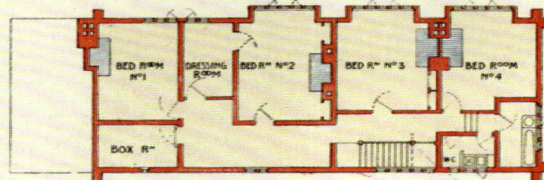

BEDROOM PLAN

BED R⁰ᵐ N⁰1 DRESSING ROOM BED R⁰ N⁰2 BED R⁰ N⁰3 BED ROOM N⁰4

BOX R⁰ᵐ

WASH HOUSE KITCHEN LARDER DINING R⁰ HALL DRAWING R⁰

COALS SCVLLERY WINE PANTRY CVPBOARD LAVATORY

GARDEN ENTRANCE

BANK

MAIN ENTRANCE

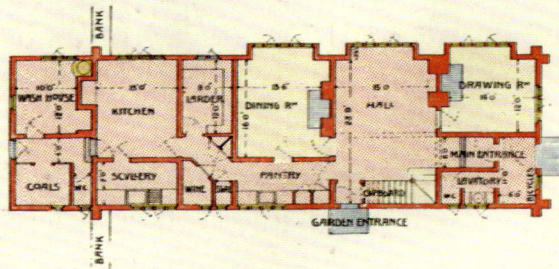

PROPOSED HOUSE FOR LIMPSFIELD, SURREY, TO BE BUILT OF BRICK AND CEMENT ROUGHCAST, WITH A
ROOFING OF GREEN SLATES, WINDOW DRESSINGS OF BATH STONE, IRON CASEMENTS, TARRED CHIMNEY-POTS

C. F. A. Voysey, Architect

Horta's tendrils as parasitic, as a kind of skin disease; but Voysey's remodellings and perhaps his new buildings were parasitic too in a sense, in that one style was inhabiting or taking over another one, and with perfect, resolved detailing at the points where the styles or periods of building fabric meet. This is more a profound kind of architectural parasite than can be achieved by a style, like art nouveau, that might go out of fashion.[34] The beautiful poise of the new elements he introduced through the facade and their balance with the old work are a revelation of what his architecture was doing, drawing attention to the physical nature of the correct constructional solution, deploying the elements of historical craftsmanship reduced to their essentials.

This was a very sophisticated way of designing, and in terms of aesthetic and intellectual coherence, very few came close to it. Lethaby's Avon Tyrrell, which was extensively published, allegorised Tudor architecture like this – that is, by turning elements of it into something new. In a sense this allegorising too is a characteristic part of the work of many of the most familiar Edwardian architects: a fine and subtle example is James MacLaren's house in Bayswater in London of 1889–90, but Charles Rennie Mackintosh clearly did it with elements of late mediaeval Scottish castle architecture. Every architect who built a white-rendered house – a kind of imitation of the plain walls of a mediaeval building – in a garden suburb was copying them. But the way in which Voysey detailed, conjoined and separated these elements out and placed them against his plain backdrop was extreme, and exciting (fig.181).

With the exception of his mediaeval Lodge Style of 1909, a homage to Pugin, Voysey's architectural elements were almost entirely drawn from the 17th century. In fact it was mostly from either the first years of that century, or the last: his hooded doorway above the front door at New Place in Haslemere of 1897, is 'William and Mary'; then in the same year, at Norney, near Shackleford, he took this motif and abstracted it further into something with no clear history. This was to be a harbinger of Edwardian work in general. In his case, however, there was little sense of wanting to convey the idea that a house had been constructed over different periods. Nor does it look as if he took any interest in the reuse of old materials.

In these last respects M.H. Baillie Scott might also be considered an architect in the first rank (figs 182–185). Writing on him to date has concentrated first on the completeness of his arts-and-crafts vision, and more recently on his original house layouts.[35] The latter were without doubt a breakthrough on a scale not seen in English houses since Pugin smashed

the rigid layouts of Georgian England with his pinwheel plans in which the axis of the major rooms revolves around a staircase hall. But it is possible to see Baillie Scott's appeal in a way which would have been more obvious to those who saw images of them without further analysis. The exteriors of his early houses drew, as might be expected, from Shaw or more probably from imitations of Shaw. In the late 1890s they were derived to varying extents from Voysey – he designed a village hall at Onchan on the Isle of Man in 1897 which is almost a direct imitation of the Voysey style. Then he stripped them back so that they looked like artistic representations of mediaeval houses with mullioned windows: Blackwell, in Cumbria, of 1898 is like this, and so is the exterior of his White Lodge at St Mary's Convent, Wantage, Berkshire, of 1898–9. Diane Haigh's analysis of his work illustrates these three together in order to present his 'breakthrough', his liberation from the Shaw type.[36] The irregular white-rendered houses that immediately followed – White House in Helensburgh, Argyll (1899–1900); Danestream in Milford-on-Sea, Hampshire (1904); The Crow's Nest at Duddleswell, East Sussex (1904); Tanglewood at Letchworth, Hertfordshire (1906–7); even his Bill House at Selsey, West Sussex, with its Voyseyesque buttresses (1906–7) – looked unresolved, however, perhaps because Baillie Scott was concentrating on their planning.[37] But from that point onwards he became a 'Tudor' and 'Jacobean' architect *tout court*. The earliest example of a house that looks precisely as if it is intended to be purely Tudor is his Landhaus Waldbühl at Uzwil, near Zurich, of 1907, perhaps because his clients had wanted an *englisches Haus*. From then on, his houses were mostly and evenly vernacular 'Tudor' or 'early-to-mid-17th century', which was the style of his cottages at Biddenham in Bedfordshire, and of the larger house in Hoddesdon in Hertfordshire where it is located next door to a house by Lucas (see fig.151). Baillie Scott had recycled material from earlier buildings at the ornate half-timbered Bexton Croft at Knutsford in Cheshire of 1894, and in 1908–9 he did it again for Longburton House, near Sherborne in Dorset, coming close this time to using a Pugin-like pinwheel plan.[38] As readers of *Country Life* (at least) will have known, designing 'Jacobean' houses that are scarcely indistinguishable from the real thing was completely normal at this point; Baillie Scott simply did it better. He increasingly gave them '17th-century' decorative detailing and interiors too, for example the plasterwork hop pattern that appears on the outside of his houses at Gidea Park, and above the fireplace of Michaels, in Harbledown outside Canterbury, designed in the same period. Home Close, at Sibford Ferris in Oxfordshire, of 1910, could be a late mediaeval building in spite of its motor house and

182. King's Close, 11 Main Road, Biddenham, Bedfordshire, by M.H. Baillie Scott, designed around 1909, three years after the publication of his *Houses and Gardens*. This small house encapsulates the architect's talents at their zenith. The entrance front incorporates another variety of the Wealden type.

battery and engine rooms.[39] Yet all this came during the period in which he protested that building a 'Jacobean' room 'must necessarily be a failure'.[40]

This approach became more striking still when Baillie Scott remodelled two old timber-framed Kentish houses: Yeomans in Great Chart, near Ashford, in 1916–17, and then Ockhams in Edenbridge in 1923. By then, his understanding of vernacular detailing was so advanced that it becomes impossible to distinguish at all between old and new, as with Devey more than half a century beforehand at Penshurst. This was even true, in so far as he was able to maintain control, of the cheap speculative houses designed with A. Edgar Beresford in the latter part of his career. Baillie Scott, like Voysey, incorporated artisan-mannerist grotesque faces into his work, too. It is possible therefore to summarise that whereas Baillie Scott is usually seen as a proto-modernist planner with advanced social views, and at the same time an unrivalled practitioner of jugendstil interiors, he was actually an architect whose awareness of the primary constructional elements of traditional building and of what Tudor architecture could convey were so comprehensive that he could design buildings that spoke of the renewal of the past in a way that countless lesser-known or unrecognised architects could imitate across England. His fine floral detailing, for example the slender white pillars on the upper floors of Blackwell, each topped with a cluster of branches of leaves, have something of the flower-fairy fantasies of the children's writers and illustrators, too.

There clearly were magical elements in the most memorable Edwardian houses. The great appeal of the drawings by Mallows, which featured extensively in the *Studio* as well as in the more specifically architectural or

183. (opposite) The garden front at King's Close, still today Edwardian in character.

184. The hall at King's Close. The house was designed at the time that Baillie Scott had declared that 'the modern Jacobean room . . . must necessarily be a failure', and yet work like this clearly indicated that this was untrue.

185. Baillie Scott's newel post at King's Close. Details such as this demonstrate that there was no inherent contradiction between rational modern planning and sentimental, almost childlike details.

professional publications, was the loveliness of the buildings in them, which usually somewhat outdid the built reality (fig.186).[41] This was also true to some extent of Arnold Mitchell, who published attractive drawings and watercolours of his houses in the new prestigious Edwardian villa-suburbs of Great Stanmore and Northwood in Middlesex. His matter-of-fact chapter on house layouts in Shaw Sparrow's *The British Home of Today* puts much emphasis on 'brightness'

and calls for the atmosphere of the home to be 'quite fresh and sweet'. The staircases of his houses in Hans Street near Knightsbridge 'having domes and galleries over them, make a very picturesque interior'.[42] These are very pretty homes. His drawings must have inspired provincial architects: in the seaside resort areas of Cliftonville, to the east of Margate in Kent, there are plenty of houses with exuberant plasterwork decorations, with garlands and cartouches across walls and

186. The Nottingham practice of Brewill & Baily employed several distinguished draughtsmen to present their work: this one of 1898, from J.H. Elder-Duncan's *Country Cottages and Week-End Homes* (1906), is by Charles Mallows, and Geoffry Lucas also contributed a drawing for them for the book.

187. Soval, a house in Rickmansworth Road, Northwood by Arnold Mitchell, now demolished, published in the *Studio* in January 1906. Mitchell's pretty plasterwork decoration, inspired by late 17th-century rural models, was copied widely by provincial architects.

188. A.N. Prentice worked convincingly as a stylist but could also create typically Edwardian combinations of '17th-century' details. Not surprisingly he was in demand as an interior designer for luxury ocean liners. This is The Retreat, Lakenheath, Suffolk, designed for the Liberal MP Sir William Dunn in the 1890s.

gables, that are more likely to be derived from Mitchell's pretty perspectives than from late 17th-century originals (fig.187).

This prettiness was everywhere; it evidently had a purpose to it in its own right. The sardonic Greenock-born architect A.N. Prentice designed a pavilion, decorated with ornamental plaster flourishes, for the Van Houten cocoa company's display at the 1901 Glasgow International Exhibition which looks like a children's-book drawing come to life.[43] A friend of Voysey, he had trained with Thomas Collcutt and after setting up his own practice in London in 1893 he also acted as draughtsman for several key figures.[44] His perspective

view of T.G. Jackson's principal's house for Brasenose College, Oxford, appeared in the first volume of the *Architectural Review*, in late 1896.[45] And at around that period he designed thatched extensions to The Retreat, at Lakenheath in Suffolk, for Sir William Dunn, the Liberal MP for Paisley. This had been a gothick *cottage orné*, and Prentice's work combined polite and rustic 17th-century styles: stout chimneys; ornate plasterwork; a porch with dwarf Tuscan columns (fig.188).[46] At Cavenham Hall in Suffolk, a drawing for which appeared in a supplement to the *Review* in 1899, he designed a formal, classical 17th-century-style house with an attached office wing

205.—BIRD'S-EYE VIEW.

206.—THE BIG MUSIC ROOM ; ONCE A BARN.

189. Prentice's later work was more severe but equally effective. Lawrence Weaver admired his remodelling of Orchard Farm, Broadway, Worcestershire, 1905, which left it looking more Tudor than before. This page from Weaver's *Small Country Houses: Their Repair and Enlargement* (1914) shows that the interior included a music room created from a barn. This design was made before W.D. Caröe's Vann (see figs 60–4): the significance of the latter was not so much its novelty but the coherence and richness of the resulting building.

190. (opposite) Halsey Ricardo's own Enchanted Castle: an upper corner of the Debenham House at 8 Addison Road, Kensington. The house, even more richly decorated with ceramics within than on its exterior, provided the only opportunity for Ricardo to realise his colour theories.

that looked like a slightly older cottage, again with ornamental pargetting – a remaking of history in a pretty way.[47] The restored farmhouse at Broadway illustrated by Weaver in his *Small Country Houses: Their Repair and Enlargement*, where in 1905 he added a new service wing and removed 'Nineteenth Century Ravages' for Lady Maud Bowes-Lyon, provides a model of the pretty, old-new Edwardian house, prettily drawn too (fig.189).[48] Less capable designers than Prentice could assemble these characteristic architectural elements in a free way, but the result only looked good in drawings; the reality was nothing like as magical or dreamlike (see fig.156). The relationship between these drawings and reality corresponds with that of the fantastical buildings in the work of writers like Nesbit, and the real houses they were based on.

Halsey Ricardo's Debenham House of 1905 was by far the most remarkable of any of his works; its sparkling polychrome tiled exterior and its mystical, ornate 'Byzantine' hall could be the setting from Nesbit's *The Enchanted Castle*, written just after it went up; perhaps she had seen that, too (fig.190). In E.M. Forster's novels, houses become the scenes of emotional responses to Englishness; that is even more true of his favourite, *The Longest Journey*, than it is of *Howards*

End where it is sometimes seen as being the central theme. The former is well known for the fact that it includes what seem to modern minds an improbably large number of unexpected deaths, but experiences like this these would have been familiar to several of the characters in this book. Alfred Lyttelton's early widowerhood, the loss of his two children, and his own premature death were all deeply felt in his circle and beyond at the time. Avebury lived through a sequence of family and close friends' deaths in 1905 and 1909–10 so terrible that it makes Forster's story seem perfectly plausible.[49] The obsessively breezy layout of Great Maytham Hall, with its narrow plan and large windows, may have sprung from personal tragedy because Jack Tennant, Lyttelton's brother-in-law, and his wife had all seen several family members die of tuberculosis. Consecutive deaths were often part of Edwardian parenthood. Reconstructing houses from the fragments of old ones is a way of bringing the dead back to life.

Rebirth

Thus the recurrent themes of rebirth, of starting again in the past, of coming back to life, or coming back from prison in the case of the vanished father of Nesbit's *The Railway Children* (1906), might easily reflect a much wider cultural interest than simply a theme in children's stories. The arrival of the Liberal government at the end of 1905 launched a 'flurry of activity' in social welfare, with a particular emphasis on the health of children, especially in schools where the dismal outcome of new medical inspections had led to pressure, from medical officers of health, for a school medical service: as G.R. Searle put it, the children of the period were being 'reconceptualized' as citizens, healthy, active, British.[50] For the politically aware Liberal, this was an exciting period. Possibly this is the significance of the fact that Clough Williams-Ellis designed homes that looked too often like doll's houses; and with his wife Amabel he became a writer of children's books. C.H.B. Quennell emerged from his declining career as an architect after the unfortunate episode of the ugly house and launched a much more successful career as a children's writer, together with his long-suffering wife Marjorie; so the pretty and much publicised nursery playroom he designed was finally eclipsed by the longer-lasting success of their children's literature. Beresford Pite, writing on house design in the *Architectural Review* in 1900 and expressing admiration for Robert Adam and the architecture of Buxton, Derbyshire, observed tellingly that 'without offence, and having come back to a happy

infancy in art, the doll's house, so well bricked, with its windows so full of panes and very green shutters, is now our unconfessed ideal'.[51]

It is striking how many of the major characters in this book recorded happy memories of childhood or enjoyed the company of children. Carrington made the study of his house at Daws Hill out of what had been the farmyard potting shed he had played in as a child.[52] In early 1906 his young son Albert Edward got hold of his mother's diary and wrote engagingly in it that 'I helped Daddy with his books, it was fun' – perhaps in that same room.[53] At the age of four he had also helped Daddy build the house, by laying a commemorative stone at the corner of the front elevation of it soon after the family had moved in, and Lady Carrington remembered that the children had been 'perfectly happy' at the time when their father was looking for a site for his new house: these moments ran deep into their memories.[54] Perhaps the contemporary interest in making homes from oast houses and windmills is also evidence of a sense of childlike fun. Herbert Gladstone, who was such a convivial host at Littlestone, in later life recalled his father as quite different to what might be assumed from the image of the austere politician that people remember from black-and-white photographs:

> But when we went to his room we found someone who thoroughly understood us, and gave himself to us when we were there. We had teaspoons of black coffee, and rides on his foot slung over his knee while he sang 'Ride a cock-horse to Banbury Cross'. He showed us things, told us stories, measured and recorded our heights. But the supreme moment came when he carried four of us at a time – two of my sisters, Henry and myself – on his back. There were little presents of things he did not want and we did. It was a daily treat. We were like little dogs who never resent exclusion but are overjoyed when they are allowed in. Our affection was secured. It was so complete and continuous that we gave very little trouble to him though much to others.[55]

In his early childhood, this 'room' of his father's was at 11 Downing Street where he was chancellor of the exchequer, and it is a curiosity of Herbert Gladstone's career that he returned there on becoming home secretary in 1905, because the Asquiths chose to remain in Cavendish Square.

The rebirth and revisiting of childhood through the recollections of fathers and sons could perhaps be a metaphor for the rebirth of England through Liberal government responses to land and tenure. The introduction to this book raised the possibility that Edwardian domestic architecture was related to the contemporary state of party politics. In two objective respects it clearly was: much private housing was built directly by Liberal Party members, and Liberal-backed legislation had introduced the Housing, Town Planning, &c. Act of 1909. Lord Carrington's promotion of smallholdings, from his position of President of the Board of Agriculture in a Liberal government, made landowners not only think about the development of their lands but calculate more finely and knowledgably about the consequences of new types of rural housing and tenure. The increasing awareness of what was required to raise health standards – the rise in public and voluntary activity related to health, to education, to physical fitness – all of which were associated with the Liberal Party during this period, meant that hospital buildings and houses where there was an emphasis on healthy living were well promoted. Arts-and-crafts architects, of whom many were Liberals, publically and professionally proclaimed the importance of fine and precise craftsmanship in building, and following decades of work by local archaeological societies and the promotion of the building trades by *Country Life* and others, the information was available to make domestic architecture more precise and more exact in meeting technical and functional specifications – as was clear from even a popular guide such as that to the Gidea Park Exhibition.

What this means is that there was a process going on across the Edwardian decade which can be compared directly to the 'realist' period of the early gothic revival, when architects had been forced by government action, in the wake of various overspending scandals, to submit detailed specifications for tender, and building contractors moved towards tendering in gross; a period in which technical and scientific processes and the vocabularies used to describe them were vastly increasing.[56] This momentum led to Pugin's gothic revival, but then it faltered, before picking up again as once more political initiatives and thought were pressing in the direction of more accurate and more logical decision making. So there remains the question of why Tudor architecture in particular should have met the requirements of the period.

The realists of the gothic revival disliked the architecture of the Elizabethan and Jacobean period more than any other except for that of stuccoed, late Georgian houses: for Pugin it represented the Protestant Reformation, and with its shallow arches and borrowing of artisan mannerist decoration it looked unprincipled. The genius of Pugin was that his doctrine of the unity of structure and function was absolutely clear and uncompromised, which meant that young architects

who were bored of the cheapened, predictable, technically failing neo-classicism of their day could latch on to it with abandon; indeed, George Gilbert Scott famously described his 'conversion' to gothic in religious terms.[57] Yet the appeal of Tudor architecture persisted. The appearance of Pugin's own houses of the 1840s is vernacular-Jacobean rather than gothic, in spite of their revolutionary plans, in part because Pugin knew that a house should not resemble a church.

There are many contradictions in the original historical period itself, however. An extraordinary Elizabethan house like Little Moreton Hall in Cheshire is on the one hand a wonder of construction: to look at it is to know how it stands up. Yet on the other hand there is something romantic and daft about it. Like English high-camp culture in general, it is unlikely but possible. Many Tudor and Jacobean vernacular buildings are characterised by the imaginative use of timber; this looks emphatically like a material that has come straight out of the earth, the earth that belonged, according to patrician Liberals, to those who lived on it and made their living through it, and not to the landowners – a central theme of Liberal Party policy over decades. It is also a material that demonstrates the hand of the craftsman in the way that masonry does not – except where that consisted of fine, ornamental brickwork as it did in the better houses of the late Stuart period. Indeed, one could almost imagine of a half-timbered Tudor house that its resident had built it himself, which no one would have said about a gothic or a Palladian home. Furthermore, these houses which were designed to look as if they had been remodelled over the centuries thus incorporated within themselves an inbuilt sense of progress, an attractive concept in a house for optimistic, committed radicals. Edward Fawcett's recent study of Liberalism concludes that the great contribution of the revered John Stuart Mill was that he found a way to blend the austere rational utilitarianism that he had absorbed from childhood with an awareness of the vitality of individual character, of private happiness.[58] Edwardian architects were thus doing much the same, using the hard facts of building that they had learned from Pugin and Devey to build romantic, beautiful, highly personal buildings (fig.191; see also fig.168).

On top of that, the romantic Tudor imagery specifically of the early 19th century cast a long shadow, in part because of the intensity and brilliance of Walter Scott's novels, and the warmth and hospitality that radiate from the drawings of Joseph Nash and his imitators. In December 1906 *Country Life*, the writers of which were surprisingly sympathetic towards the 'Tudor gothic' of the 1820s, printed a selection of these to illustrate 'The Old English Christmas', and there is something

to be said for the argument that modern Christmas too was as much late-Georgian-Tudor in its imagery as it was Victorian-German: that is clearly the case with the 'first' Christmas card, produced in 1843 for Henry Cole.[59] That touches on a further factor. One area of perpetual conflict between Liberals and Conservatives, especially over the 'long' Edwardian period from 1900 to 1914, was that of the relationship between church and state; the Conservatives were the Church of England party, the Liberals, broadly, the dissenters inside and outside it. This division between the parties fuelled the bitter debates and controversies around the role of the Church of England in state education: Arthur Balfour's 1902 Education Act, which pitted Nonconformists against Anglicans, brought all this back out into the open. It is not hard to see how the emphatically protestant architecture of Elizabethan England might appeal to Liberals in a way which was simultaneously romantic and rational. It is possible also to see a new realist element in a kind of architecture that introduced the different periods of 17th-century design under the one roof of an

191. The Wyck was 'one of those interesting places which modern taste and judgment . . . have created out of fragments of the old'. At some point shortly before 1905, when *Country Life* described it as an 'exemplar', the house was remodelled using old materials, including the red terracotta tiles used as nogging. The left-hand bay was built later in the 20th century.

apparently vernacular house (see fig.107). Their houses put these together in ways that made one look at them and think about them. Then a new story comes out of it. This is what Voysey was doing. That is what Avebury and Romaine-Walker were doing when they made the contrasting strata of Georgian and newly-laid flint a feature of the design of their castle, and avoided any visual obstructions between these walls and the lawns around it, as if the new house were a restored archaeological site. It is easy to see how this argument might have appealed to the geologist in Avebury.

The Gidea Park estate embodies this kind of architecture. Its prettiness came from its variety, and its great range of different experiments with building materials and logical, constructional forms. The effect could sometimes be very attractive where the architect was skilled enough to bring together these elements in an elegant way, as Romaine-Walker did in the farm and school buildings and the cottages that he designed for Robert Hudson in Medmenham (see figs 38 and 39).[60] Had Avebury read about them in *Country Life* before appointing his architect? Then for ten years these combinations come in floods. The great genius of *Country Life* was that it managed to combine so disciplined and so technically precise an editorial line on the architecture of both new and remodelled houses with sentimental stories and dreams and gardens, and photographs of heiresses and Highland cattle, and of happy children splashing in streams, that captivated their audience. This must have been the reason for both its commercial success and its writers' astonishing ability to understand the meaning of the buildings they saw around them.

This was true above all of the proprietor himself. Bernard Darwin wrote that Hudson's interest in country houses and gardens came about in the first place because he wanted to entertain his consumptive brother Henry by taking him on trips: 'So that which had in a measure begun as good-natured sightseeing on Edward Hudson's part became a passionate interest.'[61] In this way, *Country Life* was reborn as the primary architectural publication of its day, and Hudson and Hudson's brother mirrored the magical story of *The Secret Garden*.

Fairies I have met

There are several mysteries regarding the landscape and buildings of the area around Kingsgate Castle. One concerns the exact whereabouts of the birth of Baillie Scott. He was born in a house on Baird's Hill, the first section of the lane that leads directly to Kingsgate Castle from the village of St Peter's, the mediaeval core of Broadstairs. There were at that time a few recent villas along Baird's Hill, as well as one long, low half-timbered Tudor house nestled up against the railway line which has survived, and which appears to have been sympathetically and gently remodelled in the way that Baillie Scott himself pioneered. It is an intriguing question as to which house he was born in: was it one of the plain Victorian villas, from which his parents might have looked out towards the Tudor house with envy? Or was it the Tudor house itself, a rare beauty nestling half-hidden between undistinguished villas with the promise of warmth and richness and hospitality, like one of Nesbit's fairy-tale mansions?

I myself lived in a flat in Kingsgate Castle as a child; my mother's bedroom was in what must have been Avebury's servants' hall. When I visited it recently for the first time in decades, I found I could remember the names of nearly all the other residents from 45 years previous: Violet Ollie, Edwardian herself; Dawn Latter, chain smoking in what was once Avebury's bedroom; the squash-playing Buttifants; the elderly, hospitable Clarkes; the Haydons (Mrs Haydon was Judith Whitlock, the Australian children's author, and they had Eames playing cards amongst other improving toys); affable, knowledgeable Paul Gunn; smart Mrs Winter, otherwise in Kensington; the stiff, upright, military parents of the art critic John Berger. Thus in some form they are all still alive beyond their own families' memories. When I lived in Bethnal Green, east London, in the 1980s, having remade an old house myself, I looked out from my bedroom window onto the post-war Avebury Estate, lit at night as places still were by eerie neon-strip lights. These names have been chasing me from place to place.

Surely it was the slightly other-worldly character of North Foreland that had attracted Lord Holland to it in the first place. Pitt Rivers visited in 1868, unearthing Romano-British pottery, tools, bones and shells; at the end of the century, his son-in-law Avebury was struck by the fact that Holland House, from which he first caught sight of the Castle on the cliff top across the bay, had been built by a forebear of his wife's.[62] There are however unexplained half-traces of many great figures. Why was the house that was once the lodge to Elmwood, Northcliffe's residence, renamed in the later 20th century High Elms, the name of the Avebury house in Bromley? And why was it that the *Architectural Review*'s long three-part article on George Devey in 1907 was immediately followed by a full-page photograph of a cottage here called Pine End, which had one of Thanet's ornamental 'Dutch' gables?[63] It could well have been one of the buildings that Devey himself was fond of, for nearby Reading Street, immediately behind Northcliffe's house, is full of such gables and was one of the villages that Devey had been attracted to. But why was it published here? And who then rebuilt it as part of a house nearby, and why, well before the Edwardian mania for moving and reconstructing old farmhouses got under way?[64]

In his old age Avebury derived much pleasure from the particular atmosphere of Kingsgate: he repeatedly said so in his diary. He insisted on being driven down there when he felt that he was at the end of his life in the late spring of 1913. A few days later, he had a bed made up for him in his cloister so that he could hear his new clock chiming in the courtyard behind without being exposed to the winds, and stayed there for most of the rest of the day. He died in the

192. Lord Avebury at his favourite spot, on the Castle terrace overlooking Kingsgate Bay: this is where he chose to spend his last moments. The Captain Digby pub is just out of sight to the left, but Lord Holland's Arx Ruochim, still with its tower, can be clearly seen.

193. (opposite) The Captain Digby pub, right, visible from the terrace of Kingsgate Castle. Avebury often sat out under the archway to the left.

early morning of 28 May 1913. He had seen and regretted the recent polarisation in politics occasioned by Lloyd George's 'People's Budget' as well as the deterioration of relations with Germany; thankfully he did not live to see where that was leading. His astonishing political career, dedicated to analysis and publication, and almost incessant public activity, all of it motivated by the desire to see people treated rationally and respectfully by the British state, presaged the great national reforms introduced by the Liberal Party from 1906 until the Great War: the 1907 Education Act; the introduction of old-age pensions, of labour exchanges, and of school meals; the Irish Land Act; the National Insurance Act; the Coal Mines (Minimum Wage) Act; the Mental Deficiency Act. For Avebury himself, almost every day for decades was taken up from breakfast onwards with meetings and with the great political concerns of the day, the House of Commons, the House of Lords, the Society of Antiquaries, the scholarly institutions; the scientific elite; encounters with a Queen Empress and two further British monarchs, the President of the French Republic, the President of the United States, the German Kaiser and the King of Spain; a delegation of German mayors and the commanders of the French fleet; tea with Mark Twain; research, travel, lecturing and publication on a staggering scale, to a world-wide audience of readers from the Far East to central Africa; a life that spanned between the first outdoor daguerreotype to electric light, the motor car and the Bank Holiday – especially the Bank Holiday; everything organised, rationalised, and punctuated by continuous rounds of golf and the merry laughter of young children. 'I now seem to live,' said a shopworker after reading one of Avebury's scientific books, 'in a new world.'[65]

Avebury was one of the many Edwardians who loved children and who inspired devotion in them. Horace G. Hutchinson's biography, published in 1914 in the year following his death, retained a respectful distance in relation to most of his subject's life, but towards the end and in the Kingsgate period his writing is animated with stories that convey his subject's fascination with life and his affection for his family. How delighted the old man must have been when his young son Maurice, just two years old, asked him: 'who made the sky?' and then, having burnt his hand in a fire, burnt it again to see whether the 'nursery fire burnt too'.[66] In fact time and time again Avebury's diary reflects his concern and his affection for his children – he seems devastated each time anew when Eric in particular, a 'dear little fellow, & as good as gold', and evidently revived as intended by the bracing sea air, goes back to boarding school, and the happy time they were spending 'working at Pollen together' must come to an end, or when he, or his eldest son Johnny, or Harold, or Maurice have yet another of the many painful accidents and operations that seem to afflict them.[67] He also enjoyed entertaining Maurice's schoolfriends, showing them 'marvels through the microscope', and talking to them tactfully and unpatronisingly 'in a way that delighted them'.[68]

At one point in the last year of his life – we know from Avebury's diary that it was on 22 July 1912 – a party of these children came to visit. Avebury himself wrote in his diary that the boys 'seemed to enjoy themselves', but Hutchinson added that one of the children said to the headmaster afterwards 'Isn't he jolly to us?'.[69] He had, said Hutchinson, 'a twinkle of humour which was always lurking in the corner of [his] eye'.[70] Hutchinson also saw an echo of the lively fun of the household outside the castle wall, in the 'sometimes rather noisy exuberance of the trippers and those who are enjoying the boon, which Lord Avebury himself assured to them, of the Bank Holiday'.[71] 'These holidays', according to Avebury, 'were the first ever instituted by any legislature for the enjoyment and relaxation of the people'.[72] So the day trippers were in a way also his children, his political children.

Avebury, like Earl Carrington, died in the house that he had built. Hutchinson's final Kingsgate anecdote is so beautifully recorded that it is worth reading as he wrote it:

It was here that I saw him last, sitting in the archway of the Castle which gives out on to the terrace and on the view over the open sea beyond. He had his microscope on a little table before him, and in the clear light was examining, and exhibiting to anyone who cared to look, what to the naked eye had all the appearance of an insignificant brown beetle of so small a size that the unlearned might almost be tempted to miscall it by the monosyllabic name of another insect (of the Hemiptera, however, not the Coleoptera), beginning with the same capital letter. Seen under the microscope, it discovered a carapace studded, as it seemed, with all the jewels of the world glittering in a variety of hues and with an indescribable brilliance . . . .[73]

When the Captain Digby pub nearby, atop the cliff that faced Avebury's castle, came to be sold in 1903, it was advertised as a 'very Old Established House and occupies an absolutely unique position on the Kentish Coast. It stands in its own grounds overlooking Kingsgate Bay / And the MAGNIFICENT VIEWS therefrom attract thousands of visitors from all parts during the Spring, Summer and Autumn months'.[74] It was Avebury who had created the opportunity for the hard-worked people of Britain to have some fun, and while

they were doing so to learn a little about their country; its history; its rocks; its plants; its animals; its ancient walls. It is not a surprise to hear from Hutchinson, his convivial biographer and golf partner, that he chose to sit out his final summers, in quiet contemplation from his castle terrace of the busy holidaymakers gathering by the pub on the cliff opposite, or on the beach below.[75] He spent his last moments of consciousness in his gothic cloister, looking out across the broad horizons of the Channel. The great Edwardian Liberal archaeologist, polymath and reformer had made all this possible. He had created the entire scene.

ACKNOWLEDGEMENTS

THIS BOOK HAS ITS ORIGINS in my friendship with the Service family. In 1975, Alastair Service published his *Edwardian Architecture and its Origins*, which I, aged 14, bought hot off the press, and soon afterwards *Edwardian Architecture*, which he was kind enough to give me with a personal inscription. Unlike so many historical overviews, these two books have stood the test of time and are unlikely to be bettered. I am delighted to have had the generous support of Nick and Sophie Service in writing the present book.

It has been an honour and a pleasure to work with my editor Valerie Rose throughout, and I would also like to thank Sarah Thorowgood, Head of Editorial and Production at Lund Humphries, for the resources she provided especially in respect of preparing archival illustrations for print. My thanks too to Abigail Grater for her excellent copy editing. I am particularly grateful to a group of scholars and friends who have given me the enormous privilege of their assistance: Clive Aslet, James Stevens Curl, Mark Girouard, Hilary Grainger, Neil Jackson, Jeremy Musson, Andrew Saint (especially), and Robert Thorne, each of whom has saved me from embarrassment with their advice and suggestions. I would like to thank Lyulph, Lord Avebury, for most generously allowing me access to the first Lord Avebury's archives, and also Christian Poltera who provided access to Kingsgate Castle and to the images and records of it collected by himself and the late Paul Gunn. Rupert, Lord Carrington, kindly granted me permission to quote from the Marquess and Marchioness of Lincolnshire's diaries, and contributed the fine portrait photograph of him. I am grateful too to the University of Kent for allowing me a term's study leave in which to work on the project.

My thanks to the archivists who have been so helpful at the following collections, and in particular to the staff of the British Architectural Library at the Royal Institute of British Architects, with especial thanks there to Irene Machariah, Richard Reed and Valeria Carullo; Sarah Charlton, archivist to the Carington Estates; Nicky Hilton and the staff of the Parliamentary Archives; the staff of the Manuscripts & Rare Books and Special Collections in the Weston Library, at the Bodleian Library, University of Oxford; and to Emily Boswell, Clare Brazier and Tina Cunningham at Wycombe

Abbey School. I am grateful too to Ingrid Smits and Tudor Allen at the Camden Local Studies and Archives Centre; the City of Westminster Archives Centre; the Dorset History Centre; Gloucestershire Archives; Lucinda Walker and Graham Deacon, the Historic England Archive; the London Metropolitan Archive; Jeremy Coote, Pitt Rivers Museum; the Surrey History Centre; and to Sandy Paul, Sub-Librarian, and Jonathan Smith, Archivist and Modern Manuscript Cataloguer, Trinity College, Cambridge. I have also been greatly assisted by specialist society members and local historians: Jackie Godfrey, Walton-on-the-Hill and District Local History Society; Philip Truett, archivist, Walton Heath Golf Club; Arthur King, North Foreland Golf Club; and David Snoxell and Stuart King, High Wycombe Society.

I have received very helpful support, advice and information from Andrew, Lord Adonis; Rod Aspinall, Lympne Castle; Chris Beetles and David Wootton; Graham Booth; Mark Bostridge (who identified the infanta portrait at Gidea Park (fig.107)); Mark Bowden; Simon Bradley; Daniel Brittain-Catlin; Oliver Caröe and Mary Caröe; Alison Charles; Jonathan Deeming; Patric Dickinson, Clarenceux King of Arms; John East; James Edgar; Maggie Edgar, Cockett Henderson; Simon Edwards, for information on Horace Field; Brent Elliott; Catherine Eyre, Haslemere; John Goodall; Julia Gosling, Hand Picked Hotels; Elain Harwood; Stephen Hazell-Smith; Charles Holland; Mark Horton; Charles Lawrence, The C.F.A. Voysey Society; Rebecca Lilley, The Lutyens Trust; Karen Maibom and Bent Baggersgaard; Cheryl Marner, Danesfield House; Jeremy Melvin; Dave Morrissey of the Beech Grove Bruderhof community at the former St Alban's Court, Nonington; Damir and Sacha Novakovic; Avner Offer; Julian Orbach; Judith Patrick; Angela Paterson; Jana Pohaničova; Gillian Whitley Roberts; Hugh Routh; Chris Seaber; Chris Stewart, Sandroyd School; Annabel Watts, Munstead Wood; and William Whyte.

I would like to thank those whose generous support has enabled both the illustration programme and the production of the book: John S. Cohen Foundation; Marc Fitch Fund; Paul Mellon Centre for Studies in British Art; the Design History Society; Sophie Service; the Society of Architectural Historians of Great Britain; and the Scouloudi Foundation in association with the Institute of Historical Research. I would like to thank Professor Philippe De Wilde, Deputy Vice Chancellor Research and Innovation at the University of Kent, and his REF steering group, for their generous contribution towards photography and printing costs.

Of course I owe a great deal to Robin Forster for his photography and also to the owners of the houses who so kindly allowed us onto their property. I cannot stress enough how valuable this is for architectural historians and their readers. I am grateful to Paul Finch, Manon Mollard and Eleanor Beaumont for their generous permission to reproduce images from the Architectural Review's own archive, and to Rupert Bickersteth for handling this, and to Melanie Bryan of the Country Life Picture Library who afforded every helpful assistance. The portrait of W.H. Romaine-Walker was located by Peter Howell.

I am again very grateful to my friend Benjamin Wood for expertly preparing the historical images for publication. This entailed a great deal of work at a busy time, and I appreciate it. I would like to thank Graham Scales at F1 Colour for his work on the archival images.

The hero of H.G. Wells's The New Machiavelli of 1910 remembered 'with infinite gratitude the great uncle to whom I owe my bricks', before launching into a beautiful description of the make-believe continents he constructed with their help across his nursery floor. In my case I must thank my grandmother Phyllis Manasseh's Aunt Gladys and Uncle Josh Jacobs for giving her throughout her Edwardian childhood the very best contemporary children's literature which, fifty years on, her daughter, my mother Jennifer, then read to me at bedtime. 'If any of us have any intelligence,' she once said, 'it is thanks to my mother's family.' We all liked E. Nesbit's Harding's Luck the best and now, decades later, I have finally worked out, more or less, what it is about. And not least, I thank my other grandmother, Vera Brittain, who died in 1970, who indirectly but generously supported the production of this book through the royalties of her literary estate.

194. (previous pages) Kingsgate Bay today. From left to right along the clifftop: Kingsgate Castle; Holland House; and the Captain Digby pub. Photographed in June 2019 by Patrick O'Keeffe.

NOTES

⸻

Introduction

⸻

1.   Mark Girouard, *Sweetness and Light*, Oxford: Oxford University Press, 1977, p.10.

2.   ibid., pp.64–70.

3.   A.J.A. Morris, 'Edwards, John Passmore (1823–1911), newspaper proprietor and philanthropist', *Oxford Dictionary of National Biography*.

4.   Francis Goodall, 'Stevenson, James Cochran (1825–1905), chemical manufacturer', *Oxford Dictionary of National Biography*.

5.   Girouard, *Sweetness and Light*, pp.88–9; Sarah Bush, 'Nicholson, Joshua (1812–1885), silk manufacturer', *Oxford Dictionary of National Biography*.

6.   Girouard, *Sweetness and Light*, pp.125–6.

7.   ibid., pp.86–7.

8.   My thanks to the Jackson scholar William Whyte for this.

9.   Girouard, *Sweetness and Light*, pp.186–7.

10. ibid., p.139.

11. In a BBC Radio 3 programme entitled *Living in Quality Street*: see http://genome.ch.bbc.co.uk/be9fe50f63914a78b66c9bd96aa4b7aa. Timothy Brittain-Catlin, 'Downward Trajectory: Towards a Theory of Failure', 2011, *passim.*, describes this style in relation to the architect Horace Field; and Timothy Brittain-Catlin, *Bleak Houses: Failure and Disappointment in Architecture*, Cambridge, MA: MIT Press, 2014, pp.89–91 etc., attempts a definition of it.

12. G.R. Searle, *A New England? Peace and War 1886–1918*, Oxford: Oxford University Press, 2004, pp.126 and 205.

13. Andrew Saint, *Bedford Park, Radical Suburb*, London: The Bedford Park Society, 2016, p.21.

14. Jane Brown, *Lutyens and the Edwardians: An English Architect and his Clients*, London: Viking, 1996, pp.133–6.

15. H. Avray Tipping, 'Three Gables, Letchworth', *Country Life*, 22.1.1910, supplement, p.35.

16. *Times*, 22.12.1905, quoted by Avner Offer, *Property and Politics 1870–1914:*

Landownership, Law, Ideology and Urban Development in England, Cambridge: Cambridge University Press, 1981, p.356.

17. Offer, *Property and Politics*, p.328.

18. C.F.G. Masterman, *The Condition of England*, London: Methuen, 1909, p.30.

19. For the English translation: H. Muthesius, *The English House*, London: Frances Lincoln, 2007, vol.1, p.101.

20. Paul Readman, 'The Edwardian Land Question', in Matthew Cragoe and Paul Readman, *The Land Question in Britain 1750–1950*, London: Palgrave Macmillan, 2010, p.181.

21. A.W.N. Pugin, *The True Principles of Pointed or Christian Architecture*, London: John Weale, 1841, p.1.

22. Chris Brooks, *Signs for the Times*, London: Routledge, 1984, p.157.

23. Alastair Service (ed.), *Edwardian Architecture and its Origins*, London: Architectural Press, 1975, caption to fig.3, p.15.

24. Timothy Brittain-Catlin, 'Realism in Nineteenth-Century British Architecture', in Harry Mallgrave, Martin Bressani and Christina Contandriopoulos (eds), *The Companions to the History of Architecture*, vol.3, Hoboken: Wiley, 2017, pp.174–91; Timothy Brittain-Catlin, *The English Parsonage in the Early Nineteenth Century*, Reading: Spire Books, 2008, pp.123–6 and 199–200.

25. Timothy Brittain-Catlin, 'La Normandie de Nodier; L'Angleterre de Pugin', in Martin Kew Meade, Werner Szambien and Simona Talenti (eds), *Architecture normande en France: identités et échanges*, Marseilles: Éditions Parenthèses, 2002, pp.149–54.

26. Timothy Brittain-Catlin, 'Good Fairies', *AA Files*, no.73, 2016, pp.126–7. The opening of the sanatorium was referred to in *Country Life*, 16.6.1906, p.855, and extensively in the professional press.

27. Andrew Ballantyne and Andrew Law, *Tudoresque: In Pursuit of the Ideal Home*, London: Reaktion, 2011, pp.149–50.

28. Peter Virgin, *The Church in an Age of Negligence*, Cambridge: James Clarke, 1989.

29. Margot Asquith, *The Autobiography of Margot Asquith*, London: Thornton Butterworth, vol.1, 1920, p.23.

30. For example, 'Texture as a Quality of Art and a Condition for Architecture' (1889), reproduced in David Valinsky, *An Architect Speaks: The Writings and Buildings of Edward Schröder Prior*, Donington: David Valinsky for Shaun Tyas, 2014, pp.44–56.

31. M.H. Baillie Scott, *Houses and Gardens: Arts and Crafts Interiors*, London: George Newnes, 1906, ch.7, p.25.

32. ibid., ch.18, p.44.

33. ibid., Introduction, p.3; ch.1, p.5.

34. ibid., ch.1, p.7.

35. Brittain-Catlin, *Bleak Houses*, pp.62–7.

36. Jill Lever, 'A.T. Bolton, Architect', *Architectural History*, vol.27, 1984, pp.429–42; Elizabeth McKellar, 'C.H.B. Quennell (1872–1935): Architecture, History and the Quest for the Modern', *Architectural History*, vol.50, 2007, pp.211–46.

37. Peter Davey, *Arts and Crafts Architecture*, London: Phaidon, revised edn 1997, pp.190–91.

38. Timothy Brittain-Catlin, 'Picturesque, Modern, Tudor-Style: Edgar Ranger in Thanet', in *Twentieth Century Architecture 12, Houses: Regional Practice and Local Character*, 2015, pp.34–47.

39. See for example Paul Oliver, Ian Davis and Ian Bentley, *Dunroamin: The Suburban Semi and its Enemies*, London: Barrie & Jenkins, 1981, pp.23–5 and 27.

40. Notoriously and influentially in Nikolaus Pevsner, *Pioneers of Modern Design: From William Morris to Walter Gropius*, revised edn Harmondsworth: Penguin, 1974, p.162.

Chapter One

1. Horace G. Hutchinson, *The Life of Sir John Lubbock, Lord Avebury*, London: Macmillan, 1914, vol.1 p.15. Recent critical biographies of Avebury include Michael Thompson, *Darwin's Pupil: The Place of Sir John Lubbock, Lord Avebury, 1834–1913, in Late Victorian and Edwardian England*, Ely: Melrose Books, 2009; Mark Patton, *Science, Politics and Business in the Work of Sir John Lubbock: A Man of Universal Mind (Science, Technology and Culture, 1700–1945)*, London: Routledge, 2007; and Janet Owen, *Darwin's Apprentice: An Archaeological Biography of John Lubbock*, Barnsley: Pen & Sword, 2013.

2. Listed in Hutchinson, *The Life of Sir John Lubbock*, vol.1, p.171.

3. ibid., pp.201 and 211–15.

4. ibid., p.241; this was Harold, on 28.6.1909: Diaries and correspondence, etc., of and relating to Sir John Lubbock, 4th Bart. (1834–1913), 1st Baron Avebury (1900), British Library, Add MS 62681–62682: 1850–1913 ('Avebury Diary').

5. Timothy L. Alborn, 'Lubbock, Sir John William, third baronet (1803–1865)', *Oxford Dictionary of National Biography*.

6. Hutchinson, *The Life of Sir John Lubbock*, vol.2, p.110.

7. ibid., pp.110–11.

8. Simon Thurley, *Men from the Ministry*, New Haven and London: Yale University Press, 2013, pp.36–41.

9. Scientific and systematic: John Britton, *The Architectural Antiquities of Britain*, vol.5, London: Longman, Hurst, Rees & Orme, 1826, preface p.1.

10. Thurley, *Men from the Ministry*, p.41.

11. Hutchinson, *The Life of Sir John Lubbock*, vol.2, p.139.

12. The most recent and thorough survey of the house and follies is by Michael Cousins, '"As for paradise which is but another name for Kingsgate"', *The Follies Journal*, no.8, Summer 2009, pp.47–88.

13. British Library: Maps K. Top. 18.30.a.1.

14. Hugh Honour, 'An Epic of Ruin-Building', *Country Life*, 10.12.1953, pp.1968–9; Howard Colvin, *A Biographical Dictionary of British Architects 1600–1840*, 3rd edn, New Haven and London: Yale University Press, 1995, pp.1133–4.

15. Footnote to Thomas Gray, 'Impromptu on Lord Holland's Seat at Kingsgate, suggested by a view, in 1766, of the seat and ruins of a deceased nobleman, at Kingsgate, Kent', *The Works of Thomas Gray*, London: Harding, Triphook & Lepard, vol.1, 1825, p.187.

16. Alice Avebury, whose maiden name had been Fox-Pitt, had a family connection to the original Holland family.

17. Gilpin: quoted in Honour, 'An Epic', p.1969; Luke Val Fildes, *Luke Fildes RA: A Victorian Painter*, London: Michael Joseph, 1968, p.134.

18. Gray, 'Impromptu', pp.187–8.

19. This is how the view and plans of the building are titled in James Basire's engraving: British Library: Maps K. Top. 18.30.a.6.

20. British Library: Maps K. Top. 18.30.a.1–11.

21. Hutchinson, *The Life of Sir John Lubbock*, vol.2, p.139.

22. Laurie Dennett, *Slaughter and May: A Century in the City*, Cambridge: Granta, 1989, pp.114–15. The house has been demolished but a website called http://www.whitenessmanor.co.uk/history.html has photographs of it. A website by a member of the Slaughter family has further details: http://writingfamilyhistory.com/author/susie-gutch/.

23. Reginald Pound and Geoffrey Harmsworth, *Northcliffe*, London: Cassell, 1959, pp.118–20. The house survives, as does its former lodge (now incorporated into a larger building), but its garden, once full of ornamental trees, has been greatly subdivided.

24. ibid., pp.124 and 120.

25. ibid., p.166. The billiard room survives but the large garden pavilion had gone by the Ordnance Survey map of 1939.

26. ibid., pp.245 and 466.

27. Marks, a Moderate member of the London County Council from 1889 to 1892, and then Conservative MP for the St George division of Tower Hamlets from 1892 to 1900, was elected as member for Thanet in 1904–10. The house had been demolished by 1938 except for the lodge – which gives some indication of the style of the main house – and the ornamental walls outside. Some traces of its ornamental garden have survived.

28. Avebury Diary, 19.10.1901. An indenture for the conveyance for the Castle from its previous owners is dated 24.4.1902, so it is not clear what process Avebury was referring to. The actual ownership of the Castle was, and continued to be, very complicated. Avebury bought it in his son's name, but various transfers and further purchases or sales followed, with himself and Alice as owners or lessees, and other permutations were applied at the time and later to subsequent purchases. The legal status of the freehold was so unclear by the 1950s that sorting it out occupied the residents for about two decades.

29. Avebury Diary, 25.10.1902.

30. Private collection.

31. Hilary J. Grainger, *The Architecture of Sir Ernest George*, Reading: Spire, 2011, pp.335–40.

32. Jill Franklin, *The Gentleman's Country House and its Plan 1835–1914*, London: Routledge & Kegan Paul, 1981, p.104.

33. Mark Bowden, *Pitt Rivers: The Life and Archaeological Work of Lieutenant-General Augustus Henry Lane Fox Pitt Rivers, DCL,* *FRS, FSA*, Cambridge: Cambridge University Press, 1991, p.3.

34. Coined by Bowden in an article in 1984 but revisited in the final chapter of *Pitt Rivers*, pp.154ff.

35. Avebury Diary, 30.5.1900.

36. Hutchinson, *The Life of Sir John Lubbock*, vol.1, pp.239 and 242–3.

37. Andrew Saint, *Richard Norman Shaw*, 2nd edn, New Haven and London: Yale University Press, 2010, p.453. The house survives, and a Knight, Frank & Rutley sales catalogue of the contents of the house in the collection of sales particulars in the National Art Library indicates that it was luxuriously furnished.

38. Avebury visited Ightham on 30.8.07 and 27.4.11 (Avebury Diary), but he may have been there before. His host, Sir Thomas Colyer-Fergusson, had made internal improvements in the 1890s, using the decorative firm of Walford & Spokes: John Newman, *The Buildings of England: Kent – West and the Weald*, New Haven and London: Yale University Press, 2012, p.320. In 1906, Avebury sat next to Shaw at a Royal Academy dinner: Avebury Diary, 5.5.1906.

39. Sheila Kirk, *Philip Webb: Pioneer of Arts & Crafts Architecture*, Chichester; Wiley-Academy, 2005, p.300; Tollard Royal: Historic England list description, 1000542; attribution to Romaine-Walker: A. Stuart Gray, *Edwardian Architecture: A Biographical Dictionary*, London: Duckworth, 1986, p.314. Funeral: Diary, 10.5.1900.

40. Tanner and Walker were paid fees for it of £99.16.3 on 1.11.1890: Pitt Rivers's accounts; Dorset History Centre, D-PIT/F/79: personal, household and estate accounts book, with abstracts of accounts 1881–1892. The detailed accounts books for the earlier period in which the lodges were built have not been not located, but according to the accounts summaries brought forward in this volume, Pitt Rivers spent £5,215.15.17 and £4,698.08 on building works in 1881 and 1882 respectively, enough for both lodges and his Larmer Ground educational gardens nearby. According to the historian of Sandroyd School, Pitt Rivers was however carrying out substantial remodelling works at Rushmore during this period too. Austen Caverhill, *Rushmore: Then and Now*, Tollard Royal: Sandroyd School, 1988; a partial transcription available online at http://web.prm.ox.ac.uk/rpr/index.php/article-index/12-articles/815-austin-caverhill.html.

41. Bowden, *Pitt Rivers*, p.38.

42. ibid., p.156.

43. ibid., p.158.

44. M.W. Thompson, *General Pitt-Rivers*, Bradford-on-Avon: Moonraker Press, 1977, p.110.

45. Bowden, *Pitt Rivers*, p.160.

46. ibid., p.48.

47. Hever: Avebury Diary, 27.6.1908. The castle, unlike Kingsgate, was in *Country Life*: 12.10.07, pp.522–35, and 19.10.1907, pp.558–67. Deal: his diary suggests a familiarity with the resident, Lord George Hamilton, for example playing golf with him on 4.10.1902.

48 Avebury Diary, 29.9.1907.

49 Hutchinson also noticed the similarity with Tantallon; possibly Avebury had mentioned it to him: *The Life of Sir John Lubbock*, vol.2, p.190.

50. Reproduced at https://www.spab.org.uk/about-us/spab-manifesto, penultimate paragraph.

51. Avebury Diary, 11–12.10.1902.

52. Photographs: Lubbock family archives.

53. R.J. Cleevely, 'Rowe, Arthur Walton (1859–1926)', *Oxford Dictionary of National Biography*. Avebury's diary says simply 'Dr Rowe' and this is the obvious candidate: Diary, 27.8.02.

54. 'Expensive': Avebury Diary, 29.8.1902; plan approved, ibid., 13.9.1902.

55. Avebury Diary, 10–11.3.1903. Over time Capel Slaughter's original 'Tower Field' course was extended to include lands owned by other members of the group. Arthur King and Tony Lavender, *North Foreland Golf Club: Founded 1903*, Kingsgate: North Foreland Golf Club, 2007, pp.9 and 13.

56. Avebury Diary, 3.7.1903.

57. Information from Lyulph Avebury.

58. She certainly took charge of their decoration at Grosvenor Street, and Avebury thought that she did it 'very prettily': Avebury Diary, 30.8.08.

59. Avebury Diary, 26.12.1906.

60. Kingsgate Castle visitors' book: Lubbock family archive.

61. Avebury Diary, 16.9.07.

62. Avebury Diary, 3.8.1912.

63. 'Verandah': Avebury Diary, 19.5.1909; 'Cloister': Hutchinson, from Avebury's notes, vol.2, p.139, and family album; Avebury's Ledger, p.105, records that Paramor & Sons, the contractors, received £600 for it: Lubbock family archive.

64. Indenture of 22.9.1910: Lubbock family archive; Avebury Diary, 30.8.1905 and 8.10.1905.

65. Exceptions were the holding of the Parliamentary Gold Handicap on 7.5.04, and 'a few holes with Northcliffe', on 12.8.10: Avebury Diary.

66. Paramor & Sons received a total of £1,620 for it, and Romaine-Walker & Jenkinson a fee of £100: Ledger, p.111. It was getting on fairly well' by 26.2.2012: Avebury Diary.

67. The Avebury Diary first records, on 18.6.1905, that he hired a motor to take him to Kingsgate, and by the end of 1906 he mentioned that he had 'set up' one which arrived at the house. The family owned a Minerva at one point. Prestige garages for prestige cars were not uncommon among those who could afford to buy them and build them.

68. *Builder*, 17.5.1940, p.582; *Builder*, 21.6.1940, p.723.

69. Romaine-Walker's office address appears in *Who's Who in Architecture* for 1914.

70. Census 1901.

71. *Church History and Guide*, St Saviour's Church, Pimlico, p.16; online at https://www.scribd.com/document/255023853/Church-History-Guide. The architect himself appears as 'Walker' in all census records, but always gave it as 'Romaine-Walker' in publication.

72. Census, 1861, 1881.

73. Simon Bradley and Nikolaus Pevsner, *The Buildings of England: London 6 – Westminster*, New Haven and London: Yale University Press, 2003, p.767.

74. E.W. Leachman, *A Church in No Man's Land, being the Romance of Holy Trinity*, St Leonards-on-Sea: King Bros & Potts, 1934, p.40; R. Stephen Ayling, 'Augustus W. Tanner', *RIBA Journal*, vol.30, 1923, pp.626–7.

75. RIBA Nomination papers, RIBA Library; he was elected on 23.5.1881 at a meeting chaired by Street himself.

76. Buckingham Gate was later renamed Buckingham Street.

77. The drawing of it that was exhibited at the Royal Academy in 1884 attributed it to Romaine-Walker alone.

78. Newman, *The Buildings of England: Kent – West and the Weald*, p.175.

79. Alan Brooks and Jennifer Sherwood, *The Buildings of England: Oxfordshire North and West*, New Haven and London: Yale University Press, 2017, p.480.

80. Bridget Cherry and Nikolaus Pevsner, *The Buildings of England: London 2 – South*, New Haven and London: Yale University Press, 2002, p.502.

81. http://www.stclementspoole.org.uk/churchhistory.htm has a thorough account.

82. Michael Hill, John Newman and Nikolaus Pevsner, *The Buildings of England: Dorset*, New Haven and London: Yale University Press, 2018, p.480.

83. *Builder*, 1.9.1883, p.284 and pl., p.28

84. 'Flemish Mannerism': James Stevens Curl and Susan Wilson, *The Oxford Dictionary of Architecture*, 3rd edn, Oxford: Oxford University Press, 2015, p.285.

85. John Greenacombe (Royal Commission on the Historical Monuments of England), *Survey of London, Volume 45: Knightsbridge*, London: Athlone, 1998, pp.83–6 and 94. The site was 195 Knightsbridge. The building was demolished for Mercury House, built on the site in 1957, which in turn has itself been replaced by a block of modern flats.

86. See TG Revive, Listed Building Consultants, '7 Caledonian Road & 3 Bravingtons Walk (The Former Varnish Works) Regent's Quarter London', available at http://planning.islington.gov.uk/NorthgatePublicDocs/00349904.pdf.

87. Grainger, *Sir Ernest George*, pp.155–60; the press references are listed in the gazetteer, pp.411–12.

88. Much of the execution of the decoration of the Oratory is 20th century, however; for Richmond, see https://www.stpauls.co.uk/history-collections/the-collections/object-collection/mosaics-of-st-pauls-cathedral/mosaics-in-the-quire.

89. See Hill, Newman and Pevsner, *The Buildings of England: Dorset*, pp.174–7.

90. *Builder*, 24.8.1889, pl.; text, p.135. The wing is described in Franklin, *The Gentleman's Country House*, plan 58, p.220 and pp.221 and 258.

91. There is no sign, by comparing the Ordnance Survey maps of 1882 and 1896, of any mansion having been built.

92. *Builder*, 17.8.1889, pl. (general view); 4.7.1891, pl.; text: p.12 (hall).

93. Franklin, *The Gentleman's Country House*, p.72.

94. Historic England list description, 1167015.

95. 'Unexpected': obituary, *Builder*, 29.5.1897, p.488.

96. His career as an illustrator has been researched by David Wootton of the Chris Beetles gallery: see http://www.chrisbeetles.com/artists/walker-william-henry-romaine-ariba-1854-1940.html#. There was a posthumous exhibition of this work at Walker's Gallery in April–May 1952, with a catalogue entitled *Watercolour Drawings by Four Victorians*.

97. For Hudson senior, see Nigel Lemon, 'A Blackcountryman at Bache Hall', *Cheshire History*, vol.46, 2006, pp.91–103. The company was bought by Lever Brothers Ltd in 1908.

98. The Grayson & Ould house was called Bidston Court and it was dismantled and moved west to Royden Park in Frankby in 1929–31 by the architects Rees & Holt: Historic England list description 1242748.

99. Kirk, *Philip Webb*, p.302.

100. Nikolaus Pevsner and Elizabeth Williamson, with Geoffrey K. Brandwood, *The Buildings of England: Buckinghamshire*, New Haven and London: Yale University Press, 2003, p.468.

101. There are good photographs of the exterior and interior, albeit much refurbished in the 20th and 21st centuries, in Emma Glanfield, 'If these walls could talk! Idyllic abbey that once hosted orgies for 18th Century politicians and aristocrats is on sale for £10million and now the in-house entertainment is a spa and cinema', *Daily Mail*, 17 March 2015: http://www.dailymail.co.uk/news/article-2998691/If-walls-talk-Idyllic-abbey-hosted-orgies-18th-Century-politicians-aristocrats-sale-10million-house-entertainment-spa-cinema.html. The Historic England list description, 1310928, says that Romaine-Walker designed the west wing.

102. Pevsner, Williamson and Brandwood, *The Buildings of England: Buckinghamshire*, pp.99 and 471–2.

103. See ibid., p.469, and Historic England list description, 1310810.

104. By 1903 Gillow & Co. had displays that 'illustrated the history of every period worthy of notice': quoted in Clive Edwards, *Turning Houses into Homes: A History of Retailing and Consumption of Domestic Furnishings*, Aldershot: Ashgate, 2005, pp.124.

105. Historic England list description, 1006230. Elsewhere I have called this building as the House One for gothic-revival architects in search of an authentic mediaeval dwelling (Brittain-Catlin, *The English Parsonage*, pp.79–82 and 172). Pugin himself copied details from it and it is hard to deny that it has a magnetic attraction.

106. Bradley and Pevsner, *The Buildings of England: London 6 – Westminster*, p.554.

107. The Farm Street interior has recently been thoroughly documented and illustrated in Michael Hall, Sheridan Gilley and Maria Perry, *Farm Street: The Story of the Jesuits' Church in London*, London: Unicorn, 2016, especially at pp.68–91. The decorative and church work is generally attributed to Romaine-Walker himself rather than the partnership.

108. See 'Hursley Park, Hants', *Country Life*, 23.10.1909, pp.562–9; 30.10.1909, pp.598–605.

109. Described and illustrated in detail in *Country Life*, both when new by Lawrence Weaver (15.5.1915. pp.662–9; 22.5.1915, pp.698–705) and, following restoration, in John Martin Robinson, 'A Country Palace: Buckland House, Berkshire', *Country Life*, 11.5.2011, pp.92–7, and 18.5.2011, pp.74–9.

110. Referred to in some lists as 'Nuneham Paddox'. Moreton Hall, now an agricultural college, lost its interior in a fire in 2008; Romaine-Walker's drawings are in the Warwickshire County Record Office, CR2244: my thanks to James Edgar for drawing this to my attention. Moreton Paddox has been demolished and only estate buildings remain. See Chris Pickford and Nikolaus Pevsner, *The Buildings of England: Warwickshire*, New Haven and London: Yale University Press, 2016, p.466.

111. Bradley and Pevsner, *The Buildings of England: Westminster*, p.518.

112. Avebury was upset at his death: Avebury Diary, 28.3.08.

113. Clare Hartwell, Nikolaus Pevsner and Elizabeth Williamson, *The Buildings of England: Derbyshire*, New Haven and London: Yale University Press, 2016, pp.238–40 and 245.

114. Brooks and Sherwood, *The Buildings of England: Oxfordshire North and West*, p.164. Dated there to 1902, but Romaine-Walker had exhibited a design for it at the Royal Academy in 1890 (Algernon Graves, *The Royal Academy of Arts: A Complete Dictionary of Contributors and their Work from its Foundation in 1769 to 1904*, Wakefield and Bath: S.R. publishers and Kingsmead Reprints, 1970, vol.3 p.355.

115. 'J.', 'Knowsley Hall, Lancashire', *Country Life*, 12.7.1913, p.61.

116. *Survey of London*, vol.40, Grosvenor Estate, pp.53 and 206. Showy porch: Bradley and Pevsner, *The Buildings of England: London 6*, p.577.

117. Avebury Diary, 30.9 1908.

118. Historic England list description 1027959; the entry notes that 'This is a high quality Arts and Crafts house by a major society architect of the period'. See also Nicholas Antram and Nikolaus Pevsner, *The Buildings of England: Sussex – East, with Brighton and Hove*, New Haven and London: Yale University Press, 2003, p.553. By the time of the 1911 census Romaine-Walker was living at 9 Montpelier Terrace, Brighton.

119. Obituary: *Builder*, vol.192, 31.5.1957, p.1001.

120. ibid., without any given dates. There is an article in Slovakian on Rusovce and the significance of its style by Jana Pohaničova in *Architektúra & Urbanizmus*, vol.39, no.1/2, 2005, pp.45–64. Dr Pohaničova has kindly told me that in her research on the house she found no reference to Romaine-Walker.

121. Cadw list description 22373; accessed from http://www.swansea.gov.uk/article/5205/Listed-buildings-index. Note, this list has confused the entries for the house and the outbuildings.

122. H.W. Sheppard (ed.) (Royal Commission on the Historical Monuments of England), *Survey of London, Volume 40: The Grosvenor Estate in Mayfair, Part 2 – The Buildings*, London: London County Council, 1980, p.289.

123. Amicia de Moubray, *Twentieth Century Castles in Britain*, London: Frances Lincoln, 2013, pp.30–39.

124. *Builder*, 9.6.1900; *Architectural Review*, vol.9, 1901, p.86.

125. *Architect and Contract Reporter*, 30.10.1903, pp.281–2.

126. Jennifer Smith, 'A taste of the Raj: one of UK's first bungalows that was built in the 1880s in colonial style goes on sale for £1million', *Daily Mail*, 9 April 2015, http://www.dailymail.co.uk/news/article-3032197/A-taste-Raj-Victorian-India-style-bungalow-built-Sussex-preserved-1880s-goes-market-1million.html.

127. 'Hubert Saxton Besant, fl 1912–1926', in Antonia Brodie, Alison Felstead, Jonathan Franklin, Leslie Pinfield and Jane Oldfield, *Directory of British Architects 1834–1914*, London: Continuum, 3rd edn, 2001, p.171.

128. Avebury Diary, 28.6.08.

129. Jill Allibone, *George Devey: Architect 1820–1826*, Cambridge: Lutterworth Press, 1991, ch.4, 'Working for the Whigs', pp.53–78 and 78.

130. ibid., pp.58–60 and 163.

131. ibid., p.60.

132. Mark Girouard, 'George Devey in Kent', part 1, *Country Life*, 1.4.1971, p.745.

133. Walter Godfrey, 'The Work of George Devey', part 3, *Architectural Review*, vol.21, 1907, p.298.

134. Saint, *Richard Norman Shaw*, pp.38 and 100.

135. Allibone, *George Devey*, p.30.

136. *Architect*, 21.4.1905, p.253. Macartney's lecture was held on 17.4.1905: *RIBA Journal*, vol.12, 1905, pp.377–92.

137. Holme Lacy House: Alan Brooks and Nikolaus Pevsner, *The Buildings of England: Herefordshire*, New Haven and London: Yale University Press, 2012, pp.367–9.

138. See Brittain-Catlin, *The English Parsonage*, pp.86–94.

139. John Claudius Loudon, *An Encyclopaedia of Cottage, Farm, and Villa Architecture and Furniture*, London: Longman, 1833, p.2.

140. Avebury Diary 17.12.1905. Harmsworth had congratulated Avebury on the 'great improvement in the landscape wrought by the reconstruction': Hutchinson, *The Life of Sir John Lubbock*, vol.2, p.190. Harmsworth did not like the idea of being called Lord Elmwood as 'it's the wood they use for coffins' (Pound and Harmsworth, *Northcliffe*, p.295).

141. These are described and illustrated in 'Kingsgate Castle', a portfolio of images and texts compiled and distributed privately by the printer Paul Gunn, a long-term resident of the Castle in the 1960s and 1970s who researched the history of the building. All the extensions are clearly distinguishable in contemporary aerial photographs.

142. http://www.dover-kent.com/2015-project/Castle-Keep-Hotel-Broadstairs.html.

143. Illustrated in Gunn, 'Kingsgate Castle'.

144. There is a plan of the subdivision in the sales particulars for the flats: Kent Archives and Local History Centre, R/U1/E1/452. The plans were drawn up by C.E. Vincent, AIAS, of Ramsgate.

145. Visible on Right Move's sales particular, http://www.rightmove.co.uk/property-for-sale/property-37998505.html, image 4, in the flat used for the BBC's makeover programme *Great Interior Design Challenge*, 20.1.2017.

146. 'Typescript copy of speech given by Lord Avebury (Sir John Lubbock) at the opening of Gloucester Public Library, 31st May 1900', Gloucestershire Archives, NQ21.96S.

Chapter Two

1. Andrew Adonis, 'Aristocracy, Agriculture and Liberalism: The Politics, Finances and Estates of the Third Lord Carrington', *The Historical Journal*, vol.31, no.4, 12.1988, pp.871–97. See also Andrew Adonis, 'Carington, Charles Robert Wynn- [formerly Charles Robert Carrington], marquess of Lincolnshire (1843–1928), politician and landowner', *Oxford Dictionary of National Biography*.

2. Lady Carrington's Diaries 1892–1913, Bodleian Libraries, Oxford, MS Film 1100, 19.3.1894

('Lady Carrington Diary'); the original diaries are in the Carington Estate archives at Bledlow.

3. See Heather Clemenson, *English Country Houses and Landed Estates*, London: Croom Hill, 1982, ch.6, pp.96–106.

4. Diaries of Charles Robert Wynn-Carrington, Marquess of Lincolnshire, December 1890–July 1900, Bodleian Libraries, Oxford, MSS Film 1103 ('Carrington Diary'). De L'Isle and Dudley: 21.12.1896; the original diaries are in the Carington Estate archives at Bledlow.

5. Carrington Diary, 27.10.1897.

6. Adonis, 'Aristocracy, Agriculture and Liberalism', pp.882–3.

7. The 1896–1900 diary includes summary tables of income and expenditure at the end of each year.

8. John Martin Robinson, *James Wyatt: Architect to George III*, New Haven and London: Yale University Press for Paul Mellon Centre for British Art, 2011, p.350.

9. Carrington Diary, 1897, p.1.

10. Lady Carrington Diary, 7.7.1896; 14.7.1896.

11. Lady Carrington Diary, 26.8.1896; Carrington Diary, 9.6.1897, p.160.

12. Lees obituaries: *Builder*, 11.5.1907, p.577; *RIBA Journal*, vol.14, 1907, p.511. None of Carrington's surviving papers record Lees's Christian name.

13. Carrington Diary, 8.8.1897.

14. Carrington Diary, 3.8.1897.

15. Carrington Diary, 9.6.1897.

16. Carrington Diary, 18.12.1897; 18.3.1898.

17. Carrington Diary, 9.4.1898; 19.5.1899; 26.5.1899.

18. Carrington Diary, 29.7.1899; 30.7.1899.

19. Sales particulars, 1928, Wycombe Abbey School archives.

20. Gayhurst: K.A. Walpole, *From One Generation to the Next: A Panorama of Wycombe Abbey, Buckinghamshire*, printed privately, c.1970; by courtesy of Tina Cunningham, Wycombe Abbey School.

21. Carrington Diary, 23.10.1897; 11.11.1898.

22. Adonis, 'Aristocracy, Agriculture and Liberalism', pp.888–9.

23. See Ballantyne and Law, *Tudoresque*, ch.4, 'Tudoresque Self-Reliance', pp.105–30.

24. Adonis, 'Carington', *Oxford Dictionary of National Biography*.

25. Lady Carrington Diary, 29.1.1903.

26. I am indebted to Oliver Caröe for his very helpful observations on the house. Vann was described by Lawrence Weaver in *Country Life*, 29.6.1912, supplement, pp.7–11, and included in his *Small Country Houses: Their Repair and Enlargement – Forty Examples Chosen from Five Centuries*, London: Country Life, 1914, pp.36–41; Jennifer M. Freeman, *W.D. Caröe RStO FSA: His Architectural Achievement*, Manchester: Manchester University Press, 1990, pp.103–6; Richard Haslam, 'Vann, Surrey; Architect of 1907–1909 Additions: W.D. Caröe', *Country Life*, 26.6.1986, pp.1818–20.

27. Caröe's drawings for Vann are at the Historic England archive, Swindon, ref.CAR01.

28. J. Rady, T. Tatton-Brown and J. A. Bowen, 'The Archbishop's Palace, Canterbury', *Journal of the British Archaeological Association*, vol.144, no.1, 1991, pp.17–18, fig.11 and p.40. For Caröe's house in the light of this survey, see Jenny Freeman, 'Archbishop's Palace, Canterbury', *Country Life*, 25.4.1991, pp.84–7.

29. Freeman, *W.D. Caröe*, pp.103–6.

30. For Cave, see Judith Patrick, *Walter Cave: Arts and Crafts to Edwardian Splendour*, Andover: Phillimore & Co., 2012. Patrick describes the houses but not the barn at The Wharf on pp.87–91.

31. ibid., pp.29–31; 'Bateman's, Sussex', *Country Life*, 15.8.1908, pp.224–32.

32. Lawrence Weaver, 'The Wharf, Sutton Courtenay, Berkshire', *Country Life*, 25.10.1913, supplement, pp.7–11; Weaver, *Small Country Houses: Their Repair and Enlargement*, pp.53–6.

33. 'The Wharf, Sutton Courtenay, Berks: The Country House of Mrs Asquith', *Architectural Review*, vol.55, 1924, pp.192–5.

34. See Michael Brock and Eleanor Brock, *Margot Asquith's Great War Diary 1914–1916: the View from Downing Street*, Oxford: Oxford University Press, 2014, p.xcvi.

35. Charles Mallet, *Herbert Gladstone: A Memoir*, London: Hutchinson, 1932, p.87.

36. British Library, Add MSS 52550, letter to Lady Aberconway 123, 17.1.1928.

37. Lawrence Weaver, 'Modern Scottish Architecture: The Work of Sir Robert Lorimer – Reconstructions After a Fire', *Country Life*, 27.9.1913, pp.32–4; Kitty Cruft, John Dunbar and Richard Fawcett, *The Buildings of Scotland: Borders*, New Haven and London: Yale University Press, 2006, pp.326–7; Gavin Stamp, 'Besieged by Suffragettes: Lympne Castle, Kent', part 2, *Country Life*, 6.7.2016, pp.106–10.

38. See Lawrence Weaver, 'Lympne Castle, Kent: The Seat of Mr F.J. Tennant', *Country Life*, 12.11.1910, pp.682–9.

39. Lawrence Weaver, 'Great Maytham, Kent', *Country Life*, 30.11.1912, p.751.

40. See Brittain-Catlin, 'Good Fairies', pp.121–8.

41. *Times*, 25.1.1898: letters from Edward Warren and 'A Resident in the Hinterland'. I am indebted to Andrew Saint for the research which he contributed to this section. Address: Brodie et al., *Directory of British Architects 1834–1914*, pp.920–21.

42. *Times*, 23.6.1900; 20.7.1900.

43. *Times*, 16.8.1900; 18.8.1900.

44. 63 & 64 Vict. c.269.

45. J.C. Paget, 'The New Westminster', *Architectural Review*, vol.20, 1906, p.318.

46. 'Old Westminster', *Builders' Journal*, 28.10.1903, p.238.

47. Westminster City Archives, WCC:Acc0244/1/280 and 281, have later plans which show this layout. Text: 63 & 64 Vict. c.cclxix, s.4 (1); 42; royal assent, 6.8.1900.

48. The redevelopment was not completed until the development of the Horseferry Road end of the site in the early 1930s.

49. Census 1891: my thanks again to Andrew Saint.

50. See Bill Fawcett's excellent *The North Eastern Railway's Two Palaces of Business*, York, Friends of the National Railway Museum in association with GNER, 2006, for a comprehensive description of the offices and houses.

51. A. Morris, 'Trevelyan, Sir Charles Philips, third baronet (1870–1958), politician', *Oxford Dictionary of National Biography*.

52. Detailed in Fawcett, *The North Eastern Railway's Two Palaces of Business*, pp.47–8.

53. *Architects' and Builders' Journal*, 14.6.1911, p.630.

54. Royal Academy of Arts, *Royal Academy Exhibitors, 1905–1970: A Dictionary of Artists and their Work in the Summer Exhibitions of the Royal Academy of Arts*, Wakefield: EP Publishing, 1973–, vol.3, p.61; Graves, *The Royal Academy of Arts: A Complete Dictionary*, p.104.

55. The style matched the houses attributed to Robert William Furze Brettingham in Little Dean's Yard nearby, of 1789–90.

56. London Metropolitan Archives (LMA): GLC/AR/BR/28/U/07, with some further minor information in GLC/AR/BR/17/03677:; GLC/AR/BR/23/066222/01; GLC/AR/BR/22/BA/035940. The first references to the designs for these houses appear in August 1908. By 1912 Horace Field & Simmons, Field's practice, was working on service wing extensions to it. Like the neighbouring Field pair, the houses disappeared under 1928 extensions to British American Tobacco's Westminster House. The gas meter works and other industrial buildings can be seen on the Ordnance Survey town plan, first revision, 1895. 'Unofficial' pupil: Kirk, *Philip Webb*, pp.101 and 175.

57. The later building on the site imitates the composition.

58. Her *Times* obituary, 5.4.1932, p.16, refers to her 'entertainments' at the house.

59. Field's application was approved by the LCC on 24.1.1911. LMA: GLC/AR/BR/28/U/07 has application plans and sections at ¼":1' but no street elevations. A watercolour view was reproduced in the *Building News*, 13.10.1911 (my thanks to Simon Edwards for this).

60. *Builder*, 24.12.1898. The date of the design is from Field's 1903 RIBA fellowship nomination papers.

61. Letter from Field of 28.4.1911; permission of 12.6.1911: LMA: GLC/AR/BR/22/BA/035940.

62. For example in Mervyn Macartney, *Recent English Domestic Architecture*, London: The Architectural Review, vol.6, 1913[?], p.104.

63. Westminster City Archives, WDP/0542/04; WDP2/1257/01; submitted 18.9.1913.

64. Lutyens Trust: http://www.lutyenstrust.org.uk/portfolio-item/walking-tour-westminster/

65. GLC/AR/BR/22/BA/038166, amended plans submitted 31.12.1912. The house was bombed and rebuilt as flats by the same architect in a more conventional style in

1952–3. John Summerson noted that his The Pantiles, Englefield Green, designed shortly beforehand, had also been German in style, 'partly through the clients' influence': 'Rendel, Harry Stuart Goodhart- (1887–1959), architect', *Oxford Dictionary of National Biography*.

66. In, for example, J.H. Elder-Duncan, *Country Cottages and Week-End Homes*, London etc.: Cassell, 1906, pp.192 and 213–15.

67. The original building, designed in 1912 was by Gordon & Gunton; the extension, 1928, by Gordon & Gordon. LMA: GLC/AR/BR/22/BA/035940; GLC/AR/BR/23/066222/01.

68. Timothy Brittain-Catlin, 'Downward Trajectory: Towards a Theory of Failure', *ARQ*, vol.15, no.2 (2011), pp.139–47. 'Artistic': ibid., p.145; London Metropolitan Archives, GLC/AR/BR/22/BA/035940, letter of 28.1.1911.

69. Timothy Brittain-Catlin, 'Horace Field and Lloyds Bank', *Architectural History*, vol.53, 2010, pp.271–94.

70. *Country Life*, 24.2.1906, pp.277–9.

71. Author's collection.

72. Horace Field, and Michael Bunney, *English Domestic Architecture of the XVII and XVIII Centuries*, London: Bell, 1905, p.1.

73. Kirk, *Philip Webb*, p.86.

74. 'The Cox Family and the Houses on Hook Hill', Hook Heath Residents' Association website, http://www.hhra.co.uk/the-cox-family-and-hook-hill.htm. Sales particulars for the separated western part of the house, now called Brockhurst, in the archives of Surrey History Centre, SP/3482, record that the date of the original house was 1893–4.

75. Lawrence Weaver, 'South Hill, Hook Heath, Woking', *Country Life*, 25.6.1910, supplement, pp.7–11; Weaver, *Small Country Houses of To-day*, London: Country Life, 1911, pp.46–9.

76. Weaver, *Small Country Houses of To-day*, p.48.

77. The house was on Barnet Road at the junction with Elmbank Avenue, on the site of what is now called Kerri Close. It was published with a photograph and plans in *Family Homes*, anonymously edited, and published by Baker, London, in 1913, p.69.

78. R. Randal Phillips, 'Hook Heath Farm', *Country Life*, 15.7.1922, pp.65–6.

79. Mallet, *Herbert Gladstone*, p.169.

80. John Cash, RIBA Fellowship application papers, 1901.

81. W. Shaw Sparrow, *The British Home of To-day: A Book of Modern Domestic Architecture & the Applied Arts*, London: Hodder & Stoughton, 1904, fig.B46.

82. Reginald Blomfield, *Memoirs of an Architect*, London: Macmillan, 1932, p.96.

83. ibid., p.54.

84. Brock and Brock, *Margot Asquith's Great War Diary*, p.xciv.

85. Edward David, 'The New Liberalism of C.F.G. Masterman', in Kenneth D. Brown (ed.), *Essays in Anti-Labour History: Responses to the Rise of Labour in Britain*, London: Palgrave Macmillan, 1974, p.28; John Grigg, *Lloyd George, War Leader 1916–1918*, London:

86. Walton Heath Golf Club: https://www.waltonheath.com/our_heritage.

87. H. Matthew, 'Masterman, Charles Frederick Gurney (1873–1927), politician and author', *Oxford Dictionary of National Biography*.

88. Brown, *Lutyens and the Edwardians*, p.120.

89. The extension of the South Eastern railway from Purley to Kingswood, the closest station to Walton Heath, had been opened in 1897 under the chairmanship of Sir Henry Cosmo Bonsor, one of the founders of the golf club before Riddell bought it.

90. My thanks to Philip Truett, archivist for Walton Heath Golf Club, and to Jackie Walker for directing me to Metcalfe's *The Architectural Development of Walton-on-the-Hill from 1900 to 1930*, Walton: Walton Local History Society, 2000. There is also some recent detailed description of the area included within documents relating to a planning application for Morley Horder's Little Ambrook, submitted to Reigate and Banstead by The Heritage Advisory, in https://bdsdocs.reigate-banstead.gov.uk/Planning/StreamDocPage/obj?DocNo=2760090&content=obj.pdf (April 2014); https://bdsdocs.reigate-banstead.gov.uk/Planning/StreamDocPage/obj?DocNo=3019482&content=obj.pdf (March 2016).

91. Metcalfe, *The Architectural Development of Walton-on-the-Hill*, p.88.

92. Christopher Hussey, *The Life of Sir Edwin Lutyens*, London: Country Life, 1950, p.98.

93. Historic England list description 1295187.

94. Brown, *Lutyens and the Edwardians*, p.123; Metcalfe, *The Architectural Development of Walton-on-the-Hill*, refers to this theory on pp.13–14 and it has sunk into planning guidance: see the Reigate and Banstead local planning authority conservation officer's report quoted in the March 2016 referred to in n.90 above, para.7.1.

95. Elder-Duncan, *Country Cottages*, pp.187–8 and 201–2. The house, called Pachesham, was located grandly in an island site on the links and, with a servants' wing, was somewhat more than a 'cottage'.

96. Allibone, *George Devey*, p.135.

97. Bradley and Pevsner, *The Buildings of England: London 6 – Westminster*, p.718.

98. It was illustrated in the fifth volume of Mervyn Macartney's *Recent English Domestic Architecture*, p.34. Sadly for Morley Horder, the current owners' website describes it as 'in Lutyens' style' without giving his name. Morley Horder's Inverleith, Norwich, with A.G. Wyand, published in Weaver's *Small Country Houses of To-day* of 1911, pp.67–70, also looks remarkably like Pinfold.

99. Weaver's house, which has again been remodelled, is now number 98. He was there by 1916 and the house was presumably commissioned before the War, as Weaver enlisted in 1914. R. Randal Phillips, *The House Improved*, London: Country Life, 1931,

pp.46–51.

100. Hengrove: Mervyn Macartney, *Recent English Domestic Architecture*, vol.4, 1911, p.128; Gertrude Jekyll, 'Orchards, Surrey', *Country Life*, 31.8.1901, pp.272–9; *Architectural Review*, vol.10, 1901, pp.32–8.

101. For example in 'Architects of the Day, X: Mr Percy Morley Horder F.R.I.B.A.', *Builders' Journal*, 26.1.1910, pp.65–70.

102. Brown, *Lutyens and the Edwardians*, p.123.

103. Pinfold (former Cliftondown): sales particular, http://www.rightmove.co.uk/property-for-sale/property-30943091.html.

104. Lawrence Weaver, *The 'Country Life' Book of Cottages*, London: Country Life, 1913, pp.32–3; Metcalfe, *The Architectural Development of Walton-on-the-Hill*, pp.57 and 117. Lane End was rebuilt by Macartney in 1924 after a fire; ibid., pp.21 and 38.

105. K. Robbins, 'Grey, Edward, Viscount Grey of Fallodon (1862–1933), politician, countryman, and author', *Oxford Dictionary of National Biography*; Joe Shute, 'River retreat of the man who took Britain to War', *Daily Telegraph*, 2.8.2014, http://www.telegraph.co.uk/history/world-war-one/11006046/River-retreat-of-the-man-who-took-Britain-to-war.html.

106. John Newman, *The Buildings of England: Kent – North East and East*, New Haven and London: Yale University Press, 2013, pp.153–5; Historic England list description 1001457.

107. National Archives, LG/F/43/1/36.

108. *Who Was Who*, vol.4, 1941–1950, London: A. & C. Black, 1952, p.216.

109. In July 1946; quoted by Nikolaus Pevsner in 'Goodhart-Rendel's Roll-Call', in *Architectural Review*, vol.138, 1965, p.262.

110. Wendy Hitchmough, *The Homestead*, London: Phaidon, 1994, p.10.

111. C.F.A. Voysey, *Individuality*, London: Chapman & Hall, 1915, p.11.

112. Wendy Hitchmough, *C.F.A. Voysey*, London: Phaidon, 1995, pp.20–23.

113. Octagonal hall: David Gebhart, *Charles F.A. Voysey Architect*, Los Angeles: Hennessey & Ingalls, 1975, fig.22 p.104; Hitchmough, *C.F.A. Voysey*, pp.21, 36. Sanatorium: ibid., p.27.

114. James Williams, 'George Devey and his Work', *Architectural Association Journal*, vol.24, no.266, 1909, p.97.

115. Hitchmough, *C.F.A. Voysey*, p.23.

116. Observed by Richard Allan Woollard and recorded in Alastair Service, 'Charles Harrison Townsend', in Alastair Service (ed.), *Edwardian Architecture and its Origins*, London: Architectural Press, 1975, pp.162–82 especially pp.169–70.

117. Voysey experts are aware of this: see for example Richard Havelock, 'Recollections and Reflections of an Inveterate Voysey Visitor, Part 2', in *The Orchard*, the Journal of The CFA Voysey Society, no.6, Autumn 2017, pp.64–85, which points to explicit Devey references in Voysey's work and also sees traces of Voysey in the work that Lutyens carried out for Grove after Voysey had fallen

118. Aymer Vallance, 'Some Recent Work by Mr C.F.A. Voysey', *Studio*, vol.31, 1904, p.127.

119. See Emily Gee, '"Where Shall She Live?": Housing the New Working Woman in Late Victorian and Edwardian London', in Geoff Brandwood (ed.), *Living, Leisure and Law: Eight Building Types in England 1800–1941*, Reading: Spire Books, 2010, pp.89–109.

120. Philip Temple, Colin Thom and Andrew Saint, *Survey of London, Volume 52: South East Marylebone, Part 2*, New Haven and London: Yale University Press, 2017, pp.662–3 and 673.

121. Historic England list description 1260541; Alastair Service, *Edwardian Architecture: A Handbook to Building Design in Britain, 1890–1914*, London: Thames & Hudson, 1977, p.206.

122. See Timothy Brittain-Catlin, *19th- and 20th Convents and Monasteries* (introduction to heritage assets), 2nd edn, London: Historic England, 2016, p.16.

123. G. Tweedale, 'Lewis, John (1836–1928), department store owner', *Oxford Dictionary of National Biography*.

124. Susan Beattie, *A Revolution in London Housing: LCC Architects and their Work 1893–1914*, London: Architectural Press, 1980.

125. Historic England list entry 1358481; photographs of the interior soon after completion are in Harvard University Library; HUAM153505soc.

126. Hansard, House of Commons debate 1.11.1909, vol.12 c.1569; Hampstead Garden Suburb: local act, 6 Edw. 7 c.cxcii.

127. Osbert Lancaster, *Pillar to Post*, London: John Murray, 1938, p.56.

128. Diane Haigh, *Baillie Scott: The Artistic House*, London: Academy Editions, 1995, p.59.

129. Allibone, *George Devey*, pp.119–21.

130. Saint, *Bedford Park*, pp.12–16.

131. ibid., p.15.

132. Small Holdings and Allotments Act 1907, 8 Edw.7 c.54, s.6; Small Holdings and Allotments Act 1908, 8 Edw.7 c.36, s.13.

133. 9 Edw.7 c.44.

134. M. Pottle, 'Vivian, Henry Harvey (1868–1930)', *Oxford Dictionary of National Biography*.

135. 2 Edw. 7 c.ccxl, s.25.

136. 9 Edw.7 c.44, s.54 (1).

137. 'Thomas Adams on the Housing and Town Planning Act, 1909', *Architectural Review*, Town Planning and Housing Supplement, part 1, vol.27, January 1910, pp.52–4.

138. 9 Edw. 7 c.44., s.55 (2); see Chapter Three, notes 47–49 below.

139. 9 Edw.7 c.44., s.58 (3).

140. H.C. Dowdall, 'The Law of Town Planning', *Town Planning Review*, vol.1 no.2, 1910, pp.39–43, provides a clear overview and a comparison with the Liverpool precedent.

141. Obituary: *Builder*, 29.3.1940, p.383.

142. Hansard, House of Commons Debate 5.4.1909 vol.3, c.740.

143. ibid., c.738.

144. ibid., c.735.

145. ibid., c.752–3.

146. ibid., c.749.

147. ibid.

148. ibid., c.774.

149. ibid., c.788.

150. ibid., c.797.

151. The most useful recent descriptions of the early development of Gidea Park are the undated Twentieth Century Society guide *Return to Gidea Park*, by David Davidson and Nick Collins; and *An Afternoon Walk in Gidea Park*, July 1998, produced for the Twentieth Century Society in 1998, compiled by John East and drawn from earlier tour notes for the Victorian Society by Roderick Gradidge (1989); a publication called *The Romford Garden Suburb*, of the Gidea Park District Civic Society (1986); and the original guide to the exhibition, *The Book of the Exhibition of Houses and Cottages, Romford Garden Suburb, Gidea Park*, London: The Exhibition Committee, 1911.

152. Weaver, *The 'Country Life' Book of Cottages*, pp.70–71, assumed that land costs would have been approximately an additional £100 / quarter-acre site.

153. Lawrence Weaver, 'The Exhibition of Houses at Gidea Park', part 1, *Country Life*, 3.6.1911, supplement, p.14.

154. *The Book of the Exhibition*, p.48.

155. Brodie et al., *Directory of British Architects*, p.699; Alan Crawford, *C.R. Ashbee: Architect, Designer and Romantic Socialist*, 2nd edn, New Haven and London: Yale University Press, 2005, p.217. His partner was presumably John Bell Gripper, mentioned in Crawford, *Ashbee*, as a sometime client, p.470, whose bankruptcy papers for 1913 are in the National Archives.

156. Field and Bunney, *English Domestic Architecture*, pl.72.

157. Richard Haslam, *RIBA Drawings Monographs No 2: Clough Williams-Ellis*, London: Academy Editions in collaboration with the Royal Institute of British Architects, 1996, p.32.

158. Weaver, *The 'Country Life' Book of Cottages*, p.89.

159. Weaver, 'The Exhibition of Houses at Gidea Park', part 1, pp.13 and 16.

160. *The Book of the Exhibition*, p.87.

161. Weaver, 'The Exhibition of Houses at Gidea Park', part 2, *Country Life*, 10.6.1911, supplement, p.7.

162. *The Book of the Exhibition*, p.111.

163. Weaver, 'The Exhibition of Houses at Gidea Park', part 2, p.8.

164. Ronald P. Jones, *Nonconformist Church Architecture*, London: Lindsey Press, 1914.

165. S.D. Adshead, 'Romford Garden Suburb, Gidea Park: Cottage Exhibition and Town Plan', *Town Planning Review*, vol.2, 7.1911, pp.124–7. Bridson's house was also omitted from the Gidea Park exhibition guide, so there is no public record of it.

166. Quoted in Mervyn Macartney, *Recent English Domestic Architecture*, vol.4, p.79.

167. For example, at the junction of Wulfstan and Erconwald Streets. For history and detail, see London Borough of Hammersmith & Fulham's design guidelines, https://www.lbhf.gov.uk/sites/default/files/section_attachments/wormholt_and_old_oak_design_guidelines_tcm21-165276.pdf, and http://www.socialhousinghistory.uk/wp/wp-content/uploads/2015/10/Early_LCC_Housing_Part_3_42-Old_Oak_Estate.pdf.

168. See Mark Swenarton, 'Tudor Walters and Tudorbethan: Reassessing Britain's Inter-War Suburbs', *Planning Perspectives*, vol.17, no.3, 2002, pp.267–86.

169. *The Book of the Exhibition*, p.53.

Chapter Three

1. *The Book of the Exhibition*, pp.105, 91 and 99.

2. ibid., pp.62 and 66.

3. ibid., p.90.

4. ibid., p.29.

5. ibid., p.52.

6. ibid., p.53.

7. ibid., p.17.

8. ibid., p.18.

9. ibid., p.20.

10. ibid.

11. ibid., pp.21 and 23.

12. Quoted in Roy Strong, *Country Life 1897–1997: The English Arcadia*, London: Country Life, 1996, p.21; Bernard Darwin, *Fifty Years of Country Life*, London: Country Life, 1947, p.16.

13. Weaver's first article for *Country Life* appeared in 1906 and he contributed a few articles in 1907–8: Lawrence Trevelyan Weaver, *Lawrence Weaver 1876–1930: an Annotated Bibliography*, York: Inch's Books, 1989.

14. Darwin, *Fifty Years of Country Life*, p.16. For a further insider's view of the magazine, see John Cornforth, 'Lutyens and Country Life: 81 not out', in *Lutyens: The Work of the English Architect Sir Edwin Lutyens (1869–1944)* [exhibition catalogue], London: Hayward Gallery, 1981, pp.25–31.

15. Strong, *Country Life*, p.16.

16. A. Morris, 'Newnes, Sir George, first baronet (1851–1910), newspaper proprietor and politician', *Oxford Dictionary of National Biography*.

17. Strong, *Country Life*, p.16.

18. A. Morris, 'Riddell, George Allardice, Baron Riddell (1865–1934), newspaper proprietor', *Oxford Dictionary of National Biography*.

19. *Country Life*, 17.9.1904; 7.10.1905, p.469; 16.12.1905, p.854.

20. 'Country Notes', *Country Life*, 5.10.1907, p.471.

21. 'Country Notes', *Country Life*, 27.10.1906, pp.580–81.

22. The Duke of York, Cornwall and York on his father's accession, was invested as Prince of Wales on his return in 1901. Darwin, *Fifty Years of Country Life*, p.15.

23. John Leyland, 'Baddesley Clinton', *Country Life*, 8.1.97, pp.20–22; Horace Hutchinson, 'After-Dinner Golf', ibid., p.23.

24. John Leyland, 'Penshurst Place', *Country Life*, 29.5.1897, pp.576–8; John Leyland, 'Ascott', *Country Life*, 28.8.1897, pp.210–12; Lucy Hardy, 'The Cottage Garden', *Country Life*, 6.11.1897, pp.483–5; Lucy Hardy, 'Deserted Houses', *Country Life*, 20.11.1897, pp.552–3.

25. 'Country Homes: Albury Park', *Country Life*, 11.12.1897, pp.656–8.

26. E.B.S., 'Country Cottages', *Country Life*, 19.2.1898, pp.195–7. The author had previously written about Voysey in the *Studio*.

27. C.J. Cornish, 'New Forest Scenes III – Foresters' Cottages', *Country Life*, 15.1.1898, pp.57–9; C.J. Cornish, ibid., 'Ancient Water Mills', *Country Life*, 5.2.1898, pp.134–6; C.J. Cornish, 'Village Houses for Holiday Homes', *Country Life*, 7.5.1898, pp.552–4.

28. 'Houses for People with Hobbies, 1: A Little House with a Big Room', *Country Life*, 6.8.1898, pp.137–9.

29. Peter Quennell, *The Marble Foot: An Autobiography 1905–1938*, London: Collins, 1976, ch.1, *passim*.

30. The authoritative account of Quennell's career is Elizabeth McKellar, 'C.H.B. Quennell (1872–1935): Architecture, History and the Quest for the Modern', *Architectural History*, 50, 2007, pp.211–41.

31. Quennell, *The Marble Foot*, p.75.

32. McKellar, 'C.H.B. Quennell', pp.213 and 233; Quennell, *The Marble Foot*, p.11.

33. Emily Lutyens and her children appeared on the cover of the 22.11.02 issue, p.641, and Barbara on her own on both 30.5.1903, p.719, and 17.7.1909, p.89.

34. 'Typical English Villages: Penshurst, Kent', *Country Life*, 23.12.1899, pp.814–18.

35. 'The Penshurst Village Club', *Country Life*, 20.1.1900, pp.69–71.

36. Caröe's design, originally called Woodhouse, not exactly as built, was published with a plan and perspective views in the *Building News* supplement of 19.3.1886; short text: p.456. There is no information in either the Caröe archive at Swindon or in Jennifer Freeman's Caröe monograph on this project. For James Blyth see http://www.hundredparishes.org.uk/people/detail/james-blyth.

37. Visible in the OS map of 1898. The house, destroyed by fire in 1926, was located in Silver Street just west of the old windmill; the yard survives as private houses off Blythwood Gardens.

38. 'An Estate in the Making', *Country Life*, part 1, 18.8.1900, pp.203–7; part 2, 22.9.1900, pp.361–4.

39. 'Dairy Cottage in Anglesey', *Country Life*, 19.2.1901, pp.213–15.

40. Mark Girouard, 'George Devey in Kent', part 2, *Country Life*, 18.4.1971, p.812.

41. 'The Cottage Question' [letter to the editor], *Spectator*, 25.11.1899, p.782.

42. 'The Cottage Problem', *Spectator*, 4.11.1899, pp.651–2.

43. 'Cottages for the Labourer', *Country Life*, 30.12.1899, pp.848–9.

44. *Country Life*, 6.1.1900, pp.6–7; 3.2.1900, p.160.

45. 'Cottages for Labourers', *Country Life*, 24.3.1900, p.379.

46. ibid., pp.379–81.

47. See Stefan Muthesius, *The English Terraced House*, New Haven and London: Yale University Press, 1982, pp.33–5, for an overview.

48. *Country Life*, 2.2.1902, pp.154 and 160; 9.3.1901, pp.191–2; 'The Building Bye-Laws', *Country Life*, 16.2.1901, pp.219–20.

49. Public Health Amendment Act 1907, 7 Edw 7 c.53, s.9; See A.J. Ley, *A History of Building Control in England and Wales 1840–1990*, London: RICA Books, 2000, pp.82–5, for a description of this process.

50. 'Old Place, Lindfield', *Country Life*, 20.7.1901, pp.72–7.

51. 'Cranborne Manor', *Country Life*, 7.12.1901, pp.732–42; 'Spains Hall, Essex', *Country Life*, 11.1.1902, pp.48–53.

52. T. [H. Avray Tipping], 'Combe Abbey', *Country Life*, 4.12.1909, pp.794–805; 11.12.09, pp.840–48.

53. *Country Life*, 20.9.1902, pp.357–60; 4.10.1902, pp.421–3.

54. *Country Life*, 17.6.1905, pp.883–6; 27.2.1904, pp.319–22; 9.5.1903, pp.602–11.

55. David Cole, *Sir Edwin Lutyens: The Arts and Crafts Houses*, Mulgrave: Images, 2017, pp.203–4.

56. See Kirk, *Philip Webb*, pp.187–9 and 194–8.

57. 'Great Tangley Manor', *Country Life*, 30.7.1898, pp.109–12.

58. Edwin Lutyens, 'The Work of the Late Philip Webb', *Country Life*, 8.5.1915, p.618; Hussey, *The Life of Sir Edwin Lutyens*, p.26.

59. See Chapter One above, p.37.

60. Hussey, *The Life of Sir Edwin Lutyens*, p.17.

61. Weaver, *Small Country Houses of To-day*, p.96.

62. Tipping's own Mounton House has a grand version of this on its entrance front.

63. *Country Life*, 20.6.1903, pp.838–46; attributions from Michael Bullen, John Crook, Rodney Hubbuck and Nikolaus Pevsner, *The Buildings of England: Hampshire – Winchester and the North*, New Haven and London: Yale University Press 2010, pp.530–39.

64. 'South Wraxall Manor, Wiltshire', *Country Life*, 26.3.1904, pp.450–59; 14.1.1905, pp.54–64. The house featured also in one of Tipping's contributions to the Country Life Library.

65. Photographs of the screen in the church of St Mary the Virgin, Croscombe, Somerset, 9.4.1904, pp.518–19, suggest that it was not only houses that interested Hudson and Graham.

66. For example, those at Park Hall, Great Bardfield, Essex, *Country Life*, 4.3.1905, pp.306–14; Methley Hall, 18.5.1907, pp.702–9; Lymore, Montgomeryshire, 7.3.1908, pp.342–9.

67. *Country Life*, 12.9.1908, p.368. A photograph of Lindisfarne showing the ship was not published until the article of 7.6.1913, pp.830–42. A similar ship appeared much later at Lutyens's Lambay: *Country Life*, 27.7.1929, p.121.

68. 'The Week-End Cottage', *Country Life*, 6.6.1903, pp.753–4; 'Old Cottages Adapted to Modern Needs', 18.2.1905, pp.244–6.

69. Crosswell Cottages, Goose Lane, Hook Heath; published in Elder-Duncan, *Country Cottages and Week-End Homes*, p.180. 7–8 Dunsborough Cottages, Ripley: ibid., p.51.

70. Brittain-Catlin, 'Downward Trajectory', p.143.

71. *Country Life*, 13.4.1901, p.480.

72. W. Galsworthy Davie and E. Guy Dawber, *Old Cottages, Farm-Houses, and Other Stone Buildings in the Cotswold District: Examples of Minor Domestic Architecture in Gloucestershire, Oxfordshire, Northants*, London: Batsford, 1905.

73. 'A Model Village', *Country Life*, 14.7.1906, pp.41–3.

74. John Betjeman, 'Mackay Hugh Baillie Scott', first published in the *Journal of Manx Museum*, vol.7, no.84, 1968, reproduced in Haigh, *Baillie Scott*, p.115.

75. *Country Life*, 1.4.1905, p.468.

76. 'A Week-End Cottage' (The Stocks, Wittersham, Kent), *Country Life*, 25.3.1905, pp.404–6. For Maule at the AA, see Alan Powers, 'Edwardian Architectural Education: A Study of Three Schools of Architecture', *AA Files*, no.5, 1984, p.50.

77. *Country Life*, 12.8.1905, p.216.

78. 'A Bothy at Godinton', *Country Life*, 7.9.1907, pp.335–7; Weaver, *The 'Country Life' Book of Cottages*, pp.176–89. Historic England list description 1116143; Blomfield, *Memoirs*, p.82.

79. Weaver, *Small Country Houses: Their Repair & Enlargement*, p.xxviii; figs XII and XII, p.xxx; Haslam, *Clough Williams-Ellis*, p.29.

80. Girouard, *Sweetness and Light*, p.114; Simon Bradley and Nikolaus Pevsner, *The Buildings of England: Cambridgeshire*, New Haven and London: Yale University Press, 2014, p.83.

81. James Bettley and Nikolaus Pevsner, *The Buildings of England: Essex*, New Haven and London: Yale University Press, 2nd edn, reprint, 2010, p.528.

82. Falkner: See Nikolaus Pevsner, 'Obituary, Harold Falkner, 1875–1963', in *Architectural Review*, vol.135, 1964, p.240.

83. Elder-Duncan, *Country Cottages and Week-End Homes*, pp.70–71, 74, 81 and 91–2.

84. Weaver, *The 'Country Life' Book of Cottages*, pp.99–100. My thanks to Hugh Routh for this.

85. I am indebted to Simon Bradley for this interesting observation.

86. Public Health Acts Amendment, 7 Edw.7, c.53, s.23 (b).

87. William H. Draper, 'The Land of Homeliness',

Country Life, 10.3.1906, pp.337–40.

88. *Country Life*, 15.08.03, pp.240–47.
89. W.R. Lethaby, 'The Architecture of Adventure', a talk given at the RIBA on 18.4.1910, reproduced in the *RIBA Journal*, vol.17, 1910, pp.469–78; quote at p.469.
90. ibid., p.478.
91. ibid., p.482. The later edition is Lethaby, *Form in Civilisation*, London: Oxford University Press, 1922, p.66–95.
92. Reginald Blomfield, *Modernismus*, London: Macmillan, 1934, p.175.
93. Darwin, *Fifty Years of Country Life*, p.49.
94. For Tipping's life and writing see Helena Gerrish, *Edwardian Country Life: The Story of H. Avray Tipping*, London: Frances Lincoln, 2011.
95. Darwin, *Fifty Years of Country Life*, p.57.
96. H. Avray Tipping, 'Zuylestein, Holland', *Country Life*, 6.4.1907, p.486.
97. Tipping, 'Millmead, Bramley: An Example of Building and Building Bye-Laws', *Country Life*, 11.5.07, pp.674–8.
98. Gerrish, *Edwardian Country Life*, pp.101–10.
99. 'The Wyck, Hitchin', *Country Life*, 4.11.1905, pp.630–35.
100. A.W.N. Pugin, *An Apology for the Revival of Christian Architecture*, London: John Weale, 1843, p.38.
101. *Country Life*, 21.3.1908, pp.411–13; Gerrish, *Edwardian Country Life*, pp.84–101, does not mention the cottages but gives the overall story.
102. Gerrish, *Edwardian Country Life*, pp.20–21.
103. 'Suggestions for Small Homesteads', *Country Life*, 13.6.1908, pp.859–61.
104. For example, 22.5.1909, pp.747–9; 31.7.1909, pp.173–4.
105. 28.8.1909, pp.292–9.
106. Tipping, 'Lesser Country Houses of To-day (1), Sapperton Cottage', *Country Life*, 6.3.1909, p.353.
107. *Country Life*, 15.5.1909, pp.708–10; 26.6.1909, pp.947–51.
108. This was in relation to Little Thakeham, 28.8.1909, p.299.
109. 'Brinsop Court, Herefordshire', *Country Life*, 7.11.1914, pp.614–22.
110. Gerrish, *Edwardian Country Life*, p.29.
111. Tipping, 'Tudor House, Broadway', *Country Life*, 10.9.1910, pp.360–64.
112. 'Headley Court, Epson', *Country Life*, 6.7.1912, pp.18–25; Lawrence Weaver, 'Notgrove Manor, Gloucestershire', *Country Life*, 21.11.1914, pp.678–83.
113. Lawrence Weaver, 'Paycocke's, Coggeshall, Essex', *Country Life*, 12.7.1913, supplement, pp.7–11.
114. Lawrence Weaver, 'Normanby Hall', *Country Life*, 29.7.1911, p.174.
115. *Country Life*, 10.3.1906, p.349.
116. See Chapter Two, pp.84–91 above.
117. See Clive Aslet, 'Architecture and Agriculture', *Country Life*, 14.1.2015, pp.58–61.
118. C. Hussey, 'Weaver, Sir Lawrence Walter William (1876–1930), civil servant and architectural writer', *Oxford Dictionary of Biography*.

119. See Lawrence Trevelyan Weaver, *Lawrence Weaver 1876–1930*.
120. Lawrence Weaver, 'Sandhouse, Witley', *Country Life*, 27.8.1910, pp.296–302.
121. For the context, see Neil Jackson, *F.W. Troup: Architect 1859–1941*, London: Building Centre Trust, 1985.
122. There is a comprehensive guide to the Peasant Arts movement and the roles of Troup and King in it by Catherine Eyre at http://peasant-arts.blogspot.co.uk/.
123. The house was also published in the *Architectural Review*, in March 1903: vol.13, pp.120–24.
124. Lawrence Weaver, 'Nether Swell Manor', *Country Life*, 26.11.1910, pp.754–60.
125. Avon Tyrrell: 11.6.1910, pp.846–52; 'Giants': Weaver, *Small Country Houses of To-day*, p.xi; New Place: *Country Life*, 5.4.1910, pp.522–31; Standen: 7.5.1910, pp.666–72; Dawpool: 18.2.1911, pp.234–41; Chesters: 17.2.12, pp.244–8.
126. Wilfrid Scawen Blunt, 'Clouds', *Country Life*, 19.11.1904, pp.738–48.
127. Lawrence Weaver, 'Chesters', *Country Life*, 17.2.1912, p.248.
128. Hermann Muthesius, *The English House* (first published in Berlin as *Das englische Haus*, 1904–5), London: Frances Lincoln, 2007, vol.1, pp.114, 119 and 124; adopted, for example, in Nikolaus Pevsner's 'from William Morris to the Bauhaus' version of history.
129. Weaver, *Small Country Houses: Their Repair and Enlargement*, p.xxi.
130. Weaver, *Small Country Houses of To-day*, p.195; p.139.
131. Inverleith, Norwich: ibid., pp.67–70; published in the magazine, 8.1.1910, pp.37–41.
132. Weaver, *Small Country Houses: Their Repair and Enlargement*: Stonewall Cottage: p.80; Little Pednor Farm: p.70 and fig.103, p.73; Wolverton Court, pp.88–93.
133. Weaver, *The 'Country Life' Book of Cottages*, pp.7–8.
134. ibid., p.111.
135. *Country Life*, 25.2.1911, p.280; Bowood: 6.9.13 pp.324–31; Compton Verney: 18.10.1913, pp.528–35; Kenwood: 22.11.13, pp.710–18; A.T. Bolton, *Jacobean Architecture and the Work of Inigo Jones in the Earlier Style*, London: Architectural Association, 1911.
136. Weaver, *The 'Country Life' Book of Cottages*, pp.155 and 158. Now called Eversley, Brampton Road.
137. ibid., p.2.
138. ibid., pp.28–9; Clough Williams-Ellis, *Building in Cob, Pisé, Chalk & Clay: a Renaissance*, London: Country Life, 1919.
139. Golf club houses in detail: *Country Life*, 27.8.1910, pp.302–5.
140. Weaver, *The 'Country Life' Book of Cottages*, pp.124, 125 and 128.
141. H. Avray Tipping, 'Outdoor Dining-Rooms', in Lawrence Weaver, *The House and its Equipment*, London: Country Life, 1912, pp.156–63.

142. Weaver, *Small Country Houses: Their Repair and Enlargement*, p.xi.
143. Clough Williams-Ellis, *Lawrence Weaver*, London: Bles, 1933, p.66.
144. For example, George Ll. Morris, 'Philip Webb's Town Work', illustrated by Ricardo, *Architectural Review*, vol.2, 1897, pp.198–208.
145. Mervyn Macartney, 'The First Garden City', *Architectural Review*, vol.18, 1905, pp.14–21; H. Kempson Dyson, 'Cheap Cottages and the Exhibition at Letchworth', *Architectural Review*, vol.18, 1905, pp.108–15 and 154–6.
146. Blomfield, *Memoirs*, p.103; Nikolaus Pevsner, 'Goodhart-Rendel's Roll-Call', n.1, p.264.
147. Pevsner, 'Goodhart-Rendel', n.1, p.264. See also Peter Davey, 'Radical Delight: 120 years of the AR, 1896–1921', in *Architectural Review*, 1.2017, pp.90–92, for another précis of the early years.
148. Blomfield, *Memoirs*, p.103; Pevsner, 'Goodhart-Rendel's Roll-Call', p.259.
149. Blomfield, *Memoirs*, p.104; this is supported by the detailed description in n.3 to Pevsner, 'Goodhart-Rendel's Roll-Call', p.264.
150. Blomfield, *Memoirs*, pp.57 and 74–5.
151. ibid., p.36.
152. Pevsner, 'Goodhart-Rendel's Roll-Call', p.260
153. Blomfield, *Memoirs*, p.103.
154. *Architectural Review*, vol.2, 1897, p.97.
155. Powers, 'Edwardian Architectural Education', p.49.
156. In respect of his branch for Barclays Bank in Fleet Street, London: *Architectural Review*, vol.7, 1900, pp.163–7.
157. Paul Waterhouse, 'Life and Work of Welby Pugin', *Architectural Review*, vol.3, 1897–8, pp.167–75, 211–21 and 264–73; vol.4, 1898, pp.23–7, 67–73, 115–18 and 159–65.
158. *Architectural Review*: Scott, vol.24, 1908, pp.92–100, 147–52, 180–85 and 291–3; Bodley, vol.11, 1902, pp.130–39; Butterfield, vol.7, 1900, pp.259–62 and vol.8, 1900, pp.15–23; Bentley, vol.11, 1902, pp.155–64 and vol.12, 1902, pp.18–30.
159. Walter Godfrey, 'The Work of George Devey', *Architectural Review*, vol.21, 1907, pp.22–30, 83–8 and 293–306.
160. *Architectural Review*, vol.7, 1900, p.58.
161. *Architectural Review*, vol.1, 1896–7, pp.59–67.
162. Davey, *Arts and Crafts Architecture*, p.112.
163. Adam (by Percy Fitzgerald): *Architectural Review*, vol.7, 1900, pp.147–56 and 273–83; Elmes: vol.15, 1904, pp.230–45; Burton: *Architectural Review*, vol.17, 1905, pp.108–18 and 154–64.
164. Mowbray A. Green, 'Bath Doorways of the Eighteenth Century', *Architectural Review*, vol.17, 1905, pp.63–9 and 195–201; A.E. Street, 'London Street Architecture', *Architectural Review*, vol.17, 1905, pp.164–7, 201–14 and 245–57.
165. Davey, *Arts and Crafts Architecture*, p.86.
166. *Architectural Review*, vol.7, 1900, p.214. For Macartney, see Jan Ward, *Mervyn Edmund Macartney, Architect, 1853–1932: The Life and Work of Sir Mervyn Macartney, BA, FRIBA,*

FSA, with Particular Reference to his Houses and Clients on the Surrey/Kent Border, York: York College of Further and Higher Education Reprographics Department, 1998.

167. Halsey Ricardo, 'Some Conditions of House Design', part 2, *Architectural Review*, vol.3, 1897–8, p.49.

168. *Architectural Review*, vol.9, 1901, pp.143–4.

169. Macartney, *Recent English Domestic Architecture*, vol.2, 1909, p.iii.

170. Lawrence Weaver, 'Upmeads, Stafford', *Country Life*, 12.11.1910, supplement, pp.7–11.

171. Macartney, *Recent English Domestic Architecture*, vol.2, pp.86–8.

172. ibid., vol.3, 1910, pp.32–7.

173. ibid., vol.5, 1912, pp.4–7.

174. ibid., vol.5, pp.12–19.

175. ibid., vol.5, pp.40–44, 165–7 and 171.

176. ibid., vol.5, pp.21–3.

177. Kirk, *Philip Webb*, pp.72–3.

178. Macartney, *Recent English Domestic Architecture*, vol.3, pp.80–81.

179. W. Shaw Sparrow, *Flats, Urban Houses and Cottage Homes*, London: Hodder & Stoughton, 1906, plates following p.120.

180. *Builders' Journal*, 3.1.1900, pp.331 and 333–5; 17.1.1900, p.366.

181. *Builders' Journal*, 28.1.1901, p.1.

182. *Builders' Journal*, 16.11.1906, text: p.256; 26.1.1910, p.65; supplement.

183. Blomfield, *Memoirs*, p.153.

184. *Builders' Journal*, 4.6.1902, p.241. The bankruptcy courts, demolished in the 1950s, were a plain, institutional building to the north-west of the London Law Courts.

185. *Builders' Journal*, 11.5.1904, pp.222–3; 22.6.1904, supplement.

186. Weaver, *Small Country Houses of To-day*, p.19.

187. E.M. Forster, *The Longest Journey*, London: Edward Arnold, 1907, p.179.

188. Haigh, *Baillie Scott*, p.56. See also A. Saint, 'Unwin, Sir Raymond (1863–1940), engineer, architect, and town planner', *Oxford Dictionary of National Biography*.

189. 41 Heath Drive, Gidea Park; Macartney, *Recent English Domestic Architecture*, vol.2, pp.161–3 (Chesterfield); vol.4, pp.77–8 (Rotherwick Road, Hampstead Garden Suburb) and 83–7 (Rochdale).

190. Historic England list description 1279930 (Kildare Lodge); Elder-Duncan, *Country Cottages and Week-End Homes*, pp.185 and 193–4.

191. Macartney, *Recent English Domestic Architecture*, vol.1, pp.198–200.

192. *Builders' Journal*, 22.6.1910, p.645; 29.6.1910, pp.666 and 670–73.

193. It became the *Builders' Journal and Architectural Engineer* in 1906, *The Architects' and Builders' Journal* in 1910, and eventually the *Architects' Journal* after the War.

194. *Builders' Journal*, 3.4.1901, p.151; 4.5.1904, supplement; 21.8.1901, pp.18–19; Muthesius, *The English House*, p.153.

195. *Builders' Journal*, 26.6.1901, supplement.

196. *Builders' Journal*, 1.3.1901, supplement; 10.4.1901, supplement, and p.181.

197. *Builders' Journal*, 12.2.1902, pp.454–5. For Penty in an architectural context, see Ballantyne and Law, *Tudoresque*, pp.110–11.

198. *Builders' Journal*, 18.6.1902, supplement; 8.7.1903, supplement.

199. *Builders' Journal*, 27.7.1904, supplement.

200. For example, *Builder*, 11.3.1905.

201. *Builders' Journal*, 20.8.1902, p.1.

202. *British Architect*, 9.12.1888, p.409.

203. *British Architect*, vol.54, 5.10.1900, p.245; 16.11.00, p.353.

204. *British Architect*, vol.54, 6.7.1900, pp.1–2.

205. For example: Goddards, *British Architect*, vol.54, 9.11.1900, pp.330–35; Marsh Court, *British Architect*, vol.64, 13.10.1905, unnumbered plate.

206. *Builder*, 17.3.1900, pp.258–60.

207. *Builder*, 17.3.1900: lecture, pp.258–60; comments, pp.260–62.

208. *Builder*, 3.3.1900; 17.6.1905.

209. *Builder*, 1.4.1905, pp.352–3 and supplement; 29.1.1910.

210. Pevsner, 'Goodhart-Rendel's Roll-Call', p.262.

211. C.R. Ashbee, 'On the Dromenagh Estate at Iver Heath', *Studio*, vol.36, 1905, pp.47–52.

212. *Studio*, vol.21, 1900: October, pp.28–36; November, pp.86–95; December, pp.176–90.

213. G. Ll. Morris and Esther Wood, 'The Country Cottage and the Materials Used in its Construction', *Studio*, vol.36, 1905, pp.146–55.

214. *Studio*, vol.36, 1905, pp.199–209.

215. *Builders' Journal*, 13.7.1904, pp.14–15.

216. 'The British Homes Series', *Architectural Review*, vol.22, 1907, p.305.

217. W. Shaw Sparrow, *The Modern Home: A Book of British Domestic Architecture for Moderate Incomes – A Companion Volume to 'The British Home of To-day'*, London: Hodder & Stoughton, 1906, foreword, p.5; Hentschel: Shaw Sparrow, *Flats, Urban Houses and Cottage Homes*, endpaper viii.

218. W.H. Bidlake, 'The Home from Outside', in Shaw Sparrow, *The Modern Home*, p.24.

219. Brittain-Catlin, *The English Parsonage*, pp.172–3 and 249.

220. Lawrence Weaver, 'Morton House, Hatfield', *Country Life*, 25.2.1911, supplement, pp.7–11.

221. *Architectural Review*, vol.22, 1906, p.305.

222. Elder-Duncan, *Country Cottages and Week-End Homes*, pp.54–5, 64 and 73.

223. The word 'bungalow' started to appear in any quantity in its modern sense in British publications in the 1940s.

224. Ernest Newton, *A Book of Country Houses: A Series of Examples Erected at Hampstead & Elsewhere*, London: Batsford, 1903; C.H.B. Quennell, *Modern Suburban Houses: A Series of Examples Erected at Hampstead & Elsewhere*, London: Batsford, 1906.

225. Eventually published in book form with later commentary in Dean Hawkes (ed.), *Modern Country Homes in England: The Arts and Crafts Architecture of Barry Parker*, Cambridge: Cambridge University Press, 1986.

226. 'The British Homes Series', *Architectural Review*, vol.22, 1907, p.305.

227. Thomas Garner and Arthur Stratton, *The Domestic Architecture of England During the Tudor Period / Illustrated in a Series of Photographs & Measured Drawings of Country Mansions, Manor Houses and Smaller Buildings with Historical and Descriptive Text*, London: Batsford, 1908–11.

228. There is no reference to the recent work either in the article on it in *Country Life*, 12.9.1903, pp.368–72.

229. Ayrton's book was referred to in the *Review* but has not been located.

230. See Brittain-Catlin, *The English Parsonage*, p.81.

231. S. Carr, 'Batsford, Henry George [Harry] (1880–1951), publisher and author', *Oxford Dictionary of National Biography*.

232. Macartney, *Recent English Domestic Architecture*, vol.4, pp.66–7.

233. Arthur Martin, *The Small House: Its Architecture and Surroundings*, London: Alston Rivers, 1906, p.5.

234. ibid., front endpapers to second edition of 1909.

235. Raymond Unwin, *Town Planning in Practice: An Introduction to the Art of Designing Cities and Suburbs*, London: Benn, 1909.

236. 'Brilliant': Muthesius, *The English House*, vol.1, p.147.

237. See Introduction, p.17 above.

238. Muthesius, *The English House*, vol.1, p.145.

Chapter Four

1. For the historical significance of Pitt Rivers's experimental analytical and interpretive techniques, see for example Bowden, *Pitt Rivers*, p.172.

2. Julia Briggs, *A Woman of Passion: The Life of E. Nesbit 1858–1924*, London etc.: Hutchinson, 1987, p.171–2.

3. Nesbit, *Harding's Luck*, London: Hodder & Stoughton, 1909, p.199.

4. ibid., p.39.

5. ibid., p.210; on p.184 the Ardens are going to 'mend the houses of the tenants and to do good to the poor and needy'.

6. E. Nesbit, *The Enchanted Castle*, London: T. Fisher Unwin, 1907, p.148.

7. For example, to Whitstable: Briggs, *A Woman of Passion*, p.170.

8. De Moubray, *Twentieth Century Castles*, pp.48–61 and 74–81.

9. 'Magic world': Nesbit, *Harding's Luck*, p. 211.

10. ibid., pp.120–21.

11. ibid., p.275.

12. ibid., p.1.

13. Quennell, *The Marble Foot*, p.16; Briggs, *A Woman of Passion*, p.2.

14. Quennell, *The Marble Foot*, p.20.

15. Alison Lurie, *Not in Front of the Grown-Ups: Subversive Children's Literature*, 2nd edn, London: Sphere Books, 1991, p.131

16. Nesbit, *The Enchanted Castle*, p.280.

17. See Chapter One, p.65 above.

18. E. Nesbit, 'The Cockatoucan', in *Nine Unlikely Tales*, London: T. Fisher Unwin, 1901, fig., p.37; text: p.39.

19. For example, *Architectural Review*, supplement following p.32; vol.6, 1899 (Mallows); *Builders' Journal*, 18.6.1902, supplement; 8.7.1903 (Lucas).

20. For example, for Niven & Wigglesworth before they found Harold Falkner to do it for them: *Architectural Review*, supplement following p.32, vol.6, 1899; for Walter E. Hewitt, *Builders' Journal*, 18.6.1902, supplement; 8.7.1903.

21. Endpapers to Romaine-Walker's edition of Lewis Carroll's *Alice's Adventures in Wonderland*, London: Bodley Head, c.1908.

22. Critics' comments from the unpaginated endpapers of *Alice's Adventures*.

23. H. Avray Tipping, *Country Life*, 31.12.1910, pp.970–81; 6.10.1910, pp.324–33; 13.10.1910, pp.348–55; 20.10.1917, pp.372–9. Blomfield had in fact designed part of the garden there before the Lees's interior alterations. For before and after plans, see Somerset Plantagenet Fry, *Chequers: The Country Home of Britain's Prime Ministers*, London: HMSO, 1977, pp.90–91.

24. Blomfield, *Memoirs*, pp.84–5.

25. See Brittain-Catlin, 'Good Fairies', pp.127–8.

26. *Country Life*, 9.12.1911, p.910.

27. Frederick Greenwood, *Imagination in Dreams and their Study*, London: John Lane, 1894, pp.176–80.

28. ibid., preface, p.vii.

29. *The Book of the Exhibition*, p.40; the houses, 3–7 Heath Drive, were by Bunney & Makins.

30. Gillian Whitley Roberts, 'William Johnson Harrison Weller (1877–1960): a Wolverhampton architect in the Arts and Crafts style', unpublished MSt dissertation, University of Cambridge, 2018, pp.16–19.

31. J.W. Mackail, *The Life of William Morris*, London: Longmans Green, 1899, p.312; quoted in Davey, *Arts and Crafts Architecture*, p.77.

32. Hermann Muthesius, *Landhaus und Garten: Beispiele neuzeitlicher Landhäuser nebst Grundrissen, Innenräumen und Gärten*, Munich: F. Bruckmann, 1907, p.156.

33. The layout can be deduced from a drainage application in Camden Local History and Archives Centre, 16.8.1938, which was drawn over Voysey's plan and elevations: Drainage Records, 73 Fitzjohn's Avenue, 3185 (1). Pevsner gave the date as 1901–3 and the client as P.A. Barendt: Bridget Cherry and Nikolaus Pevsner, *The Buildings of England: London 4: North*, New Haven and London: Yale University Press, 2002, p.237.

34. I am indebted to a conversation with Maša Tatalović at the Architectural Association for this observation.

35. Analysed in Haigh, *Baillie Scott*.

36. ibid., pp.22–3.

37. For an excellent visual record of many of Baillie Scott's houses, see Ian Macdonald-Smith, *Arts and Crafts Master: The Houses and Gardens of M.H. Baillie Scott*, New York: Rizzoli, 2010.

38. ibid., pp.26–33 and 110–13.

39. See ibid., pp.142–5.

40. See Introduction, p.22 above.

41. For example, the 11 fine drawings that accompany his 'Country Cottages and their Gardens', *Studio*, vol.48, 1910, pp.283–90.

42. Shaw Sparrow, *Flats, Urban Houses and Cottage Homes*, pl. between pp.120–21.

43. *Architectural Review*, vol.10, 1901, p.49. Sardonic ('pawky'): obituary, *Architect & Building News*, 9.1.1942, p.17.

44. See the online *Dictionary of Scottish Architects*: Andrew Noble Prentice.

45. *Architectural Review*, vol.1, 1896–7, p.151.

46. Illustrated in *Architectural Review*, vol.8, 1900, p.146.

47. *Architectural Review*, vol.6, 1899, unnumbered plate.

48. The Orchard Farm: Weaver, *Small Country Houses: Their Repair and Enlargement*, pp.138–41.

49. For example, Avebury Diary, 13.8.09; 9.12.1905.

50. Searle, *A New England?*, pp.369 and 382–3.

51. A. Beresford Pite, 'Modern House Design', *Architectural Review*, vol.8, 1900, p.155.

52. Carrington Diary, 17.1.1899, p.17.

53. Lady Carrington Diary, 9.1.1906.

54. Lady Carrington Diary, 7.2.1896.

55. Quoted in Mallet, *Herbert Gladstone*, pp.18–19.

56. Brittain-Catlin, *The English Parsonage*, pp.199–200.

57. George Gilbert Scott, *Personal and Professional Recollections*, London: Sampson Low, Marston, Searle & Rivington, 1879, p.88.

58. Edward Fawcett, *Liberalism: The Life of an Idea*, Princeton and Oxford: Princeton University Press, 2014, pp.85–97.

59. A.W. Jarvis, 'The Old English Christmas', *Country Life*, 22.12.1906, pp.896–9.

60. See Chapter Three, p.123 above.

61. Darwin, *Fifty Years of Country Life*, p.23.

62. Bowden, *Pitt Rivers*, p.72.

63. Allibone, *George Devey*, p.44.

64. By comparing the photograph with the map, Pine End appears to be the cottage facing Callisgrange Farm on the other side of Callis Court Road, TR384950 68845, in the 1880 1st edition county series 1:2500 OS map; by the 1st revision of 1896 it had been demolished, but a very similar pair of gables had been built to enclose a small wing, perhaps the relocated Pine End itself, added to 6 Callis Court Road about 200 metres further south. My thanks to Damir and Sacha Novakovic. There is a drawing of Pine End based on a survey by J.P. Seddon in W.A. Scott Robertson, 'Archæological Notes on Thanet', *Archæologia Cantiana*, vol.12, 1878, p.388, but this article does not give any precise location for it. Gordon Taylor, in *Thanet's Dutch and Flemish Style Houses* (Broadstairs: Isle of Thanet Archaeological Society, 2014, p.33), thinks that it was in the centre of the village of Reading Street itself, but the Ordnance Survey maps do not support this.

65. Quoted in Hutchinson, *The Life of Sir John Lubbock*, vol.1 p.245.

66. Avebury Diary, 23.12.1902; undated entry between 27.12.1902 and 31.12.1902.

67. Avebury Diary, summary for 18.9.1907. He wrote something similar under the date itself, so it clearly affected him. Eric's health: Hutchinson wrote that Eric had become, by the age of 20, an oarsman in the Oxford Trial Eights: Hutchinson, *The Life of Sir John Lubbock*, vol.2, p.141.

68. Hutchinson, *The Life of Sir John Lubbock*, vol.2, p.280.

69. ibid., vol.2, pp.280–81.

70. ibid., vol.2, p.281.

71. ibid., vol.2, p.140.

72. Recorded in ibid., vol.1, p.121.

73. ibid., vol.2, pp.140–41.

74. Sales particulars; Kent Archives and Local History Service, EK/U1453/E39/5.

75. Hutchinson, *The Life of Sir John Lubbock*, vol.2, p.318.

BIBLIOGRAPHY

Manuscripts

Avebury Diaries: Diaries and correspondence, etc., of and relating to Sir John Lubbock, 4th Bart. (1834–1913), 1st Baron Avebury (1900), British Library, Add MS 62681–62682: 1850–1913.

Carrington Diaries: Carington Estate Archives at Bledlow, Buckinghamshire.
Earl Carrington Diary: Microfilm of the Papers of Charles Robert Wynn-Carrington, Marquess of Lincolnshire, Bodleian Libraries, MSS Film 1103.

Lady Carrington Diary: Lady Carrington's Diaries 1892–1913, Bodleian Libraries, Oxford, MSS Film 1100.

Printed sources

For consistency, all unhyphenated double surnames are listed alphabetically by the final name. Only magazine articles where the author has been identified are listed here.

Adams, Maurice B., *Modern Cottage Architecture: From the Works of Well-Known Architects*, London: Batsford, 1904.

Adams, Thomas, 'Thomas Adams on the Housing and Town Planning Act, 1909', *Architectural Review*, Town Planning and Housing Supplement, part 1, vol.27, January 1910, pp.52–4.

Adshead, S.D., 'Romford Garden Suburb, Gidea Park: Cottage Exhibition and Town Plan', *Town Planning Review*, vol.2, 7.1911, pp.124–7.

Adonis, Andrew, 'Aristocracy, Agriculture and Liberalism: The Politics, Finances and Estates of the Third Lord Carrington', *The Historical Journal*, vol.31, no.4, 12.1988, pp.871–97.

Allibone, Jill, *George Devey: Architect 1820–1886*, Cambridge: Lutterworth Press, 1991.

Anon., *Family Homes: Containing a Third Series of Over Sixty Designs by Fifty Architects for Ideal Houses and Cottages*, London: Baker, 1913.

Anon., *The Book of the Exhibition of Houses and Cottages, Romford Garden Suburb, Gidea Park*, London: The Exhibition Committee, 1911.

Anon., *The Romford Garden Suburb*, Havering: Gidea Park District Civic Society, 1986.

Antram, Nicholas, and Pevsner, Nikolaus, *The Buildings of England: Sussex – East, with Brighton and Hove*, New Haven and London: Yale University Press, 2003.

Ashbee. C.R., 'On the Dromenagh Estate at Iver Heath', *Studio*, vol.36, 1905, pp.47–52.

Aslet, Clive, *The Last Country Houses*, New Haven and London: Yale University Press, 1982.

Aslet, Clive, 'Architecture and Agriculture', *Country Life*, 14.1.2015, pp.58–61.

Asquith, Margot, *The Autobiography of Margot Asquith*, London: Thornton Butterworth, vol.1, 1920.

Ayling, R. Stephen, 'Augustus W. Tanner', *RIBA Journal*, vol.30, 1923, pp.626–7.

Ballantyne, Andrew, and Law, Andrew, *Tudoresque: In Pursuit of the Ideal Home*, London: Reaktion, 2011.

Beattie, Susan, *A Revolution in London Housing: LCC Architects and their Work 1893–1914*, London: Architectural Press, 1980.

Bartholomew. Alfred, *Specifications for Practical Architecture*, London: J. Williams, 1840.

Betjeman, John, 'Mackay Hugh Baillie Scott', first published in the *Journal of Manx Museum*, vol.7, no.84, 1968, reproduced in Haigh, *Baillie Scott: The Artistic House*, 1995, pp.114–17.

Bettley, James, and Pevsner, Nikolaus, *The Buildings of England: Essex*, New Haven and London: Yale University Press, 2nd edn, reprint, 2010.

Bidlake, W.H., 'The Home from Outside', in Shaw Sparrow, *The Modern Home*, pp.13–32.

Blomfield, Reginald, *Memoirs of an Architect*, London: Macmillan, 1932.

Blomfield, Reginald, *Modernismus*, London: Macmillan, 1934.

Blunt, Wilfrid Scawen, 'Clouds', *Country Life*, 19.11.1904, pp.738–48.

Bolton, A.T., *Jacobean Architecture and the Work of Inigo Jones in the Earlier Style*, London: Architectural Association, 1911.

Bowden, Mark, *Pitt Rivers: The Life and Archaeological Work of Lieutenant-General Augustus Henry Lane Fox Pitt Rivers, DCL, FRS, FSA*, Cambridge: Cambridge University Press, 1991.

Bradley, Simon, and Pevsner, Nikolaus, *The Buildings of England: London 6 – Westminster*, New Haven and London: Yale University Press, 2003.

Bradley, Simon, and Pevsner, Nikolaus, *The Buildings of England: Cambridgeshire*, New Haven and London: Yale University Press, 2014.

Briggs, Julia, *A Woman of Passion: The Life of E. Nesbit 1858–1924*, London etc.: Hutchinson, 1987.

Briggs, Martin Shaw, 'George Gilbert Scott R.A.', *Architectural Review*, vol.24, 1908, pp.92–100, 147–52, 180–85 and 291–3.

Brittain-Catlin, Timothy, 'La Normandie de Nodier; L'Angleterre de Pugin', in Martin Kew Meade, Werner Szambien and Simona Talenti (eds), *Architecture normande en France: identités et échanges*, Marseilles: Éditions Parenthèses, 2002, pp.149–54.

Brittain-Catlin, Timothy, *The English Parsonage in the Early Nineteenth Century*, Reading: Spire Books, 2008.

Brittain-Catlin, Timothy, 'Horace Field and Lloyds Bank', *Architectural History*, no.53, 2010, pp.271–94.

Brittain-Catlin, Timothy, 'Downward Trajectory: Towards a Theory of Failure', *ARQ*, vol.5, no.2, 2011, pp.139–47.

Brittain-Catlin, Timothy, *Bleak Houses: Failure and Disappointment in Architecture*, Cambridge, MA: MIT Press, 2014.

Brittain-Catlin, Timothy, 'Picturesque, Modern, Tudor-Style: Edgar Ranger in Thanet', in *Twentieth Century Architecture 12, Houses:*

Regional Practice and Local Character, 2015, pp.34–47.

Brittain-Catlin, Timothy, 'Good Fairies', *AA Files*, no.73, 2016, pp.121–8.

Brittain-Catlin, Timothy, *19th- and 20th-Century Convents and Monasteries* (Introduction to Heritage Assets), 2nd edn, London: Historic England, 2016.

Brittain–Catlin, Timothy, 'Realism in Nineteenth-Century British Architecture', in Harry Mallgrave, Martin Bressani and Christina Contandriopoulos (eds), *The Companions to the History of Architecture*, vol.3, Hoboken: Wiley, 2017, pp.174–91.

Britton, John, *The Architectural Antiquities of Britain*, vol.5, London: Longman, Hurst, Rees & Orme, 1826.

Brock, Michael, and Brock, Eleanor, *Margot Asquith's Great War Diary 1914–1916: The View from Downing Street*, Oxford: Oxford University Press, 2014.

Brodie, Antonia, Felstead, Alison, Franklin, Jonathan and Pinfield, Leslie, and Oldfield, Jane, *Directory of British Architects 1834–1914*, London: Continuum, 3rd edn, 2001.

Brooks, Alan and Pevsner, Nikolaus, *The Buildings of England: Herefordshire*, New Haven and London: Yale University Press, 2012.

Brooks, Alan, and Sherwood, Jennifer, *The Buildings of England: Oxfordshire North and West*, New Haven and London: Yale University Press, 2017.

Brooks, Chris, *Signs for the Times*, London: Routledge, 1984.

Brown, Jane, *Lutyens and the Edwardians: An English Architect and his Clients*, London: Viking, 1996.

Bullen, Michael, Crook, John, Hubbuck, Rodney, and Pevsner, Nikolaus, *The Buildings of England: Hampshire – Winchester and the North*, New Haven and London: Yale University Press, 2010.

Burnett, Frances Hodgson, *The Secret Garden*, London: William Heinemann, 1911.

Carroll, Lewis, *Alice's Adventures in Wonderland*, with illustrations by W.H. Romaine-Walker, London: Bodley Head, c.1908.

Caverhill, Austin, *Rushmore: Then and Now*, Tollard Royal: Sandroyd School, 1988; a partial transcription available online at http://web.prm.ox.ac.uk/rpr/index.php/article-index/12-articles/815-austin-caverhill.html

Cherry, Bridget, and Pevsner, Nikolaus, *The Buildings of England: London 2 – South*, New Haven and London: Yale University Press, 2002.

Cherry, Bridget, and Pevsner, Nikolaus, *The Buildings of England: London 4 – North*, New Haven and London: Yale University Press, 2002.

Clapham, Alfred W., and Godfrey, Walter, *Some Famous Buildings and their Story*, London: Technical Journals, 1913.

Clemenson, Heather, *English Country Houses and Landed Estates*, London: Croom Hill, 1982.

Cole, David, *Sir Edwin Lutyens: The Arts and Crafts Houses*, Mulgrave: Images, 2017.

Colvin, Howard, *A Biographical Dictionary of British Architects 1600–1840*, 3rd edn, New Haven and London: Yale University Press, 1995.

Cousins, Michael, '"As for paradise which is but another name for Kingsgate"', *The Follies Journal*, no.8, Summer 2009, pp.47–88.

Cornish, C.J., 'New Forest Scenes III – Foresters' Cottages', *Country Life*, 15.1.1898, pp.57–9.

Cornish, C.J., 'Ancient Water Mills', *Country Life*, 5.2.1898, pp.134–6.

Cornish, C.J., 'Village Houses for Holiday Homes', *Country Life*, 7.5.1898, pp.552–4.

Cornforth, John, 'Lutyens and Country Life: 81 Not Out', in *Lutyens: The Work of the English Architect Sir Edwin Lutyens (1869–1944)*, exhibition catalogue, London: Hayward Gallery, 1981, pp.25–31.

Crawford, Alan, *C.R. Ashbee: Architect, Designer and Romantic Socialist*, 2nd edn, New Haven and London: Yale University Press, 2005.

Cruft, Kitty, Dunbar, John, and Fawcett, Richard, *The Buildings of Scotland: Borders*, New Haven and London: Yale University Press, 2006.

Curl, James Stevens, and Wilson, Susan, *The Oxford Dictionary of Architecture*, 3rd edn, Oxford: Oxford University Press, 2015.

Darwin, Bernard, *Fifty Years of Country Life*, London: Country Life, 1947.

Davey, Peter, *Arts and Crafts Architecture*, London: Phaidon, revised edn, 1997.

Davey, Peter, 'Radical Delight: 120 years of the AR, 1896–1921', *Architectural Review*, 1.2017, pp.90–92.

David, Edward, 'The New Liberalism of C.F.G. Masterman', in Kenneth D. Brown (ed.), *Essays in Anti-Labour History: Responses to the Rise of Labour in Britain*, London: Palgrave Macmillan, 1974, pp.17–41.

Davidson, David, and Collins, Nick, *Return to Gidea Park*, London: The Twentieth Century Society, undated and circulated privately.

Davie, W. Galsworthy, and Dawber, E. Guy, *Old Cottages, Farm-Houses, and Other Stone Buildings in the Cotswold District: Examples of Minor Domestic Architecture in Gloucestershire, Oxfordshire, Northants*, London: Batsford, 1905.

Davie, W., Galsworthy, and Green, W. Curtis, *Old Cottages & Farm-Houses in Surrey*, London: Batsford, 1908.

Davie, W. Galsworthy, and Tanner, H., *Old English Doorways: A Series of Historical Examples from Tudor Times to the End of the XVIII Century*, London: Batsford, 1903.

de Moubray, Amicia *Twentieth Century Castles in Britain*, London: Frances Lincoln, 2013.

Dennett, Laurie, *Slaughter and May: A Century in the City*, Cambridge: Granta, 1989.

Dowdall, H.C., 'The Law of Town Planning', *Town Planning Review*, vol.1, no.2, 1910, pp.39–43.

Draper, William H., 'The Land of Homeliness', *Country Life*, 10.3.1906, pp.337–40.

E.B.S., 'Country Cottages', *Country Life*, 19.2.1898, pp.195–7.

Dyson, H. Kempson, 'Cheap Cottages and the Exhibition at Letchworth', *Architectural Review*, vol.18, 1905, pp.108–15 and 154–69.

East, John, *An Afternoon Walk in Gidea Park*, drawn from earlier tour notes for the Victorian Society by Roderick Gradidge (1989), London: The Twentieth Century Society, undated and circulated privately.

Edwards, Clive, *Turning Houses into Homes: A History of Retailing and Consumption of Domestic Furnishings*, Aldershot: Ashgate, 2005.

Elder-Duncan, J.H., *Country Cottages and Week-End Homes*, London etc.: Cassell, 1906; 2nd edn, 1912.

Fawcett, Bill, *The North Eastern Railway's Two Palaces of Business*, York: Friends of the National Railway Museum in association with GNER, 2006.

Fawcett, Edward, *Liberalism: The Life of an Idea*, Princeton and Oxford: Princeton University Press, 2014.

Field, Horace, and Bunney, Michael, *English Domestic Architecture of the XVII and XVIII Centuries*, London: Bell, 1905.

Fildes, Luke Val, *Luke Fildes, RA: A Victorian Painter*, London: Michael Joseph, 1968.

Fitzgerald, Percy, 'The Life and Work of Robert Adam', *Architectural Review*, vol.7, 1900, pp.147–56 and 273–83.

Forster, E.M., *The Longest Journey*, London: Edward Arnold, 1907.

Franklin, Jill, *The Gentleman's Country House and its Plan 1835–1914*, London: Routledge & Kegan Paul, 1981.

Forrest, H.E., *The Old Houses of Shrewsbury*, Shrewsbury: Wilding & Son, 1911.

Freeman, Jenny, 'Archbishop's Palace, Canterbury', *Country Life*, 25.4.1991, pp.84–7.

Freeman, Jennifer M., *W.D. Caröe RStO FSA: His Architectural Achievement*, Manchester: Manchester University Press, 1990.

Fry, Somerset Plantagenet, *Chequers: The Country Home of Britain's Prime Ministers*, London: HMSO, 1977.

Garner, Thomas, and Stratton, Arthur, *The Domestic Architecture of England During the Tudor Period / Illustrated in a Series of Photographs & Measured Drawings of Country Mansions, Manor Houses and Smaller Buildings with Historical and Descriptive Text*, London: Batsford, 1908–11.

Gebhart, David, *Charles F.A. Voysey Architect*, Los Angeles: Hennessey & Ingalls, 1975.

Gee, Emily, '"Where Shall She Live?": Housing the New Working Woman in Late Victorian and Edwardian London', in Geoff Brandwood (ed.), *Living, Leisure and Law: Eight Building Types in England 1800–1941*, Reading: Spire, 2010.

Gerrish, Helena, *Edwardian Country Life: The Story of H. Avray Tipping*, London: Frances Lincoln, 2011.

Girouard, Mark, 'George Devey in Kent', *Country Life*, part 1, 1.4.1971, pp.744–7; part 2, 8.4.1971, pp.812–15.

Girouard, Mark, *Sweetness and Light*, Oxford: Oxford University Press, 1977.

Godfrey, Walter, 'The Work of George Devey', *Architectural Review*, vol.21, 1907, pp.22–30, 83–8 and 293–306.

Gradidge, Roderick, *Dream Houses: The Edwardian Ideal*, London: Constable, 1980.

Grainger, Hilary J., *The Architecture of Sir Ernest George*, Reading: Spire, 2011.

Graves, Algernon, *The Royal Academy of Arts: A Complete Dictionary of Contributors and their Work from its Foundation in 1769 to 1904*, Wakefield and Bath: S.R. publishers and Kingsmead Reprints, 1970.

Gray, A. Stuart, *Edwardian Architecture: A Biographical Dictionary*, London: Duckworth, 1986.

Gray, Thomas, 'Impromptu on Lord Holland's Seat at Kingsgate', *The Works of Thomas Gray*, London: Harding, Triphook & Lepard, vol.1, 1825.

Green, Mowbray A., 'Bath Doorways of the Eighteenth Century', *Architectural Review*, vol.17, 1905, pp.63–9 and 195–201.

Greenacombe, John (Royal Commission on the Historical Monuments of England), *Survey of London, Volume 45: Knightsbridge*, London: Athlone, 1998.

Greenwood, Frederick, *Imagination in Dreams and their Study*, London: John Lane, 1894.

Grigg, John, *Lloyd George, War Leader 1916–1918*, London: Penguin, 2002.

Gunn, Paul, *Kingsgate Castle*, circulated privately, c.1970.

Haigh, Diane, *Baillie Scott: The Artistic House*, London: Academy Editions, 1995.

Hall, Michael, Gilley, Sheridan, and Perry, Maria, *Farm Street: The Story of the Jesuits' Church in London*, London: Unicorn, 2016.

Hardy, Lucy, 'The Cottage Garden', *Country Life*, 6.11.1897, pp.483–5.

Hardy, Lucy, 'Deserted Houses', *Country Life*, 20.11.1897, pp.552–3.

Hartwell, Clare, Pevsner, Nikolaus, and Williamson, Elizabeth, *The Buildings of England: Derbyshire*, New Haven and London: Yale University Press, 2016.

Haslam, Richard, 'Vann, Surrey; Architect of 1907–1909 Additions: W.D. Caröe', *Country Life*, 26.6.1986, pp.1818–20.

Haslam, Richard, *RIBA Drawings Monographs No 2: Clough Williams-Ellis*, London: Academy Editions in collaboration with the Royal Institute of British Architects, 1996.

Havelock, Richard, 'Recollections and Reflections of an Inveterate Voysey Visitor, Part 2', in *The Orchard*, the journal of the C.F.A. Voysey Society, no.6, Autumn 2017, pp.64–85.

Hawkes, Dean (ed.), *Modern Country Homes in England: The Arts and Crafts Architecture of Barry Parker*, Cambridge: Cambridge University Press, 1986.

Hill, Michael, Newman, John, and Pevsner, Nikolaus, *The Buildings of England: Dorset*, New Haven and London: Yale University Press, 2018.

Hitchmough, Wendy, *The Homestead*, London: Phaidon, 1994.

Hitchmough, Wendy, *C.F.A. Voysey*, London: Phaidon, 1995.

Honour, Hugh, 'An Epic of Ruin-Building', *Country Life*, 10.12.1953, pp.1968–9.

Hussey, Christopher, *The Life of Sir Edwin Lutyens*, London: Country Life, 1950.

Hutchinson, Horace G., *The Life of Sir John Lubbock, Lord Avebury*, two vols, London: Macmillan, 1914.

'J.', 'Knowsley Hall, Lancashire', *Country Life*, 12.7.1913, pp.54–61.

Jackson, Neil, *F.W. Troup: Architect 1859–1941*, London: Building Centre Trust, 1985.

Jarvis, A.W., 'The Old English Christmas', *Country Life*, 22.12.1906, pp.896–9.

Jekyll, Gertrude, 'Orchards, Surrey', *Country Life*, 31.8.1901, pp.272–9.

Jones, Ronald P., 'The Life and Work of Harvey Lonsdale Elmes', *Architectural Review*, vol.15, 1904, pp.230–45.

Jones, Ronald P., 'The Life and Work of Decimus Burton', *Architectural Review*, vol.17, 1905, pp.108–18 and 154–64.

Jones, Ronald P., *Nonconformist Church Architecture*, London: Lindsey Press, 1914.

King, Arthur, and Lavender, Tony, *North Foreland Golf Club: Founded 1903*, Kingsgate: North Foreland Golf Club, 2007.

Kirk, Sheila, *Philip Webb: Pioneer of Arts & Crafts Architecture*, Chichester: Wiley-Academy, 2005.

Lancaster, Osbert, *Pillar to Post*, London: John Murray, 1938.

Leachman, E.W., *A Church in No Man's Land, being the Romance of Holy Trinity*, St Leonards-on-Sea: King Bros & Potts, 1934.

Lemon, Nigel, 'A Blackcountryman at Bache Hall', *Cheshire History*, vol.46, 2006, pp.91–103.

Lethaby, W.R., 'The Architecture of Adventure', *RIBA Journal*, vol.17, 1910, pp.469–78.

Lethaby, W.R., *Form in Civilisation*, London: Oxford University Press, 1922.

Lever, Jill, 'A.T. Bolton, Architect', *Architectural History*, vol.27, 1984, pp.429–42.

Ley, A.J., *A History of Building Control in England and Wales 1840–1990*, London: RICS Books, 2000.

Leyland, John, 'Baddesley Clinton', *Country Life*, 8.1.1897, pp.20–22.

Leyland, John, 'Penshurst Place', *Country Life*, 29.5.1897, pp.576–8.

Leyland, John, 'Ascott', *Country Life*, 28.8.1897, pp.210–12.

Loudon, John Claudius, *An Encyclopaedia of Cottage, Farm, and Villa Architecture and Furniture*, London: Longman, 1833.

Lurie, Alison, *Not in Front of the Grown-Ups: Subversive Children's Literature*, 2nd edn, London: Sphere Books, 1991.

Lutyens, Edwin, 'The Work of the Late Philip Webb', *Country Life*, 8.5.1915, p.618.

Macartney, Mervyn, 'The First Garden City', *Architectural Review*, vol.18, 1905, pp.14–21.

Macartney, Mervyn, *Recent English Domestic Architecture*, six vols, London: The Architectural Review, 1908–24; vol.1, 1908; vol.2, 1909; vol.3, 1910; vol.4, 1911; vol.5, 1912; vol.6, 1913[?].

Macdonald-Smith, Ian, *Arts and Crafts Master: The Houses and Gardens of M.H. Baillie Scott*, New York: Rizzoli, 2010.

Mackail. J.W., *The Life of William Morris*, London: Longmans Green, 1899.

Mallet, Charles, *Herbert Gladstone: A Memoir*, London: Hutchinson, 1932.

Mallows, C.E., 'Country Cottages and their Gardens', *Studio*, vol.48, 1910, pp.283–90.

Martin, Arthur, *The Small House: Its Architecture and Surroundings*, London: Alston Rivers, 1906.

Masterman, C.F.G., *The Condition of England*, London: Methuen, 1909.

McKellar, Elizabeth, 'C.H.B. Quennell (1872–1935): Architecture, History and the Quest for the Modern', *Architectural History*, vol.50, 2007, pp.211–41.

Metcalfe, David, *The Architectural Development of Walton-on-the-Hill from 1900 to 1930*, Walton: Walton Local History Society, 2000.

Morris, George Ll., 'Philip Webb's Town Work', illustrated by Halsey Ricardo, *Architectural Review*, vol.2, 1897, pp.198–208.

Morris, G. Ll., and Wood, Esther, 'The Country Cottage and the Materials Used in its Construction', *Studio*, vol.36, 1905, pp.146–55.

Muthesius, Hermann, *Das englische Haus: Entwicklung, Bedingungen, Anlage, Aufbau, Einrichtung und Innenraum*, three vols, Berlin: Wasmuth, 1904–5.

Muthesius, Hermann, *Landhaus und Garten: Beispiele neuzeitlicher Landhäuser nebst Gründrissen, Innenräumen und Gärten*, Munich: F. Bruckmann, 1907.

Muthesius, Hermann, *The English House*, English translation (first published in Berlin as *Das englische Haus*, 1904–5), London: Frances Lincoln, 2007.

Muthesius, Stefan, *The English Terraced House*, New Haven and London: Yale University Press, 1982.

Nesbit, E., *Nine Unlikely Tales*, London: T. Fisher Unwin, 1901.

Nesbit, E., 'The Cockatoucan', in Nesbit, *Nine Unlikely Tales*, pp.1–47.

Nesbit, E., 'Wheredoyouwanttogoto: or the Bouncible Ball', in Nesbit, *Nine Unlikely Tales*, pp.51–84.

Nesbit, E., *The Railway Children*, London: Wells Gardner & Co., 1906.

Nesbit, E., *The Enchanted Castle*, London: T. Fisher Unwin, 1907.

Nesbit, E., *Harding's Luck*, London: Hodder & Stoughton, 1909.

Newman, John, *The Buildings of England: Kent – West and the Weald*, New Haven and London: Yale University Press, 2012.

Newman, John, *The Buildings of England: Kent – North East and East*, New Haven and London: Yale University Press, 2013.

Newton, Ernest, *A Book of Country Houses: A Series of Examples Erected at Hampstead & Elsewhere*, London: Batsford, 1903.

Nodier, Charles, Taylor, I., and de Cailleux, Alph., *Voyages pittoresques et romantiques dans l'ancienne France*, vol.1, Paris: P. Didot L'ainé, 1820.

Offer, Avner, *Property and Politics 1870–1914: Landownership, Law, Ideology and Urban Development in England*, Cambridge: Cambridge University Press, 1981.

Oliver, Paul, Davis, Ian, and Bentley, Ian, *Dunroamin: The Suburban Semi and its Enemies*, London: Barrie & Jenkins, 1981.

Owen, Janet, *Darwin's Apprentice: An Archaeological Biography of John Lubbock*, Barnsley: Pen & Sword, 2013.

Paget, J.C., 'The New Westminster', *Architectural Review*, vol.20, 1906, p.318.

Parker, Charles, *Villa Rustica*, London: James Carpenter & Son, 1832.

Parkinson, James, and Ould, E.A., *Old Cottages, Farm Houses, and Other Half-Timber Buildings in Shropshire, Herefordshire, and Cheshire*, London: Batsford, 1904.

Patrick, Judith, *Walter Cave: Arts and Crafts to Edwardian Splendour*, Andover: Phillimore & Co., 2012.

Patton, Mark, *Science, Politics and Business in the Work of Sir John Lubbock: A Man of Universal Mind (Science, Technology and Culture, 1700–1945)*, London: Routledge, 2007.

Pevsner, Nikolaus, *Pioneers of Modern Design: From William Morris to Walter Gropius*, first published 1960, revised edn Harmondsworth: Penguin, 1974.

Pevsner, Nikolaus, 'Obituary, Harold Falkner, 1875–1963', *Architectural Review*, vol.135, 1964, p.240.

Pevsner, Nikolaus, 'Goodhart-Rendel's Roll-Call', *Architectural Review*, vol.138, 1965, pp.259–64.

Pevsner, Nikolaus, and Williamson, Elizabeth, with Brandwood, Geoffrey K., *The Buildings of England: Buckinghamshire*, New Haven and London: Yale University Press, 2003.

Phillips, R. Randal, 'Hook Heath Farm', *Country Life*, 15.7.1922, pp.65–6.

Phillips, R. Randal, *The House Improved*, London: Country Life, 1931.

Pickford, Chris, and Pevsner, Nikolaus, *The Buildings of England: Warwickshire*, New Haven and London: Yale University Press, 2016.

Pite, A. Beresford, 'Modern House Design', *Architectural Review*, vol.8, 1900, pp.153–5.

Pohaničova, Jana, 'Architekti a ich Mecenasi', *Architektura & Urbanizmus*, vol.39, no.1/2, 2005, pp.45–64.

Pound, Reginald, and Harmsworth, Geoffrey, *Northcliffe*, London: Cassell, 1959.

Powers, Alan, 'Edwardian Architectural Education: A Study of Three Schools of Architecture', *AA Files*, no.5, 1984, p.49–59.

Pugin, A.W.N., *The True Principles of Pointed or Christian Architecture*, London: John Weale, 1841.

Pugin, A.W.N., *An Apology for the Revival of Christian Architecture*, London: John Weale, 1843.

Quennell, C.H.B., *Modern Suburban Houses: A Series of Examples Erected at Hampstead & Elsewhere*, London: Batsford, 1906.

Quennell, Peter, *The Marble Foot: An Autobiography, 1905–1938*, London: Collins, 1976.

Rady, J., Tatton-Brown, T., and Bowen, J.A., 'The Archbishop's Palace, Canterbury', *Journal of the British Archaeological Association*, vol.144, no.1, 1991, pp.1–60.

Readman, Paul, 'The Edwardian Land Question', in Matthew Cragoe and Paul Readman (eds), *The Land Question in Britain 1750–1950*, London: Palgrave Macmillan, 2010, pp.181–200.

Ricardo, Halsey, 'Some Conditions of House Design', part 2, *Architectural Review*, vol.3, 1897–8, pp.42–9.

Ricardo, Halsey, 'William Butterfield', *Architectural Review*, vol.7, 1900, pp.259–62 and vol.8, 1900, pp.15–23.

Ricardo, Halsey, 'John Francis Bentley', *Architectural Review*, vol.11, 1902, pp.155–64 and vol.12, 1902, pp.18–30.

Roberts, Gillian Whitley, 'William Johnson Harrison Weller (1877–1960): A Wolverhampton Architect in the Arts and Crafts Style', unpublished MSt dissertation, University of Cambridge, 2018.

Robertson, W.A. Scott, 'Archæological Notes on Thanet', *Archæologia Cantiana*, vol.12, 1878, pp.329–419.

Robinson, John Martin, 'A Country Palace: Buckland House, Berkshire', *Country Life*, 11.5.2011, pp.92–7; 18.5.2011, pp.74–9.

Robinson, John Martin, *James Wyatt: Architect to George III*, New Haven and London: Yale University Press for Paul Mellon Centre for British Art, 2011.

Romaine-Walker, W.H., *Mr Hipp, or Three Friends in Search of Pleasure*, London: Faulkner & Co., 1893.

Royal Academy of Arts, *Royal Academy Exhibitors, 1905–1970: A Dictionary of Artists and their Work in the Summer Exhibitions of the Royal Academy of Arts*, Wakefield: EP Publishing, 1973–.

Saint, Andrew, *Richard Norman Shaw*, 2nd edn, London and New Haven: Yale University Press, 2010.

Saint, Andrew, *Bedford Park, Radical Suburb*, London: The Bedford Park Society, 2016.

Scott, George Gilbert, *Personal and Professional Recollections*, London: Sampson Low, Marston, Searle & Rivington, 1879.

Scott, M.H. Baillie, *Houses and Gardens: Arts and Crafts Interiors*, London: George Newnes, 1906.

Searle, G.R., *A New England? Peace and War 1886–1918*, Oxford: Oxford University Press, 2004.

Service, Alastair (ed.), *Edwardian Architecture and its Origins*, London: Architectural Press, 1975.

Service, Alastair, 'Charles Harrison Townsend', in Service, *Edwardian Architecture and its Origins*, pp.162–82.

Service, Alastair, *Edwardian Architecture: A Handbook to Building Design in Britain, 1890–1914*, London: Thames & Hudson, 1977.

Sheppard, H.W. (ed.) (Royal Commission on the Historical Monuments of England), *Survey of London, Volume 40: The Grosvenor Estate in Mayfair, Part 2 – The Buildings*, London: London County Council, 1980.

Sparrow, W. Shaw, *The British Home of To-day: A Book of Modern Domestic Architecture & the Applied Arts*, London: Hodder & Stoughton, 1904.

Sparrow, W. Shaw, *The Modern Home: A Book of British Domestic Architecture for Moderate Incomes – A Companion Volume to 'The British Home of To-day'*, London: Hodder & Stoughton, 1906.

Sparrow, W. Shaw, *Flats, Urban Houses and Cottage Homes*, London: Hodder & Stoughton, 1906.

Stamp, Gavin, 'Besieged by Suffragettes: Lympne Castle, Kent', part 2, *Country Life*, 6.7.2016, pp.106–10.

Street, A.E., 'London Street Architecture', *Architectural Review*, vol.17, 1905, pp.164–7, 201–14 and 245–57.

Strong, Roy, *Country Life 1897–1997: The English Arcadia*, London: Country Life, 1996.

Swenarton, Mark, 'Tudor Walters and Tudorbethan: Reassessing Britain's Inter-War Suburbs', *Planning Perspectives*, vol.17, no.3, 2002, pp.267–86.

Taylor, Gordon, *Thanet's Dutch and Flemish Style Houses*, Broadstairs: Isle of Thanet Archaeological Society, 2014.

Temple, Philip, Thom, Colin, and Saint, Andrew, *Survey of London, Volume 52: South East Marylebone, Part 2*, New Haven and London: Yale University Press, 2017.

Thompson, M.W., *General Pitt-Rivers*, Bradford-on-Avon: Moonraker Press, 1977.

Thompson, Michael, *Darwin's Pupil: The Place of Sir John Lubbock, Lord Avebury, 1834–1913, in Late Victorian and Edwardian England*, Ely: Melrose Books, 2009.

Thurley, Simon, *Men from the Ministry*, New Haven and London: Yale University Press, 2013.

Tipping, H. Avray, 'Zuylestein, Holland', *Country Life*, 6.4.1907, pp.486–93.

Tipping, H. Avray, 'Millmead, Bramley: An Example of Building and Building Bye-Laws', *Country Life*, 11.5.07, pp.674–8.

Tipping, H. Avray, 'Hever Castle', *Country Life*, 12.10.1907, pp.522–35; 19.10.1907, pp.558–67.

Tipping, H. Avray, 'Two Renovated Cottages in Monmouthshire', *Country Life*, 21.3.1908, pp.411–13.

Tipping, H. Avray, 'Lesser Country Houses of To-day (1), Sapperton Cottage', *Country Life*, 6.3.1909, pp.348–54.

T. [Tipping, H.Avray], 'Combe Abbey', *Country Life*, 4.12.1909, pp.794–805; 11.12.09, pp.840–48.

Tipping, H. Avray, 'Three Gables, Letchworth', *Country Life*, 22.1.1910, supplement, pp.35–6 and 39.

Tipping, 'Tudor House, Broadway', *Country Life*, 10.9.1910, pp.360–4.

Tipping, H. Avray, 'Outdoor Dining-Rooms', in Lawrence Weaver, *The House and its Equipment*, London: Country Life, 1912, pp.156–63.

Unwin, Raymond, *Town Planning in Practice: An Introduction to the Art of Designing Cities and Suburbs*, London: Benn, 1909.

Valinsky, David, *An Architect Speaks: The Writings and Buildings of Edward Schröder Prior*, Donington: David Valinsky for Shaun Tyas, 2014.

Vallance, Aymer, 'Some Recent Work by Mr C.F.A. Voysey', *Studio*, vol.31, 1904, p.127.

Virgin, Peter, *The Church in an Age of Negligence*, Cambridge: James Clarke, 1989.

Voysey, C.F.A., *Individuality*, London: Chapman & Hall, 1915.

Walpole, K.A., *From One Generation to the Next: A Panorama of Wycombe Abbey, Buckinghamshire*, printed privately, c.1970.

Ward, Jan, *Mervyn Edmund Macartney, Architect, 1853–1932: The Life and Work of Sir Mervyn Macartney, BA, FRIBA, FSA, with Particular Reference to his Houses and Clients on the Surrey/Kent Border*, York: York College of Further and Higher Education Reprographics Department, 1998.

Warren, Edward, 'George Frederick Bodley', *Architectural Review*, vol.11, 1902, pp.130–39.

Waterhouse, Paul, 'Life and Work of Welby Pugin', *Architectural Review*, vol.3, 1897–8, pp.167–75, 211–21 and 264–73; vol.4, 1898, pp.23–7, 67–73, 115–18 and 159–65.

Weaver, Lawrence, 'Inverleith, Norwich', *Country Life*, 8.1.1910, pp.37–41.

Weaver, Lawrence, 'South Hill, Hook Heath, Woking', Country Life, 25.6.1910, supplement, pp.7–11

Weaver, Lawrence, 'Sandhouse, Witley', *Country Life*, 27.8.1910, pp.296–302.

Weaver, Lawrence, 'Lympne Castle, Kent: The Seat of Mr F.J. Tennant', *Country Life*, 12.11.1910, pp.682–9.

Weaver, Lawrence, 'Upmeads, Stafford', *Country Life*, 12.11.1910, supplement, pp.7–11.

Weaver, Lawrence, 'Nether Swell Manor', *Country Life*, 26.11.1910, pp.754–60.

Weaver, Lawrence, *Small Country Houses of To-day*, London: Country Life, 1911.

Weaver, Lawrence, 'Morton House, Hatfield', *Country Life*, 25.2.1911, supplement, pp.7–11

Weaver, Lawrence, 'The Exhibition of Houses at Gidea Park', *Country Life*, part 1, 3.6.1911, supplement, pp.13–20; part 2, 10.6.1911, supplement, pp.7–10.

Weaver, Lawrence, 'Normanby Hall', *Country Life*, 29.7.1911, pp.170–76.

Weaver, Lawrence, *The House and its Equipment*, London: Country Life, 1912.

Weaver, Lawrence, 'Chesters', *Country Life*, 17.2.1912, pp.244–8.

Weaver, Lawrence, 'Vann, Hambledon, Surrey', *Country Life*, 29.6.1912, supplement, pp.7–11.

Weaver, Lawrence, 'Great Maytham, Kent, *Country Life*, 30.11.1912, pp.746–53.

Weaver, Lawrence, *Houses and Gardens by E.L. Lutyens*, London: Country Life, 1913.

Weaver, Lawrence, *The 'Country Life' Book of Cottages*, London: Country Life, 1913.

Weaver, Lawrence, 'Paycocke's, Coggeshall, Essex', *Country Life*, 12.7.1913, supplement, pp.7–11.

Weaver, Lawrence, 'Modern Scottish Architecture: The Work of Sir Robert Lorimer – Reconstructions After a Fire', *Country Life*, 27.9.1913, pp.32–39.

Weaver, Lawrence, 'The Wharf, Sutton Courtenay, Berkshire', *Country Life*, 25.10.1913, supplement, pp.7–11.

Weaver, Lawrence *Small Country Houses: Their Repair and Enlargement – Forty Examples Chosen from Five Centuries*, London: Country Life, 1914.

Weaver, Lawrence, 'Notgrove Manor, Gloucestershire', *Country Life*, 21.11.1914, pp.678–83.

Weaver, Lawrence, 'Buckland', *Country Life*, 15.5.1915. pp.662–9; 22.5.1915, pp.698–705.

Weaver, Lawrence Trevelyan, *Lawrence Weaver 1876–1930: An Annotated Bibliography*, York: Inch's Books, 1989.

Who Was Who, vol.4, 1941–1950, London: A. & C. Black, 1952.

Williams, James, 'George Devey and his Work', *Architectural Association Journal*, vol.24, no.266, 1909, pp.95–103.

Williams-Ellis, Clough, *Building in Cob, Pisé, Chalk & Clay: A Renaissance*, London: Country Life, 1919.

Williams-Ellis, Clough, *Lawrence Weaver*, London: Bles, 1933.

Online

BUILDING HISTORIES

Grianaig (now Glen Hir), Killay, Swansea: http://www.swansea.gov.uk/article/5205/Listed-buildings-index

Hook Hill and the Cox family: http://www.hhra.co.uk/the-cox-family-and-hook-hill.htm

Lutyens houses in Westminster: http://www.lutyenstrust.org.uk/portfolio-item/walking-tour-westminster/

Peasant Art movement: http://peasant-arts.blogspot.co.uk/

St Clement's church, Poole: http://www.stclementspoole.org.uk/churchhistory.htm

St Saviour's church, Pimlico: https://www.scribd.com/document/255023853/Church-History-Guide

St Paul's cathedral, London, mural mosaics: https://www.stpauls.co.uk/history-collections/the-collections/object-collection/mosaics-of-st-pauls-cathedral/mosaics-in-the-quire

Walton Heath Golf Club: https://www.waltonheath.com/our_heritage

Whiteness Manor: http://www.whitenessmanor.co.uk/history.html; http://writingfamilyhistory.com/author/susie-gutch/

PLANNING DOCUMENTATION

Old Oak Estate, Hammersmith: https://www.lbhf.gov.uk/sites/default/files/section_attachments/wormholt_and_old_oak_design_guidelines_tcm21-165276.pdf; http://www.socialhousinghistory.uk/wp/wp-content/uploads/2015/10/Early_LCC_Housing_Part_3_42-Old_Oak_Estate.pdf

Little Ambrook: Sanderson, Mark, *Appeal Statement Little Ambrook*, March 2016, available at https://bdsdocs.reigate-banstead.gov.uk/Planning/StreamDocPage/obj?DocNo=3019482&content=obj.pdf

7 Caledonian Road, London: TG Revive, Listed Building Consultants, *7 Caledonian Road & 3 Bravingtons Walk (The Former Varnish Works) Regent's Quarter London*, http://planning.islington.gov.uk/NorthgatePublicDocs/00349904.pdf

Walton Heath: https://bdsdocs.reigate-banstead.gov.uk/Planning/StreamDocPage/obj?DocNo=2760090&content=obj.pdf; https://bdsdocs.reigate-banstead.gov.uk/Planning/StreamDocPage/obj?DocNo=3019482&content=obj.pdf

BIOGRAPHICAL

Edward Grey: Joe Shute, 'River Retreat of the Man Who Took Britain to War', *Daily Telegraph*, 2.8.2014, http://www.telegraph.co.uk/history/world-war-one/11006046/River-retreat-of-the-man-who-took-Britain-to-war.html

W.H. Romaine-Walker: Peter Wootton, 'William Henry Romaine-Walker ARIBA, 1854–1940', Chris Beetles Gallery: http://www.chrisbeetles.com/artists/walker-william-henry-romaine-ariba-1854-1940.html#

James Blyth: http://www.hundredparishes.org.uk/people/detail/james-blyth

RADIO BROADCASTS

'Living in Quality Street', BBC Radio 3, 1971: http://genome.ch.bbc.co.uk/be9fe50f63914a78b66c9bd96aa4b7aa

WEBSITES WITH INTERIOR PHOTOGRAPHY

Kingsgate Castle flat: sale particular, http://www.rightmove.co.uk/property-for-sale/property-37998505.html

Medmenham Abbey: Emma Glanfield, 'If these walls could talk! Idyllic abbey that once hosted orgies for 18th Century politicians and aristocrats is on sale for £10million and now the in-house entertainment is a spa and cinema', *Daily Mail*, 17 March 2015, http://www.dailymail.co.uk/news/article-2998691/If-walls-talk-Idyllic-abbey-hosted-orgies-18th-Century-politicians-aristocrats-sale-10million-house-entertainment-spa-cinema.html

Pinfold (former Cliftondown): sale particular, http://www.rightmove.co.uk/property-for-sale/property-30943091.html

Pleasaunce Cottage in Dormans Park, East Grinstead: Jennifer Smith, 'A taste of the Raj: One of UK's first bungalows that was built in the 1880s in colonial style goes on sale for £1million', *Daily Mail*, 9 April 2015, http://www.dailymail.co.uk/news/article-3032197/A-taste-Raj-Victorian-India-style-bungalow-built-Sussex-preserved-1880s-goes-market-1million.html

IMAGE AND TEXT SOURCES
AND CREDITS

———

All recent photography unless indicated otherwise is © Robin Forster and was photographed for this book between January and June 2019. The opening quotation from E.M. Forster's *The*

Longest Journey (London: Edward Arnold, 1907, p.56) is reproduced by kind permission of The Provost and Scholars of King's College, Cambridge, and The Society of Authors.

Introduction

———

3: public domain.
4: *R. Caldecott's Second Collection of Pictures and Songs*, London: F. Warne & Co, 1895.
5: with thanks to Andrew Saint.
6: National Portrait Gallery, NPG x13489, sepia-toned platinotype print by George Charles

Beresford, 1902, http://creativecommons.org/licenses/by-nc-nd/3.0/.
7: National Portrait Gallery, NPG P1700(86a), vintage print by Reginald Haines, *c*.1907, http://creativecommons.org/licenses/by-nc-nd/3.0/.

8: © Graham Booth; by kind permission of Graham Booth.
9: by kind permission of the Master and Fellows of Trinity College, Cambridge.
10–11: © author.

Chapter One

———

Opening quotation: *Punch*, 'Fancy Portraits no.96' [by Linley Sambourne], 19.8.1882.
Extracts from Lord Avebury's diary are reproduced by kind permission of Lyulph, Lord Avebury.
14, 21, 23–29: © Lubbock family archive; by kind permission of Lord Avebury.

15–17: private collection.
18: Paul Gunn collection; by kind permission of Christian Poltera.
30: from E.W. Leachman, *A Church in No Man's Land, Being the Romance of Holy Trinity*, St Leonards-on-Sea: King Bros & Potts, 1934, p.85; with thanks to Peter Howell and James Hughes.

34: *Builder*, 4.7.1891.
43: *Architectural Review*, vol.11, 1902, p.106.
48: RIBA Collections, RIBA20274.

Chapter Two

Opening quotation: H.G. Wells, *The New Machiavelli*, 1910, quoted in *The Book of the Exhibition of Houses and Cottages, Romford Garden Suburb, Gidea Park*, 1911.

Extracts from Earl and Countess of Carrington's diaries are reproduced by kind permission of Rupert, Lord Carrington.

53: Carington Family Archives 3/21, Bledlow; by kind permission of Lord Carrington.

64: Historic England archive: Vann No.1, CAR01/03/00234; by kind permission of Mary Caröe.

69, text: 'The Wharf, Sutton Courtenay, Berks: The Country House of Mrs Asquith', *Architectural Review*, vol.55, 1924, pp.19 and 193.

70: National Portrait Gallery, NPG P166, vintage bromide print by Baron Adolph de Meyer,

c.1911, http://creativecommons.org/licenses/by-nc-nd/3.0/.

73: © Parliamentary Archives, London: HL/PO/PB/3/plan1900/L45.

77: *Architectural Review*, vol.14, 1903, p.105.

78: Mervyn Macartney, *Recent English Domestic Architecture*, London: The Architectural Review, vol.5, 1912, p.172.

80–81: Horace Field and Michael Bunney, *English Domestic Architecture of the XVII and XVIII Centuries*, London: Bell, 1905, pl.1; pl.27.

82: by kind permission of Louise Edwards.

83: J.H. Elder-Duncan, *Country Cottages and Week-End Homes*, London etc: Cassell, 1906, 2nd edn, 1912, p.180; text: Lawrence Weaver, *The 'Country Life' Book of Cottages*, London:

Country Life, 1913, pp.198 and 202.

86: Mervyn Macartney, *Recent English Domestic Architecture*, London: The Architectural Review, vol.2, 1911, p.192.

87: W. Shaw Sparrow, *Flats, Urban Houses and Cottage Homes*, London: Hodder & Stoughton, 1906, p.140.

89–90, 96: W. Shaw Sparrow, *The British Home of To-day: a Book of Modern Domestic Architecture & the Applied Arts*, London: Hodder & Stoughton, 1904, figs B46; G36; colour plate facing p.Bviii.

95: RIBA Collections, RIBA94216.

103; 107: Lawrence Weaver, 'The Exhibition of Houses at Gidea Park, Romford – 1', *Country Life*, 3.6.11, supplement, pp.13 and 16.

Chapter Three

Opening quotation: Bernard Darwin, *Fifty Years of Country Life*, London: Country Life, 1947, p.33 (referring to the magazine's advertisements).

110: *The Book of the Exhibition of Houses and Cottages, Romford Garden Suburb, Gidea Park*, London: The Exhibition Committee, 1911, pp.98–9.

111, text: H. Avray Tipping, 'Four Beeches, Bickley Park', *Country Life*, 28.8.1909, supplement, p.38.

119: *Country Life*, 31.1 1903, p.149: Country Life Picture Library.

120: *Country Life*, 18.5.1907, p.704: Country Life Picture Library.

122: Unused photograph of 1913: Country Life Picture Library.

123: Weaver, *The 'Country Life' Book of Cottages*, p.188.

124: RIBA Collections, RIBA12698.

125: Elder-Duncan, *Country Cottages and Week-End Homes*, p.91.

126: *Architectural Review*, vol.29, 1911, p.232.

127: © Hugh Routh

128: *Country Life*, 6.12.1979, p.2154: Country Life Picture Library.

129: Weaver, *Cottages*, pp.179–80.

130: *Country Life*, 28.8.1909, p.207: Country Life Picture Library.

132: National Portrait Gallery, NPG x28057, bromide print by Walter Stoneman, 1920, http://creativecommons.org/licenses/by-nc-nd/3.0/.

133: *Country Life*, 12.7.1913, supplement, p.7: Country Life Picture Library.

134: *Architectural Review*, vol.13, 1903, p.121.

136: Shaw Sparrow, *The British Home of To-day*, B25.

137: *Architectural Review*, vol.19, 1906, p.28.

138: *Country Life*, 8.1.1910, p.38: Country Life Picture Library.

139–141: Weaver, Lawrence *Small Country Houses: Their Repair and Enlargement*, London: Country Life, 1914, pp.44, 115 and 97.

142: text: Service, Alastair (ed.), *Edwardian Architecture and its Origins*, London: Architectural Press, 1975, p.426, caption fig.2.

143: Elder-Duncan, *Country Cottages and Week-End Homes*, p.25.

144: Shaw Sparrow, *The British Home of To-day*, pl. facing Cviii.

145–6; 148: Macartney, *Recent English Domestic Architecture*, vol.5, 1912, pp.6–7 and 18.

153: *Architectural Review*, vol.15, 1904, p.115.

154–155: *Studio*, vol.48, 1910, pp.289 and 285.

156: *Builders' Journal*, 27.7.1904, supplement.

157: *Studio*, vol.48, 1909, p.47.

158: *Studio*, vol.36, 1905, p.48; text: Crawford, Alan, *C.R. Ashbee: Architect, Designer and Romantic Socialist*, 2nd edn, New Haven and London: Yale University Press, 2005, pp.271 and 471.

159: *Studio*, vol.36, 1905, p.236; text, p.233.

160: *Studio*, vol.48, 1909, pl. p.137.

161–162: Shaw Sparrow, *The British Home of To-day*, figs B47 and C14.

163: W. Shaw Sparrow, *The Modern Home: A Book of British Domestic Architecture for Moderate Incomes – A Companion Volume to 'The British Home of To-day'*, London: Hodder & Stoughton, 1906, pl. between pp.16–17.

164–165: Elder-Duncan, *Country Cottages and Week-End Homes*, pp.200 and 75.

166: © Author.

Chapter Four

Opening quotation: E. Nesbit, 'Wheredoyouwanttogoto', or The Bouncible Ball', *Nine Unlikely Tales*, 1901, London: T. Fisher Unwin, 1901, p.58.

170: E. Nesbit, 'The Cockatoucan', in Nesbit, *Nine Unlikely Tales*, fig., p.37.

171: W.H. Romaine-Walker, *Mr Hipp, or Three Friends in Search of Pleasure*, London: Faulkner & Co, 1893, unnumbered plate.

174–175: Courtesy Chris Beetles Gallery, St James's, London, WWW.CHRISBEETLES.COM

176: Frances Hodgson Burnett, *The Secret Garden*, London: William Heinemann, 1911, pl. ch.10.

181: Shaw Sparrow, *The Modern Home*, pl. between pp.64–5.

186: Elder-Duncan, *Country Cottages and Week-End Homes*, p.171.

187: *Studio*, vol.36, 1905, p.342.

188: *Architectural Review*, vol.8, 1900, p.146.

189: Weaver, *Small Country Houses*, p.140.

191, text: 'The Wyck, Hitchin', *Country Life*, 4.11.1905, pp.630 and 632.

192: © Lubbock family archive; by kind permission of Lord Avebury.

194: © Patrick O'Keeffe.

INDEX